ENERGY MEDICINE TECHNOLOGIES

"Energy Medicine Technologies persuasively presents the wisdom of some of the world's foremost authorities on ancient and modern modalities of energy medicine—the only paradigm of healing that can effectively meet our health care needs in the twenty-first century. If you read only one book about this emerging healing model, let it be this one!"

SIMONE GABBAY, AUTHOR OF *EDGAR CAYCE'S ENERGY MEDICINE* AND *VISIONARY MEDICINE: REAL HOPE FOR TOTAL HEALING*

"This meaty volume explores diseases of civilization due to electromagnetic pollution, the dangers of genetically modified and pesticide-laden foods, and other examples of what might be considered 'man's inhumanity to man.' It also recommends ways to prevent or reduce these in chapters devoted to the benefits of organic foods, light and sound energies, ozone and hydrogen peroxide therapy, as well as intercessory prayer and remote healing."

PAUL J. ROSCH, M.D., F.A.C.P., CLINICAL PROFESSOR OF MEDICINE AND PSYCHIATRY AT NEW YORK MEDICAL COLLEGE, CHAIRMAN OF THE BOARD FOR THE AMERICAN INSTITUTE OF STRESS, AND EMERITUS MEMBER FOR THE BIOELECTROMAGNETICS SOCIETY

ENERGY MEDICINE TECHNOLOGIES

OZONE HEALING, MICROCRYSTALS, FREQUENCY THERAPY, AND THE FUTURE OF HEALTH

EDITED BY
FINLEY EVERSOLE, PH.D.

Inner Traditions
Rochester, Vermont • Toronto, Canada

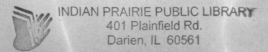

Inner Traditions
One Park Street
Rochester, Vermont 05767
www.InnerTraditions.com

SUSTAINABLE FORESTRY INITIATIVE   Certified Sourcing
www.sfiprogram.org
SFI-00854

Text stock is SFI certified

Note to the reader: This book is intended as an informational guide. The remedies, approaches, and techniques described herein are meant to supplement, and not to be a substitute for, professional medical care or treatment. They should not be used to treat a serious ailment without prior consultation with a qualified health care professional.

Library of Congress Cataloging-in-Publication Data

Energy medicine technologies : ozone healing, microcrystals, frequency therapy, and the future of health / edited by Finley Eversole, Ph.D.
    p. cm.
Summary: "New and suppressed breakthroughs in energy medicine, ways to combat toxins and electromagnetic fields, and the importance of non-GMO foods. Explores the use of microcrystals, ozone and hydrogen peroxide therapy, and how to tap in to healing antioxidant electrons from the Earth." — Provided by publisher.
  Includes bibliographical references and index.
  ISBN 978-1-62055-102-8 (pbk.) — ISBN 978-1-62055-134-9 (e-book)
  1. Energy medicine. 2. Hydrogen peroxide—Therapeutic use. 3. Ozone—Therapeutic use. I. Eversole, Finley, 1933- editor of compilation.
  RZ421.E54 2013
  615.8'51—dc23
                                       2012040342

Printed and bound in the United States by Lake Book Manufacturing, Inc.
The text stock is SFI certified. The Sustainable Forestry Initiative® program promotes sustainable forest management.

10 9 8 7 6 5 4 3 2 1

Text design by Virginia Scott Bowman and layout by Brian Boynton
This book was typeset in Garamond Premier Pro and Gill Sans with Bank Gothic and Gill Sans used as display typefaces

The Djwhal Khul quotations, from the books of Alice Bailey listed below, are used with the permission of Lucis Trust, London, and are found on the following pages:

page v — from *The Externalization of the Hierarchy*, page 163
page vi — from *Esoteric Astrology*, page 147
page vi — from *Discipleship in the New Age*, vol. 1, page 685
page 1 — from *Esoteric Healing*, page 377
page 10 — from *Esoteric Healing*, page 48
page 11 — from *Esoteric Healing*, page 535
pages 51–52 — from *The Externalization of the Hierarchy*, page 497
page 153 — from *Esoteric Healing*, page 392
page 154 — from *Esoteric Healing*, page 684

To send correspondence to the author of this book, mail a first-class letter to the author c/o Inner Traditions • Bear & Company, One Park Street, Rochester, VT 05767, and we will forward the communication, or contact the author through his website: **http://aoand.com/profile/FinleyEversole**.

Take courage. The human race is divine.

PYTHAGORAS

Humanity will become eventually the planetary savior.

DJWHAL KHUL

The people of Earth are a superpower themselves, if united.

JEANE MANNING

This time, like all times, is a very good one, if we but know what to do with it.

RALPH WALDO EMERSON

We have it in our power to begin the world over again.

THOMAS PAINE

We stand at the gateway of the new world, of the new age and its new civilizations, ideals and culture. What is coming is a civilization of a different yet still material nature, but animated by a growing registration by the masses everywhere of an emerging spiritual objective which will transform all life and give new value and purpose to that which is material.

DJWHAL KHUL

Another world is not only possible, she is on her way. On a quiet day, I can hear her breathing.

ARUNDHATI ROY

There is always a new world in the process of forming. . . . The best is yet to be.

DJWHAL KHUL

CONTENTS

ACKNOWLEDGMENTS

My first thanks go to all of the authors who have given generously of their time and wisdom to write the chapters contained in this volume, and for their quick responses to my many communications and requests.

My thanks also go to Karl Maret for writing the foreword, to Fred Walters, editor of *AcresUSA*—North America's oldest voice devoted to Eco-Agriculture—for connecting me with Melvin Epp, and to James L. Oschman, who provided valuable counsel on many occasions throughout this project.

I would especially like to thank my publisher Ehud Sperling, and Jon Graham, acquisitions editor, for approving this project when it was still only a one-paragraph idea, and for patiently waiting for it to become a reality.

Last, but not least, my thanks also go the Inner Traditions staff who have worked so hard to bring this book forth: Jeanie Levitan, managing editor, Peri Swan for the cover design, and above all, to my project editor, Anne Dillon, whose uncommon dedication and meticulous attention to every detail of this project have helped make this book be the best it can be.

Energy Medicine Technologies has been a collaborative project in every sense of the word. The twenty-first century will witness profound changes in our understanding of the human being—body, mind, and spirit—and the field of medicine will undergo profound changes as our understanding of human health deepens. May this volume help the public to think of health and healing in far broader terms than those that currently dominate the medical field, given our pharmaceutically dominated culture. True healing involves the whole human being and the whole environment. This volume is a step toward a broader understanding of that.

FOREWORD

Karl Maret, M.D.

This book is about the promising future of health care. Its authors present many new approaches within the emerging field of energy medicine that challenge us to reexamine some of the underlying causes of the increasing unaffordability of our health care system. The causes include a widespread presence of pollutants and environmental toxins, ignorance of the possible impact of genetically modified foods, and the current limited consumption of organic foods that contain significantly fewer pesticides. Useful solutions are offered by introducing the reader to a cross section of emerging energy medicine technologies, frequency therapies, ozone therapy, as well as subtle energy approaches, including the power of intention, prayer, and sound therapy. I believe that if these approaches were to become widely used, our present Western health care system would undergo a positive transformation that would reduce health care costs.

In 2013, we stand at a critical moment in the evolution of our health care system, which is, for the most part, really a "disease care" system. The unfortunate truth is that we spend more on health care than any other country in the world, yet we are not getting the best results for these expenditures. In 2008, the latest year for reliable statistics, the United States spent more than $2.3 trillion on medical care, three times more than in 1990. It is increasingly known that the majority of these expenditures deal primarily with disease, especially in the elderly. One percent of the population accounts for 30 percent of the nation's medical expenditures. The elderly (age 65 and over) made up around 13 percent of the U.S. population in 2002, but they consumed 36 percent of total U.S. medical expenditures.

Medicare, the health insurance program for the elderly, spends nearly 30 percent of its budget on beneficiaries in their final year of life. These statistics largely reflect lifelong habits of poor nutrition, lack of exercise, and lack of preventive care, accompanied by an epidemic of obesity. Two-thirds of Americans are considered overweight or obese. In addition, a 2012 report from the U.S. Institute of Medicine found a total of $765 billion of annual waste in the health care system in 2009, about 33 percent of its annual expenditures.

A preventive approach to health and healing is much talked about but not sufficiently practiced to seriously impact the system now in place. Costs keep rising every year, as do the expenditures for pharmaceuticals, over-the-counter drugs, and operative procedures. Stephen M. Davidson, Boston University professor of health policy and management, describes the challenges confronting the U.S. health care system in his book *Still Broken*. Although the need for an affordable health care system has been the focus of federal legislation and judicial review for the last several years, we are still far from a solution.

Unfortunately, the recent Patient Protection and Affordable Care Act passed by the U.S. Congress in March 2010 delivers essentially the same conventional type of care without incorporating the potential benefits of complementary and alternative medicine (CAM), including energy medicine. Recognizing the health challenges facing this nation, it is hoped that this book will contribute to a more integrative health care paradigm, one that includes an expanded understanding of energies involved in healing.

Albert Szent-Györgyi, M.D., Ph.D., recipient of the 1937 Nobel Prize in Physiology or Medicine, said, "In every culture and in every medical tradition before ours, healing was accomplished by moving energy."[1] Two widely practiced medical systems on the planet that use energies for healing are traditional Chinese medicine and the ayurvedic medical system of India. The qualitative nature of energy described in these healing traditions has names such as *chi,* or *qi,* and *prana.* These concepts are difficult to understand by Western scientists trained in reductionistic thinking and a materialistic orientation toward the life sciences. The concept of a "life force" was expunged from the life sciences in the middle of the nineteenth century, especially by the work of prominent German scientists. Specifically, it was the Berlin school of physiologists, including the physician-turned-physicist Hermann von Helmholtz (sensory physiology and conservation of energy) and Emil du Bois-Reymond (discoverer of nerve action potential and the father of experimental electrophysiology), among others, that laid the foundations for a medical biophysics that is still influencing medical thinking today.

However, the mysteries of life cannot be fathomed solely on the basis of biochemistry and electromagnetism, unless these subspecialties of physics, chemistry, and biology are framed in a larger context. What is now in the process of emerging is an integrative biophysics that embraces ideas from quantum physics, emergent properties of matter, consciousness research, and an expanded view of electrodynamics. From this modern perspective, life energy involves concepts such as the living light in our cells—called biophotons—and principles such as nonlocality, entanglement, torsion fields, coherent electric oscillations, molecular resonances, dissipative structures, and state-specific states of consciousness.

The founders of quantum physics recognized that the observer, the atomic realm, and the scientific measuring instruments formed an interconnected system where all three influence each other. From the perspective of quantum physics, the observer is an integral part of the scientific process and the act of observation influences the outcome by collapsing the wave function. As quantum physics Nobel laureate Werner Heisenberg stated, "What we observe is not nature itself, but nature exposed to our method of questioning."[2]

How can these unusual ideas of energy and life force become integrated into our current reductionistic approach to medical care? Fortunately, the winds of change are beginning to blow, and in the United States, much progress is being made at this time. Our allopathic health care system has expanded to embrace CAM in response to a public demand for a greater integration of Eastern medical approaches and ancient healing traditions. Energy medicine is now one of the four foundational pillars of CAM and has found governmental research support within the National Institutes of Health, through the National Center for Complementary and Alternative Medicine. This is a hopeful development in the creation of a more inclusive and cost-effective health care system using energy medicine and integrative biophysics modalities.

George Bernard Shaw once said, "England and America are two countries separated by the same language."*[3] By analogy, modern medicine and CAM are two medical approaches divided by a common language of energy. In traditional biophysics, the term *energy* means the capacity to do work and it describes a scalar quantity (having no direction or orientation). It exists in many forms, including mechanical energy, heat or thermal energy, electrical energy, and electromagnetic radiation. It can exist in potential energy, when it is not moving, or as kinetic energy, when in motion. Since almost everything is in motion, including atoms and their constituent subatomic particles, we live in a sea of vibrations, principally kinetic energy.

In contrast, CAM has expanded the idea of energy to also include more subtle aspects of energy typically called putative energy medicine. *Putative* means that we cannot as yet measure these "energies" with existing biophysical instrumentation to ascertain their true nature. Many aspects of this energy can be sensed, be inwardly perceived, be operated on by trained healers, and even demonstrate an unexplained action at a distance. The powerful effects of prayer and distant healing are part of this type of energy medicine, and they are discussed from a scientific perspective by physician Larry Dossey in chapter 3.

To gain a better understanding of energy in the context of energy medicine technologies, it might help to investigate the original roots of the word. The Greek philosopher Aristotle used the word *energeia,* liter-

---

The Treasury of Humorous Quotations quotes Shaw as saying this, but without giving a source. The quote had earlier been attributed to Shaw in *Reader's Digest* (November 1942). In the same vein, Dylan Thomas, shortly before his death (and published after it in *The Listener,* April 1954), commented that European writers and scholars in America were "up against the barrier of a common language."

ally meaning "to contain work." But *energeia* was contrasted with *hexis,* which meant "to possess" or "to be in the state of." *Energeia* meant doing, *hexis* meant possessing. Laying the foundation for ethical philosophy, but not science, Aristotle argued that virtue must be an activity, not just a state, to ensure happiness. Nonetheless, his ideas had a formative influence on later philosophical and scientific development.

It was not until 1807 that Thomas Young in England first used the word *energy* in the modern sense. His definition is almost the same as our current definition of kinetic energy. As the nineteenth century proceeded, Helmholtz first described the principle of conservation of energy in 1847 but used the German word *"Kraft,"* which could also mean force. During this formative time, the British self-made researcher James Joule also studied the nature of various forces and their energetic interactions. He made foundational experiments to show how chemical, mechanical, electromagnetic, and thermodynamic energy or heat can be exchanged with each other while always being conserved. The unit of measurable energy is now termed the Joule in his honor.

The great Scottish physicist and mathematician James Clerk Maxwell developed the first field theory of modern physics—the theory of electromagnetism—which he worked on for over twenty years between 1851 and 1873. Maxwell used complex mathematics, including scalar and vector potentials, which were an integral part of his field theory. Maxwell's original twenty equations were later simplified by British scientist Oliver Heaviside, using modern vector analysis, to the more recognizable four equations that every physicist and electrical engineer is familiar with.

Unfortunately, in this process Heaviside eliminated vector potentials, also known as the A-field, leaving only the magnetic field (B-field) and electric field (E-field) interactions in the modern version of his theory. With that development, modern medical scientists and biophysicists are typically unaware of these potentials and their possible impact on living systems.

British researcher Professor Cyril Smith has convincingly shown that these potential A-fields affect water, while British quantum biophysicist and biologist Mae-Wan Ho demonstrated how magnetic vector potential fields have a pronounced biological effect in altering genetic material, even in the absence of magnetic fields. If science is working with limited mathematical models, then the profound impact of electromagnetic technologies on living systems may be minimized or even dismissed.

In contrast, modern quantum physics actively makes use of these potentials in advanced theories of electrodynamics and quantum reality. The English quantum physicist David Bohm carried out research with magnetic vector potentials (Aharonov-Bohm effect), which led him to describe deeper layers of our reality. He called this the implicate order, and it involves a reality appropriate to the findings of quantum theory. It is a reality involving paradoxical concepts such as superposition, enfolding of space-time, and nonlocal space. This "implicate" reality is in marked contrast to the more familiar material reality of space and time in classical physics, which he called the explicate order. Much of what we perceive of the world is in the form of this explicate order.

To understand some of the putative energy medicine phenomena, such as distant healing, therapeutic touch, biomagnetic healing, prayer, intention, and consciousness affecting the complex human biofield, it is necessary to invoke the quantum physical nature of reality affecting living systems. We are very complex electromagnetic beings, with all the molecules interacting in a type of "quantum jazz," a term coined by Ho. Living systems have exquisite sensitivity to electromagnetic fields created by coherent modes of vibration in the biomolecules. Scientists are now beginning to define the nature of the hidden potentials, electromagnetic fields, and dynamic quantum processes that collectively interact to make up the human biofield. The energetic resonant structures within this biofield form none other than the energetic acupuncture meridian system first discovered in Asia several millennia ago.

The largest organ in the body is now understood by many to be the connective tissue matrix. It is described in chapter 1 by the energy medicine pioneering biophysicist James L. Oschman, Ph.D. If chemical toxins, heavy metals, and other biological poisons are embedded in this living matrix, the electromagnetic communication processes mediated by "living light" in the cells (called biophotons) become disrupted. In essence, abnormal electromagnetic resonances begin to occur from the toxic molecules embedded in the connective tissue, fat, and other storage sites—impairing the functioning of healthy cells and tissues. These toxins and chemical residues act as a kind of electrical "noise" in the body.

If this is not corrected, biochemical changes will begin to induce physiological disruptions and, over time, may lead to disease unless the matrix is detoxified appropriately. Modern medical students are insufficiently instructed in these matters, compared with their naturopathic medicine colleagues, who have a better appreciation for the need for good hydration, a balanced diet, and periodic cleansing of the tissues and the lymphatic system. As the research of Oschman and others has shown, electrical grounding of the body allows free electrons to be absorbed from the Earth to neutralize destructive free radicals that lead to inflammation. It is one of energy medicine's approaches to this prevalent condition and may in some cases eliminate the need for anti-inflammatory drugs.

Once readers of this book have begun to appreciate the underlying quantum physical and electromagnetic nature of life, then it may not seem so far-fetched to envision that appropriate sympathetic vibrations of the right amplitude and frequency might have a powerful healing effect. The late American physician and biophysicist Ross Adey found that the body contained specific biological windows sensitive to electromagnetic fields capable of activating cells. These are powerful triggers of biochemical changes within cells if both the appropriate low-level amplitude and correct frequencies are present in the signals. Without the presence of these unique signal characteristics, the body will not respond.

Adey's work, and that of many others in the bioelectromagnetic research community, helps us to understand why the pioneering work of Royal Raymond Rife (profiled in chapter 4) holds such promise for our future health care system. If specific frequencies and amplitudes are effective in destroying specific strains of pathogens such as bacteria, viruses, and fungi, then the need for antibiotics, which are currently used much too widely, might change. Other frequencies were found to be effective for a variety of bodily imbalances or disease states. A determined research effort in this area would be welcome to bring these frequency technologies into wider application. Today we recognize that our bodies are a symphony of vibrations involving electromagnetic and quantum processes. From this perspective, we might appreciate the tremendous impact that current telecommunications technologies appear to be having on our health.

The modern world is literally overflowing with a plethora of fields and waves, filling the entire electromagnetic spectrum. They range from slow radio waves vibrating at thousands of cycles per second (AM radio) to microwaves oscillating at billions of cycles per second and coming from devices such as cell phones, WiFi for computers, cordless telephones, and smart meters on our homes. We are all part of an epidemiological experiment to see how this spectrum of electromagnetic radiation affects our long-term health and well-being. Regulatory agencies are only concerned about the short-term thermal or heating effects of these devices and downplay the potential hazards of long-term low level or nonthermal signals emitted by these microwave transmitters. This directly contradicts the findings of hundreds of studies over the last two decades that show the biologically adverse effects of these devices at currently permitted power levels.

Although the convenience of our modern telecommunication devices makes them very attractive to use, unfortunately their powerful impact on our health is only now beginning to be recognized. In today's world, it is difficult to do effective double-blind, placebo-controlled scientific studies when environmental background levels of nonionizing microwave radiation are continuously rising. Perhaps the use of various Pulsors discovered by naturopathic physician George T. F. Yao, as described in chapter 5, may become one of several approaches to harmonizing the human biofield to the increasing levels of electromagnetic background radiation, often referred to as "electrosmog."

The importance of sound to produce healing reactions in the body is another field of research that is generally unknown in modern medicine. Early in the twentieth century, Dr. Hans Jenny in Switzerland carried out pioneering research investigating the effect of sound and vibration on all types of materials, including water. Since our body consists mostly of structured water, sound can interact with this fluid matrix. The resonances and vibrational patterns Jenny found allowed a new field of research called cymatics to emerge. The late British physician Peter Guy Manners carried out clinical research over many decades having to do with the healing effects of complex sound combinations. He achieved remarkable healings with a broad range of medical conditions, and his work has been expanded by other sound healers now actively practicing this modality.

In 2008 musicologist and healer Gary Buchanan published an especially useful book called *SONA: Healing with Wave Front Bioresonance,* which describes the power of applied cymatic methods. The symphony of life is based on a musical and sonic blueprint. In chapter 2 of this book, the neuropsychologist John Consemulder offers deeper insight into the processes by which sound, light, and energy weave this web in the cosmos as well as in our bodies. Scientists are now also discovering how the environment directly impacts our genes to restore health or create disease.

Modern molecular genetics has made great progress in deciphering the genome over the last two decades. Today, your DNA blueprint can be sequenced for less than a thousand dollars. However this approach only decodes the roughly 21,000 known genes that are actively involved in protein synthesis in the body. These exon genes make up only 1.5 percent of our DNA. In the past, much of the remaining 98.5 percent of the genome was called junk DNA because scientists did not know its purpose. Recently, scientists decoded the genome of the lowly tomato and found it contained 31,760 genes, while the highest known number of genes is around 60,000 for the protozoan causing trichomoniasis. Clearly it is not the number of human genes that is most important, but how they are activated or suppressed through internal and external environmental influences.

The functional meaning of our genome's "junk" was recently elucidated by a project begun in 2003 called the Encyclopedia of DNA Elements (ENCODE). Scientists looked at the intricate network of highly complex genetic switches that are the key to turning your genes on and off. So far, they have found 4 million switching sites, covering 8.5 percent of the genome—far more than anyone suspected. It is now believed that around 20 percent of the entire genome will be found to consist of these switching regulatory codons. The way in which these switches work is also turning out to be vastly more complicated than previously thought.

Individual switches can interact with many genes, and defects in this switching DNA can lead to faulty gene activity and expression. These switches are playing a leading role in the emerging science of epigenomics. Here the environment plays a formidable role in steering our genetic inheritance and activating protein synthesis through gene expression. Eighty percent of the entire human genome is either transcribed, binds to regulatory proteins, or is associated with some other biochemical activity. A large part of the genome transcribes RNA, not for making proteins, but rather for regulating gene activity as well as shuffling proteins, like taxi drivers, to different parts of the genome.

The epigenome is just as critical to the development of humans as is the genome. For example, by changing the diet of genetically fat and yellow agouti mice to one rich in methyl donors, found in onions, garlic, and beets, researchers have found that they could change the offspring to slim and brown mice. By epigenetic intervention, they had modulated the critical agouti gene, dramatically changing the mice's offspring. Nutrition was responsible for dimming the gene's deleterious effects, from fat and yellow mice to mice that are normal, slim, and brown. Researchers are finding that tweaking the epigenome by exposure to specific nutrients, chemicals or pesticides, or even some extra nurturing by the mother can alter the genes of the offspring, which can affect their brain for life.

It is also known that inherited errors in our "switching DNA" and brief exposure to environmental toxins during pregnancy—including electromagnetic fields—can lead to the later development of illness. In the future, health-promoting epigenetic activation of our genome via this switching DNA will form the basis of a truly preventive medicine and usher in a revolution in medicine. Scientists are now gaining their first insights into the likely mechanism by which many energy medicine technologies described in this book may have their epigenetic and physiological effects. With these developments, the conventional concept of "gene as fate" is now outdated by epigenetics. We appear to have a measure of control over our genetics.

Russian scientists, including the group working with Peter Gariaev (who has been called the father of fractal genetics), have also explored the unusual linguistic structure and electromagnetic properties of DNA. It appears that DNA's helical structure allows light (as biophotons) to spiral in a coherent manner, acting as an electromagnetic communications system inside every cell of our body. The Russians describe complex torsion fields inside living systems that interact with our very DNA. By modulating the secondary radiation from laser beams with epigenetic information they are able to positively influence the genomes of animals and help human gene expression. Using this approach, called wave genetics, they have regrown endocrine glands previously destroyed by chemical exposure, slowed the aging process in humans, and even regenerated missing teeth. It appears that an energy medicine approach to healing the genome could powerfully impact our future health care system if we are open to working in a new way.

Increasingly, a select group of scientists have recognized that the electromagnetic fields inside our body make up the high-speed communication system that coordinates our living matrix, including the energetic acupuncture system. It is a higher-level control system that then modulates the biochemical pathways in every cell and tissue of the body. In essence, there is a symphony of silent music always striving to greater harmony flowing through our body each moment—influencing all our organs, tissues, and cells. The good news is that modern medical science in the West is beginning to build a bridge to the ancient healing systems of the East, enriching both in the process.

It is my sincere hope that this book is only the first of many that will introduce readers to the wide range of energy medicine technologies and approaches that are now emerging. The importance of innovative light and laser therapies, healing with color, a wide range of pulsed electromagnetic fields, and the power of structured water and homeopathy have been extensively documented. All these modalities will undoubtedly play a formative role in the health care system of tomorrow.

I would like to close with an appeal to the reader never to forget the central importance of the spiritual dimension of our being. Modern biomedical technologies, including those of energy medicine, are but one aspect of our healing journey. If we consider that the structural, biochemical, energetic, and informational realms form an ever more subtle anatomy of our being, then our spiritual nature sits at the apex and is the source of our cyclic reappearance, life after life. Collectively, humanity now comprises a truly interconnected field of consciousness and intention.

May the coming years see the emergence of a new medical and health care system that honors both our physical and subtle energetic natures in the most enlightened manner. I sincerely hope that this book contributes to that future in a useful and meaningful way.

Emerging Paradigms in Health and Healing

Finley Eversole, Ph.D.

*There is nothing but electricity in manifestation. . . .
Everything in Nature is electrical in nature; life itself is
electricity. . . . Electrical discovery is only in the initial
stage and all that we have is simply a prelude to the real
discovery. . . . Does it mean anything to you when I say . . .
the human being is electrical in origin and nature?*

DJWHAL KHUL

*Illnesses do not come upon us out of the blue. They are
developed from small daily sins against Nature. When
enough sins have accumulated, illnesses will suddenly
appear.*

HIPPOCRATES

In this volume we take up energy medicine—an emerging paradigm that
views the human body and environment primarily in electromagnetic
terms and views healing as a way of achieving electrical balance. It has

been said that by the end of the present century, most of the medical profession will have come to understand the human body—and indeed the whole human being (body, emotions, mind, and spirit, including the living environment)—primarily as fields of electromagnetic energies. All energy is vibratory, so these same energies can also be viewed as creating musical patterns—"the music of life"—which can get out of harmony. Healing then becomes a matter of restoring harmony to the whole.

As a meditator for more than four decades, I've experienced firsthand the improvements to physical health, emotional balance, and mental clarity that come as the differing "octaves" of our being achieve greater harmonic resonance. The prevailing industrial age view of the human body as a machine whose parts occasionally break down, requiring repair only to that part without regard to the whole human being and the sources of the problem, is a health model that will increasingly be replaced by a more unified theory of what a human being truly is. By the time a problem emerges in the physical body, emotional, mental, and environmental causes have already done their work. Hence the need to address the *causes* of human illness, not just the illness itself.

Physician Larry Dossey expands our understanding of healing by bringing in the role of consciousness in healing and the influence of prayer and spiritual healers in affecting healing at a distance. Quantum physics has already established action at a distance as a proven scientific principle. On reflection, I've decided to share a personal story. In 1970 I became critically ill, dropping down from 175 to 132 pounds in six months. I developed four major illnesses, each compounding the severity of the others and defeating my doctor's efforts to aid a cure. I would learn later that two of the three doctors I'd seen had told a friend my condition was so critical that "It is unlikely he will live."

Every Monday for four months, I visited my primary physician and underwent a series of tests, waiting each time to be informed of their results. For four months, despite all of the doctor's efforts, I showed no improvement. Then one Tuesday evening a mutual friend introduced me to a seventy-six-year-old spiritual healer living on Long Island. I lived in Manhattan at the time. The healer, Lewis, told me he would begin remote healing work on me the next day, and my part was simply to relax for thirty minutes each day around 6:00 p.m. I could feel the energies as he worked on me, not only at 6:00 p.m., but also around 9:00 a.m. When I later questioned him on this point, he confirmed he was also doing a morning healing.

The Monday following the Wednesday when the healing work had begun, I made my weekly visit to my doctor. All the usual tests were run, but this time the doctor was gone far longer than usual. Finally returning, she told me all my tests would have to be redone. And again I waited quite a while for the test results. Finally, my doctor returned and asked, "Finley, are you using drugs?" I said, "No. Why do you ask?" Then she said, "I've run all your tests twice now, and something is seriously off. According to your tests—which have shown no improvement in four months—you've made a 90 percent recovery *since last Monday. But that's medically impossible!*" I then told her about the spiritual healer working on me, and she replied, "I would never have believed what is happening to you had I not witnessed it with my own eyes. I've had a long career but have *never* seen anything like this. Whatever the healer is doing is working, so tell him to keep it up."

Two weeks later I learned my father in Alabama was scheduled for surgery at 6:00 a.m. the next morning to remove a blood clot that was located above one ear. His doctors were afraid it might break loose and cause a stroke. I immediately called Louis and asked if he could help my father. "Sure," he replied. When Dad arrived at the hospital the next morning, an X-ray was taken to locate the clot for surgery. But guess what; *it had disappeared.* Dad was sent home without having the surgery. He lived another thirty years but never again had that problem.

Within a few weeks of Lewis's healing work I'd made a full recovery, and by that fall I was working eighty- to ninety-hour weeks as a university professor. My health has been excellent ever since. So do I believe in the power of mental and spiritual healing? In my experience, it works.

The ancient wisdom schools taught that all that is, *is* energy and that *energy follows thought.* As Oscar Wilde put it, "To think a thing is to cause it to begin to be." And in the New Testament we read, "As a man thinketh in his heart, so is he." And lastly, consider Victor Hugo's famous line: "There is one thing stronger than all the armies of the world, and that is an idea whose time has come." The power of clearly visualized, unselfish, and wisely directed thinking can accomplish that which, to all appearances, seems miraculous. In right thinking, when we have learned it, lies the power to transform all ills.

There is one further point I would like to make here, which Dossey does not, and that is that "death also is a form of healing." This view presupposes that we are spiritual beings in earthly bodies and that the soul lives on after the death of the physical form. The *release* of the soul from a body that can no longer serve its purposes and has become its prison is, from the standpoint of the soul, a form of healing. Not everyone will accept this view, but a 1970 survey found that 74 percent of Americans said they believe in life after death. I suspect that number is larger today given the growing number of reports of near-death experiences, which medical science itself has made possible through its ability to resuscitate many victims of cardiac arrest, electrocution, coma, and near-drowning.

Over several decades, Dutch cardiologist Pim van Lommel found that 18 percent of his heart attack patients who had flat-lined reported being conscious and having positive, life-changing experiences after brain activity had ceased.[1]* The mysteries of life are grander and more marvelous than present medical science has been willing to acknowledge. *Part of the emerging new consciousness of humanity will be an enhanced view of what a human being truly is.* This will change not only medicine, but also every facet of society. We are entering the time of the Great Awakening from the long slumber of reductionist materialism.

One other area covered in this volume is of tremendous importance, and that is the issue of healthy organic foods versus the dangers of genetically modified (GM) foods. Genetically modified organisms (GMOs) represent the first human technology that, since its release into the environment, can never again be recalled or controlled. Through pollina-

---

*On page 18 of his book *Consciousness beyond Life: The Science of Near-Death Experience,* van Lommel writes, "It is often confusing to hear bystanders or doctors declare you dead at a moment when you feel extremely alive and whole."

tion, this technology spreads indiscriminately, doing grave environmental damage.

Here we have an all-too-common example of the power of money in politics. When the first George Bush became president and Monsanto filed for Food and Drug Administration (FDA) approval of its GM crops, Vice President Dan Quayle pushed approval through in just two days. The FDA did not conduct a single study to determine the health safety of GM foods, nor did it listen to its own scientists or read a single research paper by scientists who *had* studied the damage done to the organs of animals fed with GM feeds.

In India, where Monsanto has gained enormous control over Indian agriculture, farmers are finding it impossible to survive. *Some 250,000 Indian farmers have so far committed suicide—often by drinking Monsanto's Round-Up herbicide—and another Indian farmer commits suicide every thirty minutes on average.* American farmers who refuse to use Monsanto's seed often find themselves the target of major lawsuits.

The public backlash against Monsanto is one of the largest such movements in history. Anyone concerned about his or her health needs to read about the dangers of GMOs in chapter 8, written by Jeffrey M. Smith. As Smith notes, traditional scientific methods of research have been thrown to the winds: "In the critical area of food safety research, the biotech industry is without accountability, standards, or peer reviews. They've got bad science down to a science." Nor is the U.S. government doing anything to protect the public from the dangers. With approximately 70 percent of the food in our grocery stores containing GM products, every American needs to *demand labeling of GMO foods* so consumers at least have a choice. If you care about your health and that of your family and children, eat organic foods and support organic farmers whenever possible.

A bird's-eye overview of the chapters in this volume will assist prospective readers of *Energy Medicine Technologies* in identifying the issues. Each author is a leading expert in his or her field. The information contained in this volume is not widely known to the public, nor will you find it reported in the corporate-owned media or debated by politicians or health care providers. Powerful forces, such as big pharma and the ag industry, are arrayed against it, and politicians dance to their tune.

Most readers will find themselves at new frontiers in medical thinking. New discoveries and innovations in health care described here can offer hope to many with debilitating or life-threatening diseases, such as cancer and AIDS. This does not mean traditional medicine is to be ignored, as it clearly has its proper place and role to play. I would simply urge readers to *follow the guidance* of the authors on the right uses of these healing technologies.

James L. Oschman, in chapter 1, "Moving Beyond the 'Energy Crisis' in Medicine," clarifies ancient concepts of "healing accomplished by moving energy," which are missing from our modern medicine. A key finding is the wealth of health benefits gained by simply walking barefoot on the Earth. Another is the "living matrix" system that conducts antioxidant electrons from the Earth to all parts of the body, promoting health and longevity.

John Consemulder, in chapter 2, "Life's Musical Blueprint," brings together evidence from diverse disciplines—music, mathematics, quantum physics, bioenergetics, DNA research, and sound healing—to support the thesis that we live in a musical, holographic, multidimensional, conscious, self-organizing, living universe—which calls for a new paradigm embracing cosmology, physics, biology, medicine, and consciousness studies.

Larry Dossey, in chapter 3, "Consciousness and Healing," reviews existing research on the place of prayer in healing, then offers twenty well-reasoned suggestions for future research into the role of prayer, healing intention, and consciousness as agents of healing. He says evidence to date conclusively demonstrates "the *nonlocal* nature of consciousness" and "the ability of intentionality to change the world."

Nenah Sylver, in chapter 4, "Rife Therapy," explores the work of Royal Raymond Rife—an early pioneer of Western energy medicine—and explains how modern rife technologies work and can be safely used. She also discusses some health conditions (including cancer) that can benefit from rifing, addresses the detoxification process, and takes a forward glance at the future of Rife therapies. The story of Rife's discoveries and their suppression by the medical and pharmaceutical industries is told in my earlier book, *Infinite Energy Technologies.*

R. Carole Morginsky, in chapter 5, "Harmonizing the Energies of Body, Mind, and Environment with Pulsor Microcrystals,"* examines the effects of electromagnetic fields, so all-pervasive in today's world, on the subtle energies and biofields of the body, adding to many health problems, then explains naturopathic physician George T. F. Yao's crystal-based Pulsors, which restore the body's natural energy fields and protect it from electromagnetic fields.

Nathaniel Altman, in chapter 6, "Ozone and Hydrogen Peroxide in Healing" (also called oxygen therapies), describes in detail their safe methods of application, history of research, and the spectrum of health problems that can be alleviated or diminished by their use—including heart disease, cancer, HIV, diabetes, and musculoskeletal problems. Widely used in Germany, Austria, Russia, Cuba, and elsewhere for the past sixty years, their use in the United States is permitted in some states as "experimental" therapies only.

Joseph D. Weissman, in chapter 7, "Choosing to Live," discusses the appearance of man-made toxins in our food supply, water, and environment since the start of the Industrial Revolution, especially since 1900, and the role toxins play in the spread of diseases and appearance of new ones. He tells us the human body is a toxin accumulator and urges us to eat as low on the evolutionary food chain as we can.

Jeffrey M. Smith, in chapter 8, "State-of-the-Science on the Health Risk of GM Foods," tells us that animal research into GM foods found "damage to virtually every organ and system studied in lab animals." Flawed research, a lack of regulatory oversight, the absence of a scientific review process, and suppression of information to the public conceal the dangers that GM foods hold for us. This presents a threat to all of us—especially pregnant women, children, the sick, and the elderly.

Melvin D. Epp, in chapter 9, "Organic Foods," says the average American consumes seven to ten pesticides daily in his or her food, and

---

*This product is trademark registered.

three to six more in drinking water. Children are most at risk. Until about eighty years ago, all people ate organic foods. Switching to an organic diet can reduce health risks by up to 97 percent. He explores the benefits to health and the environment of "going organic" and provides a basic guide to healthy foods.

Humanity today is embarked on a trajectory that, in the next few decades, will prove to be the most profound transformation of life, consciousness, and civilization the world has ever experienced. Numerous new technologies, new social institutions, new approaches to education, new solutions to global problems, and new dimensions of consciousness *latent* in our being and waiting to be awakened promise a future for humanity that is, at present, unimaginable. That we have serious global problems that must be solved is evident to every thinking person. And the time for their solving is now. Addressing the problems of the health care system and new and previously suppressed health cures for cancer, AIDS, and hundreds of other diseases is one of the challenges placing demands on the wisdom, skill, and conscience of every person who truly cares about the health and welfare of every person on Earth. Despite the best intentions of doctors and nurses—most of whom truly care about their patients—money and politics largely dictate the health care system available to us. This *must* change. It is my hope that this modest volume will be widely read and contribute to that change.

Take heart! The best is yet to be.

PART 1

The Body Electric and the New Age of Health and Healing

Conventional medicine itself is now the number one killer. Iatrogenic (medically caused) deaths, including fatal drug reactions, medical errors and unnecessary medical and surgical procedures, tallied in at 783,936 deaths annually, beating both heart disease (at 699,697) and cancer (at 553,251). . . . There are inexpensive, natural, non-toxic alternatives that work, but they have been largely suppressed by a profit-driven medical/pharmaceutical/ industrial complex that has monopolized markets, the legislature and the courts.

ELLEN HODGSON BROWN

For sure, we terrestrials are not isolated from the rest of the universe and are subject to influences ranging from galactic and solar forces down to local, man-made electricity and electronics.

DR. STEPHEN T. SINATRA

Electricity, in relation to human ills, is as yet an infant science, but it has in it the germs of the new techniques and methods of healing. . . . It will be seen that disease emerges into the physical body from the world of the unseen, and from the use, or misuse, of the subtler forces on the inner planes.

DJWHAL KHUL

On the basis of what is known about the roles of the electrical, magnetic, elastic, acoustic, thermal, gravitational and photonic energies in living systems, it appears that there are many energetic systems in the living body and many ways of influencing them. What we refer to as the "living state" and as "health" are all of these systems, both known and unknown, functioning collectively, cooperatively and synergistically. The debate about whether there is such a thing as "Healing Energy" or life force is being replaced with the study of the interactions between the biological energy fields, structures and functions.

JAMES L. OSCHMAN

The living organism is extraordinarily coherent: all its parts are multidimensionally, dynamically, and almost instantly correlated with all other parts. What happens to one cell or organ also happens in some way to all other cells and organs. . . . The organism is also coherent with the world around it: what happens in the external milieu of the organism is reflected in some ways in its internal milieu.

ERVIN LASZLO

Unless we put medical freedom into the Constitution, the time will come when medicine will organize into an undercover dictatorship. . . . To restrict the art of healing to one class of men and deny equal privilege to others will constitute the Bastille of medical science. . . . The Constitution of this Republic should make special provision for medical freedom as well as religious freedom.

DR. BENJAMIN RUSH, SURGEON GENERAL OF
GEORGE WASHINGTON'S ARMIES, SIGNER OF THE
DECLARATION OF INDEPENDENCE (1787)

All disease is the result of inhibited soul life, and that is true of all forms in all kingdoms. The art of the healer consists in releasing the soul, so that its life can flow through the aggregate of organisms which constitute any particular form. . . . In this release the nature of the true art of healing is hidden.

DJWHAL KHUL

1

MOVING BEYOND THE "ENERGY CRISIS" IN MEDICINE

A BIOGRAPHY AND AN AUTOBIOGRAPHY OF SCIENTIFIC BREAKTHROUGHS

James L. Oschman, Ph.D.

In every culture and in every medical tradition before ours, healing was accomplished by moving energy.

ALBERT SZENT-GYÖRGYI

INTRODUCTION

This is the story of what may well prove to be one of the simplest and most important health discoveries ever. It is also a sort of autobiography, summarizing about forty years of this author's inquiry into the rapidly growing discipline of energy medicine. In retrospect, it is remarkable how this field has quickly evolved from virtual obscurity to a major part of new health care systems that are emerging around the world. The author's focus has been on the science that explains how energy therapies work. The quote given above by Albert Szent-Györgyi defines an "energy crisis"

12

that has to be resolved in order for energy medicine to be better understood, appreciated, and more widely used. What is actually meant by healing accomplished by moving energy? And why has Western medical science, with all of its sophisticated analytical tools, been unable to understand the medicines from every culture and every medical tradition before ours? The time has come to provide a logical answer to these important questions, especially since methods are now being brought from other cultures and other medical traditions into our mainstream health care system.

The story contained herein includes some technical matters that you may find unfamiliar and perhaps a bit challenging. We all know how to use the electrical circuits that enable us to turn on a lightbulb or toaster, but the energy circuits in the body that enable us to sense the world around us and move ourselves around and regulate our biology have been elusive. However, the physics and biology of energy are important subjects that can help you better understand yourself and that you can use to have a longer and happier life. Therefore I hope you will do what I do when I come across something I do not understand. I keep on reading! Later on I usually come upon a passage that brings everything into focus. If you lose interest or get lost in the details, I suggest you jump to the last section, where all of the pieces are put together. Then, if you find the conclusions as exciting as I do, you can go back to the parts that give the details of the story.

Fig. 1.1. Albert Szent-Györgyi (1893–1986), M.D., Ph.D., known to his friends as Prof or Albi

The cast of characters in this story includes a world-famous Hungarian-American Nobel Prize–winning biochemist working at the Marine Biological Laboratory in Woods Hole, Massachusetts (figure 1.1); his wife and daughter, who became victims of cancer, stimulating him to begin a personal and passionate search for the causes of cancer and other chronic diseases; energetic subatomic particles called electrons and protons; equally energetic and essential yet highly toxic molecules produced by the immune system in response to injury; the continuous fabric of the body's cells and tissues called *the living matrix;* components of the living matrix called collagen and ground substance; some scholars of Oriental medicine; the electrically charged surface of the planet we live on; a retired cable television executive turned inventor; and a group of scientists—including the author.

Another exciting part of the story is an experience that may be familiar to you—the feeling of well-being you get when you take your shoes and socks off and let your bare feet touch the Earth. Exciting new discoveries are documenting and explaining the health benefits of going barefoot. Prepare yourself for a fascinating exploration that has helped us understand a major underlying cause of virtually all chronic diseases, including cancer, heart disease, and all of the diseases of aging. In these pages you will learn how going barefoot can provide an essential "vitamin" from the Earth beneath our feet that helps prevent or relieve virtually all of these painful and debilitating conditions. The key has proved to be inflammation, which is now recognized as the earliest stage of almost all major health challenges. An inflammatory response to an injury or to environmental stress can leave behind pockets of disturbed tissue that can persist for many years and that can slowly compromise various body functions.

We shall see that inflammation is fundamentally an energetic phenomenon and that it can be best prevented and treated by moving energy; more specifically, by moving electrons, which are nature's own antioxidants. Something as seemingly simple as a massage or other form of bodywork, or walking barefoot on the Earth, can stop inflammatory processes and lead to a surprisingly quick recovery from persistent chronic issues. This is something anyone can experience without spending a cent! These remarkable successes are explainable on the basis of energetics. Our exploration will reveal the real meaning of the terms *grounded* and *ungrounded* as used by practitioners of a variety of therapies.

ALBERT SZENT-GYÖRGYI, M.D., PH.D.

The first character in this story—and he was definitely a real "character"—is the author of the quote given at the beginning of this chapter. Albert Szent-Györgyi was considered by many to be one of the most intuitive and creative minds of the twentieth century. His pioneering research in biochemistry laid the foundation for the research of generations of biochemists who continue, to this day, to explore the molecular basis of life. In 1937 he received the Nobel Prize for his fundamental discoveries, including the purification of vitamin C from Hungarian paprika.[1]

Vitamin C, also known as ascorbic acid, is a water-soluble vitamin and is essential for the synthesis of the protein collagen, which is the basic component of the connective tissues that form blood vessels, tendons, ligaments, cartilage, bone, skin, and the inner and outer structures of all of the organs. We will have much more to say about Szent-Györgyi's research on collagen and what it means for the functioning of our connective tissues on page 28.

Throughout his career, Szent-Györgyi studied elusive substances called reactive oxygen species (ROS). These molecules are key players in the story of inflammation, chronic disease, aging, and energy medicine. They are electrically charged because they are missing one or more electrons. ROS are "eager" to replace their missing electrons and will do this by stealing electrons from any nearby structure. While this process is essential to many life processes, it can also be extremely harmful. Vitamin C is a highly effective antioxidant. It is important for neutralizing ROS wherever they are formed. Vitamin C can protect molecules in the body, such as proteins, lipids, carbohydrates and nucleic acids (DNA and RNA) from damage by ROS and other "oxidants" generated during normal metabolism as well as during the response to injury or exposure to toxins and pollutants.

We will soon see that electrons from the Earth are also antioxidants, perhaps the best and most natural antioxidants. To anticipate the conclusion of this essay, Szent-Györgyi's search for the mechanism of cancer led him to the study of the movement of energetic electrons in the molecular fabric of the human body. We now know that the movement of these electrons can help us understand and appreciate the benefits of a wide range of complementary and alternative therapies.

Sadly, Szent-Györgyi never reached his goal of finding a cure for cancer, and the last years of his life were frustrating because of it. But his studies have finally paid off by providing us with an understanding of how energy, in the form of electrons, can move from place to place within the human body. Remarkable as it may seem, this information is essential for understanding the causes of cancer and other chronic diseases, the ways other cultures and the other medical traditions before ours used the movement of energy for healing, how a wide variety of energy therapies work, and what happens when we walk barefoot on the Earth.

Skin contact with the Earth enables mobile electrons to flow from the Earth into the body. Szent-Györgyi's discoveries explain how these mobile electrons can move through our tissues to reach the places they are needed to neutralize ROS and relieve chronic pain, the cause of pain and inflammation, and prevent chronic diseases, including the diseases of aging. These discoveries can also help us understand the remarkable therapeutic effects of a wide range of bodywork, including energetic, psychotherapeutic, and movement therapies that enhance energy (electron) flows within our tissues.

THE INSTITUTE FOR MUSCLE RESEARCH

In 1949 Szent-Györgyi left Hungary and moved to Woods Hole, Massachusetts, where he set up the Institute for Muscle Research at the Marine Biological Laboratory. He continued the research on muscle that he had begun in Szeged University in Hungary. His accomplishments have been honored in Hungary by the naming of the Albert Szent-Györgyi Medical University in Szeged.

Szent-Györgyi made two fundamental discoveries that laid the foundation for modern muscle physiology and biochemistry—the study of the basic mechanisms that enable us to move. First, he discovered that the muscle protein that had been discovered in 1864 by the German physiologist Wilhelm Friedrich Kühne (1837–1900), who called it myosin,[2] is actually a complex of two proteins—myosin and actin. In a classic experiment, Szent-Györgyi found that threads made of an actin-myosin mixture called actomyosin would contract in vitro (in a glass dish) when two substances were added: the energy-rich compound known as adenosine triphosphate and calcium ions (figure 1.2).[3]

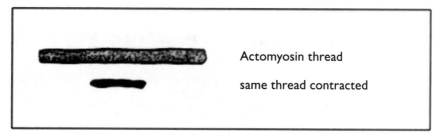

Actomyosin thread

same thread contracted

Fig. 1.2. Szent-Györgyi was the first to show that a fundamental physiological process, muscle contraction, could be accomplished outside of the body, using molecules isolated from cells.

In his autobiography, Szent-Györgyi stated that to see the threads contract for the first time was perhaps the most thrilling moment of his life.[4] In 1954 his huge discovery was acknowledged with the prestigious Albert Lasker Award for Basic Medical Research.

CANCER RESEARCH

The loss of his wife and daughter to cancer started Szent-Györgyi on a crusade to find a cure. It was obvious to him that our inability to treat the most serious diseases of our time means that something important is missing from our medicine, and his intuition was that it had to do with energy and communication. A few years after receiving the Lasker Award, in connection with his work in cancer research, he said this about the heart muscle: "The most basic property of the heart is that it is a muscle, and the chief property of muscle is that we do not understand it. The more we know about it, the less we understand and it looks as if we would soon know everything and understand nothing. The situation is similar in most other biological processes and pathological conditions, such as the degenerative diseases. This suggests that some very basic information is missing."[5]

He did not look for the reason cancer cells grow. Instead he sought the mechanisms that stop normal cells from proliferating except when required, as during embryonic development and during tissue regeneration. He suggested that the regulatory mechanisms that keep cells from becoming cancerous had originated very early in the evolution of life on Earth. The general idea was simply that when cells in the body lose their communications or their relationships with the rest of the body, they can become malignant. He came to see cancer as being ultimately an electronic problem at the molecular level.

Szent-Györgyi was mystified by the fact that biomedical researchers had little interest in energetic processes, except for those who traced the chemical reactions involved in the production and breakdown of the energetic adenosine triphosphate molecule. He realized that these metabolic pathways, some of which he had begun to identify as part of his Nobel Prize–winning research, were only a small part of the story. He had an intuition that life is too rapid and subtle to be explained by slow-moving chemical reactions and nerve impulses. He also felt that the proteins are the stage on which the drama of life unfolds. He concluded that the actors can be none other than small and highly mobile units such as electrons and protons.

In other words, he was convinced that living systems have important primordial energetic communication systems that evolved long before the nervous system did. He suspected that real progress in treating chronic diseases such as cancer would be slow until these regulatory systems were better understood.

The significance of these ideas cannot be overemphasized. At the time Szent-Györgyi was doing his research, and to this day, it was accepted that virtually all flows of electrical charges within the human body and within cells are accomplished by the movement of charged ions* or charged molecules. We are taught that nerve impulses arise entirely from the flows of ions across cell membranes. The idea that electrons might be free to move about within the body, and that some aspects of physiology might be fundamentally electronic, is never seriously considered. Note that there is an important distinction between electrical processes mediated by charged ions and electronic processes mediated by electrons. Flipping a switch to turn on a lamp is an electrical event; using a computer to write a letter or essay involves electronic processes taking place in the computer's microcircuits.

The reasons for the lack of interest in biological electronics are historical. When the electrocardiogram was developed in the early 1900s by the Dutch physician and physiologist Willem Einthoven (1860–1927), there was a need for a model to explain charge transfer between the electrically active heart and the skin surface. In 1913 Einthoven and his colleagues made the simplifying assumption that the body is a "volume conductor," or a simple bag of solution of dissolved ions.[6] This made it much easier to calculate how electrical fields produced by the heart were conducted to the skin surface, where they could be detected with the electrocardiograph.

These volume conductor models worked for a while and were extremely useful, but in the 1930s problems began to arise when it was realized that the body is actually more complicated than that; various tissues lie between the heart and the skin surface. These tissues are not composed of simple salt solutions. They have intricate structures that can significantly alter the flow of electrical charges to the skin surface. However, the idea that the body and its cells are bags of salt solution had already become a fundamental principle in physiology, and changing the concept would require revision of many aspects of physiology. To put it another way, electronic biology is a disruptive concept in that it would

---

*An ion is an atom or molecule in which the total number of electrons is not equal to the total number of protons, giving it a net positive or negative electrical charge.

require changes in the ways research is conducted, the ways physiology is taught to students, and, ultimately, the ways patients are treated. An analogy is the recognition by Copernicus and Galileo that the Earth is not at the center of the universe, as had been thought for the previous 1,500 years.

Philosophers of science refer to this situation as "meaning invariance," a serious problem that occurs again and again in science when useful tentative assumptions about nature gradually come to be taken as facts. The idea that charge could be transferred within the body in the form of small particles such as electrons and protons is something that physiologists rarely, if ever, consider. In other words, scientists have been basically discouraged from discussing electronic conduction in living tissues or have simply ignored it because it would be inconsistent or incompatible with the volume conductor assumption and all of its consequences and implications, extending throughout the fields of physiology and medicine. Meaning invariance is a phenomenon that slows progress in all branches of knowledge.

In retrospect, we can see that Szent-Györgyi's ideas about charge movement were far ahead of their time. He was convinced that something important was missing in our medicine and that energy was the missing piece. I suggest that the movement of electrons is part of the "moving energy" that facilitates healing, as stated in the Szent-Györgyi quote at the beginning of this essay. We shall see that many of the complementary and alternative healing techniques that have seemed to lack a scientific basis are made understandable in part by the ability of therapists to stimulate the movement of the mobile electrons described by Szent-Györgyi. These alternative techniques include:

Acupuncture
Alexander technique
Aura balancing
Biodynamics
Body talk
Bowen

Chiropractic

Consegrity

Continuum

Cranial-sacral

Feldenkrais

Healing touch

Holographic repatterning

Homeopathy

Massage

Meditation

Osteopathy

Pilates

Pranic healing

Polarity therapy

Reiki

Rolfing/structural integration

Therapeutic touch

Yoga

Zero balancing.

UNTIL NOW!

During the last years of his long and illustrious career Szent-Györgyi focused on the study of small and highly mobile units—electrons and protons. This work never produced the dramatic breakthrough in understanding cancer he was seeking, but, in retrospect, we can now see that his intuition had put him on the right track. The basic research he did is now paying off. Specifically, we have come to understand, on the basis of his discoveries and subsequent research, how electrons and protons move about within our bodies and act as carriers of energy and information that enable us to react far faster than can be accounted for by slow-moving chemical reactions and nerve impulses. These high-speed processes reveal themselves in peak athletic and artistic accomplishments when performers are able to sense their environment and respond to it in ways that cannot be explained by the relatively "slow-boat" communication in the nervous system.[7]

These processes also help us understand the remarkable yet silent coordination taking place within our bodies on a second-by-second basis, enabling the cooperation of the thousands of events involved in each heartbeat and in each breath. In essence, Szent-Györgyi was beginning to see and describe another fundamental communication system that is far older in terms of evolution and far faster than the nervous and hormonal systems that provide the foundation for modern regulatory physiology and biomedicine. Without an understanding of this other communication system we are unable to understand cancer, cardiovascular disease, and the many other health conditions that plague our modern world. Likewise, the physician or biomedical researcher does not know where to begin to explore and explain the mechanisms involved in the various alternative and complementary therapies.

We will also see how disturbances of energy and information flow go hand in hand with chronic inflammation. By this statement I mean that compromised energy flows can both cause and be caused by inflammation. To be specific, we will see that the mobile electron is nature's antioxidant, and when our bodies become deficient in electrons or when electron flows are disturbed the result can be chronic inflammation.

This is a very timely observation because contemporary medical researchers around the world are documenting the relationships between chronic inflammation and virtually all of the most serious diseases of our times, including the diseases of aging. The following passage from a widely used medical text describes the centrality of inflammation.

These are heady times for inflammation research. Besides advances made possible by the molecular revolution, it is now clear that inflammatory injury underlies some of the most prevalent and devastating diseases, such as atherosclerosis and perhaps Alzheimer's disease. In addition, the mechanisms regulating inflammatory events . . . overlap with those underlying normal and abnormal development and cancer. The increased understanding of molecular pathways has galvanized a mushrooming biotechnology effort focused on the holy grail of therapy: the discovery of agents that preserve the "salutary" effects of inflammation—first stated by John Hunter in 1793—and prevent its harmful effects.[8]

Despite the fact that the work of Szent-Györgyi was generally ignored by the scientific community at the time (the 1970s and 1980s), we now have a more accurate paradigm, or scientific model. In every culture and in every medical tradition before ours, healing was accomplished by moving energy.

A PUBLIC LECTURE IN WOODS HOLE

My introduction to Szent-Györgyi's work began in 1969 when I was a summer investigator at the Marine Biological Laboratory in Woods Hole. Szent-Györgyi gave a public lecture titled "Electronic Biology and Cancer." The whole community came to this event, in recognition of the fact that the speaker was one of the most famous citizens of Cape Cod at that time. I was fascinated with his highly animated demonstrations of concepts that were completely new to me, and I wanted to know more. I vividly recall to this day how he poured solutions from one huge test tube to another, showing us dramatic color changes revealing events taking place at the quantum physics level (figure 1.3). Eventually the ideas presented in this lecture were published in a book with the same title as his lecture.[9]

On the way out of the auditorium after the talk I saw a friend who was a muscle biochemist and asked her how her colleagues viewed the remarkable ideas Szent-Györgyi had just presented to us with such infectious enthusiasm. Her answer startled me. Szent-Györgyi did very significant work in the past, she said, but his current research was not important. "He should be given a modest grant in acknowledgement of his previous accomplishments, so he can putter around in the laboratory for his remaining days, but certainly nothing of significance will come of it." Somehow this statement did not seem to resonate with Szent-Györgyi's

*Fig. 1.3. Szent-Györgyi demonstrating an
experiment during a lecture*

vibrant and exciting presentation. Many years later I found this same
opinion stated again by J. T. Edsall in an article that explained why Szent-
Györgyi's peers had rejected his grant proposals for cancer research.

> His ideas on cancer research never seemed really promising to me,
> and I was distressed when the NIH (National Institutes of Health)
> insisted on my serving on a panel that was to visit his laboratory
> and evaluate the quality and promise of his research. We regretfully
> came to the conclusion that the underlying conceptions did not look
> promising compared to research that was going on elsewhere. We
> did recommend some continuation of funding, but of course Albert
> wanted funding at a far larger level. I felt, with pain, that he had
> lost the special touch and instinct that had guided him aright in his
> brilliant pursuit of significant problems in the past.[10]

Szent-Györgyi responded to the rejection of his grant request by writing some articles, including "Looking Back" in 1971[11] and a note titled
"Dionysians and Apollonians," published in *Science* in 1972.[12] In the lat-
ter article Szent-Györgyi made a distinction between the Apollonian scientist, who tends to develop established lines of research to perfection,

and the Dionysian, who instead relies on intuition and is more likely to open new and unexpected avenues for research.

These classifications reflect extremes of attitudes found in art, painting, sculpture, music, dance, and other endeavors. The future of mankind depends on scientific progress, he said, and scientific progress depends on support from research grants. He explained that the methods of distributing grants unduly favor the Apollonian, who can clearly see future lines of research and has no difficulty writing a logical proposal.

Not so the Dionysian, who knows only in which direction he wants to go out into the unknown; he has no idea what he is going to find there or how he is going to find it. He explained that he had been asked to write a plan for several years of research for the grant reviewers to evaluate, but this was not only a painful process, it also was impossible. His way of doing research was to go to the laboratory and do an experiment on one day, digest the results during a good night's rest, and then decide what to do the next day. For him to provide a detailed plan for several years of future research would not only be impossible, it would be dishonest. The creative process that leads into the unknown and to new discoveries cannot be mapped out in advance. He had not, as Edsall suggested, "lost the special touch and instinct that had guided him aright in his brilliant pursuit of significant problems in the past."

The problem was that his kind of pioneering exploration was simply not encouraged by the granting agencies, nor was it understandable to most members of the scientific community. Szent-Györgyi explained that funding criteria should be redefined as science grapples with one of nature's mysteries—cancer—which may demand entirely new approaches: "A discovery must be, by definition, at variance with existing knowledge. During my lifetime, I made two (the synthesis of Vitamin C and the contraction of actin and myosin). Both were rejected offhand by the popes of the field. Had I predicted these discoveries in my applications, and had these authorities been my judges, it is evident what their decisions would have been."[13]

His articles presented resounding critiques of the way government research funds are allocated. They triggered a wide-ranging discussion in the scientific community. A Canadian scientist, Alexander A. Berezin, explained how the competitive granting process was inefficient, expensive, discouraging to innovation, and marginalizing of truly exploratory research, with its frequently uncertain outcome. A better system, he said, would be one that bases funding on a scientist's prior successes—the long-term track record of applicants rather than their ability to make a proposal that fits with the current paradigm.[14]

Since the peer reviewers are members of the scientific establishment, they tend to understand and support projects that fit established protocols rather than innovative research. Berezin said, "Christopher Columbus may never have left harbor if his travel plans had been subject to the prior approval of an expert peer review panel!" These discussions were definitely not well received by the granting authorities. We will never know what would have happened had Szent-Györgyi received significant government funding for his research.

One purpose of this article is to show that Szent-Györgyi's special touch and instincts were leading him in a very promising direction that was too far ahead of its time to be appreciated by most of his scientific colleagues. We now know that the research that was going on elsewhere and thought to be more promising, as mentioned by Edsall, and that followed the traditional and acceptable and fundable procedures has not led to a solution for the epidemic of cancer and cardiovascular diseases. Many dedicated researchers and clinicians are working on cancer and the other chronic issues, but the scope of their inquiries is limited by the paradigms they have learned and whose boundaries they are working within. We also know that the something important that was missing in our health care, as mentioned earlier, is still missing, as witnessed by the deteriorating overall health of Americans. That something is missing in the health equation can also be documented, for example, by comparisons of life expectancy at birth by country, with the United States now ranking forty-ninth in the world. This is an absolutely devastating statistic given the fact that our health care system is the most expensive one in the world.[15]

THE NATIONAL FOUNDATION FOR
CANCER RESEARCH

Due to the interest and skill of a remarkable man, Szent-Györgyi was able to continue his research despite the loss of government funding. In April 1971, Szent-Györgyi gave a talk at the National Academy of Sciences and was interviewed afterward by the *Evening Star* newspaper. In the interview, published in the April 29, 1971, issue, Szent-Györgyi described his financial hardships and his current funding dilemmas. He was surprised, a short time later, to get a contribution of twenty-five dollars from Washington, D.C., attorney Franklin Salisbury.

Major funding bodies had not backed Szent-Györgyi's research, but Salisbury was familiar with the importance of unconventional scientific ideas and decided to send Szent-Györgyi a donation. Soon after, Salisbury received a heartfelt handwritten letter of thanks from Szent-Györgyi. Salisbury thought it was odd for a Nobel laureate to be so touched by such a small contribution.

A year later, Salisbury offered to put together a nonprofit cancer research organization built around the cause of this older scientist who still seemed to have so much to offer. Within a few years, mainly through direct-mail solicitation, the National Foundation for Cancer Research (NFCR) had raised enough money to support not just Szent-Györgyi's research, but the labs of others working on the cancer question as well. The NFCR became a "laboratory without walls" that enabled scientists from around the world to work in loose collaboration, with Szent-Györgyi as its intellectual leader. Today the foundation continues to fund more than fifty laboratories around the world that are working on innovative, multidisciplinary approaches to cancer. The foundation also selects a cancer researcher each year for the Albert Szent-Györgyi Prize for Progress in Cancer Research.

Again, while much progress has been made, this research still has not led to the dramatic breakthrough in electronic biology Szent-Györgyi was looking for. From conversations with some of the investigators who have been supported by the NFCR, it is apparent that few of them have followed Szent-Györgyi's passion for electronic biology. Most have gone off in different directions. While important discoveries have been made in the process, it can be said that Szent-Györgyi's original direction more or less fizzled out—until now!

THE FRAMEWORK OF LIFE

Many years have elapsed since Szent-Györgyi's pioneering and largely ignored investigations in the fields he named submolecular biology and bioelectronics (he also "wrote the books" on both fields, published in 1960 and 1968, respectively).[16,17] These works received little attention from American science, although they profoundly influenced many researchers in Europe, Eastern Europe, and Russia, such as Franco Bistolfi[18] in Italy, Włodzimierz Sedlak[19] in Poland, and Konstantin Korotkov[20] in Russia.

Szent-Györgyi knew that most biochemists were studying the water-soluble enzymes that could be easily extracted from cells and that this popular technique was leading to dramatic discoveries in biochemistry and molecular biology. But in the process of doing these investigations, researchers were breaking apart the physical frameworks of cells and tissues and discarding them. The discarded materials consisted of the extracellular matrix, or connective tissue, which is the basic fabric of the body (see figures 1.4 and 1.5) and is made mainly of the protein called collagen, a gel material known as ground substance, and the cellular framework known as the cytoskeleton.

Szent-Györgyi explained that he was studying the material that other biochemists were throwing down the sink. He was studying the structural fabric of the body and of life itself. By discarding the material framework of the body, the other biochemists were simply unable to study that system as a conductor of energy. When Szent-Györgyi studied the insoluble protein collagen (shown to the left in figure 1.4) from the electronic perspective, he found that it was a semiconductor* capable of transferring

---

*A semiconductor is a material that has an electrical conductivity due to flowing electrons—as opposed to ionic conductivity—that is intermediate in magnitude, that is, between that of a conductor and an insulator. Devices made from semiconductor materials are the foundation of modern electronics, including radios, computers, telephones, and many other devices.

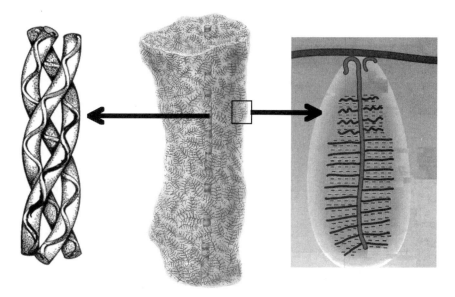

Fig. 1.4. Connective tissue (center) has two main components. The illustration at left shows the triple-helical collagen molecule with its water, or hydration, shell. Electrons are semiconducted through the protein backbone and protons through the hydration shell. The ground substance (right) binds vast numbers of electrons (shown as dashes).

electrical charge as free or mobile electrons. He also discovered that the water surrounding collagen, known as the hydration shell, conducted protons.[21] Hence, electron and proton conduction in the molecular and aqueous framework of the body could provide the basis for high-speed energetic communication systems, and these might be the systems that are compromised in cancer and other chronic diseases.

We shall see that modern research has confirmed and extended these ideas. We now know that many of the molecules in our bodies are semiconductors.[22] This fact is well-known and taken advantage of in one of the fastest growing branches of technology—known as the molecular or nanoelectronics industry. A recent review of this field acknowledges the pioneering work of Szent-Györgyi.[23]

Metals conduct electricity because they contain energetic electrons that are free to move from place to place under the influence of an electric field. It is the movement of those energetic electrons through the fila-ment of a lightbulb that produces the light that enables us to read and to do other things for which sight is necessary at night. Likewise, both the human body and the surface of the Earth are electrically conductive. Szent-Györgyi's research sought to identify the ways electrons can move about within the body; a number of mechanisms have now been identi-fied on the basis of his work and that of others.[24]

The universal conductivity of the Earth's surface varies somewhat from place to place, depending on water and mineral content, vegeta-tion, and other factors. Farmers know that soil that does not conduct well will not produce good crops. Likewise the human body is not uni-formly conductive. Some regions are more conductive than others, and these conductivities are indicative of our health status. This matter is well known to acupuncturists, who measure the conductivity between acupuncture points to evaluate energy flows in the body. It is impor-tant that we appreciate the importance of maintaining the conductivity of the living matrix within us as well as the conductivity of the liv-ing matrix beneath our feet, in the soil that produces the nutrients that sustain us.

Within the human body, the blood, for example, is highly conductive, and fatty tissues are not. However, local variations in the conductivity of the surface of the Earth and within the human body have relatively little effect on the ability of an Earth connection to allow mobile electrons to flow from the Earth to the body. When a person's skin is in contact with the Earth, the body quickly becomes saturated with mobile electrons from the Earth. The soles of modern footwear are insulators and block this vital connection.

My personal interest in Szent-Györgyi's work was inspired in part by curiosity as to why the scientific community was ignoring his research. When I asked my colleagues for a serious critique of his studies, they usu-ally confessed they did not really understand what he was talking about well enough to comment. At the time, very few scientists were interested in the biomedical implications of electronics and quantum physics. I was shocked by the willingness of my colleagues to make negative judgments about the quality and promise of Szent-Györgyi's research when they did not really understand it. This just did not seem right.

I therefore spent a decade studying Szent-Györgyi's research, talking to his colleagues about it, reading his books and papers, and teaching myself quantum physics. I was never part of Szent-Györgyi's research team; I had my own research projects and occupied the laboratory across the hall from his institute. I became good friends with a number of scientists working with Szent-Györgyi and had many valuable conversations with them. I had an intuition that someday the understandings I was gaining by studying his work would eventually reveal the breakthrough Szent-Györgyi was looking for. That time has now come.

A PASSION FOR CONNECTIVE TISSUE

Szent-Györgyi's ideas excited me, and I wondered how they might fit into the larger schemes of biology and biophysics. Some twenty years of looking at cells and tissues in the electron microscope led to a fascination with connective tissue, the ubiquitous material that touches every cell in the body and that provides the structural framework for every organ and every tissue. Subsequently I learned that a group of German and Austrian researchers led by Alfred Pischinger[25] and Hartmut Heine[26] had named this the "ground regulation system." They referred to it as the largest organ in the body because it is the only organ that touches all of the other organs. The connective tissue is the matrix that sustains life, the forest, so to speak. It is so ubiquitous that researchers often do not notice it because they are so busy looking at the trees. For example, surgeons cut through the connective tissue to get to the organs or tissues they are looking for, and physiologists pass over it in their fascination with the more familiar and more tangible systems and functions. Textbooks often refer to the skin as the largest organ of the body, not realizing that the skin and all of the other organs are mainly made of connective tissue.

On the basis of some forty years of basic and clinical research, Pischinger and Heine identified the ground regulation system as the place where diseases and disorders begin and the place to focus both prevention and treatment. Interestingly, a similar conclusion had been reached by Andrew Tyler Still, the founder of osteopathy. Still's insights have actually been incorporated into a wide variety of modern complementary and alternative therapies. He wrote, "The fascia [connective tissue surrounding nerves, muscles, bones, etc.] is the place to look for the cause of disease and the place to consult and begin the action of remedies in all diseases."[27]

Note how these concepts related to the ground regulation system are converging on Szent-Györgyi's original insight that cancer and other chronic diseases result from a failure of regulatory communications. These ideas about the clinical significance of the ground regulation system or connective tissue matrix contrast sharply with the dominant paradigm of modern biomedicine, known as cell pathology, which was established in 1858 by Rudolph Virchow.[28] As Pischinger and Heine wrote, "The concept of a cell is, strictly speaking, only a morphological abstraction. Seen from a biological viewpoint, a cell cannot be considered by itself without taking its environment into account."[29]

The modern perspective, based on Virchow's work, is that all illness arises in cells and is therefore best treated by biochemical and pharmacological approaches that affect cellular metabolism. The concept of the ground regulation system acknowledges that cells can become dysfunctional, but recognizes that pathologies actually originate in the cellular environment—in the ground regulation system. One of the themes in the various complementary and alternative therapies is the importance of the quality of the matrix and how energy "blockages" (such as those produced by old scars and by persistent chronic inflammation) can compromise energy and information flows and thereby lead to diseases and disorders and slow the communications involved in injury repair.

Since collagen is one of the main components of connective tissue, and since Szent-Györgyi and his colleagues were describing how collagen behaves as a semiconductor, I wondered if electronic semiconduction might be taking place throughout the connective tissue system that extends everywhere in the body. If this is the case, electronic and protonic conduction in the connective tissues could provide the basic system for high-speed, whole-body conduction of energy and information; these could be the systems that are compromised in cancer and other chronic diseases; these could be the systems that enable athletes and performers to accomplish remarkable physical feats; these could also be the systems that are the focus of the various complementary and alternative medicine approaches, including acupuncture, shiatsu, acupressure, healing touch, therapeutic touch, zero balancing, and reiki (refer to the list on page 20).

On one occasion I asked Szent-Györgyi if he thought the connective tissue could be the organ that conducts electrons throughout the body. He responded that he had quite enough work to do with figuring out the processes taking place in molecules, and that it would be good for me to look into that subject. As fate would have it, I had already decided to go in that direction.

In 1982 I was invited to present a talk at the annual meeting of the American Society of Zoologists, held in Louisville, Kentucky. In my talk I summarized some of these ideas about Szent-Györgyi's research. I was asked to write an article about my talk and decided to dedicate it to Szent-Györgyi to commemorate his ninetieth birthday. The main thesis for the talk and the paper was the interconnection between the various fiber systems in the connective tissues and in the cells embedded in them. From a thorough review of the histology and ultrastructure of various kinds of cells and tissues, I realized something that seemed profound: biologists studying connective tissue had known for a long time that the spaces between collagen fibers are filled with a hydrated and electrically charged gel-like material called the ground substance (shown in figure 1.5).

Likewise, cytologists had noticed that the interiors of cells were also filled with another negatively charged material they referred to as ground substance. Finally, cytologists and geneticists described a gel-like matrix within the cell nucleus and also referred to *it* as ground substance. Therefore the title of my paper was "Structure and Properties of Ground Substances."[30]

Two key discoveries led to my profound idea that these ground

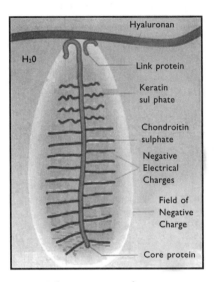

Fig. 1.5. The anatomy of connective tissue

substances might share similar properties and might be connected to each other. The first was the discovery by Mark Bretscher at Cambridge University in England that there are proteins extending across cell surfaces, connecting the cytoskeleton of every cell with the surrounding extracellular connective tissue matrix that pervades the body.[31] Second, Ronald Berezney and colleagues from Johns Hopkins University in Baltimore, Maryland, found that there are also connections across the nuclear envelope, joining the cytoskeletal matrix with the nuclear matrix.[32] Taken together, these observations meant there is a continuous physical system or matrix that actually extends throughout the body and that reaches into every part, even into the nucleus and the DNA.

As a body-wide system this continuum needed a name. After trying several different ways of identifying it, in 1993 my wife, Nora, and I named it the living matrix,[33] and this name has been recognized as a valuable concept by the complementary and alternative medicine community (figure 1.6).

When I received reprints of my article from the *American Zoologist,* I gave a copy to Szent-Györgyi. He wrote me a little note saying he thought

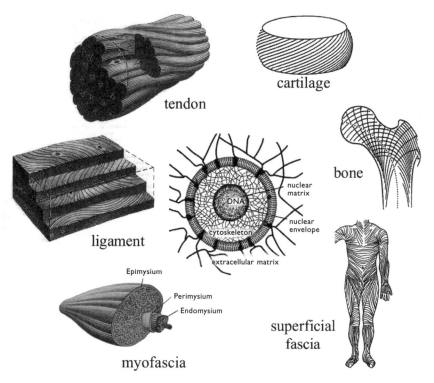

Fig. 1.6. The living matrix is the continuous fabric of the body that includes every cell and nucleus as well as the fibrous system of the connective tissue, including tendons, ligaments, the myofascia around the muscles, the superficial fascia under the epidermis, the bone fibers, and cartilage.

the ideas I had summarized were correct. Coming from this hugely respected Nobel laureate, this was tremendous validation for the years I had invested in exploring these ideas.

On the basis of the observations of Szent-Györgyi and his colleagues, it was obvious to me that this body-wide system could be the material substrate that rapidly conducts energy and information between every part of the body and every other part, with electrons and protons acting as the carriers of the energy and information. This high-speed electronic system could be the basis for Szent-Györgyi's idea that life is too rapid and subtle to be explained by slow-moving chemical reactions and nerve impulses. Failures of communication within this ancient system could be the key to chronic diseases such as cancer. The successes of a wide variety of complementary and alternative therapies might be accounted for in part by their ability to maintain and restore this vital system—generally unrecognized or unexplored by modern biomedical researchers.

These ideas definitely seemed worthy of further exploration, but something was still missing. Could there be some way to bring all of these new concepts into sharp focus and attract the interest of medical researchers? For this to happen, a lot more detail had to be fitted into the picture. This has now been accomplished through the discoveries that will be described next.

ACUPUNCTURE AND OTHER FORMS OF ENERGY MEDICINE

Acupuncture gained attention in the United States when President Nixon visited China in 1972. Traveling with Nixon was *New York Times* reporter James Reston, who had an emergency appendectomy and was so impressed with the postoperative pain relief he felt as a result of having had acupuncture that he wrote an editorial about it in the *New York Times* upon his return to the United States. This was one of the first times the American public was introduced to the practice of acupuncture in a major way.

Acupuncture is based on an ancient concept of health and healing, which is accomplished by the movement of energy. As such it is one of many traditional and modern medical systems widely thought to be entirely unsupported by modern science. Of course, acupuncturists and other energy therapists would like to find a way of validating and reconciling their work with modern biomedicine. We will soon see that Szent-Györgyi's discoveries have contributed to this reconciliation and validation.

A few years after Reston's report in the *New York Times,* one of the leading acupuncturists in Asia, James Tin Yau So (1911–2000), came from Hong Kong to teach the first acupuncture course in the United States. The class took place in 1974 in the back room of Redwing Book Store in Cambridge, Massachusetts, the first U.S. bookseller to concentrate on complementary medicine. So's classes evolved into the New England School of Acupuncture, the first acupuncture school in the Western Hemisphere.

Some years later I was asked to teach a class in science to the acupuncture students. I met faculty members Stephen Birch and Kiiko Matsumoto, who were teaching a Japanese style of acupuncture and have since become known internationally as acupuncturists, teachers, and authors. They asked me to give some lectures in their classes. I learned from them that modern acupuncturists were passionately interested to know if there might be some science to describe the energy flows that seemed so obvious during their clinical work. Acupuncture and related methods such as reflexology and shiatsu are based on ancient ideas of the movement of energy through the body and how compromised energy flows can compromise health.

Matsumoto and Birch became very excited about the possibility of semiconduction of electrons and protons through the acupuncture channels in the body. Perhaps Szent-Györgyi's ancient high-speed regulatory system is the actual physical substrate of the acupuncture meridian system! In 1988 Matsumoto and Birch published some of Szent-Györgyi's ideas and my interpretations of his discoveries in their book, *Hara Diagnosis: Reflections on the Sea*.[34] The concepts were of interest to the acupuncture community and to practitioners of other energy-based therapies (listed earlier on pages 20–21).

I began to further explore the details of this idea in various articles and in my book *Energy Medicine: The Scientific Basis*, published in 2000.[35] The concepts were of sufficient interest that I was invited to present them at conferences and workshops around the world. But the biomedical, clinical, and research communities took little notice, since acupuncture and other forms of bodywork—energetic and movement therapy—were not regarded as significant components of the health care system at that time.

This situation has changed dramatically during ensuing decades, as has been documented by David Eisenberg and colleagues at the Harvard

Medical School. They did two demographic studies in the 1990s show-ing that alternative health techniques, defined as methods that are not taught in medical schools, were becoming extremely popular among patients. Billions of dollars were being spent by patients out of pocket, since the methods were not covered by health insurance.[36,37] Since then scientific research has begun to document both the physiological mech-anisms and clinical effectiveness of these techniques. Numerous energy medicine modalities have grown from total obscurity to widespread and enthusiastic acceptance. For example, reiki, healing touch, and therapeu-tic touch began to be offered to patients in major medical centers around the United States, and hospital doors are opening for many of the other techniques listed on pages 20–21.

A number of acupuncture schools were created to serve various regions nationwide, and thousands of practitioners were trained in this ancient art. Many physicians became interested in acupuncture, and the American Academy of Medical Acupuncture was formed to nourish their fascination with Oriental medicine. Other schools emerged to teach a wide range of energy therapies.

Many of the methods listed on pages 20–21 take advantage of the properties of the acupuncture meridians and other ancient energetic channels. However, the meridian system that is the basis for acupunc-ture theory continued to be a mystery to biomedical researchers, resulting in ongoing skepticism in the medical community, which has slowed the acceptance of energy medicine—until now!

BAREFOOT

Remarkably, the key studies that have enabled this validation are based on what happens when you take your shoes and socks off and walk bare-foot on the surface of the Earth. While the entire skin is conductive to the mobile electrons that flow from the Earth into your body, there is one particularly important area of the foot known to acupuncturists as Kidney 1 (figure 1.7).[38]

As antioxidant electrons from the Earth enter the body through

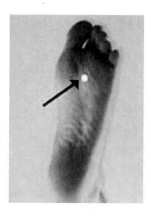

Fig. 1.7. Kidney 1 is the termination of the Kidney meridian, and ultimately connects via the living matrix to all of the other meridians, and thereby delivers Earth's antioxidant electrons to every nook and cranny of the body.

the bottoms of the feet and flow throughout its framework—the living matrix—they neutralize the free radicals widely thought to be responsible for the cumulative damage that leads to chronic diseases and aging.

GROUNDING THE MATRIX OF LIFE

A final and remarkable piece in the puzzle being presented here was contributed by Clinton Ober, a retired cable television executive (figure 1.8). Ober knew a lot about grounding because television cables are shielded to prevent the TV signal from leaking out and to prevent external signals from leaking in. When the cable leaks, the TV picture turns to "snow." This rarely happens these days because modern shielding and grounding are virtually perfect, thanks in part to the essential work of Ober and his engineers.

Some years after retiring from the cable TV industry, Ober began to wonder what would happen if the human body was grounded. These thoughts were inspired in part by a simple observation: the people he saw walking around were insulated from the Earth because they were wearing shoes with soles made of plastic or rubber, both of which are insulators. Shoes with traditional leather soles—electrically conductive—were rapidly disappearing. Note that the leather used in the past to make the soles of shoes and moccasins is actually a semiconductor. Leather is made from the hides of animals and is electrically conductive because it includes a

Fig. 1.8. Clinton Ober, who perfected the art of grounding

layer of dermal connective tissue known as superficial fascia (see figure 1.6). Leather is mostly made of collagen, which Szent-Györgyi had shown to be a semiconductor.

Ober wondered what would happen to the human body if it was grounded by connecting it to the Earth. He already knew that many people like going barefoot and that it somehow made them feel good. This was important to Ober because he had recovered from a nearly fatal illness and had constant pain from prior back surgery. Because of this pain, it was hard for him to sleep at night. So he decided as an experiment to connect himself to the Earth while sleeping. He devised a crude grounding system by placing some conducting materials on his bed and connecting them to a wire that went out his bedroom window to a steel rod inserted into the Earth. As soon as he lay down on this simple grounding system he quickly fell asleep, and suddenly it was the next morning! He hadn't slept that well in a long, long time.

Ober decided to share his experience with some friends who also had trouble sleeping, all of whom experienced improved sleep. Moreover, several of his friends told him they no longer needed to take pain medications before going to bed. Ober realized he might have stumbled on a discovery of some importance, and the rest of the story is history. It has been fully explained in the book *Earthing,* by Ober, Stephen T. Sinatra, and Martin Zucker.[39]

Subjective reports of subjects in a study, who slept grounded, include the following reactions.

Fell asleep faster and easier
Able to fall back asleep after waking up
Wake up refreshed instead of exhausted
General quality of sleep improved
Sleeping much deeper
No more daily headaches
Decreased food cravings
Decreased bloating
Decreased depression and hot flashes
No more nightmares
Digestion improved
Less constipation and nausea
Less neck pain
Fewer leg and foot cramps
Arm and lower back pain gone
Improvement of temporomandibular joint problems
Don't need coffee in the morning to get going
Less backache
Less PMS
More even-tempered
Greater sense of well-being
Subtle sense of lightness and ease
Diminished stress
Less fatigue because of less pain
Fibromyalgia improved, diminished pain and fatigue
Felt more rested and feel like I need an hour less sleep
Deeper relaxation
Allergies definitely lessened
Stopped clenching jaw at night

Sleeping fewer hours

Have more energy

Stopped snoring

Less numbness in hand and fingers, especially at night

No longer wear brace at night

Feeling better physically and emotionally

Dreams more vivid

Stress and tension improving

Calmer and better mood

More centered and patient

More relaxed

Stomach reflux has disappeared

Less heartburn.

Ober refined his first makeshift system by designing a sophisticated conductive fabric with carbon or silver threads woven into it. He gave these sleep systems to many people, asking only that they tell him how it affected them. The results were astounding. People reported that they not only slept better, but they also had more energy and fewer aches and pains both during the day and night. These results were so encouraging that Ober decided to recruit some scientists to verify his results and help him figure out what grounding was actually doing to the human body.

This did not prove to be easy. As Szent-Györgyi had experienced, most people in the science world thought Ober's ideas were very strange. His lack of a scientific background made it difficult for him to find any interest in the science world. Eventually he found a physician, Maurice Ghaly, who decided to set up an experiment that would prove Ober was wrong. Ghaly was convinced that sleeping while grounded to the Earth could not possibly have any of the benefits Ober was describing. Contrary to his expectations, Ghaly found that sleeping grounded did, indeed, improve sleep. Moreover, the subjects in his study reported a wide variety of other benefits (see the list above. A key discovery was that sleeping grounded normalizes the day-night rhythm of the stress hormone cortisol. Ghaly and his colleague, Dale Teplitz, reported these results in 2004.[40]

Research continues on grounding, or earthing, the human body. The studies have involved more than a dozen scientists in the United States and Canada. The next and final section of this article will summarize the discoveries that have been made.

EARTHING, ELECTRONS, AND INFLAMMATION: PUTTING THE SCIENCE TOGETHER

This story began with a description of some remarkable research conducted by a prominent scientist at the Marine Biological Laboratory in Woods Hole, Massachusetts. Szent-Györgyi's motivation: to defeat the enemy, cancer, that had taken away two of the beloved women in his life. His discoveries and the way they were interpreted were ahead of their time and were generally ignored by the American scientific community. Now, some thirty years later, those discoveries are proving to be the key to understanding an equally remarkable discovery—the effects of connecting our bodies to the surface of the planet we live on. And when these two stories are put together they begin to answer another important question: How do bodywork and energetic and movement therapies produce such remarkable results when other methods have failed?

After making two historic discoveries in the fields of biochemistry and physiology, Szent-Györgyi finished out his career "lost in the twentieth century" (the title of his autobiography).[41] But we are now able to see that his wanderings into the unknown were not in vain. He was merely solving a puzzle that had not yet been thoroughly defined. We can now define the puzzle in more precise terms.

PRECISELY WHAT IS MEANT BY "HEALING BY MOVING ENERGY"?

The final chapter in this story is a simple description of how inflammation works, how chronic inflammation creates so many disease conditions, and how both biological grounding (also known as earthing)

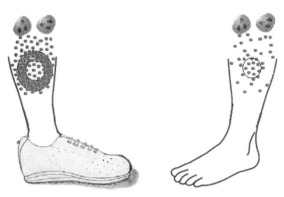

Fig. 1.9. Response to an injury in an ungrounded person (left), with the inflammatory barricade shown as the gray circle, and in a grounded person (right)

and complementary and alternative methods can bring quick relief from chronic disorders. The actors in this part of the story are injury, aging, the immune system, white blood cells called neutrophils, a process known as the oxidative burst that releases reactive oxygen species (ROS), the ground substance, collagen, the living matrix, and electrons. These actors can function together naturally to protect us from inflammation and disease and slow the aging process. All of these valuable mechanisms are compromised when we become electron deficient by disconnecting ourselves from the Earth. The picture of inflammation in the ungrounded versus the grounded body is depicted in figure 1.9.

As seen in figure 1.9, without grounding, the connective tissue ground substance reservoir is electron deficient. Any stored electrons are gradually consumed by neutralizing free radicals produced during metabolism. The injury attracts white blood cells called neutrophils that secrete free radicals. These molecules are missing one or more electrons and are therefore highly reactive. The free radicals destroy any bacteria that might have entered the injury site, and they break down damaged cells and necrotic tissue to make way for the repair process.

However, the absence of electrons in the ground substance allows free radicals to escape from the injury site and damage nearby healthy cells. This can cause the formation of an inflammatory barricade and a pocket of chronic inflammation, as shown in the image on the left in figure 1.9. Hans Selye, the great Canadian scientist who devised a new medical context for the term *stress* and who documented the hormonal consequences of trauma and other stressors, based on his work done in the 1950s, found that these pockets of inflammation can cause chronic disease by leaking toxins into the body fluids over long periods of time.[42]

In figure 1.9, on the right, we see the way electrons stored in the ground substance reservoirs in the grounded person can neutralize any free radicals that might stray from the injury site. Grounding thereby protects healthy tissues from free radical damage, widely thought to be a cause of aging. The grounded person shows little or no inflammation, the injury heals quickly, the inflammatory barricade does not form, and the risk of developing chronic disease is greatly reduced.

The key to chronic inflammation and the cause of chronic disease is the inflammatory barricade. This quotation is from a popular medical text on inflammation: "Inflammation normally is a localized, protective response to trauma or microbial invasion that destroys, dilutes or walls-off the injurious agent and the injured tissue."[43]

The "walling-off" of a site of inflammation leaves behind a pocket of fluid surrounded by connective tissue.[44] Selye accidentally discovered that injection of air under the skin of rats produces a stable bubble, or pocket, that can be used to study inflammatory reactions (figure 1.10). These pockets came to be called inflammatory, or Selye, or granuloma pouches. More than a thousand articles have been published on the effects of injecting bacteria and various irritants into inflammatory pouches.[45] Our research on grounding indicates that these pouches probably will not form or will be minimal if a person is grounded before, during, and after an injury.

Fig. 1.10. Rolf reproduced Selye's concept of an inflammatory pouch produced by injecting air into fascial sheaths.

Selye's work tied inflammatory responses to stress, cortisol secretion, and adaptation. Selye's work, and that of others, proved that the necrotic tissue breakdown products created in inflammatory pockets, which slowly leak across the barricade and enter the blood and lymphatic circulation, produce progressive atrophy in various organs a distance from the original site of trauma. For example, on page 161 of the first edition of his classic book *The Stress of Life,* Selye mentions that he was able to inject inflammatory pouches in rats with irritants and microbes that produced a syndrome characterized by inflammation of the heart valves (endocarditis), which was very similar to what was occurring in children suffering from rheumatic fever.[46] Under some conditions this was accompanied by inflammation of the kidney (nephritis) and excessive stimulation of the blood-forming organs.

The inflammatory pouch concept explains how local pockets of inflammation in our bodies can trigger a variety of chronic diseases and disturbances, many of which frustrate physicians because it is difficult to locate their cause. "Silent inflammation" refers to a condition in which the inflamed site is not painful and may go undetected for years, while gradually causing chronic problems elsewhere in the body. The phenomenon was described long ago in dentistry, beginning with twenty-five years of root canal research by Weston Price,[47] but it currently receives little attention except from "biological" dentists. Price demonstrated that pockets of inflammation remaining after a root canal procedure can give rise to a variety of chronic diseases.

The existence of walled-off areas, as described by Selye, is known to practitioners of bodywork and energetic and movement therapies (figure 1.10). Ida P. Rolf, in her book on Rolfing, states, "In practically all bodies, in one muscle or another, small lumps or thickened non-resilient bands can be felt deep in the tissue. The lumps may be as small as small peas or as large as walnuts."[48]

Rolf also states, "Some similarly injurious process no doubt gives rise to the lumpy knottings we have noted." A consistent observation is that these palpable lumps gradually disappear during a series of sessions of bodywork.

Since the wall of the inflammatory pocket is composed of connective tissue, which is made of collagen, electrons can probably cross the barrier by semiconduction much more readily than can the much larger antioxidant molecules, such as those that can be provided in the diet. This is a simple explanation of how electrons from the Earth can percolate through the living matrix and enter the inflammatory pockets, where the electrons can neutralize residual ROS. Likewise, various therapeutic technologies introduce or induce electric currents to flow within tissues. Examples include frequency specific microcurrent,[49] pulsing electromagnetic field therapy,[50] Ondamed,*[51] and related technologies.

There are several mechanisms that can explain how Rolfing (also known as structural integration), massage, shiatsu, and other forms of bodywork, as well as energetic and movement therapies that involve applying pressure or bringing movement to the tissues, can bring about the natural reduction or elimination of pockets of inflammation left over from old injuries. One mechanism involves piezoelectricity, or pressure electricity, using the electric fields that are set up when pressure is applied to crystalline materials such as connective tissue and bone. A second mechanism uses the induced movements of electrons stimulated by the energy fields from the hands of the therapist even before physical contact is made with the skin surface.[52] (Finally, it is known that the ground substance gel can dissolve or depolymerize temporarily when exposed to physical forces such as pressure, electricity, or magnetic fields.[53] Hence the therapies that introduce physical pressure, electric currents, or magnetic fields into the body may temporarily render the inflammatory barricades more permeable or even cause them to dissolve as the ground substance depolymerizes.

CONCLUSIONS

One important step is identifying the place on the bottom of the foot that provides the best connection with the Earth. As described on pages 38–39 this is the point on the ball of the foot known to acupuncturists

---

*Ondamed is a registered trademark.

as Kidney 1 (see figure 1.7). This point connects to the Kidney meridian that, in turn, connects to all of the other meridians extending throughout the body and to every tissue and every organ. From the biological perspective it appears that the living matrix system and the acupuncture meridian system form a continuous network that connects to every part of the body and is therefore capable of delivering mobile antioxidant electrons to any part, even to the interiors of cells and nuclei (figure 1.11).

Fig. 1.11. Science is now proving that our connection to the Earth is more significant than we had previously realized.

This chapter describes the connections between several remarkable discoveries and how they support and explain each other. Szent-Györgyi's research on the movement of charged electrons through the protein framework of the body, conducted during the 1970s and 1980s, had little impact on modern biomedicine. The author's explorations of the living matrix have proved valuable to complementary and alternative therapists, especially when asked to explain to their curious patients how they were able to produce such remarkable clinical results, often when other medical approaches have failed.

However, the living matrix concept has not yet percolated into conventional medical training. For example, most medical texts show an entirely incorrect picture of the cell as a bag of solution, leaving out the cytoskeleton and its interconnections with both the extracellular matrix and the nuclear matrix, as shown in figure 1.6. Finally, the measurable phenomena associated with grounding the human body are most readily explainable on the basis of a living matrix and a meridian system that extends throughout the body and can conduct antioxidant electrons to protect healthy tissues at any place where ROS form, whether from normal metabolism or from immune responses to injury or exposure to toxins or pollutants.

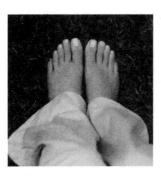

Fig. 1.12. We can halt inflammatory processes in our body by walking barefoot on the Earth.

Our story concludes with some obvious suggestions that can support recovery from an injury, prevent chronic disease, and slow the aging process. Complementary and alternative therapists can easily grasp and use these concepts since they are familiar with the consequences of being ungrounded. Moreover, the concepts that have emerged provide a sound scientific basis for many of the profound therapeutic outcomes that previously seemed to defy scientific logic (figure 1.12).

Some Recommendations
- Spend as much time as you can in barefoot contact with the Earth.
- If you are injured, it is desirable to connect your body with the Earth as soon as possible.
- If you are engaged in a sport or other activity in which you risk injury, spend fifteen minutes with your bare feet on the Earth before you begin, to saturate the electron reservoirs in your connective tissue.
- When it is not possible to be outside with your bare feet on the ground, use devices that conductively connect you to the Earth (see Earthing, www.earthing.com; accessed November 12, 2012). These include grounded sleep systems, grounded floor mats, wrist and ankle bands, and conductive patches, any of which can be

connected with a wire to a ground rod inserted into the Earth or to a properly tested ground port in your electrical system.*

- Patients should be connected to the Earth for at least fifteen minutes or so before and after therapeutic treatments of any kind. It is likely that any therapy will work better if the patient has saturated his or her ground substance reservoirs with electrons.

- Likewise it is wise for both therapists and their patients to be connected to the Earth during therapy sessions. This will prevent patients with extensive inflammation from drawing electrons from the therapist. If the patient has pain in a particular part of his or her body, a grounded conductive patch can be placed on or near the area.

- Patients should be connected to the Earth before, during, and after any surgery. This will probably reduce pain and inflammation and facilitate the healing and recovery process.

- Pets that stay mainly indoors should have a grounded pad to sleep on (see Dr. Goodpet, www.goodpet.com; accessed November 12, 2012).

---

*An electrician can check your electrical system to determine if it's properly grounded.

THE SCIENCE OF VIBRATION

The world to a thinker is the magic motion produced by the Orphic singer.

SOME THOUGHTS ON THE GITA

See deeply enough, and you see musically; the heart of nature being everywhere music, if you can only reach it.

THOMAS CARLYLE

The universal vibratory energies were called by the ancient Egyptians the Word or Words of their gods; to the Pythagoreans of Greece they were the Music of the Spheres; and the ancient Chinese knew them to be celestial energies of perfect harmony. The Cosmic Tones, as differentiations of the OM, were the most powerful force in the universe according to the ancients, for these Tones were the universe—the very source of the Creation itself.

DAVID TAME

You cannot have Motion in Matter without generating vibration; and all vibration is fundamentally Sound; all vibration is changeable into Sound. . . . Sound without which form cannot be, Sound which is the builder of form, which generates form, every Sound having its own form, and every Sound being of this triple character, that it generates form, that it upholds form, that it destroys form.

ANNIE BESANT

The study of sound and the effect of sound . . . will put into man's hands a tremendous instrument in the world of creation. Through the use of sound the scientist of the future will bring about his results; through sound, a new field of discovery will open up; the sound which every form in all kingdoms of nature gives forth will be studied and known and changes will be brought about and new forms developed through its medium. One hint only may I give here and that is, that the release of energy in the atom is linked to this new coming science of sound.

All vibration, it must be remembered, travels along waves of living substance. . . . The forces of evolution vibrate more rapidly than the forces of involution.

DJWHAL KHUL

Like the musician, if we touch the strings that vibrate in harmony, we have melody—sweet music. If we set in vibration discordant tones, we have inharmony—confusion of sound. To understand and comply with the law of harmonious attunement is the great need of humanity.

W. H. WILLIAMS

Many people are aware that sound is always associated with color—that when, for example, a musical note is sounded, a flash of color corresponding to it may be seen by those whose finer senses are already to some extent developed. It seems not to be so generally known that sound produces form as well as color, and that every piece of music leaves behind it an impression of its nature, which persists for some considerable time, and is clearly visible and intelligible to those who have eyes to see. . . . Some such forms are very striking and impressive, and naturally their variety is infinite. Each class of music has its own type of form, and the style of the composer shows as clearly in the form which his music builds as a man's character shows in his handwriting.

ANNIE BESANT AND C. W. LEADBEATER

2
LIFE'S MUSICAL BLUEPRINT

HOW SOUND, LIGHT, AND ENERGY WEAVE THE WEB OF LIFE

John Consemulder, M.Sc.

Nothing rests; everything moves; everything vibrates.

HERMES TRISMEGISTUS

Music in the coming centuries will play a greater role than the roles played by physics, chemistry, and engineering combined. Through the utilization of sound, many scientific discoveries will be rendered obsolete. It will be possible through music to lead nations and humanity to a higher realization of divine principles.

TORKOM SARAYDARIAN

Since the difference between one dimension of reality and another is its rate of vibration, the key to the transformation of spirit also lies within music.

EVAN T. PRITCHARD

IN THE BEGINNING

In different spiritual traditions and cultures, our connection to the source of being is accomplished using sound and vibration. Ancient seers, mystics, and psychics have talked about the music of the spheres, *aum* (or *om*), the word, logos, soundless sound, and the celestial song. All sacred knowledge and mystical exercises are based on knowledge of the word and sound. In shamanic rituals, reaching the spiritual world without using sound is almost unthinkable. In all spiritual traditions we find knowledge concerning the power of sound, vowels, and the spoken word. In the Hindu Upanishads, one of the oldest esoteric teachings, sound is regarded as the essence of being, sound being a particular quality of the ether or akasha, the primal element.

In this essay, my aim is to show that your essence really is sound and that important relationships exist between sound and music, scalar electromagnetics and light, and form and consciousness itself. We live in a multidimensional, vibrational, and energetic universe, but also in a harmonic and truly musical universe, as both microcosmic and macrocosmic evidence will show. Increasingly, "new" scientific discoveries are reflecting important esoteric knowledge from all ages. Science is now rediscovering what the ancients knew all along—that there is a multidimensional, holographic, and musical blueprint of sound, light, and energy patterns that is connected nonlocally to consciousness and intention, and that they create the physical universe and all that we call matter!

SOUNDING ATOMS

In her book *The Secret Doctrine,* author and mystic H. P. Blavatsky (1831–1891) talks about a fundamental law in the occult: in nature there is no rest or silence. She writes, "What might seem like rest is only the transition from one form to another; the change of substance going hand in hand with that of form. Knowledge of this law helps to use Siddhis or supernatural powers and can also help in disintegrating matter or moving objects from one place to another." And in the same book she says this:

"Atoms are called 'Vibrations' in occultism, also 'Sound'—collectively. The waves and undulations of Science are all produced by atoms propelling their molecules into action from within. Atoms fill the immensity of space, and their continuous vibrations are that MOTION which keeps the wheels of life perpetually going. It is that inner work that produces the natural phenomena called the correlation of Forces. Only, at the origin of every such 'force,' there stands as the *conscious* guiding noumenon thereof—Angel or God, Spirit or Demon—ruling powers, yet the same."[1]

The ancients associated sound or speech with the ether of space—which we now refer to as akasha, zero point energy, or the vacuum—of which sound is a fundamental characteristic.

All motion and vibration produces sounds, which we may or may not be able to hear, depending on the range of auditory perception. All music is based on certain numerical relations between sounds, which brings us into direct contact with mathematics. In the words of author Alain Daniélou, "Numbers correspond to abstract principles, and their application to physical reality follows absolute and inescapable laws. In musical experience we are brought into direct contact with these principles; the connection between physical reality and metaphysical principles can be felt in music as nowhere else. Music was therefore justly considered by the ancients as the key to all sciences and arts—the link between metaphysics and physics through which the universal laws and their multiple applications could be understood."[2]

Of course, music and sounds can evoke in us, both in a magical and real sense, emotions, feelings, sensations, images, and connections to the "music of the spheres" because of correspondences between certain aspects of the manifested world and the laws of music. And of course sound has a relationship to color and light because both are based on vibrations, which are frequencies, and frequencies and ratios of frequencies relate to numbers because of their vibrational speeds. Also remember, according to the Bible, God said, "Let there be light." And the phenomenon known as sonoluminescence in contemporary physics demonstrates the relationship between sound and light in water.

Harmony between heaven and Earth comes via attunement and

resonance through a symbolic vibrational representation, much as a tuning fork sets up a sympathetic vibration in another tuning fork of the same frequency. Resonance and entrainment, two key concepts in sound healing, are also basic to understanding nonlocal energetic healing and the influence of consciousness and intention on health. I refer to these as the blueprint of life.

Music represents the connecting forces between the many elements of creation and the manifest world and also regulates these forces as they find expression in form. In the words of grammarian Bhatrihari, "This science of sounds is the chemistry of the universe."[3] The whole universe may be viewed as a musical instrument, giving rise to what Pythagoras called the "music of the spheres."

SYMPATHETIC VIBRATIONS AND JOHN WORRELL KEELY

More than a century ago, inventor and free energy pioneer John Worrell Keely worked out a science he called sympathetic vibration physics, which used musical notes and chords. To activate his machines, he used a vibrating bow held above a tuning fork. When he did this, the tuning fork acted as a generator of invisible but incredibly powerful forces. These forces in turn were able to move large, normally unmovable objects, causing them to levitate.

In addition to levitation, Keely was able to produce disintegration and antigravity phenomena with the use of sound. He also experimented with free energy motors, which ran by means of vibrations. Authors Theo Paijmans[4] and Dale Pond[5] and researcher and author Leonard G. Horowitz[6] all point to the fact that Keely considered the vibration ratios of the thirds, sixths, and the ninths as extremely powerful. As it turns out, these ratios are also important clues in Marko Rodin's math, in Harmatt Muller's lifewave math, and in astrophysics. "Physical manifestation or materialization specifically occurs only at certain node points, reflecting the 3–6–9 matrix of fourth dimensional (i.e., spiritual) mathematics," according to Horowitz.[7] In his earlier writings, Horowitz described these as the same numbers one gets by summing the six frequencies of the ancient solfeggio tones[8]—sound used in ancient Gregorian chants and viewed as the original frequencies of creation.[9]

Keely proved that the "antagonistic thirds vibrations" were "a thousand times more effective" than heat in separating hydrogen and oxygen in water. In his formula of water disintegration, Keely notes that he found that a stream of antagonistic vibrations—in the form of thirds, sixths, and ninths—forced matter to divide itself progressively into all molecular divisions and disintegrate. This principle applied equally to all combinations of elements, gasses, and solids.

Herein lies the hidden power of sympathetic vibration as developed by Keely. A concordant waveform, composed of harmonic frequencies, tends to pull subatomic particles together. On the other hand, discordant waveforms will tend to split or explode the particle or aggregate. In Keely's words, "The rhythmic relations in which force acts are everywhere, under all conditions, and at all times, the same. They are found experimentally to be universally expressible by the mathematical relations of 'Thirds.'"[10] Keely worked, without success, on the theory that polar and depolar current actions were circular, but found success when he found and proved that these forces act with a spiral-vortex motion. Since we can now see that spirals are governed by sixths (inversion thirds, according to musical theory) we begin to get an idea of what Keely called "triune polar flow."

Given this, we begin to understand why the monuments of the ancients show evidence of accomplishments we have been unable to duplicate. They did with simple whole numbers what we've been unable to do with our high-powered computers working with complex irrational numbers. As musical inversion (a music theory principle) demonstrates, we can skip the entire heavily unworkable math when we work with whole numbers. This helps us grasp why Keely was able to do so much with so little a hundred and thirty years ago.

Around the turn of the twentieth century, scientists were looking for a harmonic relationship, but Keely demonstrated the importance of looking for a musical relationship. Pythagoras taught that the lower the numbers in a relationship, the greater the harmony between two frequencies.

According to Keely, this translates into greater bonding force or denser material aggregation. The opposite applies to greater number relations (for instance, 1:1 being the unison versus 13:8 being the major sixth).

Keely recognized the relative pitches between atoms and stated that this is just as important as the vibrational frequencies of the atoms themselves. After all, what value has a frequency when unrelated to another frequency? Not much and probably no value whatsoever. When the two relative frequencies are brought together we have music intervals, modulation, and demodulation of each other, and the whole host of phenomena associated with the merging of vibratory influences.

OCCULT KNOWLEDGE ECHOED IN NEW SCIENTIFIC DISCOVERIES

If we compare ancient and occult knowledge with our new scientific discoveries, it is clear that the *new* sciences are validating what ancient civilizations and spiritual traditions already knew and have long used on a daily basis.

A few interesting points can be made if we compare the knowledge that the ancients possessed with new findings from quantum mechanics, bioenergetics, psychoenergetics, electrogenetics, bioholographic studies, biophoton research, research into acoustical and electromagnetic influence from and on DNA, biogeometry, structured water studies, digital biology, electromagnetic (EM) homeopathy, scalar electromagnetics studies (done by scientist and author Thomas E. Bearden), zero point energy (also called akasha) studies, and crop circle research. First, it seems to me the old ether theory is returning through the backdoor,[11] which is shown by a renewed interest in zero point energy studies, nonlocality research, and the unified akasha field literature coming from authors like Ervin Laszlo.[12] Vortex action and spin are very significant concepts in this new science, but it is also very important to realize that the ancients already recognized these actions as the vibrating movements of atoms and spheres.

Second, authors such as Thomas E. Bearden,[13] Lynne McTaggart,[14] James L. Oschman,[15] and Peggy Phoenix Dubro and David P. Lapierre[16] clearly show that there remains much more to say (and change) about the currently accepted theory of electromagnetism. For instance, we ought to view electricity and magnetism as effects instead of as causal forces, as forces existing only in their interactions with matter. These insights into so-called scalar electromagnetics and scalar waves (which Russian scientists call "energetics"), which can be coupled to intention and consciousness, could have far reaching consequences.[17]

Third, sound, light, numbers, and geometry really are related to each other in fundamental ways, and this fact reflects the knowledge the ancients already possessed and our new sciences now finally seem ready to rediscover (or perhaps remember).

Fourth, nonlocality and the principles of entanglement and interconnectedness should be brought into our explanation models now more than ever. Actions working from a distance have always been commonplace in parapsychology but are now are also being accepted as occurring in quantum mechanics, scalar wave physics, and bioholographics.

Fifth, I think it advisable for us to work our way toward a multidimensional paradigm that will allow us to discover more of the unseen worlds, higher bandwidths, and higher octaves of our musical and holographic universe.[18]

SCALAR WAVES, CONSCIOUSNESS, AND HEALING MORPHIC FIELDS

The now commonly accepted theory of electromagnetism of Oliver Heaviside and Heinrich Rudolf Hertz is only a partial and simplified version of the more original theory of Scottish physicist and mathematician James Clerk Maxwell, according to Bearden.[19] Our current knowledge of electricity, magnetism, and gravity is incomplete. We understand them as effects, not as causes.

Oschman explains that when we say a magnetic field induces a current flow in a conductor, such as a wire or a living tissue, it is actually the potential component of that field, and not the field itself, that underlies the effect.[20] The potentials are of two kinds, called electric scalar potentials and magnetic vector potentials. In 1959, Yakir Ahoronov and David

Bohm showed in their experiments that the potentials have a physical reality. Hence, in destructive interference (in which the waves are exactly out of phase, their amplitudes subtract, and they can partially or completely cancel or destroy each other), where the classical fields cancel each other, there nonetheless remain electrostatic scalar potentials and magnetic vector potentials!

According to Bearden, the traditional transversal electromagnetic waves actually are longitudinal electromagnetic waves and functions thereof. In his book *Energy from the Vacuum,* Bearden says bluntly:

> Every charge in the universe already freely and continuously pours out EM energy in 3-space in all directions, without any observable EM energy input. That is the well-concealed source charge problem, known but ignored by the leaders of the scientific community for a century. All EM fields and potentials and their energy come from those source charges, according to electrodynamics itself. Either we must give up the conservation of energy law entirely, or else we must accept the fact that unobservable virtual EM mass and energy are continuously absorbed from the vacuum by the source charge, transduced into real observable EM energy, and then re-radiated in 3-space in all directions as observable EM energy, creating the associated fields and potentials reaching out across the universe. That this problem continues to be ignored by the scientific community— some forty-five years after the basis for its solution has been proven and is well known in particle physics—is totally inexplicable.[21]

Bearden speaks about so-called scalar waves (others have called these Tesla waves, torsion waves, or vortex action), which are longitudinal waves (similar to the concepts of Nikola Tesla, who spoke about "non-hertzian waves," and Keely, who used sound as a vibratory force for his free energy machines by influencing the etheric force).

A scalar wave is characterized by magnitude only. However, with respect to polarization, scalar photon is a term used for a "time-polarized" photon where the electromagnetic energy oscillates along the time axis.

Hence, a scalar wave is an electromagnetic wave composed of scalar photons whose electromagnetic energy is oscillating along the time axis. The term *scalar* with respect to polarization implies only that there is no vector in 3-space, while there exists one along the time axis. So only the presence and combination of the time-polarized photon and the longitudinal photon in every point of the electromagnetic wave make this wave "observable." The local polarization of the vacuum creates the electromagnetic wave in space. Scalar waves can be regarded as electromagnetic sound waves, the result of two phase-conjugated electromagnetic waves (the wave and its antiwave, both in phase spatially, but 180 degrees out of phase temporally).

Scientists like U. V. Nachalov and Anatoly Akimov made very clear that whenever there are electrostatic or electromagnetic fields in space, torsion fields (scalar waves) also exist in that part of space. These scalar waves can be used in a process Bearden calls "precursor engineering" and can be coupled with intention and consciousness.

According to Bearden, the work of scientist Edmund Taylor Whittaker from 1903 and 1904 has been picked up by Russian scientists and secretly used in their super weapon technologies[22] (see work by Russian scientists Dr. Vlail Kaznacheyev and N. D. Devyatkov). The same principles of Whittaker's work, however, can also be used for healing purposes. In his book *Oblivion*, Bearden reflects on the work of the scientists Raymond Pautrizel and Antoine Prioré, who managed to actually cure cancer and also bring the immune system back to a previous state where the disease had not yet manifested itself.[23] Bearden states that the traditional model of the electromagnetic wave is an erroneous result of replacing the effect with the cause in the electrodynamics of Maxwell. Mass is a component of force; there are no forces in mass-free space. Forces and force fields only exist when they interact with matter.

In my view, it is very interesting that more than a century ago Keely mentioned that you cannot separate force and matter.[24] According to Keely, they are one and the same; force is liberated matter, and matter is force in bondage. A simple analogy is that of dynamite, a harmonious substance when at rest, one that is held together by the molecular and atomic component frequencies. The introduction of a strong impulse from a dynamite cap destroys its homogeneous integrity, and the component subatomic particles are liberated from their bonds. The electromagnetic input into nature is not visible because nature doesn't reveal its real source. Energy is not being produced but captured from the vacuum and transformed. What we measure with today's equipment therefore can only be the integrated and combined transversal electromagnetic field effect waves, not the more fundamental longitudinal waves. These longitudinal waves are force free, except when they come in touch with matter (this explains Bearden's term "force-free precursor engineering").

Whittaker's 1903 discovery that sets of longitudinal waves are the actual basis of all electromagnetic waves, fields, and potentials means that these "ordinary" electromagnetic waves can undergo substantial changes and can therefore be engineered. It is possible to give these "ordinary" electromagnetic waves hidden internal field vectors and dynamics; "deterministic Whittaker infolding of bi-directional electromagnetic plane waves is the key to direct engineering of the Schrödinger equation itself, hence of all physical change."[25]

These principles can be used for healing at a distance, for a cure for specific diseases, or to fight the aging process, depending on the specific "engine" used. Bearden shows that "physical reality itself is deterministically tunable, changeable, engineerable, and not fixed at all."[26] He also makes very clear that "we can engineer it to be either a heaven or hell, the choice is strictly up to us."[27]

Bearden, in his book *Gravitobiology,* states, "The true 'living electromagnetic energy' of biological systems is internalized, infolded electromagnetic energy. It is the infolded and hidden electromagnetic energy of the organized bi-directional electromagnetic wave systems inside the Whittaker potential. It is photon-structured graviton energy. This is not the externalized electromagnetic energy of the electromagnetic wave envelope, with which Western science is presently so preoccupied. This energy does not appear in the electrical engineering or electrical physics textbooks. Nonetheless, our health and our very lives depend on it."[28]

Scalar waves appear to interact with atomic nuclei rather than with electrons. Such interactions are described by quantum chromodynamics.[29] The waves are not blocked by Faraday cages or other kind of shielding; they are probably emitted by living systems, and they appear to be intimately involved in healing (see the work of Robert Jacobs[30] and Glen Rein[31]). According to Bearden, scalar electromagnetics is a unified field theory of electromagnetics and gravitation, since it recaptures the scalar wave portion of electromagnetics, erroneously discarded by Oliver Heaviside and Willard Gibbs.

Some scientists also think the brain receives and sends out scalar waves. Valerie V. Hunt, professor emeritus of physiological science at UCLA, has shown that human brain waves contain hidden order.[32] According to Bearden, "Hunt's experiments with extreme low frequency bands (ELF) of human brainwaves clearly show that hidden deterministic substructures of hidden electromagnetic order exist concealed inside human brainwaves. Since Dr. Hunt has deliberately selected multiple frequency bands, this implies that this hidden order probably represents deterministically created and infolded multiple electromagnetic bidirectional waves in Whittaker potentials. This is strong evidence that the human brain utilizes Whittaker-potentials and Whittaker-infolding in its internal communications—directly correlating with the Soviet approach by Kaznacheyev, Devyatkov, and Lisitsyn."[33]

We can understand by now that in addition to the *externalized* energy balance of nature, there is a heretofore unsuspected (by Western reductionists) *internal* energy balance of nature. This internal energy balance is of vital importance when we consider how the planet is polluted. "We are steadily polluting the very intercommunication and intracommunication fields that sustain life as we know it. . . . We are steadily contaminating and poisoning the entire planetary potential, and each and every year we are dramatically increasing this deadly effect," says Bearden.[34]

He also states, "Each living cell of a biological organism is itself a complete biological organism. Each cell has its own individual bio-quantum potential. Insofar as that cell is concerned, its 'species' bio-quantum potential is the body bio-quantum potential of the whole animal of which the cell is a part. . . . Even organs of an animal have their own biopotentials, as does every physical structure and division of everything in the universe. And everything intracommunicates and intercommunicates via hidden electromagnetic energy. . . . Literally, the planet is a living being, and a special kind of Gaia exists."[35]

Ervin Laszlo employs the image of a jazz band, borrowed from British quantum biophysicist and biologist, Mae-Wan Ho, to explain this phenomenon. No matter how diverse the cells, organs, and organ systems of the organism, in essential respects they act as one; every player responds immediately and spontaneously to however the others are improvising. The super jazz band of an organism never ceases to play in a lifetime, expressing the harmonies and melodies of the individual organism with a recurring rhythm and beat but with endless variations. Always there is something new, something made up, as it goes along. It can change key, change tempo, or change tune as the situation demands, spontaneously and without hesitation. There is structure, but the real art is in the endless improvisations, where each and every player, however small, enjoys maximum freedom of expression, while remaining perfectly in step with the whole. The "music" of a higher organism ranges over more than seventy octaves.

Bearden further explains what he calls the "window of magnitude" that most often exists in weak electromagnetic induction of biological effects in living systems: "Only at or above the minimum threshold does sufficient resolution of the pattern signal for biological activation occur. Above the maximum threshold, the infolded pattern or 'image' (this sounds similar to holographic representations) is no longer discriminated."[36] Bearden's important statement that each cell has its own individual bioquantum potential sounds similar to the view of Jacques Benveniste and James L. Oschman that each molecule has its own electromagnetic signature (as Benveniste's digital biology lab also has shown).

Energetic transfer of information (nonlocal, without biochemical contact) via energy fields constitutes the electromagnetic signature—or what I prefer to call the blueprint—of the field called digital biology.

The so-called law of attraction states that everything you focus your attention on gets drawn to you by attraction. We have all heard this saying:

"Be careful what you wish for." These things come to mind when we read a fascinating perspective from Bearden concerning his view on evolution: In the gravitons composing the vacuum potential, one photonic element is "time forward" and the other is "time-reversed." These are phase conjugates. Thus, any pattern consistently happening to the species diffuses into the vacuum potential, where its opposite, or "negative feedback," component is automatically selected or created by phase conjugation.

> The bottom line is this: the external factors causing stress on a species automatically (but slowly) generate a time-reversed response in the activation of the vacuum potential. That is, the species' need-charge generates an activated phase conjugate response charge, effectively charging up (integrating) the very ghost form or forms in the virtual state of the vacuum that can fulfill that need. As is well known in physics, a virtual entity can become real and observable if energy is added to it.
>
> Thus the species-need is steadily causing just such an 'addition of energy' to the virtual state ghost form that answers that need. When sufficient energy has been added (when it has been sufficiently charged or activated), the ghost form starts emerging into the observable state, in the conceptions (via impulse discharge) taking place in the species. Then species members start being born with that evolutionary change already fully established.[37]

This view, to me, sounds very similar to, and might extend theories and concepts like, the law of attraction, the morphogenetic field theory of Rupert Sheldrake, and the hundredth monkey effect, and even resonates with bioholographic and regenetics ideas (more to come), and co-creation findings in crop circle research.

THE HOLOGRAPHIC WORLD OF DNA

Our DNA is capable of producing and receiving sound (phonons) and light (photons). DNA can even trap photons in a photon lattice (see the research of Professor Fritz-Albert Popp and the Biophysics Institute in Neuss, Germany).[38] Because of its sacred double spiral, DNA is able to spiral light around its double helix structure instead of letting it proceed along a linear path. DNA is a kind of a lens that can attract electromagnetic energy into itself.

Authors Stephen Linsteadt and Maria Elena Boekemeyer emphasize, "Every biochemical reaction is preceded by an electromagnetic signal." The matrix that is produced and sustained by frequency oscillations "provides the energetic switch boarding behind every cell function, including DNA/RNA messengering. . . . Cell membranes scan and convert signals into electromagnetic events as proteins change shape to vibrations of specific resonant frequencies."[39]

It is interesting to note that in 2008 Bruce Lipton also suggested that the cells themselves have the ability to perfectly reprogram their own DNA when the external environment demands it.[40] Harvard geneticist John Keams proved this remarkable hypothesis in his experiment with bacteria that were able to reprogram their DNA. In the words of Iona Miller and Richard Miller, "Life is fundamentally electromagnetic rather than biochemical, the DNA blueprint functioning as a biohologram which serves as a guiding matrix for organizing physical form."[41] The same happens with sound, creating standing wave patterns. Scientists Milo Wolff and Geoff Haselhurst are now working together on a theory called the wave structure of matter, which states that matter is the focal point of a standing wave, the result of two interfering waves. More than a century ago, William Clifford had suggested, "All matter is simply undulations in the fabric of space."

Chromosomes are arranged in a holographic grid, which is designed to interpret and produce highly stable spiraling standing waves (frequency oscillations) of sound and light. These spiraling standing waves direct and control all biological functions. In the words of Iona Miller and Richard Miller, "The genetic code is being transformed into physical matter by means of sound and light signals."[42]

Dolphin research by Michael Hyson has shown that dolphins use their phonators to produce high-frequency sounds and to work with phase control, sound aiming, and sound cancellation to produce a kind of holographic communication.[43]

Scientist Dan Winter—presenting a kind of physics called implosion physics—proposes a theory of a wave-coupling mechanism showing how the "e-motion" energy (energy in motion, feelings such as love, joy, and anger) of the mind and heart (golden mean, *phi*-related in the case of attunement with true feelings of love) is delivered to our own DNA.[44] Electrons should not be regarded as particles, but as standing wave patterns—interference patterns created by vortex action and combined ether vortexes that form a torus—at discrete distances from the nucleus, which might explain why an electron does not crash into the nucleus and how its radiated energy gets replenished.

In a way a torus is like a little black hole, attracting light into itself and creating gravity. The torus shape can also be seen as a form that can be described by a set of phi (golden mean) spirals. DNA itself, measuring 34 × 21 angstroms for every full spiral, happens to be exactly phi-related. According to Winter, the cascade of golden mean electromagnetic sine waves that gain an ever-increasing velocity, breaking the speed barrier of light, is what gravity really is. It now seems clear that our DNA can be influenced by acoustic, electromagnetic, and scalar waves.

According to Jeremy Narby, our DNA can even be "read" or "rewritten" as a textual (and acoustic) genetic code.[45] Research by the Russian group of Pjotr Gariaev strongly suggests that chromosomes both produce and receive the information contained in the DNA "texts" in order to encode and decode them.[46] Chromosomes assemble themselves into a holographic lattice designed to generate and interpret highly stable standing waves of sound and light that direct all biological functions. The linguistic DNA findings of Gariaev's research group reflect the occult teaching, "In the beginning, there was the word."

The biophysics scientist Herbert Fröhlich suggested in 1988 that oscillations (vibrations) set up within a certain area of the DNA create information signals that are spread throughout the whole body, where they deliver energy to certain protein structures.[47]

Living matter is highly organized and exceedingly sensitive to the information conveyed by coherent (laser-like) signals, having collective or cooperative properties of the entire being. The living matrix and the circulatory system are obvious candidates for the medium through which the DNA oscillations become entrained with molecules throughout the body (scientist Harold Saxton Burr has similar ideas concerning this).[48] The Gariaev group showed that chromosomes function much like reprogramming holographic biospiritual computers, using the DNA's own laser radiation.[49] Their discovery of the grammatical syntax of the DNA language led to experiments in which they managed to modulate certain frequency patterns onto a laser beam—also modulating radio waves and adding meaning (semantics) to the carrier wave—thereby influencing DNA frequency information and its communication. Spoken language can be modulated on the correct carrier wave frequencies, by which we can reprogram our DNA.

In the words of Iona Miller and Richard Miller, "In the quantum holographic DNA-wave bio-computer theory, DNA is a self-calibrating antenna working by phase conjugate (remember scalar waves and phase conjugation) adaptive resonance capable of both receiving and transmitting quantum holographic information stored in the form of diffraction patterns-quantum holograms."[50]

The Gariaev team developed machines that influenced cellular metabolism by means of sound waves and light waves, both coupled to human language frequencies. The genetic code, especially of potential DNA, follows uniform grammar and usage rules virtually identical to those of human languages. Using this method, Gariaev showed that chromosomes that are damaged by X-rays, for instance, can be repaired by simply applying vibration and language, or sound combined with intention, or words to DNA. Here, once more, we see the powerful influence of words, another thing the ancients knew quite well.

Glenn Rein and Rollin McCraty discovered and proved experimentally that emotions such as anger and fear can compress DNA; they have the power to contract the DNA molecule.[51] However, emotions of joy, gratitude, and love unwind the DNA, decompressing it. Here we find a direct connection between torsion energy (scalar waves) and life-affirming emotions, especially unconditional love.

Now consider the implications of Winter's theory that e-motions can program our DNA and Masuru Emoto's findings that human consciousness affects the molecular structure of water. This is especially true of high-quality water, which forms beautiful crystalline patterns in response to affirmation techniques and positive visualization in general—especially when coupled with healing sounds. Maybe the Beatles were right all along (as were the ancients): "All we need is love."

Gariaev's work also showed that DNA looks similar to the workings of a network computer—their research showing that DNA is able to influence quantum subspace.[52] Our "junk DNA" has some impact in the universe at large. Genetic expression has been found to impact the infinite matrix of space—our DNA sending and receiving powerful data through a universal network of ether. Small, magnetized wormholes of a subquantum nature (equivalent to the Einstein-Rosen bridges in the vicinity of black holes) can be produced by these electrogenetic effects.

MUSIC OF THE GENES

Certain electromagnetic and bioacoustic frequencies can be turned on to trigger or suppress genes. Such genetic expression is bioelectrically mediated through liquid protein crystal matrices throughout the body. Matter can be structured and reshaped through sound frequencies and energized waves (particles being just the focal node points of waves) to vibrate our sacred geometries into physical realities.

Remember that not only, "In the beginning, there was the word," but also, "God said let there be light; and there was light." Holy persons have said that light and sound are one. Author Sol Luckman states, "When properly activated by sound combined with intention, the superconductor that is DNA is designed to re-harmonize the entire bioenergy blueprint."[53]

Dr. Merrill Garnett talks about "a musical or harmonic element within the organism. . . . This is molecular music, fragile, dependent, recurring

under the right conditions, based in quantum echoes and hidden physics."[54] The work of Keely (as recounted in Dale Pond's *Universal Laws
Never before Revealed: Keely's Secrets*), Joachim Ernst Berendt (*The World Is
Sound*), Michael Hayes (*High Priests, Quantum Genes*), and other authors
such as Horowitz suggests that, as the ancients have told us for centuries,
this truly is a musical universe, not just a harmonic one. We live in a holographic, vibrational, harmonic, but most importantly, a musical universe.

Sol Luckman refers to James Hurtak's book *The Book of Knowledge:
The Keys of Enoch* in regard to DNA's four basic nucleotides that form
sixty-four different "words" used to build a virtually limitless number
of "sentences" out of genes.[55] In Luckman's words, "The keys of Enoch
is an elaboration of the 'keys' for creating a higher energy body." These
"letters" are reflected in the points Gregg Braden brings out in his book,
in which he demonstrates that the ancient four-letter Hebrew name for
God—YHVH, the tetragrammaton—is actually code for DNA based
on DNA's chemical composition of nitrogen, oxygen, hydrogen, and
carbon.[56]

Significantly, there are sixty-four keys (similar to the sixty-four combinations in the I Ching). "Hurtak is clearly writing about actualizing a
transformational potential in our genetics," Horowitz says. "This musical mathematics determines the sacred geometry of DNA. It is a perfect
five-sided pentagon for each helical spiral of the molecule. Double this to
construct the twin helix, with each full helical spiral rotating 36 degrees,
and you end up with a decagon formed from the two pentagons. (It is not
likely coincidental that the highest level possible in the hierarchy of the
global elite's secret society, Freemasonry, is also 36; wherein 3 + 6 = 9 or
completion in Pythagorean mystery school math)."[57]

We now know DNA can be influenced by scalar waves and acoustics.
Bearden discusses the major mechanism for a "translation between different frequency bands," which is already well-known in the theory of forced
oscillations, called subharmonic oscillation, and which might be important to our musical genes discussion here. He says, "Subharmonic oscillation is very important in Whittaker-structuring. A Whittaker-structured
potential is already harmonically structured—essentially from 0 Hz to

infinity. The Whittaker-structuring is a spatial and harmonic structuring of a partial potential component of the total space-time potential. Subharmonic resonance plays a major role in this structured lattice—far more than we have previously suspected in our study of subharmonic resonance in nonlinear gadgets."[58]

In subharmonic oscillation, a frequency that is a subharmonic of some higher, even much higher, resonant frequency can trigger the higher-frequency oscillation—much the way multidimensional sound can resonate with the higher frequencies of light. Subharmonic oscillation is particularly applicable to living systems. It is very important for healing in my opinion. Bearden continues by saying:

> The implication of high biological nonlinearity and subharmonic oscillation is that Kaznacheyev cytopathogenic optically-induced effects can readily be translated to cytopathogenic microwave-induced effects—because they already are! An optical Devyatkov information substructure can also be translated to a microwave Devyatkov information substructure. Further, if the optical Kaznacheyev cellular disease-inducing signal sets captured from a diseased cell culture are phase-conjugated, this yields a specific curative signal complex for that specific disease. This optical curative signal structure can then be subharmonically translated and Whittaker-infolded to yield a curative microwave Devyatkov information signal. This is the basic mechanism for direct engineering of electromagnetic healing apparatuses, such as were successfully developed by Antoine Prioré and properly tested by eminent French scientists working with him, in the 1960s and 1970s.[59]

ENLIGHTENMENT
BY SOUND HOLOGRAMS

The task of the Human Genome Project was to identify the complete structure of the human DNA and map its triplets and genes. It is now known that of the complete chain of triplets in a complete DNA string only 3 percent is used for coding and reproduction of proteins. The other 97 percent is called junk DNA!

Evidence now shows that this so-called junk DNA might be more important than the encoding codons. The sequence of the DNA molecule's codons can be reprogrammed. This seems to me to lead to another startling conclusion, not unlike scientist Karl Pribram's findings that when we remove a lot of brain tissue, cognitive functions and memory still seem to remain intact.[60] Pribram proposed a neural holographic process of creating life wherein images are reconstructed when their bioacoustic and associated electromagnetic representations, in the form of distributed data within neurological information systems, are appropriately engaged.

According to Iona Miller et al., "These representations act as screens or filters. The temporal organization of cortical columns and the arrival of impulses at neuronal junctions converge from at least two sources, forming interference patterns. These patterns are made up of classical postsynaptic potentials, coordinated with awareness. This microstructure of slow energy potentials is accurately described by the equations that describe the holographic process."[61]

The quantum mechanistic, nonlocal, fractal, and holographic biowave computer workings of our brain surpass the slower biochemical and neurotransmitter signaling and processing of neurons. Water and the circulatory system would also seem very important sound-wise and (scalar) electromagnetically in relation to these findings, especially since the ventricles in the brain are filled with fluid. Furthermore, if it really is not just a holographic universe but also a musical universe, our DNA "texts" may be rewritten to another musical "score." Sound and light are one, the ancients said. Maybe we will soon find out that our electromagnetic fields are actually concentric spheres of multidimensional sound.

It is now known that the rest of our junk DNA contains what are being called transposons.[62] Scientist Barbara McClintock received the Nobel Prize in 1983 for her discovery. A transposon is a term for "jumping" DNA. It can actually break loose from a certain area and jump to another area. In this way transposons can change and rewrite the DNA code, working through RNA. Clearly, junk DNA was prematurely dismissed. More than 90 percent of our DNA does not code for protein synthesis. In the 1990s, three Nobel Prize winners proved that the primary function of our DNA is not protein synthesis but the reception and transfer of electromagnetic energy.

Findings from other genetic research show that sound can produce light, a concept quite similar to the so-called regenetics field of research. In 1975, an article by Richard Allen and other researchers appeared in *Psychoenergetic Systems* titled "A Holographic Concept of Reality." They outlined a model of "precipitated reality," stating, "Superposed coherent waves of different types in the cells interact to form diffraction patterns, firstly in the acoustic (sound) domain, secondly in the electromagnetic (light) domain. . . . This leads to the manifestation of physical form as a 'quantum hologram'—a translation between acoustical and optical holograms."[63]

It is very important to note that this sound-light transformation process creates reality functions in the genome, in our DNA. Maybe the Hermetic principle "as above, so below" also goes here. The mathematical relationship to "above" and "below" can also be expressed by phi, or the golden mean. When you raise the frequency of sound by forty octaves, you enter the frequency bandwidth of light. Conversely, if you slow down light frequencies by a factor of forty, you get sound frequencies. Maybe the theory of forced oscillations and the principle of subharmonic oscillation might also be involved in the translation from sound to light.

We now see that the conclusions from Richard and Iona Miller et al. and the Gariaev group are also relevant to author Michael Talbot's suggestions,[64] and may also be relevant to Hyson's dolphin research. Dolphins, but also whales and bats, use a kind of acoustic sonar, echolocation, vortex ring production, and phase locking techniques for orientation and communication, and they sometimes use sound to numb their prey. Dolphins routinely produce acoustic waves and electromagnetic fields capable of causing bioresonance and entrainment, which science now proves are factors exquisitely involved in therapeutics and healing.

Entrainment causes systems to vibrate more in phase, or synchronistically. When the phases of two oscillations match (resonance), most energy will transfer between them. It is as if a more dominant wave "couples" to another wave and "pulls" it to its own frequency. Steven Birch showed that entrainment of the human EEG occurred during and after swims with free dolphins. The EEG of the human subjects reduced in frequency and increased in power. Again, this energy entrainment effect is mediated through DNA.[65]

Dolphins' senses encompass a broader bandwidth than ours. They can cause water to steam (called cavitations); work with "time-reversed acoustics" (a very important field for future healing with sound, which has shown some good results in cancer research); and produce micro-bubble formations (much like medical ultrasound), sonochemistry heating effects, sonoluminescence, piezoelectric effects, and more. In my view, it seems clear all these amazing (and highly important) things dolphins can do are very important for healing and future vibrational and energy medicine, and they show how sound and light (and geometry and energy fields) work together.

It is very important, I think, to study the exact mechanism by which dolphins create their acoustic-light holograms and the amazing effects they are able to produce. Not only does water know the answers, but so also do some of nature's creatures who live in it.

Jonathan Goldman, an internationally known sound healer (his formula is frequency plus intention equals healing), states, "The language of light, of course, is multidimensional sound."[66] Goldman described a remarkable experience he had in a Mayan site in Palenque, Mexico.[67] This was in 1987, during the Harmonic Convergence. He and his group were taken to a spot people are normally not allowed to visit. When they arrived, Goldman was asked to "tone"—make sound with his voice. When he did this, using the overtones his voice created, he noticed something extraordinary; the dark room he and his group were in became subtly lighted. He could see the contours of the group, which he couldn't see before he started making sound. In his experience, this was not the light we can see from a lamp or a sonoluminiscent light; it was a light field created by harmonic vocal toning.

Some authors seek to explain the phenomenon Goldman experienced by implicating the pineal gland, a brain structure that is very important electromagnetically, but highly underrated in neuropsychology. Thirty percent of the pineal gland structure is highly sensitive magnetically, and more importantly, the pineal gland has been shown to have light-producing properties (bioluminescence).

The pineal gland is a small, pine-cone-shaped gland located in the middle of the head. It is closely associated esoterically with the ajna chakra, which is located between the eyes, and is often associated with the "third eye," which, according to Descartes, is "the seat of the soul." It is also known to be a light-sensitive clock affecting sleep and the sex glands. The pineal gland is rich in neuromelanin, which, according to scientist Frank Barr, is a phase-timing, information-processing interface molecule that is a photo transducer. This is a substance that has the ability, among other traits, to absorb and convert light energy into sound. It also has the ability to turn sound energy into light. While this phenomenon is not widely known, there are references to it in certain texts. Dhyani Ywahoo, a Native American medicine woman, writes that in the ancient mystery schools, initiations were held in total darkness.[68] The initiates had to be able to produce their own light. Maybe this was done through the creation of vocal harmonics.

Barr believes melanin and its brain counterpart, neuromelanin, may be the keys to the link between the mind and the brain.

ENTER THE MATRIX

Oschman refers to research done by I. Peterson.[69] Peterson showed that DNA has a tendency to pack together in crystalline arrays. Living crystals are composed of long, thin molecules, soft and flexible. They are liquid crystals (also check the work of Ho in this regard). We can find use of crystals in the esoteric and spiritual literature, but crystals are also used in old phonographs, radios, and all kind of electronic devices, where they are responsible for making highly tuned circuits. In fact, in living systems crystals are the rule, not the exception. We find them in arrays of phospholipid molecules forming cell membranes and myelin sheaths of nerves, collagen arrays forming connective tissue and fascia, contractile arrays in muscle, arrays of sensory elements in the eye, nose, and ear, arrays of microtubules in the brain, microfilaments and other fibrous components of the cytoskeleton in nerves and other kind of cells, and arrays of chlorophyll molecules in a leaf.

Oschman describes his theory of how energy and information circulate through what he calls "the living matrix." Other researchers who have contributed to this electromagnetic view of the living organism are Albert Szent-Györgyi, Robert O. Becker, Herbert Fröhlich, Donald Ingber, K. J. Pienta, and Donald S. Coffey. The conclusion drawn by Oschman from scientific research is that the matrix structures of the nucleus, the cytoplasm, and the extracellular grids form a continuous and interconnected communication system. Electric signals, photons, acoustic signals, and piezoelectric signals are working together with solid-state biochemistry.

In this living matrix all kinds of essential integrations of functions are being accomplished, for instance, the bodily repair functions and protection against disease. Movement, pressure, and other energies circulating through this system are in interaction with our metabolism and our genetic material, our DNA!

It's interesting to note here that, according to Becker, our immune system doesn't heal anything. Becker's[70] important research suggests that repair and healing are accomplished by the badly studied regeneration system (also shown by the fascinating studies on salamanders by Harold Saxton Burr and other studies by Reinhard Voll.)[71]

VIBRATION CREATES FORM AND THE UNIVERSE: CYMATICS

Sound vibrations create form (structure, geometry). This is what cymatic research clearly shows. Cymatics (the Greek word *Kyma* means "wave") can be defined as the study of how vibrations generate and influence patterns, shapes, and moving processes. It is all about the study of wave phenomena. The so-called Chladni figures, the Lissajous figures, harmonograph studies, and especially the work of Hans Jenny[72] clearly show that form does not follow function but is created by its underlying vibration.

Sound affects physical matter. If we tone the sacred Hindu syllable *om* (*aum*) and other spoken sounds or sound vibrations, their corresponding forms appear in paint, sand, dust, or powder (or water, we now know from Emoto's work). We can see all kind of geometric patterns emerge while uttering this mantra. When correctly uttered into a tonoscope, with a substance on its vibrating plate, the sound produces a circular "O," which is then filled in with concentric squares and triangles, finally producing, when the last traces of the "m" have faded, a "yantra"—the sacred geometrical pattern found in many of the world's religions.

Goldman states, "Sound is an extremely powerful tool for creating sacred space" (something shamans also know). He adds, "Almost any place can become a sacred space and power spot if the individuals present use the formula of vocalization + visualization = manifestation to create the field. . . . Sound builds upon itself; this is especially true of sacred sound—chanted with sacred intention (certain sacred words have lost much of their power because they are no longer chanted with sacred intention). A sacred sound that has been activated through constant chanting is charged and particularly powerful."[73]

So cymatics is closely related to geometry and sacred geometry and therefore also to the golden mean, Fibonacci ratios, spirals, platonic solids, and interference patterns like the vortex action Laszlo describes in his akasha unified theory.[74] In Ervin Laszlo's example, the action might be compared to the interference effects created by two stones thrown in the water, but here the water is the Dirac Sea, or quantum vacuum, where all energy and matter are connected. Not only do the cymatic images sometimes resemble crop circle formations and geometric patterns, but they also resemble mandalas and sometimes even the Sri Yantra, and platonic solids can be created by use of sound.

Nada brahma, the world, is sound. Cymatic patterns created by sound can also look like the shields of turtles, the structures in leaves and trees, or shelves, and sometimes look very similar to the branching of neurons and the column structure of the cortex of the brain. I have witnessed a cymatic video entitled *Hidden World: Cymatics,* by Alexander Lauterwasser, who is a scientist, cymatics researcher, and the video's producer. In the film, a musical instrument was utilized. When the pitch started to rise, the geometry changed, and different forms began to emerge (maybe began to "collapse" is even a better way of describing it). The higher the pitch, the more complex the structure in the sand became (not unlike crop circle images, which seem to get more complex while energy frequency readings seem to get higher each season).

Hans Jenny, using his tonoscope, began to study the forms that came into existence when vowels of ancient languages like Sanskrit and Hebrew were toned with the voice. The fascinating result was that the sand actually took the form of the respective letter shapes, like frequency fingerprints. This did not happen with modern languages, including English. (Horowitz states that the English language in reverse is mathematically related to Hebrew, but is electromagnetically, bioacoustically, and spiritually backward.) These findings were later replicated by Dan Winter and Stan Tenen using the Hebrew alphabet. According to Horowitz, "This knowledge lays the foundation for understanding creationism in the strict sense from Yah's spoken word as detailed in the Bible."

In Jenny's work we also find acoustic clues to antigravity. In one instance, Jenny has a plate filled with liquid that is being vibrated, and holds this plate on a slanted position. The vibrating liquid was able to resist gravity and did not fall to the floor. However, when Jenny stopped the vibration process, it did. But even more curious, when Jenny managed to start vibrating the plate in time once more, the liquid remained on the plate and continued its process of creating form.

Swāmi Hariharānand Saraswati explained the fundamental interdependence of sounds and forms as follows: names and the things named are parallel manifestations resulting from the union of *brahman* (the undifferentiated principle) and *māyā* (appearances), like waves appearing in the sea.[75] From brahman united with *sakti* (energy) issues the order of the manifest world. On the one hand, we have the principle of naming, starting with the monosyllabic *om,* and from the *om* all words and sounds. On the other hand, we have the principle of forms giving rise to all worlds and living beings. Between those two aspects of manifestation there exists an unbroken relationship. There is a fundamental identity between the principle of naming and the principle of forms, as well as between words and objects.

Author and sound healer John Beaulieu points out that a relationship exists between cymatic images and quantum particles.[76] For both it is true that what seems like solid form is a wave also. Both are being formed and organized by a pulse. This is what makes sound so special: a form that looks solid is actually created by its underlying vibration. This is real magic indeed.

Fig. 2.1. Image courtesy of Erik Larson

In Sanskrit the universe is called *jagat,* that which moves. The beautiful cymatic images, as well as the sciences of astrology, alchemy, sacred geometry, and magic, seem to reflect this wisdom. Nothing exists but by combinations of forces, vibrations, and movements. Resonance, entrainment, symbolism, and metaphysical correspondences . . .

LIFE'S MUSICAL, HOLOGRAPHIC, AND MULTIDIMENSIONAL BLUEPRINT!

This article can be seen as a summary of the essentials found in my Dutch book *Blauwdruk: de Multidimensionale Werkelijkheid van Creatie en Manifestatie.* A new book titled *Science Action: The Truth about Antigravity, Free Energy, and Other Impossible Facts!* is almost finished. Can we use the aforementioned knowledge and insights to lift the veil by which matter hides itself from the real reality? Can we move toward a multidimensional and bioenergetic science of reality, consciousness, and healing? The answer seems to be a resounding yes.

I would like to end this chapter with some concluding remarks. First, the universe is not a static, reductionistic, mechanistic, and predictable kind of a machine. The universe manifests as a dynamic, organic, vibrating, harmonic, musical, holographic, multidimensional, self-organizing whole and is very much alive! All matter is filled with a rich kind of emptiness (zero point energy, energy from the vacuum, akasha, vril, orgone, *prana, chi,* life energy) that permeates and interconnects anything and everything.

Then there are the concepts of entanglement, wholeness, and interconnectedness. In biophysics we see that the boundaries between the cell and its environment seem to become blurry.

In psychoneuroimmunology we see that the immune system, the endocrine system, and the neuronal system interact with each other. This is wholeness, but still confined within the body. But the body is not the "master hologram."

One step further takes us to a form of consciousness and intention-filled space, a field of consciousness that extends beyond the body and influences our DNA and biological (life) activity, even outside of our bodies. Think of the work of Cleve Backster, Robert Becker, Glen Rein, Rollin McCraty, Iona Miller, Dan Winter, Bruce Lipton, and the many Russian scientists (such as Pjotr Gariaev, Vlail Kaznacheyev, Alexander Trofimov, Konstantin Korotkov, and Alexander Gurvich). This could be described as a consciousness-driven, nonlocal transfer of information. Therefore, the terms nonlocal biophysics, digital biology, radionics, and electromagnetic homeopathy are all relating to the concept of "radiating" fields of information energetics. This is achieved using a carrier wave, modulated by words, intention, or consciousness.

Another one step further would bring us to a consciousness-driven, nonlocal astrobiological or planetary-cosmic field where everything is interconnected and there are no "physical boundaries," only transitions of form and densities. In such an energy world everything is *one*!

All is one, as the ancients already knew. If we radiate our energies out into the world, it is equally true that the world impresses us with its radiations, and it does. Think of Alexey Dmitriev's "space weather" or the cosmoplanetary studies of N. A. Kozyrev, V. Kaznacheyev, Alexander Trofimov,[77] and many others, and we know this to be the case.

What I call the "real reality," the blueprint, seems to be a musical, holographic, and multidimensional world working with interference patterns, standing waves, and vortex energies in sound, light, and water. Thought forms, emotions, and consciousness itself seem to create interference patterns (fields) that are able to crystallize into form or matter (think of cymatics). Consciousness seems to precipitate matter on a holographic level; think of Bearden's "precursor engineering" concept, where reality isn't fixed and is engineerable, for ill or the greater good.

Even the "illusory concept of time" seems to be part of all this, again proof of nature's multidimensional character. Time seems to be some kind of nonlinear energy flow. (Some authors say time and energy are dual variables.) Remember Bearden's time-reversed waves (scalar

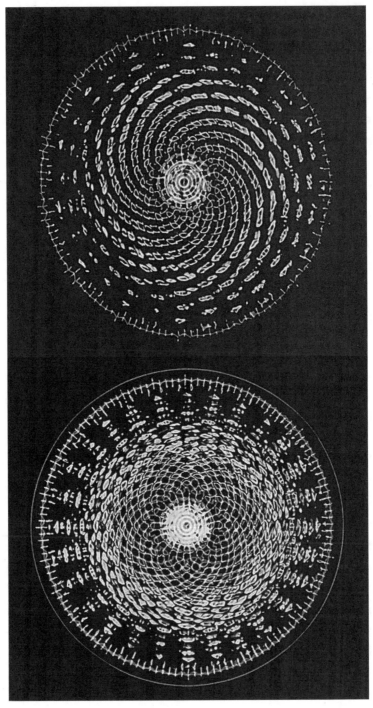

Fig. 2.2.

waves), and think also of William Braud's experiments showing we can time-reverse even a prerecorded outcome of a parapsychological intention experiment, after the fact. Also think of the work of Kozyrev, Kaznacheyev, and Trofimov, experimentally showing that if we mimic the electromagnetic properties of our planet and even time itself, we can manipulate their parameters in experiments and witness the different effects they produce.

Then there are the studies done by Prioré and Pautrizel showing we can "go back into time" and treat a disease (even cancer) by returning to the state before the disease "kicks in," before the actual manifestation of the latent information energetic signaling the onset of "dis-ease." Now think of the "memory of water" in homeopathy—and all intra- and extracellular signaling and communication in the body—and Gariaev's phantom DNA effect. (The informational changes in the energetics of the environment brought about in the presence of DNA remain active for weeks even if we get rid of the DNA.)

James Hurtak showed me some "anomalous" light pictures showing an energetic field after chanting with intention and a picture of psychic Uri Geller that showed a bent spoon (performed by a child) with the "light body" of the spoon still intact. Remember the sentence in the Bible: "Nothing is broken in the Kingdom of Heaven." I also remember a scientific study that showed that if rats are sedated in a certain physical location, the second round of rats in that location are more easily sedated. How about that for a hundredth monkey effect? Also think of Sheldrake's morphogenetic field theory and his concept of "backward causation" of time, and see the resemblance and importance in the psi and ESP research of presentiment (and Bearden's evolutionary concepts, where the vacuum can be "loaded with the needs of a species," allowing a new form to arise following a "critical mass" of information transfer coming from the collective needs of the species).

Speaking about the collective, resonance, intention, and the concept of coherence, now think of Roger Nelson and Dean Radin's global consciousness studies and Cleve Backster, Glen Rein, and William Tiller's nonlocal intention experiments, and the pictures become clear. Like the emergence of a new hologram, we need a new paradigm in physics, astrophysics, consciousness studies, biology, medicine, science, and life in general.

The new paradigm has to be based on the nonlocal, musical, holographic, and multidimensional world of sound, light, and "energy information" transfer, which are interconnected to infinite and nonlocal consciousness. Of course, we need to realize that even terms like interconnected, relations, and transfer of information do not truly cover the concept of a master hologram where every part is connected to the whole and contains the blueprint of the whole. Global unity and the universal brotherhood of humanity are but two of the many implications of these new sciences.

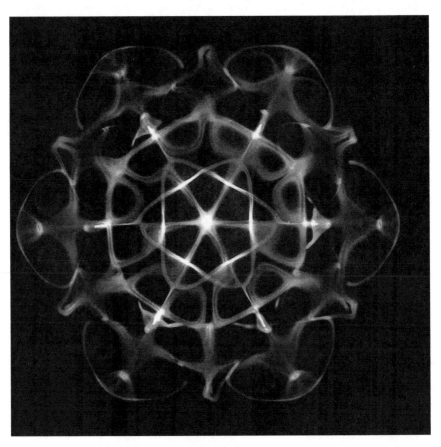

Fig. 2.3.

We need a form of nonlocal, interconnected, and multidimensional cosmoplanetary geo-bio-information physics and consciousness to finally resolve our many planetary problems and crises. Human potential and human evolution appear to be cosmophysical and consciousness-related states of affairs. I think it is time we literally become *whole* again!

In the words of a Hopi prophecy, "We are the ones we've been waiting for."

3

CONSCIOUSNESS AND

HEALING

WHAT WE KNOW
AND WHAT WE DON'T KNOW

Larry Dossey, M.D.

NOTE: This chapter is based on an address to the International Society for the Study of Subtle Energies and Energy Medicine that was given in Boulder, Colorado, on June 22, 2008.

> *The greatest mistake in the treatment of disease is that there are physicians for the body and physicians for the soul, although the two cannot be separated.*
>
> PLATO

> *Something unknown is doing we don't know what.*
>
> SIR ARTHUR EDDINGTON

> *Not everything that counts can be counted, and not everything that can be counted counts.*
>
> ALBERT EINSTEIN, ATTRIBUTED

> *No directions came with this idea.*
>
> WILLIAM MAXWELL

Our ignorance about healing vastly exceeds our understanding. Some people see this mystery as a good thing. For example, when I published a book in 1993 that attempted to clarify these questions—*Healing Words: The Power of Prayer and the Practice of Medicine*[1]—a reviewer wrote, "Life, ultimately, is a mystery. . . . In the past year, I have found myself yearning for the mystery, faith, and rapture to be restored to my spirit. I want more prayer and less analysis."[2]

This point of view—that some things should not be subjected to dissection, analysis, and the empirical methods of science—has a long history. Benjamin Jowett (1817–1893), the great nineteenth-century Plato scholar, theologian, and master of Balliol College at Oxford University, felt this way. He grumbled, "Research! Research! A mere excuse for idleness; it has never achieved, and will never achieve any results of the slightest value."[3]

Even Albert Einstein occasionally emphasized the limitations of science. He is reported to have said (although it may be apocryphal), "If we knew what we were doing, it would not be called research, would it?"[4]

HEALING RESEARCH:
THE BEGINNING

We've been bumping into the mysteries and paradoxes of healing intentions and prayer since the very first prayer study, an 1872 survey by Sir Francis Galton, the cousin of Charles Darwin. Galton reasoned that, since monarchs and highly placed clergy were regularly prayed for ("God save the queen!"), their health and longevity should exceed that of ordinary people if prayer is effective. He discovered the opposite—that sovereign heads of state lived the shortest lives "of all who have the advantage of affluence."[5]

Skeptics love to quote Galton's study, but it was a dreadful exercise, a retrospective stab in the dark that was, one might say, too cute by half. Galton failed to take into account a host of confounding factors, one of which has been pointed out by theologian John C. Polkinghorne, a physicist and fellow of the Royal Society. He suggests that one of the main reasons sovereigns lived shorter lives was because they were exposed to one of the greatest health hazards of the day—the continual ministrations of the medical profession.[6] If you were a European monarch in the nineteenth century, there simply was no escaping the brutalities of physicians and the often lethal effects of their leeching, bleeding, and purging.

The classic American example of this phenomenon involved the death of George Washington, our first head of state. Some historians believe he was essentially bled to death by his team of well-meaning physicians.[7]

MODERN PRAYER-AND-HEALING STUDIES

Paradoxes abound in prayer research. For example, if prayer is effective, many people say "the more the better." Perhaps not. Rupert Sheldrake, the British biologist who spent years in India, was intrigued by the fact that most married couples in India prefer having sons and that they routinely ask holy men to bless their marriage. Toward this end, Indian holy men pray incessantly. With roughly one-sixth of the Earth's population in India, that's a lot of prayer for male babies. But when Sheldrake compared the incidence of male births in India and England, where the preference for sons is not as strong, he found the same statistic: 106 male births to 100 female births, which is the same in nearly all countries.[8]

Modern prayer-and-healing research was launched around the midpoint of the twentieth century. Between 1951 through 1965, three studies explored the correlation of intercessory prayer with psychological well-being, childhood leukemia, and rheumatoid arthritis, respectively.[9] While one study claimed statistical significance, the other two did not. These studies were not well designed and were poorly reported. They contribute little to our understanding of healing intentions. We can, however, give these researchers a nod of appreciation for getting the ball rolling.

The most famous prayer study is that of cardiologist Randolph Byrd, published in 1988.[10] This controlled clinical study took place at University of California, San Francisco School of Medicine and San Francisco General Hospital. It involved 393 patients admitted to the coronary care unit for heart attack or chest pain. Although there was no statistically significant difference in mortality between the groups, those receiving assigned prayer did better clinically on several outcomes. Areas of statistical significance included less need for CPR, less need for potent medications, and a lower incidence of pulmonary edema and pneumonia in the group receiving intercessory prayer from prayer groups around the United States. These differences, although statistically significant, were not earthshaking—on the order of 5 to 7 percent in favor of the prayed-for group.

Although it was the first major prayer experiment, the Byrd study is not the best; it could have been improved in many ways, as I've described in *Healing Words*.[11] Byrd deserves great credit, however, for this coura-geous effort, which could hardly have embellished his career as an aca-demic cardiologist at one of the nation's best medical schools. His great contribution was establishing a principle that came as a shock to most physicians, including me: one can study prayer in a clinical setting, much as one studies a physical intervention such as a new medication.

If we fast-forward to the present time, we can identify around two dozen major controlled studies in humans, approximately half of which show statistically significant results favoring the intervention group toward whom healing intentions were extended.[12]

Around eight systematic or meta-analyses of studies involving heal-ing intentions and prayer have been published in peer-reviewed journals.[13] The majority have arrived at positive conclusions. The most thor-ough analysis is that of Dr. Wayne B. Jonas, the former director of the National Institutes of Health's National Center for Complementary and Alternative Medicine, and Jonas's co-researcher Cindy C. Crawford.[14] In their 2003 review, they state, "We found over 2200 published reports, including books, articles, dissertations, abstracts and other writings on spiritual healing, energy medicine, and mental intention effects. *This included 122 laboratory studies, 80 randomized controlled trials,* 128 summaries or reviews, 95 reports of observational studies and non-ran-domized trials, 271 descriptive studies, case reports, and surveys, 1286 other writings including opinions, claims, anecdotes, letters to editors, commentaries, critiques and meeting reports, and 259 selected books" (emphasis added).

The categories of these data include:

- Religious practice
- Prayer
- Energy healing
- Qigong (laboratory research)
- Qigong (clinical research)
- Laboratory research on bioenergy
- Direct mental interaction with living systems, such as remote influence on electrodermal activity or remote staring
- Mind-matter interaction, such as the remote influence of individuals or a group on random event generators, so-called fieldREG experiments
- Healing in a group setting.

In assessing the quality of healing studies, using strict Consolidated Standards of Reporting Trials criteria, Jonas and Crawford give the highest grade, an "A," to lab-based mind-matter interaction studies, and a "B" to the prayer-and-healing studies. Religion-and-health studies get a "D" because they are epidemiological-observational studies and are not blinded and controlled.

This context does not permit us to review even the main healing studies, which I have done elsewhere.[15] So too has Dr. Daniel J. Benor, whose pioneering contributions in this field deserve special recognition.[16]

Neither can we examine the main skeptical responses to prayer-and-healing studies in general. David Hufford, of Penn State College of Medicine, and I have discussed them elsewhere.[17]

What do these studies tell us? In their assessment of this field, Jonas and Crawford conservatively conclude, "There is evidence to suggest that mind and matter interact in a way that is consistent with the assumptions of distant healing. Mental intention has effects on non-living random systems (such as random number generators) and may have effects on living systems. While conclusive evidence that these mental interactions result in healing of specific illness is lacking, further quality research should be pursued."[18]

This conclusion is so cautious many healers insist that it does not go far enough. I disagree. The key question is not how large the effects are, but whether they exist at all. In fact the conclusion of Jonas and Crawford is radical, because it suggests what conventional science considers unthinkable: that human consciousness can act *nonlocally* to affect the so-called material world at a distance, beyond the reach of the senses. This involves a fundamentally new way of thinking about the nature of human consciousness and its place in the world.

These findings represent more than a new tool in the physician's black bag. While it's true that intentionality, including prayer, has been used throughout history to heal illness, this practical side is not the primary contribution of the emerging evidence. The key significance is the *nonlocal* nature of consciousness that is suggested by these studies. This implication dwarfs whatever pragmatic benefits these studies convey.

Many skeptics realize what's at stake here. If only a single one of these studies is valid, then a nonlocal dimension of consciousness exists. In this case the universe is different than we have supposed, and the game changes. Therefore, *all* these findings must be rejected, or the conventional, cherished views of consciousness as a completely local phenomenon will be subverted. That is why many critics seem to consider skepticism a blood sport and why they pursue a scorched-earth policy, in which *all* studies in the field of healing are categorically condemned, often for the flimsiest reasons.

What about the hundreds of studies dealing with nonhuman, inanimate systems? Overall, these studies demonstrate the highest quality of the various categories of intentionality experiments. Many of these studies, such as those done at the Princeton Engineering Anomalies Research lab, have demonstrated astronomically high levels of statistical significance and have been consistently positive across decades.[19] Healing studies involving inanimate systems, therefore, buttress the human studies and are potent evidence supporting the remote effects of healing intentions.

We need to take *all* the studies in intentionality into consideration because, when taken together, they affirm a principle that is highly prized in science—the concatenation, or interconnectedness, of things that appear unrelated. If we examine the array of categories analyzed by Jonas and Crawford, we find intentionality effects at the macroscopic level, as in healing studies involving whole persons; at the tissue level, as in studies involving populations of various types of cells; at the microbial level, as in studies involving growth rates of bacteria, yeasts, and fungi; at the molecular level, as in studies involving enzyme kinetics and biochemical reactions; and at the subatomic level, as in random event generator experiments where people attempt to influence the distribution of ones and zeroes. The fact that intentionality effects are demonstrated across this enormous spectrum of nature, from the macro-, to the meso-, and to the microworld, suggests that we have discovered a general, pervasive principle in nature—the ability of intentionality to change the world. This unity of knowledge from disparate domains is called *consilience* by sociobiologist Edward O. Wilson.[20]

THE STEP STUDY

The second-best-known prayer-and-healing experiment is the Study of the Therapeutic Effects of Intercessory Prayer (STEP) by physician Herbert Benson and colleagues from Harvard Medical School, published in 2006.[21] The purpose of the STEP study was to assess the impact of certainty and uncertainty on the possible effectiveness of intercessory prayer in patients undergoing coronary bypass surgery.

Many proponents of prayer and healing have called the STEP study a "STEP backward" or a "misSTEP." The impact of the STEP study, however, has been significant. Because of its negative outcome, it has become the darling healing experiment of skeptics. Many critics consider "the Harvard study" as the final nail in the coffin of remote healing research. To the great glee of critics of this area, it has had a chilling effect on future research in this field because of the gravitas associated with Harvard-based science. Unfortunately, few critics take the time to ask whether the study was well conceived and whether its conclusions are valid. But there is another side to the STEP study. It has actually contributed to healing research, because some of the most instructive experiments are those that fail.

Methods

STEP involved 1,802 patients undergoing coronary artery bypass surgery in six different U. S. hospitals. They were assigned to three groups:

- In one group, 604 patients were told they might or might not be prayed for, and were (which we'll call Group A).
- In another group, 597 patients were told they might or might not be prayed for, and were not (which we'll designate as Group B).
- In the last group, 601 were told they would definitely be prayed for, and were (which we'll call Group C).

The intercessors were members of two Catholic groups and one Protestant group. They prayed for the subjects for two weeks, beginning on the eve or day of surgery. The intercessors were given a prescribed prayer, following which they were permitted to pray their customary way. They were also given the first name and the initial of the last name of those for whom they were praying.

Results

- In Group A: Of the 604 patients who were told they might or might not be prayed for, and were, 52 percent had post-op complications, which was not statistically different from Group B.
- In Group B: Of the 597 patients who were told they might or might not be prayed for, and were not, 51 percent had post-op complications.
- In Group C: Of the 601 who were told they would be prayed for, and were, 59 percent had post-op complications, a statistically significant difference from Groups A and B.

In other words, the group that received prayer and was certain they would do so had the worst clinical outcome of all, implying that prayer might be harmful. The response of the media to these findings was enthusiastic and often playful. A banner in the April 10, 2006, issue of *Newsweek* magazine, read, "Don't Pray for Me! Please!"

Analysis

Let's imagine what the results of the experiment might have been under three conditions: (1) if prayer is effective, (2) if prayer is ineffective, or (3) if prayer is harmful.

1. **If prayer is effective,** Groups A and C should have benefited equally from it, with C having the added benefit of the placebo response owing to the certainty of receiving prayer. Group C, then, should have had the best clinical outcome of the three groups. This was not the case; C had the worst outcome. So "effective prayer" is unable to explain the outcome of the STEP study.
2. **If prayer is ineffective,** it should not have exerted any effect on any of the three groups, but Group C should have done better because of the certainty of receiving prayer, thus benefiting from the placebo effect. But Group C did the worst of all the groups. So "ineffective prayer" is unable to explain the outcome of the experiment.
3. **If prayer harms,** both Groups A and C should have demonstrated worse outcomes than Group B, which was spared prayer, in which case B would have done better than the other two groups. But B responded equally with A. Therefore harmful or negative prayer cannot explain the results of the STEP study.

The STEP researchers essentially ignored the possibility that prayer might be harmful in their report, simply saying that the worst outcome in Group C "may have been a chance finding." They were taken to task for this in a scathing rebuke in the *American Heart Journal*.[22] The criticism is appropriate in view of the anthropological evidence that negative beliefs and intentions can be lethal (curses, hexes, spells), as well as the controlled laboratory studies showing that negative intentions can retard or harm living, nonhuman systems.[23]

What other possible explanations are there for STEP's outcome?

Extraneous Prayer

Randomized, controlled studies in prayer in humans acknowledge that patients in both treatment and control groups may pray for themselves and that their loved ones may pray for them as well, but it is assumed that the effects of this extraneous prayer are equally distributed between the intervention and control groups and do not create statistical differences between the two. This assumption may or may not be true, and in any case does not eliminate the problems posed by extraneous prayer in controlled studies. The positive effects of extraneous prayer, if they exist, may diminish the effect size between the two groups, therefore limiting one's ability to detect the effects of assigned prayer in the intervention group. As one of the coauthors of the STEP study said in a news release from Harvard Medical School, "One caveat [of STEP] is that with so many individuals receiving prayer from friends and family, as well as personal prayer, it may be impossible to disentangle the effects of study prayer from background prayer."[24]

An analogy would a pharmaceutical study in which the intervention group is treated with 10 mg of the drug being tested, and the control group with 9 mg. Even if the medication were effective, could the effect be detected?

No one knows how extraneous prayer could be eliminated in human prayer-and-healing studies. It may be impossible to do so, especially in American culture, where the great majority of individuals pray routinely when they are *well*. Trying to eliminate prayer in a control group may be unethical as well, for who has the right to extinguish personal prayer and prayer by loved ones during sickness? In contrast, extraneous prayer can be handily eliminated in nonhuman studies involving animals, plants, or microbes. They presumably do not pray for themselves, and neither do their fellow beings pray for them. In these studies, one often sees profoundly positive effects of healing intentions.[25]

Randomization Differences

In May 2008, Hannah Ariel, Lana Dvorkin, and colleagues examined the demographic differences between the three groups in the Harvard study and found that group C, which had the highest rate of post-op complications, may have been predisposed to do worse.[26] This group had a higher incidence of chronic obstructive pulmonary disease (emphysema and chronic bronchitis), a higher incidence of smoking history, a higher rate of three-vessel coronary bypass surgery, and a lower rate of beta-blocker use prior to surgery, which many experts consider to be cardioprotective during coronary bypass surgery, when compared with the other two groups. For a fair trial of prayer, the study should have established a level playing field between all three groups through proper randomization, such that no group was worse off than any other going into the study.

Psychological Factors

The overall design of the study may have created psychological dynamics in Groups A and B that could have led to the results that were observed. Patients in A and B were told they might or might not be prayed for by the intercessors. Think for a moment what this means. Surveys show that around 80 or 90 percent of Americans pray regularly when they are well, and it can be assumed that even more pray when they are sick. Faced with the prospect of being denied prayer in the study, the subjects in A and B may therefore have aggressively solicited prayer from their loved ones to make up for the possible withholding of prayer in the experiment, and they may have redoubled their personal prayers for themselves. Thus a paradox may have resulted, in which Groups A and B received more prayer, not less, than Group C, even though this was not the intent of the study. If prayer is effective, this additional unforeseen, extraneous prayer may have lifted A and B above C in terms of clinical outcomes, accounting for the study's results.

Another possibility is that patients in Group C, who knew that many outsiders were praying for them, felt stressed and pressured to do well. Moreover, "It might have made them uncertain, wondering, 'Am I so sick they had to call in their prayer team?'" said cardiologist Charles Bethea, a member of the STEP research team.[27] "We found increased amounts of adrenalin, a sign of stress, in the blood of patients who knew strangers were praying for them," said STEP researcher Jeffrey A. Dusek, Ph.D., associate research director of Harvard's Mind/Body Medical Institute at Massachusetts General Hospital. "It's possible that we inadvertently raised the stress levels of these people."[28]

Experimenter Effects

One of the most consistent findings in parapsychological research is that the preexisting beliefs of the experimenter often correlate with the outcome of his or her experiment.[29,30] This so-called experimenter effect is assumed not to exist in modern clinical research, because it is believed that the subjective attitudes of an experimenter cannot penetrate a controlled study and "push the data around." Yet, any study that attempts to evaluate the effects of prayer should entertain the possibility of experimenter effects. After all, the assumption of an experimenter effect in a healing study is no more radical than the hypothesis being tested—namely, that the beliefs and intentions of intercessors might influence clinical outcomes. If the beliefs and intentions of intercessors can change the physical outcomes of an experiment, then why shouldn't the beliefs and intentions of experimenters also affect the results?

Ian Stevenson, the late physician and researcher of the University of Virginia, addressed experimenter effects in his 1989 presidential address to the Society for Psychical Research, titled "Thoughts on the Decline of Major Paranormal Phenomena."[31] By "major" he meant "phenomena so gross that we require no statistics for their demonstration." One reason he gave for this decline was the influence of an increasingly pervasive mechanistic and materialistic worldview. As he put it:

The possibility [exists] that spreading materialism has had an inhibiting effect on paranormal phenomena through paranormal causes. Critics tell us that allegations of their having an adverse effect on the phenomena are mere evasions of the painful truth that they have improved vigilance and tightened controls, so that the alleged phenomena do not occur in the presence of the controls they recommend. This may be true in some instances, and I am far from saying that we can learn nothing from critics. However, we for our part have obtained abundant evidence of the effect of the participants' beliefs on the delicate balance for or against paranormal effects in experimental situations.[32] An atmosphere of completely unqualified belief appears to facilitate and may indeed be essential for the occurrence of paranormal *physical* phenomena,[33,34] and I think this may be equally true of paranormal *mental* phenomena. *If belief facilitates them, disbelief can block them,* as Schmeidler's experiments showed many years ago.[35,36] (emphasis added)

Psi researcher Gertrude Schmeidler showed that the scores of subjects in card-guessing experiments tended to be high or low according to whether an experimenter was *wishing* the percipient to succeed or fail.[37,38] Other experiments suggest that unfavorable influences may not reach the level of an overt wish that a percipient fail, says Stevenson, but the desire may remain largely unconscious. Moreover, Stevenson cites experimental evidence that a person need not be physically present to adversely affect an experiment in extrasensory perception.[39]

Are these findings from psi research relevant to the biological domain? Almost certainly the answer is yes. I reviewed several studies in nonhumans in which negative thoughts and intentions of experimenters were correlated with negative biological effects in a variety of living systems.[40] During the late nineteenth century, several experiments by Pierre Janet, Charles Richet, and others showed that certain subjects could be put to sleep by suggestions directed at them from a long distance.[41-44] Experiments in the twentieth century by Leonid Leonidovich Vasiliev showed that this effect could operate under conditions of electromagnetic shielding.[45,46] The anthropological literature provides abundant evidence suggesting that negative intentions can harm or even kill individuals at a distance, beyond the range of sensory influences, even when the victim is unaware the attempt is being made.[47]

A surprising number of Americans embrace the possibility that thoughts, intentions, or prayers may harm others remotely. A 1994 Gallup poll found that 5 percent of Americans have prayed for harm to come to others.[48] It is likely that the percentage is much higher, since many individuals may be reluctant to admit to pollsters they are attempting to harm other people through prayer.

Could an experimenter effect explain the results of the Harvard prayer study? We cannot say with certainty, because we do not know the preexisting attitudes and beliefs of the experimenters. We can say, however, that the Harvard group were not generally known to be advocates of the nonlocal, *inter*personal effects of intercessory prayer prior to the study; rather, the group is widely known and admired as proponents of the *intra*personal, mind-body perspective, toward which they have made admirable, even landmark, contributions for decades.

Experimenter effects may not be limited to the immediate investigators, but may involve the larger experimental surround. No one knows where experimenter effects begin or end. Could the negative attitudes of skeptical or hostile scientists in the larger Harvard scholarly community have been a factor in group C's negative results? Might the effects of negative thoughts, intentions, wishes, or willing extended even further? The STEP study, more than any other healing study on record, was the subject of media attention for years before it was published. While still on the drawing board, it commanded interest from interested parties in both America and Europe. Several scholars predicted this experiment would decisively settle the controversy about the effectiveness of prayer, and most of the predictions of which I am aware were that prayer would fail. Some critics gleefully anticipated a failed experiment and the demise of such studies. Did these negative beliefs and intentions affect the results? In view of the evidence for nonlocal experimenter effects, this possibility cannot be handily dismissed.

It may be difficult to assess the preexisting beliefs of experimenters even if we try. Some investigators may claim they are neutral toward the remote effects of intentionality and prayer even though they may disbelieve them, because the scientific ideal is openness, not close-mindedness. Sometimes prejudice slips out, however, as with a peer reviewer who rejected a paper on the nonlocal manifestations of consciousness with the comment that he would not believe such a thing, even if it were true.[49,50]

STEP: A SUMMARY

We can make several general statements about the STEP study:

- Nowhere in the world is prayer used as in the STEP study. People universally say they pray for their "loved ones." This suggests that they intimately know them, they pray unconditionally for them, and they love and care for them with empathy and compassion.

    In their critique of the STEP study, researchers Marilyn M. Schlitz and Dean Radin say, "None of the clinical trials [of distant healing intention] has made use of what scientists call 'ecological validity.' This means the trials were not designed to model what happens in real life, where people often know the person for whom they are praying and with whom they have a meaningful relationship. In the Harvard study, for example, prayer groups were instructed for the sake of standardization to use a prescribed prayer that was different from what those who prayed used in their normal practice. So the Harvard study did not really test what the healers claimed works for them. In addition, in most of the clinical studies, the investigators were tightly focused on medical outcomes, and hardly any attention was paid to the inner experiences of the healers and patients."[51]

- Patients in the STEP study were not known to the intercessors. Neither were the subjects offered unconditional prayer. Two of the three groups were essentially told, "We may or may not pray for you." The perceptions of the subjects could hardly have been those of unconditional love and caring. To grasp the significance of uncertainty of prayer, imagine going to the bedside of a loved one the evening prior to cardiac surgery and saying, "I have not decided whether or not I am going to pray for you."

- People do not ordinarily pray scripted prayers in real life, but pray from the heart in ways that vary according to their individual temperament, personality, and spiritual beliefs. Some pray for specific outcomes, others pray in an open-ended, nonspecific way—"thy will be done" or "may the best outcome prevail." Scripted prayers degrade the ecological validity of real-life prayer.

- Ritual and context help strengthen the emotional bond in real life between intercessors and subjects (community prayer, prayer in religious settings, etc.) We are not told about the context in which the STEP prayers were offered.

- Strangely, the study could not generate a placebo effect, suggesting that factors were afoot in the study that were not taken into account by the research team.

- Although it is the largest and most expensive prayer study to date, STEP is not the most rigorous and scientific. Several other studies appear much more thoughtful, such as the strongly positive study of Jeanne Achterberg that used native Hawaiian healers, which we shall examine in the next section.[52-54] Although published just prior to the STEP study, this positive study generated almost no media attention, illustrating the media's preference for controversy and bad news.

The most important criticism of the Harvard prayer study is that prayer was employed in ways that simply do not occur in ordinary life. "Prayer in the wild" in "free-range humans" does not resemble STEP prayer. In fairness, this criticism applies not just to the STEP study, but to nearly all randomized, controlled clinical trials of prayer in humans as well.

Large randomized, controlled clinic trials of prayer in humans contain so many pitfalls that even the most assiduous researchers may not be able to anticipate them all. This does not mean that this type of trial should be abandoned, because research methodologies in any young, growing field in medical research generally improve with time. And some of the more carefully done controlled trials have produced positive results. But perhaps it's time to focus on healing research in humans in ways that preserve the ecological validity of prayer, even though these methodologies depart from the cherished randomized, double-blind protocol. As we'll now see, some researchers have begun to do exactly this.

THE ACHTERBERG FUNCTIONAL MAGNETIC RESONANCE IMAGING STUDY

Researcher Jeanne Achterberg, who is well known for her decades-long research in imagery, visualization, and healing intentions, moved to the "Big Island" of Hawaii to investigate healing.[55] She spent two years integrating with the community of healers, who accepted her and shared their methods. After gaining their trust, she and her colleagues recruited eleven healers. Each was asked to select a person he or she had worked with previously using distant intentionality, and with whom he or she felt an empathic, compassionate bond. The healers were not casually interested in healing; they had pursued their healing tradition an average of twenty-three years each.

They described their healing efforts variously—prayer, sending energy or good intentions, or wishing for the subject the highest good. Each recipient was placed in a functional magnetic resonance imaging (fMRI) scanner and was isolated from all forms of sensory contact with the healer. The healers sent forms of distant intentionality related to their own healing practices at two-minute random intervals that could not be anticipated by the recipient. Significant differences between the experimental (send) and control (no send) conditions were found; there was less than approximately one chance in ten thousand that the results could be explained by chance happenings ($p = 0.000127$). The areas of the brain that were activated during the "send" periods included the anterior and middle cingulate areas, the precuneus, and the frontal areas. This study suggests that remote, compassionate, healing intentions can exert measurable effects on the recipient and that an empathic connection between the healer and the recipient is a vital part of the process.

Strictly speaking, this is not a healing study, because no one was sick. It can be considered a healing analogue, however, because the healers were performing what they usually do during healing rituals.

CONSIDERATIONS FOR
FUTURE RESEARCH

What can we learn from these studies? Where do we go from here? What should we do differently in future experiments? I have several suggestions.

1. Experiments involving prayer should replicate, not subvert, how prayer is employed in the daily lives of ordinary people. Therefore it is time to question whether the randomized, double-blind protocol favored in conventional clinical research is adequate for healing experiments.

   Because all double-blind prayer experiments employ the uncertainty of receiving prayer, all double-blind protocols distort real-life prayer. The double-blind protocol, therefore, while useful in other areas of medical research, is not ideal for assessing intercessory prayer.

   Obsessive reliance on double-blind protocols to test healing intentions may reflect what researcher Edward F. Kelly of the University of Virginia calls "methodolatry"—blind worship of a particular method of investigation. Kelly states, "Laboratory research using random samples of subjects, control groups, and statistical modes of data analysis can be wonderfully useful, but obsession with this as the only valid means of acquiring new knowledge readily degenerates into 'methodolatry,' the methodological face of scientism. . . . The experimental literature itself is replete with examples of supposedly 'rigorous' laboratory studies which were in fact performed under conditions that guaranteed their failure from the outset."[56]

   Inserting uncertainty of receiving healing intentions or prayer erodes trust between healer and healee, and trust is considered crucial in real-life prayer and healing. As physicist Russell Targ and healer Jane Katra state, "Rapport [is] . . . paramount [in healing]. . . . Commonality of purpose and mutual trust are essential prerequisites. . . . Such agreement and coherence among individuals

. . . can be attained whenever people surrender their individual identities and join their minds together, focusing their attention on creating a common goal. . . . The trust and rapport can then be quickly achieved."[57]

A more appropriate experimental approach may be that of Achterberg et al., which we've examined. This experiment maximized the key features of intercessory prayer: trust, rapport, empathy, compassion, and unconditionality of healing intent. This true-to-life approach is more likely to capture whatever effects of prayer and intentionality may exist.

There is no need to apologize for departing from a double-blind, controlled approach to prayer. Where healing is concerned, one should adapt the experimental methodology to the technique and not vice versa, as is often done. This is not only common sense, but good science as well.

2. Single case reports of single individuals' responses to healing efforts should be encouraged.

It may not be accidental that the most dramatic responses to prayer are reported not in randomized, controlled trials, but in instances in which single individuals receive prayer from family, loved ones, the faith community to which they belong, or from healers whom they know and trust. These individualized settings maximize the trust, unconditionality, love, empathy, and compassion on which healing depends, while controlled trials do not.

When dramatic responses occur in conventional randomized clinical trials involving pharmaceutical treatments, they are usually dismissed as "statistical outliers" and ignored. In healing experiments we need to treat them not as an inconvenience or embarrassment, but as a possibly meaningful response to healing efforts, as emphasized by authors Caryle Hirshberg and Mark Ian Barasch in *Remarkable Recovery,* an admirable review of this field.[58]

3. In view of the evidence for experimenter effects, the preexisting beliefs of prayer experimenters should be ascertained and recorded as part of the study. The longitudinal assessment of this factor, over many decades and scores of studies, would help clarify whether the experimenter effect applies to healing-and-prayer studies, as it does in studies in other areas, as we have seen.

4. Studies involving healing intentions should not be conducted in the full glare of the media. Healing studies are best done out of the way, with a minimal amount of fanfare and public attention. This will minimize any influence of extraneous intentions—experimenter effects—from both cordial and hostile sources.

5. Careful consideration should be given to the selection of intercessors or healers. We have made only halting efforts at gauging the skills of healers, although the fields of therapeutic touch, healing touch, and reiki have taken steps in this direction through certification programs. Some of the most successful studies have employed healers with years or decades of experience who considered themselves professional healers.[59,60] A competing approach seeks to democratize healing by using relatively unskilled healers and intercessors. This reflects a desire to show that healing abilities are widespread or universal, present in some degree in perhaps everyone. Democratizing healing abilities is a noble effort, but the evidence so far suggests that this often results in marginal or nonsignificant outcomes.

   Prodigies exist in every area of human endeavor, such as athletics, music, mathematics, and art. Throughout history they have existed in healing as well. Selecting seasoned, experienced, veteran healers should not be seen as an exercise in elitism, but as an effort to provide an experiment with the optimal chance of success. And if the use of veteran healers is considered elitist, it is a "democratic elitism" to which all are invited through training and experience.

   If we wish to know whether humans can run a four-minute

mile, we test exceptional athletes to find out. To determine whether prayer is effective, why not test the most experienced, seasoned intercessors or healers? The strongly positive Achterberg study[61] and the positive study in advanced AIDS by physician and researcher Elisabeth Targ and colleagues[62] illustrate this principle.

6. The actual techniques of healing and prayer deserve attention. According to a Buddhist saying, "When the wrong person uses the right method, the right method works in the wrong way." In healing, we want the right person to use the right method. The right person may be a veteran healer, as mentioned, but what is the right method?

Many researchers consider healing to be a black box and pay little or no attention to the techniques that are used. This is akin to regarding all pharmaceuticals as drugs, without distinguishing between antibiotics, antiarrhythmics, anti-inflammatories, chemo-therapeutic agents, and so on. Want to get better? Take a drug; don't ask what it is. Our failure to differentiate healing method-ologies may be equally naive.

Our efforts to distinguish the efficacy of different healing techniques are compromised because many studies use a variety of healers simultaneously. How would we know which one worked and which ones did not?

Yet we must be careful when using a homogeneous group of healers or intercessors. This has led to a charge of religious favor-itism toward some studies, including the celebrated 1988 Byrd study, in which only born-again Christians were recruited as inter-cessors. Religious agendas, whether real or implied, are a guarantee for criticism of this field.

Thus far, evidence suggests that religious affiliation in prayer-and-healing studies does not greatly matter. Successful studies have used secular healers, spiritual-but-not-religious healers, or devotees of a variety of faiths. Thus far, no particular faith tradi-tion appears to have cornered the market on effective healing.

In a world aflame with religious zeal and narrow fundamentalism, healing researchers should not add to the epidemic of religious intolerance and bigotry. This caution may seem unnecessary, but I believe otherwise. An example involved a physician friend of mine who is a sincere proponent of religious-based healing at a leading medical school. He suggested to me that we need a prayer-and-healing contest. Healers of various faith traditions would be invited to participate in a uniform healing experiment, and their results would be quantified and compared. This would be a "pray-off," rather like a play-off in professional sports. In the end, the healers of a single religious tradition would be crowned the winner. He called this the "Elijah Test," after the Old Testament prophet who trounced a group of pagan priests in a head-to-head contest of sorts (1 Kings 18). Although I initially thought my friend's proposal was a joke, he was quite serious. "Why do you want to do this?" I asked. "I just want to bring praise to the Lord," he replied with incandescent enthusiasm. He had no doubt that his own religion would triumph. He seemed not to care that his proposal would evoke divisiveness and enmity between faiths. I am happy that a pray-off has not been conducted, and I hope it never is. In healing, we should not be promoting winners and losers.

7. We should determine whether certain conditions are more susceptible to healing with prayer and intention than others.

In conventional medicine, appendicitis is easier to cure than brain tumors, and some brain tumors are easier to cure than others. Is this true where healing intentions are concerned? Are some illnesses more responsive to healing than others? We don't yet know, but we should be prepared for surprises. It may turn out that some serious illnesses are more susceptible to healing intentions than mild ailments.

Many years ago I had a conversation about this issue with Elisabeth Targ, when she and her research team were designing their landmark healing study. I had just learned that she had decided to use subjects with advanced AIDS for the experiment. I called her and said something like, "Elisabeth, why on earth did you pick advanced AIDS? There's no good *conventional* treatment for this problem [this was prior to the use of multiple antiretrovirals]. Why do you think *healing* is going to work? Why not pick a milder illness, like the flu? I'm afraid you're going to give healing a bad name!" She laughed heartily. "Larry," she chided, "I thought you believed in healing!" She patiently explained her reasons. "If we can make a difference in advanced AIDS, skeptics can't say that healing did nothing because the illness would have got better anyway. Besides, healers like a challenge. They'd much rather work on patients with a problem like AIDS than someone with the flu."

She was right. Her study found that the patients with advanced AIDS who were extended healing intentions did better on several counts. They had a lower incidence of AIDS-associated illnesses that kill AIDS patients, such as pneumocystis pneumonia, encephalitis, and so on. They had a lower rate of hospitalization. If they were hospitalized, their stays were briefer. They had a higher quality-of-life score than the control subjects, and there was no correlation between their outcomes and whether they believed they were receiving healing intentions.[63]

8. We should determine whether specific healing techniques are compatible or incompatible with conventional drugs and surgical procedures. Some healers say there's never a conflict with conventional therapies, while others say incompatibility is always a problem. Experiments using single healing methods would help answer this question.

9. We should seek to understand the interconnections between healing, prayer, and meditation. Several studies have compared experienced meditators versus nonmeditators in performing certain psi tasks. Regarding his psi research, Radin says, "The meditators

almost always perform better, usually significantly better. . . . These abilities have something to do with the subtle aspects of mind. . . . The phenomena seem to bubble up from our unconscious, so the more that we are aware of what's going on in our unconscious, the better people are likely to do."[64]

Do skilled meditators make better healers? As far as I know, there have been no healing studies that have specifically used only skilled meditators. There needs to be.

10. What is the difference between prayer and focused intentionality? When patients respond to intercession, what is responsible for their response—intercessory prayer itself or focused attention such as one sees in skilled meditators? And is the prayer mediated by a higher power, or is there a direct, mind-to-matter interaction, which psi researchers called psychokinesis? No one knows for sure.

Most religious-based healers insist that the effects of prayer are mediated by a higher power. Yet not all religions are theistic. The classic example is some forms of Buddhism, in which healers pray not to a specific deity but to the universe at large. What mediates Buddhist healing prayer?

I confess that I cannot conceive of an experiment that would tease apart this question. After all, there are no "God meters" in science. Perhaps this is an indication that we ought to leave this question open and encourage people simply to pray in the way that feels most genuine and authentic to them, without trying to prove "what did it." After all, the person who is healed is more concerned with the *fact* of her healing than *how* it happened.

11. More attention should be paid to a tiered and rotating experimental design in prayer-and-healing studies. A tiered design means a backup group of intercessors who simply pray for a successful outcome of the overall study, in addition to a group of intercessors who pray specifically for the subjects. The MANTRA II study by Michell Krucoff, Suzanne W. Crater, and colleagues at Duke

University Medical Center added a tiered feature at a certain point in the experiment. While the overall study was not statistically significant, analysis revealed that significant results were achieved beginning with the addition of the tiered feature.[65]

A rotating design means that prayer assignments are rotated during the course of the experiment, so that by its conclusion all patients have been subjected to the prayers and healing intentions of all the intercessors or healers. This helps minimize any difference in the skills of healers by ensuring that efforts of healers who may be uniquely gifted are conveyed to all the patients in the treatment group, not just to a few. Targ and her colleagues employed this method in a positive study examining healing intentions in patients with advanced AIDS, as we've seen.[66]

12. Close attention should be paid to the duration and frequency of the healing therapy that is used. These factors vary so widely in experiments to date that comparison between studies is often difficult. For example, prayer duration has varied from only a few minutes[67] to hours.[68] One "minutes-only" prayer study involving patients receiving renal dialysis actually prohibited the intercessors from praying more than just a few minutes a day, whereas the Targ study in patients with advanced AIDS required healers to extend healing intentions for hours a day. The Targ study was successful, while the "minutes-only" study was not.

This does not necessarily mean, however, that more prayer and healing intentions are always better. There does not appear to be a dose-response curve in healing, like we see with medications. Almost certainly we will find that it is not just quantitative factors such as the frequency and duration of healing intentions that matter, but also qualitative factors—the degrees of genuineness, sincerity, compassion, empathy, and love that are offered. For my part, if I were sick I would prefer the brief prayers of a single empathic, loving individual to those of a hundred people who were bored stiff.

13. We should acknowledge that healing research may not be for everyone. In conventional science, it is believed that any researcher can investigate any subject, provided he or she has the requisite expertise. But we've noted that the conscious and unconscious beliefs and intentions of a researcher may influence the outcome of a carefully designed experiment. If intentions and beliefs matter, it is best that those who are hostile to the possibility of remote healing bypass this field of investigation, because their negative beliefs may poison their efforts.

Barbara McClintock, the Nobel Prize–winning geneticist, expressed a similar idea. She believed that her success depended in large measure on what she called a "feeling for the organism."[69] Those who have no "feeling for the organism" in healing should cede this research area to those who do.

14. Healing researchers should familiarize themselves with the accomplishments of parapsychology. Research involving human intentionality has been done in the field of parapsychology for decades, including hundreds of careful studies in a variety of living systems.[70,71] However, prayer-and-healing researchers generally appear oblivious to this work. For example, one can read the literature review sections of healing papers and see no mention of prior intentionality studies in parapsychology. To compound this situation, most healing researchers seem not to have learned very much from prior studies *in their own field*. Protocols meander in every direction without incorporating features of earlier studies that have been successful. Some studies have even duplicated features of prior *failed* studies.

This willful ignorance is dreadful, because psi researchers have dealt for decades with issues that are critical in healing research. Decline phenomena and experimenter effects are examples. Moreover, theory development and hypothesis formation in the psi literature is leagues ahead of the situation in healing research in medicine.

No healing researcher should venture into this area without familiarizing himself or herself with the basic literature in parapsychology. This is no longer a daunting task. Several excellent books are now available; please find them listed in the Additional Resources section on page 314. Every healing research team should include one or more coinvestigator, advisor, or consultant with experience in parapsychology research. Not doing so is like conducting brain surgery without a neurosurgeon.

15. We should emphasize more bench science and proof-of-principle studies. There are a great many advantages to simple healing studies involving not humans but animals, tissues, cells, biochemical reactions, plants, or microbes. Some of the issues we've examined—whether skilled healers are preferable to lay people, whether some healing methods are more effective than others, or questions about the duration and frequency of healing intention—are more easily approached in nonhumans.

The mother of all questions is whether the healing effect is real or whether we're fooling ourselves. I believe this question has been answered in the affirmative and that the most decisive proof is not in human studies but in nonhuman ones.

In order to further answer these pressing, fundamental questions, Jonas and Crawford have wisely suggested that we need to develop a biological model for healing. They say, "Laboratory models allow for rigorous and controlled studies to test mechanisms and theories of healing. . . . A bioREG (biological random event generator) is one focus for development. Other models might include a cell biology model of cancer and a neuroscience model examining the neurological correlates of healing and consciousness technologies such as functional MRI and PET, MEG or qEEG."[72]

A promising example along these lines is a recent study examining the effects of therapeutic touch on the proliferation of normal human cells in culture, compared to sham and no treatment.

These researchers found that therapeutic touch administered twice a week in ten-minute intervals for two weeks significantly stimulated proliferation of fibroblasts, tenocytes, and osteoblasts in culture ($P = 0.04$, 0.01, and 0.01, respectively) compared with untreated control subjects.[73]

16. The goal of a single "killer study" in healing, which would sweep all opposition before it, should be abandoned, because such a study is unnecessary. As historian Thomas S. Kuhn maintained in his landmark book *The Structure of Scientific Revolutions,* paradigm shifts in science usually occur as a result of an increasing number of exceptions to prevailing views, not because of a single experiment that suddenly demolishes conventional thinking.[74] This is already happening in healing research, as more data points are being added to the healing canon.

17. Experimenters should strive to conduct their experiments in surroundings that are cordial to the idea and possibility of healing.

It may matter greatly *where* one does healing research. For example, the Big Island of Hawaii, where Achterberg, as we've seen, did her positive fMRI study involving healers, is often called the Healing Island. There, healing seems to be in the air, assumed to be a part of everyday life. In contrast, in many academic settings remote healing is considered an embarrassment to the institution—heretical, blasphemous, antiscientific, implausible, impossible, or threatening. Inimical situations such as these can suffocate the best efforts of healers and perhaps prevent the effects that experimenters are investigating.

Stevenson was an authority on children who claim to remember past lives. He and his colleagues investigated thousands of these cases. They found that few of them originate in the United States. Stevenson attributed this largely to the inhibiting effects of our materialistic mind-set. He said, "If I were advising a young scientist entering psychical research today, I would reverse Horace

Greeley's advice to young Americans of the mid-nineteenth century and say 'Go East, young man.'"[75] That is where the cultural atmosphere is friendliest to such phenomenon. I'm not suggesting that healing studies literally be conducted in the East, but in surroundings that are at least cordial to the possibility of healing.

18. We should consider a temporary moratorium on healing studies. At the risk of sounding censorious, I suggest a temporary halt to prayer-and healing studies.

Currently, researchers seem to wander almost without direction in this field, with little awareness of what has worked and what hasn't. A make-it-up-as-you-go-along philosophy often seems to prevail. A time-out is needed to assess where the field has come from and where it is headed. All healing studies need to be critically assessed, analyzed, and dissected. Which factors correlate with success and which with failure? Of the many hypotheses that have been advanced to account for remote healing, which hold promise?

We need a healing summit that would bring together key healing researchers to confront these questions. Healers should also be a part of this discussion. Too often they are marginalized and their opinions ignored in favor of the intellectual gyrations of investigators, who may be clueless about the inner dimensions of healing that are important to the healers themselves.

19. Healing research should be conducted with respect.

Before she died in 2002, Elisabeth Targ told me, "When I go into my lab to do a healing experiment, I feel as if I am walking on sacred ground." She compared her experiments to invitations. "I set up the experiment as if I'm opening a window to the Absolute. If She enters, the experiment works. If not, it's back to the drawing board to figure out how to make the experiment more inviting the next time." Targ's healing experiments were all about invitation, not manipulation or control. She knew that the words *healing, wholeness,* and *holy* are related. Targ believed it is not enough for healing researchers to be clever; one's inner life is also important. I agree completely. In fact, I have never known a healing researcher who made a significant contribution to the field who did not have a rich inner life and who was not following a spiritual path.

We will never compel or bludgeon healing to yield its secrets. A light touch is required, such as Targ's gentle, respectful invitation, by which one approaches the world like a lover.

20. We should shed our timidity about what has been accomplished in healing research.

Healing research hardly existed forty years ago. If someone had told me, when I graduated from medical school, that I would see studies in remote healing conducted at some of the finest medical schools in the world—Harvard, Columbia, Duke, UC-San Francisco, and others—I'd have considered that person a lunatic. We should be proud of these achievements. But that is possible only if we know our history—what studies have been done, what they showed, why they worked, or why they didn't.

People working in this field are what medical futurist Leland Kaiser calls "edge runners"—risk takers who are out front in controversial territory.[76] But edge runners can get discouraged, because they are always swimming upstream.

I recently had a conversation with a healing researcher who was having a really bad day. She lamented, "We have learned almost nothing from all these experiments. It's as if we are back where we started." So I had the opportunity to talk her down from that ledge. I told her that, in my opinion, we have decisively demonstrated that consciousness operates nonlocally to change the state of the physical world. We've learned that these effects occur throughout nature, including in the context of health and illness. History, I said, will record this as one of the most remarkable contributions in human history, perhaps *the* most remarkable.

And I reminded her that she was partly responsible for this breakthrough. She said, "Really?" and we shared a laugh.

But we have to be realistic. Those of us who work in this field will continue to face skepticism, which is as it should be, because science cannot progress without it. But we will also continue to meet willful ignorance, prejudice, and bigotry. The best response is simply to do our work patiently and take the long view. Radin has described this situation accurately. In a fascinating review of the scientific evidence for time-reversed effects, he offers predictions that apply also to healing research, saying, "These implications, of course, are heresies of the first order. But I believe that if the scientific evidence continues to compound, then the accusation of heresy is an inescapable conclusion that we will eventually have to face. I also believe that the implications of all this are sufficiently remote from engrained ways of thinking that the first reaction to this work will be confidence that it is wrong. The second reaction will be horror that it may be right. The third will be reassurance that it is obvious."[77]

In the end, it is unclear how much we *can* know about the abundant mysteries of healing and the nature of human consciousness. William James, the father of American psychology, said, late in life, "I firmly disbelieve, myself, that our human experience is the highest form of experience extant in the universe. I believe rather that we stand in much the same relation to the whole of the universe as our canine and feline pets do to the whole of human life. They inhabit our drawing-rooms and libraries. They take part in scenes of whose significance they have no inkling. They are merely tangent to curves of history the beginnings and ends and forms of which pass wholly beyond their ken. So we are tangents to the wider life of things."[78]

These mysteries are certain to exhaust us before we exhaust them. But this is no concession or admission of defeat. In the human drama, it is the journey, not the destination, that is most important.

TWO HEALERS

In our enthusiasm for healing, we ought always to bear in mind that, in the end, all the attempts of healers to eradicate illness fail. Everyone dies; so far the statistics are quite impressive. This is a blessing for human life in general, because if all the prayers for the eradication of illness were answered, few would die, and the Earth would have become overpopulated and rendered unfit for habitation long ago.

But in another sense healing never fails, because the very fact that remote intentionality exists reminds us that our consciousness is nonlocal, or infinite in space and time. This means that immortality is our birthright. It is part of our original equipment. We do not have to acquire it. It comes factory installed.

Two remarkable women reminded me of this fact, both of whom were extremely influential in advancing the art and science of healing.

One was Charlotte McGuire. Many of her colleagues remember her guiding principle, "Love is the essence of healing."[79] At the height of her nursing career, "Charlie" was vice president and director of patient care for nineteen hospitals in Texas. She was corporate America. However, in 1981 she had the guts to say, "I quit," and she founded the American Holistic Nurses Association (AHNA). This happened at the gentle nudging of Dr. C. Norman Shealy, who was one of the founders of the American Holistic Medical Association. Today the AHNA has almost six thousand members and is a champion for healing in nursing worldwide. Holistic nursing has matured so greatly that it has recently been officially recognized as a subspecialty within nursing by the American Nurses Association.

On April 22, 2008, Barbara, my wife, and I journeyed to Charlie's Buffalo Woman Ranch near Dove Creek, Colorado, to see her for the last time. Barbie was a founding member of the AHNA and one of Charlie's earliest collaborators. Charlie was dying of metastatic breast cancer and was in her final days. She was bald, battered, and beautiful. We knew this was our last time to see her, so we didn't waste time with idle chatter and neither did she. Barbie asked her, "Charlie, have you seen the other side?"

She nodded yes. "What's it like?" She said softly with a smile, "It's beautiful. So beautiful!" She died a few days later in perfect peace.

I wish also to honor the late physician and researcher Elisabeth Targ, whom I have mentioned many times. Elisabeth was one of the great geniuses of healing research. She had the distinction of being able to do something many scientists simply are incapable of; she could produce a positive study in remote healing, not least because she was herself a healer and knew healing from the inside out. Shortly before her death she said her fondest wish was to return as "the Virgin Mary's assistant to help people love and heal."[80]

It is to the memory of these two extraordinary women—Charlotte McGuire, R.N., M.S. (1942–2008), and Dr. Elisabeth Targ (1961–2002)—that I dedicate this essay. May our efforts be worthy of their memory.

PART 2

Electromagnetic and Frequency Therapies

The nature of the pulsatory energy component that animates all living things, and is absent from their corpses, remains an enigma to official science. . . . Failure to address this most significant element in all biology has some strange consequences as technology advances. Medical engineers have produced, through a multi-million dollar investment, an artificial heart driven by electrical power. Yet these same medical engineers do not know where the power comes from that pulses the healthy heart naturally. . . . Orthodoxy protects itself well against such disturbing information.

TREVOR JAMES CONSTABLE

What if someone invented an electronic device that would destroy pathogens, bacteria, and even viruses with no toxic side effects? What if that same device could wipe out cancer by altering the cancer's cellular environment or by killing cancer viruses with an electronic or ultra-sonic beam?

That was accomplished years ago. The researcher who invented and perfected this device had an odd name, Royal Raymond Rife. But his associates and colleagues knew him as Roy Rife.

AUTHOR UNKNOWN

The first recorded use of electricity for health was found in Egyptian tombs, estimated to be inscribed around 2750 BC. The drawings showed them touching electric eels for treatment. In the 1st century AD the Greeks were doing the same and recorded various health benefits, including pain relief. In the early days of the USA, Benjamin Franklin invented a device which produced electricity and he was experimenting with it on people with epilepsy. In 1752 Johann Schaeffer published the book Electrical Medicine. At that time many physicians were using electricity on their patients. In 1858 Dr. Francis, a Philadelphia physician, was the first to describe the relief of dental pain by electricity. After 164 successful tooth extractions using what he called "galvanism" he received a patent on May 25, 1858. His methods then spread throughout the USA and Europe. By the late 1800s the use of electricity for medical purposes was wide spread and described in such medical texts as Osler's Practice of Medicine. Around 1900 there was much corruption in the business world and there were many medicines and devices being advertised as a cure for all kinds of ailments although some of the claims were exaggerated or false. This situation came to be as a result of an almost total lack of standards in medical education and practice. To investigate this situation, the Carnegie Foundation established a commission headed by Abraham Flexner and subsidized by John Rockefeller, who had just purchased stock in pharmaceutical companies. The commission's final report, in 1910, produced an almost instantaneous revision of medical education, and electromedicine was prohibited from being taught in medical schools. The report basically discredited electromedicine, and doctors using electrical instruments (which was most of them before this report) began to stop using the devices because the pro-drug efforts were causing them to look like quacks. In spite of the virtual disappearance of all electrical therapy some investigation continued and new diagnostic and therapeutic devices were still becoming available. An electrotherapy book was published in 1916 and it described AC powered devices which had various transformer outputs for applying alternating current to the patient as well as being able to power a large dual-electrode glass vacuum tube that output X-rays which were for taking radiographic photos of bones (with the damaged limb between the tube and an X-ray sensitive plate).

THE INVESTIGATION OF ELECTROMEDICINE

In reality, it is not the bacteria themselves that produce the disease, but the chemical constituents of these microorganisms enacting upon the unbalanced cell metabolism of the human body that in actuality produce the disease. We also believe if the metabolism of the human body is perfectly balanced or poised, it is susceptible to no disease.

ROYAL RAYMOND RIFE

4

RIFE THERAPY

AN INNOVATIVE ADVANCE IN ELECTROMEDICINE

Nenah Sylver, Ph.D.

One of the most effective and noninvasive healing modalities is frequency therapy based on the principles discovered by Royal Raymond Rife. Though initially hailed by physicians in the 1930s and 1940s as a major breakthrough for curing cancer and other diseases, Rife's technology was disparaged and censored, reemerging only in the last twenty years. Did this technology really work? If so, why was it suppressed? And how can we use it today?

Modern devices using Rife's technology work differently from his original equipment, but to simplify matters I will yield to popular nomenclature and call them "rife machines." The act of giving oneself a rife session has been made into the verb *rife,* with its conjugates *rifing* and *rifed,* and the noun *rifer* (someone who rifes). For a much more detailed explanation of Rife and his technology, see my 2011 book, *The Rife Handbook of Frequency Therapy and Holistic Health.*

FUNDAMENTALS

Principles of Holistic or Complementary Medicine

The word *healthy* comes from an old Anglo-Saxon word meaning "to heal, make whole." Rife's technology is best understood in the context of holistic or complementary health, which is different from allopathic (Western) medicine.

Allopathic medicine regards the body as a machine that is the sum of its parts. If something breaks, attempts are made to "fix" it—either by surgically removing the body parts that aren't working or by administering drugs that substitute for the function of the broken parts. Usually, the uncomfortable symptoms are relieved with pharmaceuticals, but numbing doesn't address the cause of the problem or cure it.

Holism treats the person as a unified organism greater than the sum of its parts. Since all parts are interconnected, there are no isolated symptoms. Restoration of health involves eliminating the poisons that clog the system and reestablishing cell function. Therapies may consist of specialized foods, nutritional supplements, herbs, or treatment with electromedical devices.

Allopathic medicine has its place—for example, when a passenger injured in an auto accident requires surgery or someone in a diabetic coma needs insulin. By definition, emergencies involve immediate intervention. But degenerative diseases take time to develop. If biochemical and energetic imbalances were managed as they arose, drastic intervention might not be needed. With allopathic medicine invasiveness is the norm, not the exception. With preventive medicine, the body's natural healing abilities are respected, so intervention is needed less often.

Contributors to physical disease are interrelated. They include:

- **Nutrient starvation:** Nutritional deficiencies are due to poor-quality foods, fake foods, or even nutritious whole foods that are indigestible, unabsorbed, or in the wrong proportions.
- **Sleep deficit:** The body needs adequate sleep for repair. During sleep, waste removal is more efficient, as tasks normally done during waking hours are set aside. Even the brain restores itself, promoting memory retention.
- **Chemical toxicity:** *Toxin* literally means "poison." Poisons negatively impact biochemistry, cell structure, and organ functions.

They enter the body through the skin, respiratory tract, and gastrointestinal tract. Most drugs are poisonous (note the warnings on the labels). But thousands of everyday chemicals are also dangerous, such as aromatic solvents, petroleum-based synthetics, persistent organic pollutants, volatile organic compounds (including formaldehyde, toluene, and benzene), and heavy metals (including arsenic, cadmium, lead, and mercury). One or more of these chemicals is found in adhesives, antifreeze, carpet, disinfectant, fertilizers, furniture, insecticides, laundry detergent, fabric softener, pesticides, polishes, shampoo, varnish, and even packaged foods.

- **Injury:** When the body is injured—whether from trauma or infection—it often becomes inflamed. During inflammation, scavenger cells gather at the site to ingest dead and damaged tissue and to barricade the damaged area from the surrounding healthy cells. Inflamed sites can become infected when, due to impaired blood and lymph circulation, the tissues stagnate and putrefy, providing a breeding ground for microbes. At this point, infection and inflammation overlap. What began as mechanical stress is now a biochemical soup of stress hormones, microbial waste, accumulated white blood cells, and other debris.

- **pH imbalance:** pH refers to the acid and alkaline levels of various bodily tissues. Of all biological systems, the bloodstream must maintain the most rigid margin of alkalinity; otherwise, the person dies. When the bloodstream is threatened by too many (usually acidic) wastes—whether from microbial toxins, stress hormones, or ingested chemicals—the acids are moved to other areas. The poisons in these tissues cause symptoms we call disease.

- **Proliferating pathogens:** Pathogenic microbes are an obvious component of illness. But often, worse than the pathogens themselves are the *mycotoxins* they excrete. (Mycotoxins are wastes consisting mostly of foreign proteins.) Since bacteria, viruses, parasites, and fungi thrive in an unbalanced pH environment, the same terrain that causes tissue deterioration also allows microorganisms to proliferate. Microbes thrive on sugars, chemical wastes, and heavy metals.

- **Toxic bodily responses:** Illness also results from noxious biochemicals and hormones produced by the body *in response to these mycotoxins.* For example, a cyst is a sac of fluid that forms around foreign material in the body to contain it and prevent it from poisoning the rest of the system. Allopathic doctors usually perceive the cyst as the medical condition itself, rather than as an expression of a deeper disturbance. The cyst is labeled the cause of the problem rather than an effect. A holistic approach recognizes that the body's formation of cysts is related to an impaired waste removal function.

- **Oxygen scarcity:** Not only would we die without oxygen, but our tissues also require oxygen for repair. Some of the most dangerous microbes thrive in an anaerobic (oxygen-deprived) environment.

- **Emotional states and belief systems:** "E-motion" is energy in motion, which we call love, joy, anger, grief, and so on. This energy has electrical and chemical components. An electrical charge is the communications system for the nervous system, while hormones circulate throughout the body as chemical messengers. (For instance, fear occurs simultaneously with certain neurological responses and with the outpouring of the fight-or-flight adrenal corticosteroid hormones.) When we deny or suppress our emotions or do not channel them into appropriate action, the electrical impulses and hormones remain in the tissues, where they can cause damage. Psychoanalyst Wilhelm Reich, and the many body-mind therapists who followed him, described this process in depth.

- **Electromagnetic toxicity:** The word *toxin* usually evokes thoughts of environmental pollutants, drugs, assorted chemicals, and sometimes radioactivity, all of which overburden the body with wastes that prevent it from functioning properly. But harmful electromagnetic (EM) fields also pollute, due to their ability to change the polarity and voltage of cells. (Electromedicine uses beneficial EM fields.)

Electrotherapy's Place in Complementary Medicine

Electrotherapy (or electromedicine) is a medical modality that uses EM, electric, and magnetic energies for therapeutic purposes. Since ancient times, humans have used EM fields from the sun (far infrared [FIR] and ultraviolet [UV] radiation), visible light (different colored wavelengths), electricity (lightning), and magnetism (lodestones) for healing. These energies stimulate circulation and normalize the body's cells and tissues. Sometimes they disable and destroy pathogens.

By the early 1900s—a hundred years after the discovery of electrical current—electromedical equipment was considered mainstream. Alternating current, direct current, low frequencies, high frequencies, static electricity, diathermy, infrared rays, and UV rays were used for treatment. Conditions treated included muscular aches and pains, skin problems, gynecological disorders, some heart conditions, respiratory ailments, gastrointestinal disorders, acute and chronic infections, and degenerative diseases.

Today, machines using EM fields, electricity, and magnetism are used for diagnosis, such as the electrocardiogram (EKG; to assess the health of the heart) and magnetic resonance imaging (MRI; to show the inside of the body). Given the widespread historical use of electromedicine and the modern use of machines for diagnosis, it seems remarkable that more practitioners and the general public don't use electromedicine in their daily lives for healing. There is so much more to electromedicine than, for instance, the FDA-approved current-emitting transcutaneous electro-nerve stimulator (TENS) unit to manage pain—and which doesn't even heal, as it "manages" pain by numbing the nerves instead of restoring cell function.

Unlike pharmaceuticals, which have side effects and must be taken in volume by one person (and for just one or two conditions), electromedical devices:

- Are noninvasive.
- Support the body's innate ability to heal, instead of substituting for its natural functions.
- Are fairly easy to use, by lay people as well as professionals.

- Address many conditions, so can be used over the course of a lifetime.
- Can be used by more than one person. (Some devices are configured to treat an entire group of people or animals at the same time.)
- Are relatively inexpensive, considering their range and scope.

The bioelectrical nature of our bodies is often overshadowed by their more obvious mechanical aspects. But every cell is a transmitter and receiver of EM information (which is why electronic equipment is successful in testing). The entire body is a living electrical circuit. Cells and tissues act as conductors (allowing for electron flow), as insulators (inhibiting electron flow), as semiconductors (allowing for electron flow in only one direction), and as capacitors (accumulating and storing charge, later to release that charge). Human beings, animals, and plants all contain and respond to EM fields, as each cell has its very own frequency with which it oscillates. These various EM frequencies precede and correspond to biochemical functions. For instance, healthy cells oscillate at higher frequencies than do unhealthy cells like cancer. The lower frequency of cancer is reflected by (and causes) the aberrant biochemical reactions within the cell. Conversely, the biochemical differences between normal healthy cells and cancer cells correspond to the differences in the electrical properties of each. Variations in magnetic fields likewise correspond to either favorable or unfavorable changes in biological activity.

Cells respond constructively to minute EM stimuli as long as certain criteria are met. The stimulus must be from the correct region of the EM spectrum and, if necessary, be further refined to an exact frequency or combination of frequencies. It must be of a sufficient intensity (power) and have the correct wave shape. It must be administered in the correct amounts. And it must be accurately and precisely aimed at the target. Once a cell is exposed to EM radiation, its fields start to move. Then, the corresponding biochemical responses are activated, such as electrolytes (liquid minerals) moving through a cell membrane or wastes being excreted.

Electromedical therapies use many portions of the EM spectrum: electrical current, magnetism, visible light, FIR and UV rays, and heat (in the form of specific FIR wavelengths). Rife's technology first used EM fields, and later, electrical current, to convey the frequencies used for healing.

A Brief History of Royal Raymond Rife

Born in Nebraska in 1888, Rife was truly a Renaissance man. Educated in optics, electronics, biology, and chemistry, he studied at Johns Hopkins University and even trained for two years to perform eye surgery. Rife designed and built many medical research instruments, but one of his most famous inventions was the 200-pound, 5,682-part Universal Microscope, completed in 1933. The Universal Microscope had extraordinary magnification powers and depth of field, rendering live organisms as small as single viruses visible—something that conventional scopes and even the later electron microscopes could not accomplish.

Reasoning that once he could see how living organisms responded to stimuli he could find a way to destroy them, Rife built a ray that devitalized microbes via a specific EM field. The first machine prototype lined Rife's entire laboratory wall. It delivered frequencies in the radio frequency (RF) range by sending an electrical current through a tube filled with noble gases. The gases would transform into plasma and light up the tube, which transmitted the frequencies. It was the EM radiation, rather than the luminescence from the light, that disabled or killed the pathogens.

Each microorganism required a different frequency to devitalize it. Rife called a microbe's resonant frequency—or the number of cycles per second at which it vibrated—its mortal oscillatory rate. To find the exact frequency, Rife would turn the dials of the ray machine to input a frequency, switch on the power, and then examine his specimen under the microscope to see if he had found the correct resonant frequency. Once the virus or bacterium began to vibrate and then grew weak or broke apart, Rife knew that he had found the correct frequency.

The destruction of a microbe was often analogized to the cliché of a soprano whose pure, focused tone shatters a glass. Although Rife's equipment was not based on acoustics, the analogy conveys the basic principle. The physics behind the occurrence is described by biophysicist James L. Oschman as follows:

In the living body, each electron, atom, chemical bond, molecule, cell, tissue, organ (and the body as a whole) has its own vibratory character. . . . Any object has a certain natural or resonant frequency. Strike it, bump it, pluck it, or heat it, and it will tend to vibrate at a specific frequency. This applies to a bone, a piece of wood, a molecule, an electron, or a musical instrument. . . . In terms of vibrations, the human body can be compared to a symphony orchestra. Each molecule corresponds to a particular instrument. Each bend, rotation, or stretch of a chemical bond has a certain resonant frequency, and will give off certain "notes" if it is energized. . . . When two objects have similar natural frequencies, they can interact without touching; their vibrations can become coupled or entrained. For electromagnetic interactions between molecules, the word "resonance" is used more often than entrainment. In the older literature you will find the term "sympathetic vibrations."[1]

Once the microbes were disabled, the body's immune cells could eliminate them. Rife's technology was safe and effective. A frequency administered at low power can devitalize a microbe, but does not harm an animal or human because much less power is required to kill a simple one-celled pathogen than its larger, more complex-structured host.

Rife was praised in hundreds of newspapers and journals. His colleagues and supporters were among the most prestigious doctors and scientists of the time. Throughout the United States and Europe, doctors administered Rife's therapy to treat many types of infections, including those caused by *E. coli*, *Streptococcus*, *Staphylococcus*, and *Salmonella*. People recovered from cancer, tuberculosis, typhoid, tetanus, gonorrhea, pneumonia, and other ailments. Even most patients given "terminal" diagnoses by their doctors became well when treated with the ray device.

Fourteen highly effective units were made by the Rife's Beam Rays Corporation before a smear campaign was begun in 1939 against Rife, his inventions, and his colleagues. Virtually everyone who attacked Rife was funded by or connected to the pharmaceutical industry. The allopathically oriented American Medical Association, American Cancer Society, and

Memorial Sloan-Kettering Cancer Center in New York City began a heavily organized campaign to publicly discredit anything connected to Rife. Articles appeared in journals claiming that the technology did not work. Practitioners were maligned by the press and threatened with the loss of their licenses if they continued to use the machines. Rife's laboratory was raided: photographs, medical records, reports, and valuable equipment (including pieces of the Universal Microscope) were stolen. The abundant funds and resources that Rife had enjoyed in the 1930s were no longer available, making the mass production of a Rife ray machine impossible.

If Rife's supporters could be pressured to withdraw their financial backing—and in some instances even deny knowing him, despite public documents that indicated otherwise—imagine what the general public, which had no firsthand experience of the man or his inventions, could be swayed to think. In 1961, Rife wrote:

> They spend millions on drugs but nothing on electronics, unless it will supplement drugs like X-ray and radioactive treatments, which put terrible scar tissue and burns inside the body. And then the person has to have a great amount of dope and pain killers to keep the pain down. The drug racketeer makes ten billion dollars annually on cancer alone [at that time], and with this money they have been able to have an unconstitutional law put on the books which stated that people will only be treated for cancer by medical doctors with X-ray, radioactive treatments, and surgery.[2]

Although Rife's equipment focused on undermining pathogens, Rife recognized the need to keep the terrain (body) healthy so that microbes would be unable to proliferate. Nevertheless, disabling pathogens is a very important part in keeping healthy.

RIFE EQUIPMENT AND SESSIONS

Machine Basics

Fortunately, Rife's technology did not die with him in 1971. Modern rife machines range from simple to elaborate, but all possess the following features:

- **Computerized function generator:** Responsible for the signal processing, the electronic components are usually housed in one box. The smallest unit is the size of a pocket calculator; larger ones may be housed in desktop computers.
- **Built-in dials, push buttons, or numbered keypads:** Some units attach to a laptop computer to program the unit.
- **Digital display panel:** Built into the body of the device, the display shows the frequencies you have programmed into the machine, the time period for which the frequencies have been set, and other data. Devices connected to a laptop provide additional data.
- **Frequency-emitting component:** The unit, programmed with the desired frequencies, sends the electrical signal to either a radiant plasma light tube or metal electrodes (which come in various styles). Occasionally a frequency device comes with other accessories, such as LEDs.

Reliable units are accurate: the frequency you program in is what comes out. Some desirable features include memory (so a string of frequencies can be entered at one time) and the ability to program different time durations for different frequencies in succession.

Most quality rife machines cost from one to five thousand dollars, depending on the features. For units that don't operate on batteries, a good surge protector will prevent the delicate components from being damaged by unwanted power surges, as during lightning storms. This equipment may save your life, so make the extra investment.

A good frequency device should be well made, easy to use, have a warranty with an accessible manufacturer or dealer in case the unit needs repair, and (very important) configure the signal in such a way that the frequencies can be used by the body.

Radiant Plasma Light Units

Freestanding radiant plasma light units have a one- to three-foot tube that rests in, on, or near the generator. The tube may be cylindrical, round, or cylindrical with a bulge in the middle. The gases inside are usually argon and neon, and occasionally krypton or helium. The glass may be Pyrex or quartz. If the plasma light system uses two tubes, touching the tubes (one in each hand) completes the circuit and ignites the gases.

The light on Rife's original ray device got very hot, emitted RF waves, and could not be touched. Some plasma lights on modern units also become hot, but others don't, depending on the unit's construction. The tubes that are designed to be touched for extended periods do not become overly warm.

People who prefer freestanding tube units enjoy having their hands free to do other tasks while rifing. Also, for some rifers the generalized EM field provides more thorough and comprehensive penetration than what they obtain with electrode devices. (See "Precautions and Contraindications" on page 133 for information on when not to use plasma light machines.)

Electrode Devices

All rife machines that use electrodes come into contact with the body. Electrodes (also known as pads) come in many forms:

- Metal cylinders held in the hands
- Flat metal plates on which the feet rest
- Patches that adhere to the skin (commonly used with TENS units)
- Flexible metal strips covered with wet cloth that are held or affixed to the skin with stretchable cloth bandages
- Pans of water, in which the hands or feet are placed, to which current-carrying wires are attached with alligator clips.

Although pad units diminish mobility—the person must remain connected to the unit—there can be advantages to electrodes. Chinese medicine practitioners often prefer pads because they place them at a meridian, which affects the corresponding organ, gland, or system deep inside the body. Specific areas can also be treated by placing the two electrodes on either side, or at the front and back, of the targeted tissue. Electrodes can be very useful for injuries such as muscle sprains.

All medical device manufacturers advise against putting electrodes on the face, although for dental infections, some people successfully use pad units, set at very low power, with electrode patches on the cheeks or jaw. Do not place electrodes over the carotid artery; this can severely disable or even kill you!

The closer together the electrodes are placed on the body—or the lower the frequency is that you use—the more intense the signal, so you may want to turn down the amplitude (volume) in such cases. (See "Precautions and Contraindications" below for information on when not to use electrode machines.)

Biological Compatibility and Signal Acceptance

Different rife machines are designed using various engineering principles to ensure signal penetration. This includes using certain wave shapes (usually square) or augmenting the machine's transmission power by using an easily penetrating RF carrier wave, on which the main frequency is transported. (RF is so named because radio broadcasts are transmitted within that range of high frequencies).

Some people subscribe to the paradigm, "If a little is good, more is better." Thus, they are understandably tempted to blast the signal even if it hurts (this applies to electrodes). But bombarding the body isn't optimal or effective. The body's acceptance of the signal doesn't necessarily correspond to the power with which the signal is being sent. The host body (and a microbe) can become resistant to a steady, unwavering signal, similar to how a constant tapping on your arm will first be noticed but eventually ignored if the signal doesn't vary. This is why it's important to ensure that the signal will penetrate the tissues. To accomplish this, manufacturers manipulate the wave in various ways. The device may produce a square wave or generate a sharp spike on the waveform, and/or have a "gate" feature built into the signal (which turns the signal on and off rapidly).

Precautions and Contraindications

As with any healing modality, there are conditions under which one may safely use Rife therapy, may use it if medically supervised, or should not be using it at all. Which category you belong to depends on your physical health and the type of unit you're using.

If You Have a Heart Condition, but Are Not Wearing a Pacemaker

- **Electrode unit:** Do not use any type of electrode! The electrical current may disrupt the beating of your heart and could even kill you. (These same warnings apply to other electrical devices that touch the body, such as ultrasound and TENS machines.)
- **Plasma light unit:** This technology is considered safe. However, your unit may come with an optional foot plate for grounding, which is similar to an electrode, so do not use the foot plate.

If You Are Wearing a Pacemaker for Your Heart Condition

A pacemaker is a small electronic device implanted under the skin on the left side of the chest (usually below the collarbone) and connected to the heart with wires. It monitors the heart rhythm. If the heart starts to beat too slowly, the pacemaker sends electrical impulses to the heart, causing it to contract. All pacemaker function is interrupted by even mild electrical current that touches the body. But older pacemakers, which are not shielded, also malfunction when exposed to both RF waves and microwaves (which can be emitted by leaky microwave ovens).

Around the mid-1980s, pacemaker manufacturers began shielding the devices so they would continue functioning even when exposed to various EM signals in the environment. (These signals include emissions from idling car engines, high-tension electric wires, high-voltage sites, cell phones, defibrillation, electrical cauterization, radiation treatments for cancer, and MRIs and other modalities that use oversized magnetic fields.) Although new pacemakers are theoretically shielded, it's possible not all of them are—especially if they're being used in less technologically developed countries. Older people with pacemakers implanted years ago are also more likely to have unshielded models. But even shielded-pacemaker customers must be cautious, as EM interference can affect a pacemaker's function by readjusting its settings.

- **Electrode unit:** Do not use any type of electrode! The electrical current may disrupt the beating of your heart and could even kill you. (These same warnings apply to other electrical devices that touch the body, such as ultrasound and TENS machines.)
- **Plasma light unit with RF:** You could be at risk if you use this technology, so consider the pros and cons carefully. If you want to use an RF light unit, ask your doctor and pacemaker manufacturer if your pacemaker is shielded. And ask your company representative if the device uses RF and explain why you need to know. Most of the rife researchers I asked have assured me privately that radiant light units with RF are perfectly safe—at least for those wearing shielded pacemakers—because the RF isn't strong enough to interfere with pacemaker function. Nevertheless, to ensure safety they suggest sitting six feet from the unit, beyond the range of the RF (RF waves dissipate exponentially over distance). Some plasma light units that emit high levels of power are excellently constructed, while others do emit enough EM interference to, for example, interfere with TV reception. Even a loose cable can be responsible for severe RF leakage.

  So if you have any doubts that aren't assuaged by the rife machine or pacemaker manufacturer, don't use a plasma light unit with RF. Personally, I would avoid all RF equipment if I were wearing a pacemaker. If your unit comes with an optional foot plate for grounding, this is similar to an electrode. Therefore, do not use the foot plate.
- **Plasma light unit without RF:** This technology is considered safe, as the machine is not using RF to drive the frequencies into the body. Double-check with your company representative to make sure the device does not use RF and explain why you need to know. If your unit comes with an optional foot plate for grounding, this is similar to an electrode, so do not use the foot plate.

If You Are Pregnant

Nutrients that the mother ingests, chemical pollutants to which she is exposed, and the hormones she secretes all travel through her bloodstream into the fetus. So will the microbial waste and other toxins that flood the system as a result of rifing. Since a developing fetus can't eliminate toxins as efficiently as an adult can, it's wise to avoid experimenting with rife frequencies when pregnant unless there is an emergency or a holistic doctor is consulted. However, if it's a choice between taking antibiotics or rifing, I would always choose rifing.

- **Electrode unit:** Under no circumstances should an electrode unit be used, since electrical current in the body could adversely affect the fetus.
- **Plasma light unit with RF:** Do not use RF units during pregnancy, for reasons similar to those given on pages 134–35 for pacemaker wearers.
- **Plasma light unit without RF:** If the mother wants to use the technology, a radiant unit that uses high voltage or another means rather than RF is recommended. Your unit may come with an optional foot plate for grounding. This is similar to an electrode, so do not use the foot plate.

If You Are Nursing

"Do not use when pregnant or nursing" is a standard disclaimer found on the labels of drugs, herbs, and even homeopathic remedies. This is because nutrients that the mother ingests, chemical pollutants to which she is exposed, and the hormones she secretes migrate to her milk to become part of the baby's diet.

Although I have not heard any reports of babies being harmed by nursing when their mothers are rifing, it's wise to avoid combining the two. However, a nursing mother can still rife if she needs to. Before the first session, pump out extra breast milk and refrigerate or freeze it. This way, the baby will have an adequate milk supply while you're using the machine. To prevent the milk from drying up, pump your breasts as often as necessary during the rifing period, and throw away the milk since it might contain too much microbial waste. As soon as you feel well, stop rifing and resume nursing.

If You Have Blood Clots

Frequencies can dissolve blood clots. If a clot breaks off into small pieces, it can travel through the bloodstream and lodge in the brain, causing strokes. If you have a history of blood clotting or strokes, check with your doctor before using this equipment.

If You Are Taking Pharmaceuticals
or Natural Substances Like Herbs

Many types of electromedical devices improve cell function, thus lessening (or eliminating entirely) the need for drugs. Once the cell's voltage is normal, there is better absorption—of oxygen, nutrients, and even medications. What may previously have been an appropriate amount of medications may be too high or even toxic. Even vitamins, minerals, and herbs can cause imbalances if they are more readily absorbed, as they may now produce intensified effects. Consult a doctor who understands rifing, especially if you are receiving chemotherapy.

If You Are Wearing Implants

The type of implant (and unit) may determine whether you experience negative reactions. A metal implant could attract too much current from an electrode unit, whereas there may be no reaction from a plasma tube unit.

With titanium screws used in hip replacements and other metal implants, occasionally you may feel warmth or tingling in the implant area. These sensations are caused by the transfer of energy within the metal object. Metal implants, like biological tissue, can act as receivers, depending on the wavelength of the signal. If the area feels warm, this may or may not indicate internal burning, so consult your doctor.

With stents (tube-like structures inserted into blood vessels or ducts to dilate them), no problems have been reported. The effects on breast implants are unknown. However, it might possibly be harder for the frequencies to penetrate as dense a material as silicone, so you might need extra time with the equipment.

If You Cannot Adequately Eliminate
the Toxic Waste Materials Released by the Rife Sessions

The immune cells, liver, lymph system, kidneys, and colon help neutralize and eliminate the mycotoxins that are released by the dying or killed pathogens. This therapy may be less effective—and in some cases could actively harm you—if these detoxification and elimination pathways are substantially impaired. If you don't know whether you can handle the effects of rifing, consult with a health practitioner who's knowledgeable about cleansing. You may have to build up one or more systems before you rife. This is especially true for people with cancer, Lyme disease, and other severely debilitating conditions.

No matter what your condition, you *must* drink water. Water prevents the body from being overloaded by microbial die-off (for more about this, see "The Importance of Water" on page 140).

If You Want to Give Sessions to an Infant or Small Child

To my knowledge, reliable studies in the United States on the effects of Rife therapy on infants or younger children do not exist (aside from parents' anecdotal reports). Therefore, we must be guided by natural health principles and common sense.

Infants are fragile. Their brain and nervous system, digestive tract, reproductive organs, endocrine system, and immune response are still developing. Natural medicine points out that it may be unwise to use the technology for routine and relatively mild childhood illnesses (such as the German measles) unless the child is excessively ill and uncomfortable. These illnesses stimulate the body to produce antibodies (proteins that catalyze the body to defend itself against foreign microbes). Once the antibodies are produced, the system's immunity to those particular microbes is established, and the body can better protect itself against these and other diseases in the future. Like a muscle that becomes stronger when given a moderate workout, an immune function that is "exercised" matures and strengthens.

However, should your children ever become ill enough to warrant a doctor's prescription for antibiotics, that may be the time to rife them instead. If my own infant or small child had a dangerous disease for which a doctor wanted to administer toxic drugs, I would not hesitate to use my rife machine first. Unlike drugs, rifing does not contain chemicals that poison the body. Some parents have reported success rifing even three-month-old infants. Consult a holistic health care provider as to the suitability of rife sessions for your child.

With children, it's safer and easier to use a freestanding plasma light unit than an electrode unit. Run each frequency for the same amount of time as you would for an adult.

If You Want to Give Sessions
to a Pet, Farm Animal, or Zoo Animal

Many people rife their dogs, cats, rabbits, hamsters, mice, and birds. A number of rifers reported that they initially bought a device for their pet, and the animal improved so much they began using the equipment for themselves. There are many accounts of how the animals would jump on their laps or sit on the floor next to the units, waiting to be rifed.

Some farmers use this technology for their cows, sheep, goats, pigs, chickens, ducks, and other animals. Even exotic animals are being rifed. One vet states that she used a machine to help a lion at a nearby zoo. And there's a growing market for frequency devices in the lucrative show horse and racehorse industry.

Especially if your animal is seriously ill and you have any doubts about its ability to eliminate the microbial debris resulting from a session, consult your vet. And give it more water; otherwise, toxic waste will accumulate. If the animal won't drink more water on its own, either put more liquid into the food or give the animal liquids that it likes.

If You Are Especially Sensitive to
High Levels of Concentrated EM Radiation

Some individuals have strong negative reactions to certain EM emissions. These fields may be generated by hair dryers, vacuum cleaners, or even sonic alarms beyond the range of human hearing (such as those installed in banks). The emissions from radiant plasma light devices are often better tolerated by sensitive individuals than the electrical current from electrode devices. Sometimes, rifing may rectify whatever is causing or contributing to your EM sensitivity, but on rare occasions you might feel worse. So if you have EM radiation sensitivity, use equipment from Pulsed Technologies or an electromagnetic energy machine (EMEM) unit specially designed without a spark gap.

The Importance of Water

Everyone who rifes should drink plenty of water during and after the session (for at least twelve hours afterward), regardless of their condition or what device is being used. This may mean one or two quarts of water, depending on one's size. Water flushes out the toxic debris that rife sessions release. Since ingesting too much water at once can flush out minerals, add electrolytes, vitamin C, lemon juice, Celtic sea salt, or chlorophyll to the water. *If you won't drink, don't do the therapy.*

Children who won't drink water may have unsweetened juice or chicken soup. Some animals will naturally drink more on their own after rife sessions, but if not, give chicken soup to dogs and (preferably raw, not pasteurized or homogenized) milk to cats.

How Do the Frequencies Work?

The frequencies work in two ways: by negatively affecting the microbes and by positively affecting the body. One popular film sequence, often included in documentaries on Rife and shown on many Internet sites, depicts a protozoan "undergoing evisceration, membrane transport disruption, and disintegration"[3] as it's being exposed to a plasma wave of 1,150 Hz. The actual shattering of a microorganism—although compelling and visually dramatic—is probably the exception, rather than the rule, of how frequencies disable microbes. If the waves do not outright shatter a microorganism, they may:

- Disable specific enzymes or proteins in the microorganism
- Disrupt the microbe's ability to metabolize, replicate, or reproduce.

Some frequencies used by rifers were taken from Rife's original lab notes. Many others were computed using live blood analysis, muscle testing (also called applied kinesiology), or by observing pathogens through a microscope. (The modern Ergonom microscope from Germany can view live viruses.) Charlene Boehm received a patent for her discovery that microbe mortal oscillatory rates can be calculated by applying a complex mathematical formula to measurements of structures in the pathogens' DNA. Frequencies have also been determined by in vitro studies. Living microbes on slides are exposed to frequencies and then examined through a microscope to see how they responded. Alternatively, microorganism colonies in petri dishes are exposed to different frequencies, allowed to incubate, and weighed and counted at regular intervals. The frequency's success rate is determined by how slowly the microbes were able to reproduce or if they died outright.

Frequency therapy appears to do one or both of the following, independent of killing or disabling microbes:

- Focuses the attention of the body's immune cells on an organism that was not previously recognized as a threat
- Normalizes or stimulates organs, glands, tissues, and body functions by beneficially reorganizing the RNA and DNA and making the flow of ions across cell membranes more efficient.

A recently deceased colleague of Rife, Dr. Robert P. Stafford, believed that the frequencies stimulate the adrenal glands and provide other immune-enhancing properties. Chiropractor James Bare, who holds the patent on the Bare-Rife device, also focuses on immune response, referring to studies showing that "pulsed EM fields activate heat shock proteins that act to stimulate the dendritic cells of our immune system."[4]

However one explains the benefits of rifing, it's clear that as EM beings, when our cells have the proper resistance, capacitance, and inductance—that is, possess the proper EM signature—we will function efficiently and be resistant to microbes. Any electrotherapy device that improves the electrical charge of a cell or disables pathogens will assist with healing. Cells that are too weak or diseased to contain the charge needed for health will lose their structural integrity and become part of the body's waste load, as they should. Microbes that absorb more energy than they can hold will undergo a similar fate.

Conditions Helped by Rife Therapy

Rife technology can be used for all types of infectious and degenerative diseases. My 2011 release, *The Rife Handbook of Frequency Therapy and Holistic Health,* lists all the (cross-referenced) conditions in alphabetical order—either as stand-alone entries or in categories according to type of pathogen, affected body part or system, medical name for the disease, or common name of the condition. The categories include: Arthritis and Joints; Bacteria; Blood Sugar Levels; Bone and Skeleton; Cancer; Candida, Fungi, Molds, and Yeasts; Chemical Poisoning/Detoxification; Dental (Mouth and Gums, Teeth); Ears; Eyes; Gastrointestinal Tract (Systemic Conditions, Colon/Large Intestine, Small Intestine, Stomach, and Esophagus); Glands (Adrenals, Pancreas, Parathyroid, Pineal, Pituitary, Thymus, Thyroid); Headache; Heart, Blood, and Circulation; Injuries; Insect Bites; Liver and Gallbladder, Lymphatic System; Men (Penis, Prostate, Sexual Functioning, Testicles, Urinary); Mind and Emotions; Muscles; Nervous System and Brain; Parasites, Protozoa and Worms; Regeneration and Healing; Respiratory Tract (Lungs, Nose and Sinuses, Throat and Lymph Nodes, Vocal Cords); Skin; Tuberculosis; Tumors, Benign; Ulcers; Urinary Tract (Bladder and Urethra, Kidneys); Viruses; Women (Breasts; Menstruation and Menopause; Sexual Functioning; Uterus and Cervix, Ovaries, and Fallopian Tubes; Vagina and Labia).

Effects of Rifing

Rifers react differently to sessions. Bright yellow urine can indicate killed pathogens that are being excreted as waste. Some people report finding large numbers of parasites or worms in their stool within a day after rifing.

Occasionally, with lower-range frequencies, one feels sensations resulting from the effects of the signal on the nervous system. These sensations may be perceived as relieving or unpleasant. However, this is usually a physiological response to the signal, rather than the effects caused by the disabling of microbes, which may take longer to occur. If the signal affects the body by improving cell function, the subject may feel better—either during the session itself or shortly thereafter. "Better" may mean lighter, clearer, less congested, a decrease in pain, or a partial or complete elimination of symptoms. However, we should distinguish between our own body's physiological sensation and the reaction of a microbe to its mortal oscillatory rate. So, while sensations experienced during a session can provide clues about which frequency is affecting you physiologically, you may not be able to tell which frequency is responsible for disabling a microorganism. Nevertheless, some people can sense when microbes are disabled.

Sometimes people temporarily experience an irregular heartbeat during or after rifing. This may denote microbial die-off. Often it indicates mineral depletion, since the body uses up its nutrient stores trying to rebalance itself. Specific minerals are discussed in the "Replenishing Minerals" section on page 149.

If you are very ill, it may be difficult to detect which frequency is doing the job, since pain and discomfort can overwhelm all other sensations. But if you feel nothing while rifing, don't be concerned. What happens after the session is more important.

Detoxification Responses

Normally, wastes are broken down by the liver and excreted via the colon and urinary tract. But if there are more toxins than the body can handle, they are released into the bloodstream—free to enter any cell—and eventually leave through the skin.

Our bodies manage waste removal in various ways. Fever literally "cooks" microbes to death. Most microbes cannot survive in high heat. Coughing, which is a natural reflex, expels germs embedded in the mucous membrane lining of the lungs. Sneezing eliminates foreign particles such as dust or pollen that have migrated up the nose. The body produces excess mucus to trap microbes and other debris that might otherwise seep into the bloodstream. Lymph nodes in the neck swell from the extra white blood cells they produce to fight infection. Vomiting and diarrhea are ways of discharging poisons, such as spoiled food or dangerous chemicals in the stomach. And a rash or boils indicate waste levels high enough to be expelled through the skin.

We experience what we call "symptoms" when there is too much debris for the body to comfortably eliminate it all. Excess waste can produce a sore throat; dizziness, moodiness, irritability, and inability to focus; fatigue; pain, aching, or swelling in muscles and joints; heavy perspiration and night sweats; nasal congestion; churning stomach, cramping, nausea, and vomiting; headaches; malaise; itching, flushing, and rashes on the skin; a temporarily irregular heartbeat or quickening of the pulse; slower or faster breathing rate; and watering eyes.

Allopathic medicine tries to alleviate or abolish symptoms. But when you prevent the body from doing its job by suppressing fevers, coughing, vomiting, diarrhea, or rashes, poisonous material remains in the system. The way to expel the garbage is not by suppressing or closing the exit channels, but by allowing the body to complete its elimination process.

This discussion directly relates to Rife therapy because some people initially feel worse from rifing. When pathogens in the body are correctly targeted by the frequencies, mycotoxins and other poisons are released, causing an elimination cycle—sore throat, skin rash, nausea, and diarrhea, for instance. This explains why you must have clear and efficient detox pathways before using a rife machine. An elimination cycle should be allowed to finish, as long as the symptoms themselves are not life-threatening or intrinsically weakening to the system on a long-term basis.

That said, there are important differences between a healing response and a disease crisis. A healing response is often called a Herxheimer reaction, after the Austrian physician who discovered and catalogued the body's responses to the proteins eliminated by dying microbes. Symptoms become dangerous when the body, no longer able to eliminate waste, begins to degenerate. A healing response is ultimately revitalizing, whereas a disease crisis is degenerative. At that point, medical intervention may be required.

TABLE 4.1. HEALING RESPONSE VS. DISEASE CRISIS

HEALING RESPONSE	DISEASE CRISIS
Person feels bad, but then feels better.	Person feels bad, with little or no relief.
The response occurs over a short period. A general rule is one month of healing for every year the person has been ill.	The response occurs over a long period. A health care professional can help assess how long is "too long."
There is a retracing of prior symptoms, often from decades ago.	There is a continuation of prior symptoms, often with the addition of new ones.
Organs, glands, and the body in general function better.	There is a wide-ranging degeneration of organs, glands, and perhaps the body in general.

If your colon, kidneys, or liver are clogged or sluggish, herbs and other natural substances can support, cleanse, and, if warranted, stimulate them. Sometimes the body is too weak to undergo rigorous cleansing and needs gentle support first, so consult your complementary health care practitioner about the appropriate protocol.

Session Duration and Regularity

Rife therapy is both an art and a science. Pace yourself, based on your condition, unique physiology, intuition, and health care provider's advice. If you feel better after your session, you can rife the next day. If you have an extreme negative reaction, wait until you feel substantially better before rifing again, unless you have a severe, progressive illness like cancer. Most rife researchers suggest that people with cancer do rife sessions twice daily, so the rate at which abnormal cells are spreading is slowed and ultimately reversed.

For most conditions, each frequency is administered for three minutes. However, sometimes a single frequency is used from thirty minutes to one hour or even more—as in the settings for pain relief or for very serious conditions such as Lyme disease and cancer. The time needed for each frequency also depends somewhat on the power (and hence penetration ability) of the unit.

No matter what frequencies are employed, know that larger microbes often harbor other, smaller microbes inside them, much like the peeling of an onion. Parasites can harbor bacteria, which in turn harbor viruses. Therefore, the removal of a single pathogen may not always eliminate symptoms. It's useful to have a diagnosis, or at least an educated guess, as to the exact pathogens you're dealing with.

The guidelines in the following sections are general and for some of the most common conditions. *But no matter what you are treating yourself for, be aware that staying on a frequency for too brief a time may cause the targeted microbes to become resistant to rifing. Similarly, too lengthy an intermission between sessions may also cause the microbes to mutate. So be vigilant; don't stop your sessions!*

Cancer

Cancer requires an aggressive approach. It may take ten days to two weeks to halt the spread of cancerous tissue before the body can reverse the abnormal growth of cells. Depending on the stage of cancer and the strength of your detox pathways, use one of the following schedules.

- **Main protocol:** Regular sessions every day with no days off. Two sessions per day, one in the morning and one in the mid- or late afternoon. Sessions normally last between 1½ and 2½ hours each, depending on the power of the unit. This twice-daily protocol is followed for at least six months.
- **Alternate protocol:** Regular sessions every day for five days, with two days off to give the body time to eliminate accumulated waste. Two sessions every day, one in the morning and one in the mid- or late afternoon. Sessions normally last between 1½ and 2½ hours each, depending on the power of the unit. This twice-daily protocol of five days on and two days off is followed for at least six months.
- **Follow-up maintenance:** Most rife researchers recommend that after the cancer is gone—and the person is either pronounced "cured" (as established through lab reports) or "in remission"—she or he follow a maintenance program. This entails:

One rife session once a day for several weeks or one month. Gradually add intervals of days, and then weeks, between sessions.

One rife session every other day for several weeks or one month. Gradually add intervals of days, and then weeks, between sessions.

One rife session once a week for several weeks or one month. Gradually add intervals of days, and then weeks, between sessions.

Lyme Disease

With Lyme disease, the die-off can be so severe that most people need to rife every other day, every three days, or even every four days. Listen to your body. Most people have not healed from Lyme disease from rifing alone, however. Explore additional protocols such as using Samento (also known as cat's claw or *Uncaria tomentosa*) and other herbs, and colloidal silver.

Candida albicans

Rifing every day is best. But as the acetaldehyde waste from the *Candida* fungus is highly toxic to the brain and bodily tissues, be prepared to undergo a massive systemic cleanup. Replenish the beneficial intestinal flora. Flora eat the *Candida* and also produce vitamin B_7 (biotin), which prevents the yeast form of *Candida* from fruiting into its more dangerous fungal form. Activated charcoal, taken at least one hour before and two hours after meals and supplements, will help the body mop up and excrete the toxins.

Parasites and Worms

These nasty critters not only lay eggs, they also have different forms for all their developmental cycles. Thus the same parasite requires several different frequencies to accommodate its many stages of growth. Supplementary herbs (typically black walnut, cloves, and wormwood) are needed along with the frequencies.

The Sauna for Toxin Removal

Natural health recognizes the role that toxins play in illness. When a cell is engulfed by its own metabolic waste products, nutrients cannot easily cross the membrane to feed the cell. The cell continues to malfunction, causing even more waste to accumulate. With the additional burden of microbial toxins released by rifing, the body needs more help than ever with garbage removal. Aside from drinking mineralized water, one of the best adjunctive therapies is the sauna.

Sauna therapy is thousands of years old. Heating chambers made of many different materials have been used in native cultures all over the world, for one simple reason: it's cleansing to sweat.

Ideally, a sauna should raise the internal body temperature by at least two degrees, to approximate the effects of a fever. A fever is the body's way of combating infection by "cooking" pathogens, as most microbes cannot survive in temperatures over 104°F (40°C). During a fever, the body increases the production of endorphins (biochemicals that suppress pain) and enzymes needed by white blood cells to destroy pathogens. Nerve and tissue fibers become more pliable, providing greater pain relief and relaxation. But the most valuable benefit of sauna therapy may be the elimination of toxins that reside in the interstitial fluid (between the cells) and in the fat cells.

Many poisonous chemicals, from food additives to toxic metals, are fat soluble. Storage of these poisons in the fatty tissue keeps them out of the bloodstream, preventing them from damaging organs and muscles. Sweating—whether from playing sports, exercising, or a sauna—relieves the lymph system, urinary tract, and liver from the burden of processing toxins. Since wastes from cell metabolism and chemicals tend to be acidic (low pH), sweating out these wastes can raise the pH of some tissues to a more alkaline state, which is why people feel better after perspiring.

The most beneficial wavelengths of heat are in the FIR band, about 9.4 microns long. These wavelengths are biocompatible with living tissue, promoting growth and life. FIR emissions penetrate about an inch into the body. Saunas that use FIR rather than steam heat permit more evaporation of sweat.

One twenty-minute sauna session with deeply penetrating heat can increase blood flow to the skin by 50 percent or more. A profusely sweating person can lose between 1½ to 3½ quarts of water per hour, so drink plenty of water during and after the sauna. Also add electrolytes to the water, as sweating depletes minerals. After the sauna, shower or bathe to prevent the accumulated toxins from being reabsorbed into the skin. For more comprehensive information on the history, physiology, and "how to" aspects of taking saunas, as well as which sauna construction materials to use for people with allergies and special needs, see my book *The Holistic Handbook of Sauna Therapy.*

If you are rifing, adding sauna detoxification to your repertoire may cut your healing time in half.

Replenishing Minerals

The body uses minerals to process debris created by rifing. These include magnesium and selenium, which are vital to heart function, along with potassium, calcium, sodium, and even zinc. Drinking water to flush the system—and then sweating to reduce the debris—further depletes the system of major and trace minerals. Make sure your minerals are chelated (bound) to other substances to make them more absorbable. High-quality salt with its trace minerals intact (such as Celtic Sea Salt) may supply enough minerals to fight a detox response.

The Role of Enzymes

Enzymes also lessen detox reactions. Lymphocytes (immune cells) use enzymes to scavenge pathogens and debris. In Germany, a formula containing high levels of pancreatic enzymes is the most popular non-prescription anti-inflammatory product. When taken on an empty stomach, enzymes directly enter the bloodstream and are used to repair and rebuild tissues, provide immune support, and fight pain rather than digest food. Enzymes are safe in large amounts. Raw foods, especially fresh squeezed vegetable juices, are excellent sources of enzymes, vitamins, and minerals.

THE FUTURE OF RIFE THERAPY

People often ask, "If frequency therapy is so effective, why haven't I heard about it?" Many countries, including Germany and Romania, conduct serious research on Rife therapy and have approved it for medical purposes. Frequency devices are common in European hospitals, clinics, doctors' offices, and private homes. In Germany, people are given frequency protocols by their doctor, who devises a program based on medical diagnosis. The clients administer sessions to themselves with a take-home model, which is then presented to the doctor at their next visit for reprogramming with a new protocol. Some clinical trials are posted at www.rife.de (accessed November 12, 2012).

In the United States, Rife therapy is relatively unknown because it is systematically disparaged and unpublicized. The alliance between the pharmaceutical industry, the FDA, and the American Medical Association ensures the prevalence of drugs and surgery rather than nondrug, nonsurgical protocols—and hence, the support of allopathic rather than natural health practitioners.

Rife therapy is opposed by allopathic medicine proponents for many reasons. It's much more successful, and thus more cost effective, than medicines. Although one rife machine typically costs more than one bottle of pills, drugs are much more expensive long term. Drugs—which generally don't eliminate the cause of illness but only suppress symptoms—create repeat customers who might spend tens of thousands of dollars a year for them. Drugs also require repeat visits to a doctor who will authorize the prescription. But rife equipment is bought once, to be upgraded or replaced only occasionally. Rife machines can be used by more than one person. And rifing eliminates the "need" for medication: rifers tend to use far fewer drugs than nonrifers. Moreover, most sessions can be self-administered without doctor supervision. When rifers do seek medical help, they are inclined to consult holistic, rather than allopathic, practitioners—the very professionals who are harassed by medical authorities for promoting safe, noninvasive healing modalities.

Undoubtedly to discourage the demand for electromedicine in the health-oriented marketplace, it costs companies hundreds of millions of dollars to test their protocols for FDA approval. Drug companies can quickly recoup their investments because testing fees are built into the price of the drug. But no electromedical device company possesses equivalent funds. The rare device company that does obtain FDA approval receives it for pain management rather than for a specific illness, because pain management studies cost far less and are more likely to be approved. The phrase *pain management* is vague and does not explain the mechanism by which a device heals. But since device companies are legally forbidden to disclose what their equipment can really do and how it works, *pain management* has to suffice. And the consumer must then find out from other sources the range and scope of the equipment.

Thus, due to laws favoring an allopathic mind-set—as well as an extremely low profit margin compared with that of pharmaceuticals—rife machine manufacturers cannot compete with big pharma, which has virtually unlimited revenue and resources and government sanction.

The U.S. media also contribute to people's ignorance of electromedicine. Many respected M.D.s and Ph.D.s who submit research to medical journals on electromedicine and holistic treatments report having their articles rejected—or else so heavily edited that the articles no longer provide worthwhile or scientifically valid information. If medical journals don't publish clinical trials on Rife therapy, newspapers, magazines, and TV cannot report on it. The public has been taught that if a modality is not discussed on the six o'clock news, it's not worth considering. Although publicity obviously does not equal quality, many people don't have the time, energy, mind-set, or information to evaluate electromedicine or any other holistic protocol. While this vicious cycle can be dismantled in part by public education, helping to make people more aware takes time. (Ironically, over the past several decades over two thousand articles on using frequencies for healing disease and chronic conditions have been published in respected medical journals. Not surprisingly, Rife's name is not mentioned in any of these articles. And the general public and even most doctors are not aware of this research. A sample of these articles is featured in appendix D of my book *The Rife Handbook of Frequency Therapy and Holistic Health,* "Selected Published Studies in Electromedicine," and they are also discussed on the website www .rifehandbook.com (accessed November 19, 2012.)

Rife therapy represents a radically different paradigm than that promoted by mainstream corporate medicine. Used correctly, electromedicine can increase cell energy, normalize membrane conductivity, lessen oxidative stress, reduce the amounts of inflammatory chemicals in the blood, improve protein synthesis, boost feel-good endorphin levels, restore depleted adrenals, and enhance immune function. The restoration of metabolic processes leads to the regeneration of tissue as well as resistance to disease. Depending on which machine is used, Rife therapy may help with these functions, although it was originally publicized as devitalizing dangerous microbes.

There are some conditions that rifing may not be able to correct: damage caused by nutritional deficiencies, drugs, or toxic chemicals; severe trauma due to surgery or mechanical injury; and damage due to continued exposure to EM radiation. Nevertheless, rifing holds great promise. In North America, more manufacturers make frequency devices as consumers continue to buy them. Rife therapy is sophisticated enough to appeal to holistically oriented health care professionals, yet simple enough to be used by lay people willing to play an active role in their own healing.

Electromedicine, including Rife therapy, can no longer be debunked, ignored, or suppressed. People are seeking alternative treatments— alternative, that is, to the allopathic model most commonly promoted— because they refuse to settle for less than genuine healing. Rife therapy is compatible with all holistic modalities, such as acupuncture, chiropractic, and naturopathy. It can even be used with selected allopathic procedures. It's time to make Rife therapy freely available to everyone, everywhere.

TRANSCENDING
THE FEAR OF DEATH

Men fear Death, as children fear to go in the dark; and as that natural fear in children is increased with tales, so is the other.

SIR FRANCIS BACON

The fear and the morbidness which the subject of death usually evokes . . . is based . . . upon an innate fear of loneliness and the loss of the familiar. Yet the loneliness which eventuates after death, when the man finds himself without a physical vehicle, is as nothing compared to the loneliness of birth. At birth, the soul finds itself in new surroundings and immersed in a body which is at first totally incompetent to take care of itself or to establish intelligent contact with surrounding conditions for a long period of time. The man comes into incarnation with no recollection as to the identity or the significance to him of the group of souls in bodies with which he finds himself in relationship; this loneliness only disappears gradually as he makes his own personality contacts, discovers those who are congenial to him and eventually gathers around him those whom he calls his friends. After death this is not so, for the man finds on the other side of the veil those whom he knows and who have been connected with him in physical plane life, and he is never alone as human beings understand loneliness; he is also conscious of those still in physical bodies; he can see them, he can tune in on their emotions, and also upon their thinking, for the physical brain, being nonexistent, no longer acts as a deterrent. If people but knew more, birth would be the experience which they would dread, and not death, for birth establishes his soul in the true prison, and physical death is only the first step towards liberation.

DJWHAL KHUL

It is the secret of the world that all things subsist and do not die, but only retire a little from sight and afterwards return again. Nothing is dead; men feign themselves dead, and endure mock funerals . . . and there they stand looking out of the window, sound and well, in some strange new disguise.

RALPH WALDO EMERSON

As we live through thousands of dreams in our present life, so is our present life only one of many thousands of such lives which we enter from the other more real life and then return after death. Our life is but one of the dreams of that more real life, and so it is endlessly, until the very last one, the very real life of God.

LEO TOLSTOY

Know that everything that is of true spiritual value is persistent, ageless, immortal and eternal. Only that dies which is valueless.

DJWHAL KHUL

Live so that thou mayest desire to live again—that is thy duty—for in any case thou wilt live again!

FRIEDRICH NIETZSCHE

Our birth is but a sleep and a forgetting;
The Soul that rises with us, our life's Star,
Hath had elsewhere its setting,
And cometh from afar.

WILLIAM WORDSWORTH

5

Harmonizing the Energies of Body, Mind, and Environment with Pulsor Microcrystals

The Breakthrough Technology of George T. F. Yao

R. Carole Morginsky, Ph.D.

INTRODUCTION

Among the values people want most in their lives are peace, harmony, and abundant vitality. However, the increased levels of stressors in contemporary life interfere with the attainment of those values. While stress has always been an integral part of life, we are now assaulted by increasing numbers of stimuli and disruptors as life becomes more complicated.

155

Stress can involve emotional tension in response to environmental and other life occurrences that challenge us, and there is also physical stress, which involves and taxes our physiological coping mechanisms. Stress comes from many sources, including other people's demands and emotions, our hurried and hectic schedules, and the disruptive electromagnetic radiation that surrounds us. Since humans are not equipped to safely process the high levels of stressors with which we are currently challenged, what we need is a means of neutralizing environmental stressors and of destressing ourselves. Pulsor* microcrystal devices provide that means.

DISRUPTIVE ENERGIES

Environmental Sources

Electromagnetic fields (EMFs) are everywhere. Some are inherent in nature, but human technology increasingly adds to the number and variety of EMFs to which the human body is exposed. Natural sources include the sun, the Earth's magnetic field, cosmic radiation, and atmospheric electric charges associated with thunderstorm activity. These provide essentially the same levels of EMF radiation experienced by our ancestors. However, human-made sources are adding substantially to our EMF exposure. These include the use of devices that emit radio waves, microwaves, infrared rays, visible light, ultraviolet rays, X-rays, and gamma rays. The human-made sources, while necessary for our way of life, are having profound effects on our health and well-being.

The United States is wired with at least 150,000 miles of high voltage power lines to accommodate our massive electrical needs. Lines on poles that carry electrical wires range from 2,400 to 12,000 volts, while steel electrical towers have lines carrying an incredible 60,000 to 500,000 volts. Changes in telecommunications have resulted in the existence of about a half-million microwave links for wireless communication in addition to the broadcasting transmitters that permeate our airwaves. Also contributing to the levels of EMF radiation are millions of electromagnetic devices

---

*Pulsor is trademark registered.

employed by United States industry and military, a wide array of domestic appliances, and hundreds of millions of video and television screens and computers used in homes and businesses. Use of electrical devices has increased at an incredible rate and undoubtedly will continue to increase, particularly with the addition of new and densely populated geographic markets.

EMF radiation is so pervasive and omnipresent that it is commonly referred to as electromagnetic smog. This smog not only has the potential to affect health and human functioning worldwide, but there also is substantial evidence that this effect is already a reality. EMFs propagate from their source in all directions equally, given no interference from other electromagnetic sources. Associated with electromagnetic waves are directional components known as scalar waves that travel longitudinally and carry radio and cell phone signals and the energy from electrical devices. These are also the waves that carry the EMF overload and discordance into our bodies.

Besides the vastly increased EMF levels, another aspect of the problem lies in the nature of the radiation. The EMFs produced by power lines and electronic appliances and devices have an incoherent nature, and that incoherence has a disruptive effect on the sensitive energy fields of humans. As exposure to EMFs continues, there is a cumulative effect through kindling (small stimuli of low intensity that have a cumulative effect resulting in sensitization). The kindling effect eventually leads to cell damage and weakening of the immune system. The EMFs that are potentially most damaging to living organisms are of extremely low frequencies (ELFs), such as those emanating from appliances and wiring that use power frequency (60 hertz). These, of course, we all have in abundance in our homes and workplaces. Power frequency fields have a wavelength of more than three thousand miles and can generate weak electric currents in humans and animals, thereby having the potential to affect health.

We currently live in an environment in which the combined natural and human-made electromagnetic radiation is hundreds of millions times more intense than the radiation our ancestors received from the sun and other natural sources.[1] Our bodies, while equipped to process the amounts of ambient radiation received from natural sources, cannot adequately and safely deal with the radiation overload to which we are now exposed.

Compounding the EMF problem, metallic objects such as electrical wiring, electrical circuits, water pipes, and jewelry or other metal worn on the body can "collect and radiate disorienting energy waves and can alter natural polarities of the biophysical body."[2] Consequently, the many appliances and devices that exist to enrich and expand our lives, while providing tremendous benefit, also present the potential for harm to us from enormously increased levels of EMF pollution.

What is needed is a means of neutralizing the effects of the EMFs and of strengthening individual human energy fields, thus making those fields less susceptible to influence from external energy sources. While it is possible to shield against simple EMFs using Faraday shields and other similar devices, protecting against the accompanying scalar waves is more complex. It is not, however, impossible, as proved by George T. F. Yao, N.D., an aeronautics engineer, molecular physicist, and naturopathic doctor who developed devices that he called Pulsors, which convert the harmful-to-life aspects of scalar waves to a more innocuous form and also clear and balance the bioenergetic fields of humans and other life-forms.

The Effects of EMFs on Living Organisms

Our bodies both receive and broadcast energy waves in a continual energy interaction with the environment. External energy waves exert an entraining effect on our personal energy fields. Entrainment, or sympathetic resonance, is the tendency of an object to vibrate at the same frequency as that of an external stimulus. Environmental energies that are in harmony with our own energy do not present a problem. Difficulties occur when external and personal energy frequencies are incompatible. Continuous exposure to EMF waves distorts the natural and necessary internal information flow that is vital for optimum functioning of our individual energy organization. If our own frequencies become entrained to incompatible external frequencies, distortion is produced in the rhythms of the body's various systems. When our energy flow is in its natural state, we experience health and a feeling of well-being. When, however, our natural energy fields are altered and distorted, there are resulting physical and psychological effects such as anxiety, headaches, fatigue, and depression. If we are subjected to this inner energetic disruption for long enough, it becomes integrated into our bodies through kindling on all levels—the mental, the emotional, and the physical. We experience tension, frustration, apprehension, pain, and even disease. Nevertheless, a causal relationship between electromagnetic radiation and illness has been difficult to prove, although there is evidence suggesting a correlation between continued exposure to EMF pollution and appreciable deterioration of one's health.

A significant area of concern that has prompted considerable research is the possible relationship between an increased incidence of several forms of cancer in children and living in close proximity to power lines. Although the association has not received strong confirmation, the balance of evidence seems to indicate a connection, in particular, between continued exposure to power lines and childhood leukemia. In 2007, the World Health Organization (WHO) found supporting evidence for that association, but not strong enough to be considered causal. The same study also stated, "A number of other adverse health effects have been studied for possible association with ELF magnetic field exposure. These include other childhood cancers, cancers in adults, depression, suicide, cardiovascular disorders, reproductive dysfunction, developmental disorders, immunological modifications, neurobehavioral effects and neurodegenerative disease."[3]

The WHO Task Group concluded that scientific evidence supporting an association between ELF magnetic field exposure and an array of health effects is not as strong as is the evidence for an association with childhood leukemia. Another investigative panel, the WHO International Agency for Research on Cancer, classified power-frequency EMFs as "possibly carcinogenic to humans" based on a fairly consistent statistical association between a doubling of the risk of childhood leukemia and exposure to magnetic fields above 0.4 microtesla, which is equivalent to 4 milligauss.[4]

Research thus far has primarily tended to study gross effects on the body associated with EMF exposure, since Western science does not fully understand the body's subtle energy systems and the energy dynamics involved in the interactions between the body's subtle energy and EMFs and ELF fields. However, the effects of EMFs (through the process of kindling) can be far subtler and may require longer cumulative exposure before easily measurable effects are perceivable. Experiential and anecdotal evidence, on the other hand, is plentiful. Many of the common disorders for which there seem to be no known medical basis are thought to be caused or aggravated by excessive EMF waves. This is a reasonable hypothesis if EMFs have a cumulative harmful influence on the immune and endocrine systems. Although research has not been conclusive and science does not yet have the tools to directly measure subtle energy effects, many people have reported symptoms that they believe have resulted from continual exposure to low-level electromagnetic waves. In addition, the number of studies supporting this belief continues to increase.

One major research study presenting substantial support for the supposition that EMF exposure is harmful, the Reflex Study, was funded by the European Union, Switzerland, Finland, and Germany and conducted by twelve research groups in twelve countries from 2000 to 2004.[5] This study investigated the in vitro effects of exposure to extremely low frequency EMFs and radio frequency EMFs. Even though only short-term exposure was studied, it was found that radiation from cell phones resulted in DNA breakage and chromosomal abnormalities in human fibroblasts (skin cells). An additional finding noted that cell phone radiation promoted the growth of neuroblastoma cells by 12 percent, which is important in light of the increased incidence of childhood leukemia with exposure to EMFs. The researchers suggested that free radicals might be responsible for the DNA and cell abnormalities, but they offered no explanation for how EMFs might increase free radicals.

A mechanism by which the DNA damage might occur was proposed by Andrew Goldsworthy, Ph.D.[6] former lecturer in biology at Imperial College, London. He reported that weak electromagnetic radiation removes calcium ions from cell membranes, which then weakens the membranes and makes them more prone to pore formation and leakage.

The membrane leakage can be so severe that even large molecules are able to pass through, allowing the entry of toxins and other pollutants. Goldsworthy suggested that the DNA damage found in the Reflex Study was probably due to digestive enzyme leakage from lysosomes within the cells and increased permeability of membranes, which no longer provided an effective barrier to harmful substances or energies. Interestingly, Goldsworthy proposed that people who are extremely sensitive to electromagnetic radiation might be so as the result of having lower levels of calcium before exposure, which is then, of course, made worse with exposure.

Personal Sources of Disruptive Energies

While environmental sources of disruptive energies are a major factor in disturbing the energy fields of individuals, these fields can also be affected by either harmonious or inharmonious energies emanating from other people. Consider the influence of someone who is in a happy and peaceful state versus someone who is angry or irritated. While spending time with either individual, whoever is with that person will begin to be affected by whichever energy quality is being emanated. The affected person will find himself or herself in an emotional state similar to that of the affecting individual without recognizing the reason. Emotional states have an energy that can entrain the energy fields of others, resulting in a similar emotional state in the other person. The degree of influence and who is affected also depends on which individual of the pair has the stronger energy field. For example, strong and charismatic leaders are particularly adept at producing this entrainment effect. We have all observed this when a powerful orator is able to influence a crowd, not with words, but rather by his or her very presence. The obverse is also true that an individual with a weaker energy field will be more easily influenced and affected. This influencing effect can be explained by the principle of resonance.

All objects have a frequency or set of frequencies with which they naturally resonate. Consonant harmonic resonance amplifies vibration through summation of the interacting vibrations. Similarly, a person's energy field can be amplified through the application of a harmonically resonant device. The healthful, natural frequencies of the body need to be amplified in order to fortify and protect an individual's personal bio-energy field. In conjunction with harmonic amplification, there can also be interference patterns produced that cancel unhealthful frequencies. For example, harmful thought patterns or emotional energies that have become blocked by trauma can be canceled and the energies released with exposure to the appropriate interfering frequencies.

Just as the thoughts and emotions of others can affect a person's energy field, so too can one's own thoughts and emotional patterns. A harmful thought pattern establishes a frequency within the nervous system. When that thought pattern is repeated many times, it is amplified through resonance and becomes a more entrenched energy blockage. This energy interruption then produces a distortion of the body's natural energy flow, resulting in disturbances at all levels—physical, emotional, and mental energy systems. These malfunctions in energy flow can, in turn, interfere with proper functioning of the body's natural healing mechanisms.

SOLVING THE PROBLEM OF DISRUPTIVE ENERGIES

Energy Medicine

Stress has always been part of the human condition, but the stressors that are simply an aspect of being alive and of dealing with life events are now compounded by the greatly increased stressors emanating from environmental pollution, including EMF sources. The American Medical Association has stated that stress is the cause of 80 to 85 percent of human illness and disease. Stress is, either directly or indirectly, a major contributing factor to coronary artery disease, cancer, respiratory disorders, accidental injuries, cirrhosis of the liver, and suicide—the six leading causes of death in the United States. In fact, 75 to 90 percent of doctor visits can be attributed to stress-related disorders, as reported by the American Institute of Stress.

According to noted psychologist Irving L. Janis, psychological stress can be thought of as resulting from environmental changes or events that "induce a high degree of emotional tension and interfere with normal patterns of response."[7] Evidently it is our response to and attitude about the stressors that is most significant, not the stressors themselves. This definition of stress applies more to occurrences that are within the conscious realm; however, environmental pollution, such as EMFs, is not ordinarily within conscious awareness. Nevertheless, their disruption of our normal energy balance produces physiological stress and requires adjustments within ourselves in order to function. Continued physiological stress has a weakening or distorting effect on the immune system, which then can lead to various illnesses, in part due to the constant adjustments that tax our personal resources. The approach traditionally used by Western medicine for dealing with this stress has been antianxiety and antidepressant drugs, primarily palliative approaches, which do not result in a permanent correction of the underlying problem.

Energy medicine serves as a valuable adjunct to modern Western medicine by providing a means of understanding the balanced relationship between the human body's various energy fields and its physical well-being and by using therapeutic intervention at the nonphysical level to address physical conditions. Not only is the understanding of the importance of that balanced relationship the basis of many centuries-old healing traditions practiced throughout the world, but now modern physics also recognizes that the human body is, in its essence, a vibrating field of energy.

While modern Western medicine has only recently begun to acknowledge the effectiveness of energy medicine practices, the general population has been for some time increasingly interested in this approach, as evidenced by greater numbers of people turning to energy medicine modalities. Biofeedback, homeopathy, massage, acupuncture, reiki, feng shui, t'ai chi, yoga, and therapeutic touch are just some of the practices that are gaining new adherents. Medical schools throughout the United States and worldwide now offer courses in some of these therapeutic energy modalities, indicating an increase in mainstream acceptance. In addition, many medical doctors are beginning to incorporate these methods into their patients' treatment regimes, often finding that the healing response is thereby enhanced and treatment time substantially reduced.

Although these energy medicine methods might be useful in ameliorating some of the harmful effects of environmental and personal stressors on the body's energy systems, they do not provide an effective means of protecting against disruptive energies or of neutralizing those energies before they can have an effect on the individual. A person's energy might perhaps be enhanced and cleared through various energy medicine modalities; however, there still needs to be some method or device that can additionally maintain that balance, strengthen the individual's energy field, and provide protection against environmental stressors that would destroy that balance.

Pulsor

Pulsor Vortex Energy Stabilizer* devices have, for the last forty years, been used successfully by many thousands of people throughout the world to deal with the problems resulting from the harmful effects of stressors. One reason for this great success is that the technology, developed by Pulsor's inventor, George T. F. Yao, N.D., and embodied in every Pulsor product, reflects an understanding of the relationship between the material world and subtle energy. The model of energy/material interaction underlying the development of Pulsor technology posits that what is affected by Pulsors is the interface between subtle and physical energies. This basic energy interface between the prephysical and the physical universes was recognized by Yao and named the vortex polarity system. He realized that with an understanding of this energy interface one could address the profound impact that subtle EMFs exert on the human body. Combining his understanding of ancient energy medicine with the principles of modern physics, Yao invented products that successfully counteract the harmful effects of EMF fields and balance and strengthen the body's own energy systems.

Since his early life in China, Yao had been fascinated by both science and healing. This dual interest led him to earn a degree in chemical engineering and to study natural healing techniques and methods by training

---

*Vortex Energy Stabilizer is trademark registered.

with various masters. When he then immigrated to the United States in the 1950s, he retained his strong interest in traditional Chinese philosophy, healing, and feng shui. These interests prompted him to study naturopathic medicine, becoming a doctor of naturopathy, and to also receive training in polarity therapy, with its originator, Dr. Randolph Stone, and in acupuncture. Eventually he combined his university training as an engineer with his knowledge and understanding of natural healing methods. The ultimate result of this combined approach was the invention of Pulsors.

In the late 1960s, while working in California as an aerospace engineer connected to the NASA space program, Yao discovered the underlying principles that would eventually enable him to create Pulsors. He developed a crystal-based technology that had the capacity to affect the bioenergy field in a beneficial manner. The first Pulsors he created were intended to be gifts for his friends and relatives. These early-stage Pulsors amazed the recipients by the positive effects produced on their health as well as on their homes and automobiles.

By the early 1970s, encouraged by the large number of enthusiastic reports from early Pulsor users, Yao resigned his aerospace position in order to commit himself more fully to the development of Pulsor technology. He began using Pulsors to do energy balancings and continued to receive highly favorable feedback. As the beneficial effects of Pulsors became increasingly evident, Yao began to envision the vast potential of the discovery he had made and the extent of the applications that would be possible. He then dedicated the next thirty years, until his passing in 1998, to his life's calling—perfecting Pulsor technology, inventing new Pulsor products, and making them internationally available. Through seminars and workshops that he conducted worldwide, countless people have learned about and benefited from this unique life-enhancing technology.

Yao's many former students around the world continue to expand his work and vision by using Pulsors to help themselves and others through teaching and therapeutic work.

What, then, are Pulsors? They are solid-state electronic transceivers and transducers that correct and amplify the body's natural energy field and vortex polarities. These easily worn or carried (two-inch diameter or less) devices are energized by contact with existing energy fields (such as the bioenergy field of the person wearing a Pulsor) and require no external source of energy (figure 5.1). (Using an electrically powered device would be counterproductive by exposing the user to disorienting frequencies.) When coming into contact with a potentially harmful and disruptive EMF, the Pulsor establishes a corrective resonance that restores coherence, harmony, and balance. Pulsors achieve these effects via an innovative microcrystal technology.

Fig. 5.1. Sampling of Pulsors used for treating personal energy field

Each Pulsor consists of millions of specially designed and processed quasi- or semi-intelligent microcrystals imbedded in a plastic matrix; each crystal particle can store and discharge energy at specific frequencies. Together the particles form a unique proprietary crystalline matrix that self-organizes in lattice and grid patterns in response to the body's minute biomagnetic waves. The crystalline mix used in Pulsors is sensitive to a wide range of environmental frequencies, the particular range depending on the variety of Pulsor. These microcrystals constitute a dynamic energy cell "with a multitude of quasi-electronic tank circuits acting as traps and wave filters of various frequencies of the vortex energy systems."[8] Unlike crystals in their natural state, which absorb energy frequencies of fields that they encounter, Pulsor technology transmutes that energy into a form that is benign in relationship to human functioning. One can imagine it as a filter that takes in contaminated energy and emits clean, healthful energy.

Due to their unique properties, crystals have long been used in electronic devices, such as radio and television transmitters and receivers. Since the body's energy centers are also energy wave broadcasters and receivers, crystal technology can be adapted to establish and maintain the user's personal energy pattern via the crystal property called frequency centering. The microcrystal technology employed in Pulsors is able to normalize a person's vibrational state, amplify his or her energy field, and protect it from entrainment by outside energies.

According to Yao, Pulsors have an effect on the spin of subatomic particles at the subtle energy level. He stated that counterclockwise, or centrifugal, motion is the particle spin that represents disintegration and decay. On the other hand, clockwise, or centripetal, spin can be thought of as compressive, coming together, and life giving; it is the energy of materialization. It is this clockwise spin, for example, that makes negative ions beneficial for living organisms. Yao stated in *Pulsor: Miracle of Microcrystals,* "Pulsor is in effect a passive solid state negative ion effect generator."[9] This statement refers to vortex polarity spin, which is a mirror image of electromagnetic spin. The vortex energy system provides a subtle energy blueprint for the electrical system (as well as other systems and structures) of the body. If spin is normalized in the vortex energy system, then that normalization is reflected in the material body as well.

Subatomic energy spin can be affected by both electromagnetic force fields (EMFs) and conscious thought—by the environment and a person's inner emotional and mental state. Consequently, one can understand the mechanism by which reactions to psychological stress can distort the personal energy field. Our emotions and thinking can, quite literally, change the energy within and around us. If our thoughts and emotions were always positive, we would be creating a blissful state of being. However, we are human and cannot maintain constant, consistent positivity. In addition we, of course, also live among other people whose energy fields can entrain our own and in a world permeated with EMFs that disturb our bioenergetic balance.

Clearing, balancing, and enhancing effects on the bioenergy field can be achieved by wearing Pulsor devices, by using techniques for self-balancing, or by receiving a balancing from a Pulsor therapy practitioner. Employing Pulsor devices in any of these methods results in an automatic correction of spin at an individual's natural vortex polarity centers, thereby bringing the energy centers into balance and enhancing the personal energy field. If spin at a vortex polarity center is impeded, energy flow is blocked, just as would occur with a break in an electrical circuit. When Pulsor technology is applied at a blocked vortex polarity center, the blockage is cleared and the energy flow returns to its natural state. As the microcrystals in Pulsors establish a sympathetic resonance, the similar pulses combine to create a higher harmonic resonance, which amplifies the personal energy field of the individual being treated with or influenced by Pulsor technology. As a result, the surrounding bioenergy field can be doubled or tripled in size.

When worn, Pulsors are effective energy-enhancing and protective devices that maintain and expand the bioenergy field. Harmful waves in the environment are detected and transmuted by Pulsors without allowing the disorienting energy to affect the person or area within the Pulsor's range of influence. The surrounding field of beneficial energy created then protects against the potentially damaging effects of electromagnetic pollution as well as other energies and vibrations that are detrimental to a balanced, healthy state. One's personal energy system is thus strengthened and freed from the burden of keeping distorting energies at bay, allowing one's internal energy to be used, as was intended, for the optimal functioning, healing, and growth of the individual.

Sensitive people have reported that, when wearing Pulsors, they no longer feel emotionally depleted by other people. This effect is especially strong for those in the therapeutic professions, who tend to be more attuned to others and so more vulnerable to bioenergy disruption. These therapists report still having energy at the end of the day after working with clients—unlike their previous experiences.

Although emotional and mental benefits are difficult to quantify, some beneficial physical effects of Pulsor technology have been clearly demonstrated by research involving blood studies. A 1980 research study compared the effects of fluorescent light exposure on three groups of rats for a three-week period.[10] The experimental group, which was exposed to the fluorescent lights while in the presence of Pulsor protective devices, was able to maintain normal blood enzyme levels and had blood components similar in value to the control group, which was not exposed to fluorescents. The third group, which was exposed to the fluorescent lights but received no Pulsor protection, on the other hand, had diminished numbers of blood components and enzyme levels as much as 20 percent lower than the Pulsor group. In addition, the Pulsor group ate less and gained less weight than the other two groups, perhaps reflecting a calmer state.

Additional research conducted by Christa Uricher, N.D., using dark field microscopy, examined live blood after cell phone usage and also after subsequent exposure to Pulsors.[11] Blood taken from subjects who were not treated with Pulsors showed evidence of being overly acidic (and, therefore, more susceptible to disease formation). After Pulsor treatment, the blood no longer showed signs of being acidic. Also, the red blood cells, instead of being clumped together as in the untreated sample, were normally spaced—translating into smoother blood circulation and easier flow through tiny capillaries.

Probably the most experientially powerful way to use Pulsors is with Pulsor energy balancing. When used in this manner, Pulsors are potent therapeutic tools. These balancing techniques result in the release of energetic blockages and accumulations that we gather by simply being alive and that lead to mental, emotional, and physical dysfunctions.

Many, if not most, people go through life in a state of mental, emotional, or physical discomfort without a conscious realization of that condition. If pain (physical or emotional), mental fog, and distress are one's daily experience, then discomfort and mental cloudiness feel normal. Those who are aware of feeling profound discomfort usually have no idea of its sources or origins. People generally create many of their problems with their minds and then attempt to escape from or solve those problems using that same mind. This is not a particularly effective approach, when one considers how ingrained thought patterns usually are. Pulsor technology, on the other hand, by changing energy flow, facilitates clearing of old thought patterns and emotional baggage. When unencumbered by the old, one can function more optimally in the present and can be free to establish new, healthier patterns without the barnacles of past fears, mishaps, and other turmoil.

Therapeutic balancing with Pulsors enables brain wave patterns to easily shift into alpha, theta, and even delta frequencies (depending in part on which Pulsor devices are used), resulting in deeper states of calmness, relaxation, and physical well-being. The degree of relaxation and peacefulness achieved with Pulsor energy balancing is usually reported as being the deepest the subject has ever experienced.

These microcrystal devices can also be incorporated with other energy and alternative medicine modalities. Bodyworkers, energy medicine practitioners, and other therapists have been able to increase the benefits clients receive from the various therapy modalities by adding Pulsors to the treatment. Additionally, the therapists, by wearing Pulsors, are less likely to pick up negative energy from their clients and are of greater benefit to their clients by having balanced energy themselves.

Pulsors can be used not only to stabilize and balance the energy fields of living things (animal or plant), but also to render benign the harmful field effects of electrical equipment and the environment. Using Pulsor technology within one's surroundings neutralizes the negative effects of electrical devices and geopathic fields. Many feng shui practitioners have found Pulsor technology to be an invaluable tool for clearing environmentally caused energy imbalances. Indeed, the Pulsor Vortex Energy

Filter* device (designed to correct the energy within buildings) has been described as "high-tech feng shui" (figure 5.2). When it is plugged into the electrical system of a home or other building, the disorienting subtle energy components generated by the electrical current are neutralized, and a positive harmonious environment is created. Pulsors of various kinds can also be attached directly to electrical devices, telephones, cell phones, automobile batteries, and water and gas supplies, thereby neutralizing disruptive energies from those sources. On a more personal level, they can be used to treat food and drink and to clear jewelry and crystals of accumulated charge. Pulsors are themselves self-clearing and do not accumulate charge.

Fig. 5.2. The Vortex Energy Filter, a high-tech feng shui environmental treatment device

A demonstration of the environmental effectiveness of Pulsor applications was reported by Ulrich Arndt in the August 2000 issue of *Esotera*. Pulsor devices were installed in a Swiss business having thirty-five employees, who were not aware of the experiment. After one year of working in the presence of Pulsors, 70 percent of the employees reported an increased sense of well-being. As a result, the company realized improved attendance and performance. This experience has been replicated in a number of companies in Germany, Austria, and Switzerland.

---

*The Vortex Energy Filter is trademark registered.

CONCLUSIONS

Experiences with using Pulsors range from subtle and gradual change in oneself to dramatic transformation, and from physical to emotional, mental, and even spiritual changes. People who have experienced pain from various disorders, even sometimes for decades, find themselves with diminished or no pain. One Pulsor user experienced her disability from multiple sclerosis reduced from considerable and heading toward severe, to minimal, with the help of Pulsors. Her disease not only did not progress, it actually reversed—a virtually unheard of experience with multiple sclerosis. Many Pulsor users who have had surgery have heard their physicians express amazement at how quickly their incisions were healing. There have been many cases in which Pulsors were applied to burns and wounds as soon as the injury occurred. Within a few minutes all evidence of the wounds disappeared.

The mental clarity and profound relaxation felt after a Pulsor balancing and as one wears and uses Pulsors can be life changing and often is. Pulsor users find they are able to release the energy from long-held trauma and other deeply experienced events and emotions. One person likened the Pulsor balancing experience to having always lived with constant static and interference on the line and then suddenly being able to experience everything in high fidelity. There is a cumulative effect as well. The more and longer one uses and wears Pulsors, the greater are the benefits. People experience what can be described as a peeling away of layers of old "stuff"—the emotional and mental stuff that gets in the way of optimal, healthy functioning.

Pulsor users report feeling calmer and stronger, more emotionally stable and energized. This balanced state of being enables people to grow, change, and function in healthy, more creative ways because their energy is available and no longer appropriated as much by self-protection and survival needs. With Pulsor technology providing protection from disruptive energies and keeping the bioenergy fields clear and balanced, it becomes possible to maintain a peaceful, nurturing environment wherever one might happen to be. A healthful environment is carried within and surrounds the Pulsor-protected person.

6

OZONE AND HYDROGEN PEROXIDE IN HEALING

A SAFE, EFFECTIVE, AND LOW-COST TREATMENT FOR A WIDE SPECTRUM OF DISEASES

Nathaniel Altman

Although used by well over 10 million patients in Europe since the early 1960s, the therapeutic use of medical ozone and hydrogen peroxide (technically known as *oxidative therapies* and popularly called *oxygen therapies*) is largely a mystery to North Americans. In Europe, these oxygen therapies are hailed as a safe, effective, and low-cost treatment for a wide spectrum of diseases (including candida, cancer, heart problems, diabetes, and HIV-related infections) in Europe, and proponents feel that they can go far in resolving America's health care crisis, where complicated, risky, and expensive health care treatments have become the norm.

However, physicians who have tried to use these therapies in the United States are often harassed by local medical societies and threatened with loss of license. As a result, every year hundreds of patients have been forced to seek out physicians in Germany, Russia, and even Cuba, where oxygen therapies are an accepted part of the medical mainstream. Others spend tens of thousands of dollars for bogus ozone and hydrogen peroxide cures from unlicensed practitioners here and abroad who ignore established protocols. Many end their lives in both poverty and despair.

What is the truth behind oxidative therapies? Are they a panacea to our health care crisis, or are ozone and hydrogen peroxide ineffective and even dangerous to health? And despite decades of clinical success, why are they still considered experimental and not approved by the U.S. Food and Drug Administration (FDA)? In this chapter, let's examine some of the major issues concerning oxygen therapies and their role in the human health care picture.

WHAT ARE OXYGEN THERAPIES?

Oxygen therapies involve administering small amounts of diluted ozone or hydrogen peroxide into the body for the prevention and treatment of disease. Ozone therapy was first used by German physicians during World War I and achieved more widespread use beginning in the early 1960s. Although the medical use of hydrogen peroxide was first reported by the *Journal of the American Medical Association* in March 1888, modern hydrogen peroxide therapy was developed in the United States, primarily by the late Dr. C. H. Farr during the late 1980s and early 1990s.

These therapies have been studied in major medical research centers throughout the world, including Baylor University, Yale University, the University of California, Los Angeles, and Harvard University in the United States, as well as in medical schools and laboratories in Great Britain, Germany, Italy, Russia, Canada, Japan, and Cuba.

Some of this research has been medically significant. During the 1960s, for example, researchers at Baylor University in Texas discovered that hydrogen peroxide has an energizing effect on the heart muscle that could be of great benefit to patients suffering heart attacks. Myocardial ischemia, or lack of oxygen to the heart muscle, was relieved with hydrogen peroxide.[1] Writing in the journal *Circulation,* Dr. H. C. Urschel Jr. reported that ventricular fibrillation—a life-threatening condition involving extremely rapid, incomplete contractions of the ventricle area of the heart—was completely relieved through the intravenous administration of hydrogen peroxide.[2]

The researchers at Baylor also studied the effect of intravenous hydrogen peroxide on the accumulation of plaque in the arteries. They found that not only could hydrogen peroxide remove plaque buildup efficiently, but also its effects were long-term.[3] While these findings offered hope to individuals destined for expensive, dangerous, and often ineffective heart bypass operations, the Baylor studies were largely ignored by the medical establishment.

Despite the lack of acceptance of hydrogen peroxide and ozone therapy by mainstream medicine, between fifty and one hundred scientific articles are published each month about the chemical and biological effects of ozone and hydrogen peroxide.

OXIDATIVE STRESS FOR HEALTH?

The philosophy behind oxidative therapies is simple. The use of hydrogen peroxide and ozone in medicine is based on the belief that the accumulation of toxins in the body is normally burned up by oxidation, a process wherein a substance is changed chemically because of the effect of oxygen on it.

Oxidation breaks the toxins down into carbon dioxide and water, and eliminates them from the body. However, if the oxygen system of the body is weak or deficient (whether through lack of exercise, environmental pollution, poor diet, smoking, or improper breathing), our bodies cannot eliminate the toxins adequately, and a toxic reaction can occur. The result is commonly known as chronic *oxidative stress,* which has been linked to a wide range of degenerative diseases such as diabetes, cancer, heart disease, and yeast problems and infections. Medical research has also connected chronic oxidative stress to premature aging.

Mainstream physicians tend to believe that oxidative stress is always harmful to health. They cannot understand how a powerful oxidizer like ozone or hydrogen peroxide could possibly be safe, let alone promote healing for a wide variety of health problems like cancer, eye problems, diabetes, wounds, heart disease, and circulatory problems.

Though an apparent contradiction, the medical potential for oxygen therapies like hydrogen peroxide and ozone is based on both transient and long-term biochemical reactions that take place when these substances are introduced into the body.

Dr. Velio Bocci, emeritus professor of physiology at the University of Siena in Italy and the author of two groundbreaking medical texts on ozone therapy, believes that transient oxidative stress is the reason why oxygen therapies work. In *Ozone: A New Medical Drug,* he wrote, *"Blood exposed to ozone undergoes a transitory oxidative stress* necessary to activate biological functions without detrimental effects. The stress must be adequate (not subliminal) to activate physiological mechanisms, *but not excessive* [enough] to overwhelm the intracellular antioxidant system and cause damage"[4] (emphasis added).

So how does this work? Ozone is a form of superactive oxygen. When it comes in contact with blood inside an ozone-resistant glass bottle ex vivo (this is the preparative phase of major autohemotherapy, explained in the "Major Autohemotherapy" section on page 185), it immediately reacts with blood plasma and other body fluids, such as those found in the skin and the mucous membranes, thus generating a number of chemical "messengers" like antioxidants and polyunsaturated fatty acids.

This reaction yields two results: First, it produces hydrogen peroxide, along with other chemicals collectively known in scientific literature as *reactive oxygen species* (ROS) and *lipid oxidation products* (LOPs). The ROS are believed to be responsible for immediate negative biological effects, such as free radical production. Second, however, within a few seconds the oxidized antioxidants are recycled back in reduced form, leading to more positive biological effects. Over the longer term, the ROS target the erythrocytes (red blood cells containing hemoglobin whose main job is to transport oxygen), resulting in improved oxygen delivery to the body; the leukocytes (blood cells whose main job is to engulf and digest bacterial and fungi), thus stimulating immune system activation; and the blood platelets, which stimulate the release of growth factors, which are substances made by the body that regulate cell division and cell survival.

The biological effects of their "partner," LOPs, are both positive and more long-term. Through the continual circulation of blood, LOPs can reach virtually any organ of the body and stimulate important biological functions like the generation of cells with improved biochemical characteristics ("supergifted erythrocytes" with the ability to deliver more oxygen to ischemic tissues) and the upregulation of antioxidant enzymes in the blood.

Antioxidant enzymes have been found to neutralize oxidative stress, perhaps explaining some of the extraordinary clinical results of ozone therapy. Bocci also believes that LOPs can mobilize endogenous stem cells (stem cells already inside the body), which can promote regeneration of ischemic heart tissue (tissues of the body damaged by heart disease) and other tissues.[5]

OXYGEN THERAPIES AND IMMUNE RESPONSE

Through both transient oxidative stress and the biochemical reactions that take place within the body over time, therapeutic ozone and hydrogen peroxide stimulate the body's immune system. Because they are not designed to treat specific symptoms, these modalities enjoy both numerous and varied clinical applications, often with unexpected beneficial side effects. For example, a person undergoing successful ozone therapy for Lyme disease could well discover that his or her chronic asthma symptoms have improved as well.

According to Dr. Frank Shallenberger, who is best known in the United States for treating patients with a holistic protocol including ozone, oxidative therapies have effects in the human body in the following ways:

- They stimulate the production of white blood cells, which are necessary to fight infection.
- Ozone and hydrogen peroxide are virucidal.
- They increase oxygen and hemoglobin disassociation, thus increasing the delivery of oxygen from the blood to the cells.
- Ozone and hydrogen peroxide are antineoplastic, which means that they inhibit the growth of new tissues like tumors.
- They oxidize and degrade petrochemicals.
- They increase red blood cell membrane distensibility, thus enhancing their flexibility and effectiveness.
- Oxidative therapies increase the production of interferon and tumor necrosis factor, which the body uses to fight infections and cancers.
- They increase the efficiency of the antioxidant enzyme system, which scavenges excess free radicals in the body.
- They accelerate the citric acid cycle, which is the main cycle for the

liberation of energy from sugars. This then stimulates basic metabolism. It also breaks down proteins, carbohydrates, and fats to be used as energy.

- Oxidative therapies increase tissue oxygenation, thus bringing about patient improvement.[6]

HYDROGEN PEROXIDE: THERAPEUTIC USE

Hydrogen peroxide (H_2O_2) is made up of two hydrogen atoms and two oxygen atoms. A powerful oxidizer, hydrogen peroxide kills bacteria, viruses, and fungi; most of us have used a 3 percent solution of hydrogen peroxide externally to disinfect wounds. Higher concentrations of hydrogen peroxide are used extensively in the agricultural, food, and chemical industries as a disinfectant, water purifier, and bleaching agent. It is also a common ingredient in contact lens cleaners, eyedrops, and mouthwashes.

Hydrogen peroxide is involved in all of life's vital processes and must be present for the immune system to function properly. The cells in the body that fight infection (known as granulocytes) produce hydrogen peroxide as a first line of defense against invading organisms like parasites, viruses, bacteria, and yeast. It is also required for the metabolism of protein, carbohydrates, fats, vitamins, and minerals. As a hormonal regulator, hydrogen peroxide is necessary for the body's production of estrogen, progesterone, and thyroxine; it also helps regulate blood sugar and the production of energy in cells. Hydrogen peroxide has long been used medically as a disinfectant, antiseptic, and oxidizer, but has only recently been found to successfully treat a wide variety of human diseases with a minimum of harmful side effects.

HOW DOES HYDROGEN PEROXIDE AFFECT THE BODY?

We mentioned before that hydrogen peroxide is both an effective oxygenator and a powerful oxidizer. Numerous physiological effects of hydrogen peroxide have been described in medical and scientific literature for over sixty years.

Effects on the Lungs

Hydrogen peroxide helps stimulate the process of oxygenation in the lungs by increasing blood flow so that blood has more contact with air; it also helps red blood cells and hemoglobin carry oxygen to the cells of the lungs. This helps remove foreign material, including dead and damaged tissue from the alveoli, the tiny air sacs in the lungs where oxygen is taken into the bloodstream.

Effects on Metabolism

As mentioned previously a number of hormonal effects are regulated by the actions of hydrogen peroxide, including the production of estrogen, progesterone, and thyroxine as well as the inhibition of bioamines, dopamine, noradrenaline, and serotonin. Hydrogen peroxide also stimulates (either directly or indirectly) certain oxidative enzyme systems. Enzymes are complex proteins that are able to bring about chemical changes in other substances; digestive enzymes, for example, are able to break down foods into simpler compounds that the body can use for nourishment.

Effects on the Heart and Circulatory System

Hydrogen peroxide can dilate (expand) blood vessels in the heart, the extremities, the brain, and the lungs. It is also able to decrease heart rate, increase stroke volume (the amount of blood pumped by the left ventricle of the heart at each beat), and decrease vascular resistance (which makes it easier for blood to move through the blood vessels). As a result, it can increase total cardiac output.

Sugar (Glucose) Use

Hydrogen peroxide is said to mimic the effects of insulin and has been able to stabilize cases of diabetes mellitus type 2.

Immune Response

As stated in the "Hydrogen Peroxide: Therapeutic Applications" section on page 180, granulocytes are a type of white blood cell that the body uses to fight infections. When the body is infused with hydrogen peroxide, the number of granulocytes in the body first goes down and then increases beyond the original number.

Intravenous treatment with hydrogen peroxide has also been found to stimulate the formation of monocytes, a type of white blood cell that scavenges, hunts, and kills bacteria; stimulates T-helper cells (white blood cells that orchestrate the immune response and signal other cells in the immune system to perform their special functions); and helps increase the production of gamma interferon, a protein found when cells are exposed to viruses as well as other cytokines (cellular messengers) that promote healing. Noninfected cells that are exposed to interferon become protected against viral infection.[7] According to Farr:

> Hydrogen peroxide is manufactured by the body and is maintained at a constant level throughout our life. It is part of a system that helps the body regulate living cell membranes. It is a hormonal regulator, necessary for the body to produce several hormonal substances such as estrogen, progesterone, and thyroxine. It is vital for the regulation of blood sugar and the production of energy in all body cells.
>
> Hydrogen peroxide helps regulate certain chemicals to operate the brain and nervous system. It has a stimulatory and regulatory effect on the immune system and may either directly or indirectly kill viruses, bacteria, parasites, yeast, fungi, and a variety of harmful organisms. Our studies demonstrate a positive metabolic effect of an intravenous infusion of hydrogen peroxide. Its ability to oxidize almost any physiological and pathological substance, in addition to producing increased tissue and cellular oxygen tensions, has proved to have therapeutic value.[8]

HYDROGEN PEROXIDE: THERAPEUTIC APPLICATIONS

There are several ways to administer hydrogen peroxide therapeutically.

Intravenous Infusion

The most common form of hydrogen peroxide therapy used by doctors calls for it to be administered as an intravenous drip. An intravenous infusion is prepared by diluting 30 percent reagent-grade hydrogen peroxide and diluting it with equal amounts of sterile distilled water to make a 15 percent "stock solution." This is then passed through a Millipore 0.22 mm medium flow filter, both to sterilize the solution and to remove any particulate matter from it. The stock solution is refrigerated in 100 ml sterile containers until needed.

At the time of application, physicians normally use 5 percent dextrose in water or normal saline solution as the carrier. By adding 0.4 ml of the stock solution to 200 ml of dextrose in water, one has a 0.03 percent concentration, which is the recommended strength for most intravenous infusions.

Interarticular Injection

Farr discovered and reported the use of 0.03 percent hydrogen peroxide injected into joints and soft tissues. He found that the swelling and inflammation of rheumatoid arthritis and other types of inflammatory arthritis responded quickly to intra-articular injections of hydrogen peroxide. He also found that it was especially effective when injected into osteoarthritic joints such as fingers and knees. Trigger points in muscles and tendons are rapidly relieved with the same type of injection. Some physicians have reported good results in reconstruction of joint surfaces and spaces using hydrogen peroxide injections.

Hydrogen Peroxide in the Bathtub and as a Spray

Some individuals like to add a cup of 35 percent food-grade hydrogen peroxide to a bathtub of warm water. The hydrogen peroxide is absorbed through the skin, and the ROS that result enter the bloodstream.

Another safe way to enjoy a hydrogen peroxide bath is to spray the body with 3 percent solution of hydrogen peroxide (either diluted from food-grade hydrogen peroxide or using the common drugstore variety). Place the hydrogen peroxide in a small spray bottle and apply on the entire body after a shower. The peroxide can then be massaged lightly into the skin. Avoid contact with eyes. The primary disadvantage to this method may affect men with body hair: it will likely turn their hair reddish blond. Those who use this method claim that the spray offers the same benefits of a hydrogen peroxide bath; some have reported that it clears up skin blemishes very effectively.

Oral Ingestion?

Some have recommended drinking a glass of water to which several drops of food-grade or reagent-grade hydrogen peroxide have been added. Although there have been reports of improved health with this method, physicians like Farr believe that taking hydrogen peroxide orally can have a corrosive effect on the stomach and small intestine and advise against it.

OZONE AND ITS MEDICAL VALUE

Ozone (O_3) is an energized form of oxygen with extra electrons. It forms the protective ozone layer around the planet, yet becomes a pollutant when mixed with hydrocarbons (like carbon dioxide) and nitrogen oxide from automobile and factory emissions. Because scientists have focused on the negative effects of inhaled ozone, the medicinal aspects of the gas when applied intravenously or through the skin have been largely overlooked.

Because ozone was found to be an effective bactericide and fungicide during the mid-1800s, it was first used to purify drinking water in a number of European cities. Today, over two thousand municipalities around the world—including Montreal, Paris, Los Angeles, and Moscow—purify their drinking water with ozone. It was used to disinfect swimming pools during the 1984 Summer Olympics in Los Angeles. More recently, ozone has been found effective in controlling aflatoxin, a naturally occurring cancer-causing chemical that is a by-product from the fungus *Aspergillus flavus*. Found primarily in corn, cottonseed, and peanuts, aflatoxin can find its way into the products of animals that feed on corn (such as meat and dairy products) and foods made from corn and cornmeal, like corn chips, muffins, and breakfast cereal.

In addition to aflatoxin, ozone can also kill *Erwinia* bacteria, a pathogen found in potatoes and other vegetables that causes rot after harvesting. After the bioterrorist attacks with anthrax on United States Postal Service facilities in 2001, scientists at the U.S. Department of Energy's

Idaho National Engineering and Environmental Laboratory—who had tested ozone on potato crops—discovered that ozone can also kill anthrax spores, leading some American scientists to believe that it may be able to play a role in homeland security.

MEDICAL APPLICATIONS OF OZONE

Ozone was not used medically until 1915, when it was found to be an effective disinfectant of wounds and skin diseases in Germany during World War I. It was later found that ozone has the ability to "blast" holes through the membranes of viruses, yeast, bacteria, and abnormal tissue cells, therefore killing them.

Ozone was the focus of considerable research in Germany during the 1930s, where it was successfully used to treat patients suffering from inflammatory bowel disorders, ulcerative colitis, Crohn's disease, and chronic bacterial diarrhea.

Over the past sixty years, over a dozen methods have been developed in the application of ozone in medical therapy. Some have undergone extensive testing under clinical conditions and have been determined safe and effective by leading physicians and professional groups like the International Ozone Association and the Medical Society for Ozone Application in Prevention and Therapy (Ärztliche Gesellschaft für Ozonanwendung in Prävention und Therapie) in Germany, while others have not. New methods are being introduced on a regular basis, including some that are considered highly experimental.

In most cases, tiny amounts of ozone are added to pure oxygen (consisting of 0.05 parts of ozone to 99.95 parts of oxygen for internal use and 5 parts of ozone to 95 parts of oxygen for external applications). Doses are usually expressed in terms of micrograms of ozone per milliliter of oxygen (mg/ml). For example, if a physician were to require 1,200 mg of ozone, he or she would select a concentration of 12 mg/ml and use a volume of 100 ml of oxygen. Because exact amounts of ozone are usually indicated for medical use, only ozone generators that allow measurements of precise concentrations should be used.

The exact amount of ozone to be used is determined on a case-by-case basis, after a careful medical diagnosis by a practitioner with extensive training in ozone therapy. Protocols can change over time, and the medical needs of each patient must be determined on an individual basis before an oxidative therapy is used. There are five major methods of ozone administration that are widely accepted among ozone physicians and researchers alike.

Rectal Insufflation

First pioneered by Erwin Payr and Paul Aubourg in the 1930s, this method uses a mixture of ozone and oxygen that is introduced through the rectum. In the past, it was believed that the ozone was absorbed into the body through the intestine. In fact, ozone reacts with the luminal content immediately and only some of the generated chemicals produced during the reaction are absorbed: this has been scientifically measured both in the portal and in general circulation by Bocci and his colleagues.[9] Used for a wide variety of health problems—including arterial circulatory disorders, general immunoactivation, adjuvant cancer therapy, and to treat hepatitis A, B, and C—this method is considered one of the safest. Typically, between 100 and 800 ml of oxygen and ozone (for an average adult of normal body weight) is insufflated into the rectum, a process that takes between ninety seconds and two minutes.

Rectal insufflation is considered a safe and simple method of ozone delivery that is particularly suited to the elderly (whose access to veins is often difficult), to babies and young children, and to others who don't like getting stuck with hypodermic syringes. While it usually is administered under medical supervision in Germany, Russia, and Cuba, a growing number of private individuals in the United States have used this method for self-treatment for cancer, HIV-related problems, heart and circulatory disorders, diabetes, and other degenerative diseases. It has also been found useful in treating localized health problems like proctitis and colitis.

Major Autohemotherapy

Major autohemotherapy (MAHT) is perhaps the most popular form of generalized ozone therapy. Major autohemotherapy has been analyzed and evaluated under a wide variety of clinical conditions.

MAHT typically calls for the removal of up to 250 ml of the patient's blood. Ozone and oxygen are added carefully (to avoid bubbling) into the blood for several minutes, and then the ozonated blood is reintroduced into the vein in the form of an IV drip. Bubbling causes foaming that damages blood cells and must be avoided.

Like rectal insufflation, described in the previous section, MAHT has been found to activate red blood cell metabolism, increase adenosine triphosphate production and oxygen release, activate the immune system with the release of cytokins (such as interferon and interleukins), aid in immune system modulation, and increase the body's antioxidant capacity.[10] For these reasons, it has been used successfully to treat a wide variety of health problems, including herpes, arthritis, cancer, circulatory disorders, and HIV infection. It is probably the most commonly used type of ozone therapy today.

Body Ozone Exposure

Body ozone exposure (BOEX) uses ozone pumped into a "sauna bag" (which leaves the head uncovered), and it is now being used to treat generalized health problems, such as HIV infection, circulatory problems, and diabetes. Typically the patient will take a warm shower and get into the bag. Pure oxygen mixed with small amounts of ozone are then pumped into the bag for a period of twenty to thirty minutes, making contact with all skin surfaces. The skin interacts with the ozone, and only the oxygen and ozone-reactive products are absorbed. According to Dr. Gerald Sunnen, "Surprisingly, the mixture is able to penetrate far enough into the capillary networks to raise blood oxygen pressure. Presumably then, ozone is able to exert its biochemical influence."[11]

Another BOEX delivery system calls for the patient to sit in a steam cabinet. In addition to steam, a mixture of oxygen and ozone is pumped into the cabinet through a tube from an ozone generator. Wet towels are placed around the patient's neck and a ventilating fan is placed behind the head so that ozone is not breathed into the lungs.

A session will normally last from ten to twenty minutes or until the patient feels uncomfortable from the heat. Like the sauna bag technique described on page 185, the theory behind this method is that the ozone will react with the surface of the skin, and the oxygen and ozone-reactive products will be absorbed and eventually find their way into the bloodstream.

BOEX with a steam cabinet can easily be done at home with a minimum of technical skill, and many enjoy it as a spa treatment or in health maintenance programs. A growing number of physicians and patients have expressed enthusiasm for the steam cabinet method for treating a wide variety of health complaints, although more scientific research needs to be done. In addition, standardized protocols need to be developed for this relatively new form of ozone application. While the method itself is considered very safe, ozone must not be inhaled, even in small amounts. For this reason, the steam cabinet must be sealed to prevent ozone leakage and the room in which treatment takes place must be adequately ventilated.

Transdermal Ozone: Bagging and Cupping

This noninvasive method uses a special ozone-resistant plastic bag. The bag, which contains some water, is placed around the part of the body to be treated (i.e., hand, arm, or foot). When the bag is infused with oxygen and ozone, the water vapor makes contact with the skin, facilitating the chemical reaction. Ozone bagging is primarily recommended for treating leg ulcers, gangrene, fungal infections, burns, and slow-healing wounds. Without water in the bag, ozone is practically ineffective. A normal treatment takes ten to twenty minutes using approximately 80 to 100 microns of ozone.

Another form of transdermal ozone application is ozone cupping, which uses a small glass cup with a funnel attached to administer ozone to specific areas of the skin. The cupping funnel has an ozone destructor (an instrument that causes the ozone to decompose into oxygen by a catalytic reaction) and an ozone line to introduce ozone into the funnel. The physician first applies a small amount of water to the skin, and then the glass cup is applied firmly to the area being treated. A mixture of oxygen and ozone is pumped into the cup, and the oxygen and ozone-reactive products penetrate the skin. This method has been found to be especially effective in treating poorly healing wounds, abrasions, skin infections, herpes, decubitus ulcers, fungal skin infections, burns, and radiodermatitis. A typical treatment involves a low flow of ozone administered from ten to fifteen minutes.

Ozonated Oil

Ozonated oil has been used to treat skin problems for over a century. Although not yet widely available in pharmacies, it became quite popular in Europe during the 1950s and is currently marketed by mail through a number of ozone suppliers in the United States and Canada. Ozone gas is added to olive oil and applied as a balm or salve for long-term, low-dose exposure. Other bases (such as sunflower oil) for salves and creams have been developed in Cuba, where their effects have been extensively documented in hospitals and clinics.

Ozonated oil has been found to be useful in treating a wide variety of skin problems, including dermatitis, bacterial infections of the skin (including staphylococcal diseases such as cellulitis, impetigo, ecthyma, and scalded skin syndrome), fungal infections (including infections of the nail bed and athlete's foot), fistulae, leg ulcers, bedsores, gingivitis, herpes simplex, hemorrhoids, vulvovaginitis, bee stings and insect bites, acne, furuncles and carbuncles, infections of the sweat glands (hidradenitis suppurativa), and yeast infections of the skin including candidiasis (caused by *Candida albicans*). It is also useful in the postsurgical treatment of wounds, and Cuban physicians are using capsules filled with ozonated oil to treat gastroduodenal ulcers, gastritis, giardiasis, and peptic ulcers.

OXYGEN THERAPIES: BROAD SPECTRUM HEALING

Because oxygen therapies stimulate the body's natural immune system, they offer a tremendous range of medical applications. These applications include:

Heart and Blood Vessel Diseases

- Peripheral vascular disease (poor circulation)
- Cerebral vascular disease (stroke and memory loss)
- Cardiovascular disease (heart disease)
- Coronary spasm (angina)
- Cardioconversion (heart stopped)
- Cardiac arrhythmias (irregular heartbeat)
- Gangrene (of fingers and toes)
- Raynaud's disease ("white finger")
- Temporal arteritis (inflammation of the temporal artery)
- Vascular and cluster headaches

Pulmonary Diseases

- Chronic obstructive pulmonary disease
- Emphysema
- Asthma
- Bronchiectasis (dilatation of bronchus or bronchi)
- Pneumocystis carinii pneumonia (PCP, or AIDS-related pneumonia)
- Chronic bronchitis

Infectious Diseases

- Influenza
- Herpes zoster (shingles)
- Herpes simplex (fever blister)
- Systemic chronic candidiasis (candida)
- Epstein-Barr virus (chronic fatigue syndrome)
- HIV-related infections
- Acute and chronic viral infections
- Chronic unresponsive bacterial infections
- Parasitic infections

Immune Disorders

- Multiple sclerosis
- Rheumatoid arthritis

- Diabetes mellitus type 2
- Hypersensitive reactions (environmental and universal reactors)

Other Diseases

- Parkinson's disease
- Alzheimer's disease
- Migraine headaches
- Chronic pain syndromes (due to multiple causes)
- Pain of metastatic carcinoma
- Cancers of the blood and lymph nodes[12]

Let's examine some of the recent medical research on oxygen therapies in several important areas of health: heart disease, diabetes, AIDS, dentistry, and musculoskeletal problems.

Heart Disease

One of the reasons why oxygen therapies are successful in treating cardiovascular disorders is their ability to alter the structure of blood and the way it flows through the veins and arteries. The "pile of coins" erythrocyte formation, which is typical of arterial occlusion disease, is reversed through changes in the electrical charge of the erythrocytic membrane. At the same time, the flexibility and elasticity of the erythrocytes are increased, improving the blood's ability to flow through the blood vessels.[13] This increases the supply of life-giving oxygen to the heart and other vital body tissues.

Studies using ozone to treat patients suffering from poor blood flow to the extremities were first undertaken by the Austrian physician Ottokar Rokitansky in the early 1980s with notable success. Some of the more recent research has been undertaken by clinicians at the Second University of Naples. A 2000 study involved twenty-seven patients suffering from peripheral occlusive arterial disease (clinical stages II–III). All received autohemotherapy. Thirty minutes after treatment, significant improvements in their blood were recorded, while the blood of the control group members (who received an autohemotherapy transfusion without ozone) showed none. The researchers reported, "Ozonized auto-hemotransfusion [autohemotherapy] may be useful to improve both the poor rheological properties of the blood and the oxygen delivery to tissues in patients suffering from peripheral occlusive arterial disease."[14]

A group of Spanish researchers from the Radiation Oncology Department at the Doctor Negrin University Hospital in the Canary Islands studied the effects of ozone therapy on muscle oxygenation. Twenty-three patients and three healthy volunteers were evaluated after three auto-hemotherapy treatments over one week. Tissue oxygenation (measured as mm/Hg) was directly measured after the first and third sessions. The researchers concluded, "Ozone therapy can modify oxygenation in resting muscles, particularly of those that are the most hypoxic. Our results suggest that ozone therapy could be used effectively as a complementary treatment of hypoxic and ischemic syndromes and that the therapy warrants further investigation for possible application in other clinical conditions."[15]

Diabetes

The earliest clinical research using ozone to treat diabetes began in Cuba during the early 1990s and in Russia toward the end of the decade. Results were consistently positive, especially in decreasing the need for insulin and in avoiding amputation.

Perhaps the most ambitious clinical research was reported in the *European Journal of Pharmacology* in 2006 by a team of scientists affiliated with three Cuban medical institutions (the University of Havana, the Ozone Research Center, and the Institute of Angiology and Vascular Surgery) and two in Italy (the University of Ancona and the University of Milan).

The randomized clinical trial involved 101 patients with type 2 diabetes and diabetic foot who were divided into two groups. One group of 52 was treated with ozone (both locally and through rectal insufflation), while the other group of 49 was treated with topical and systemic antibiotics. Both groups were evaluated after twenty days of treatment.

The results among the patients treated with ozone were impressive, even though they were given only fifteen insufflations over the three-week period. There was a greater decrease in the size of the lesions in the group treated with ozone, which resulted in fewer amputations. The average duration of hospital stays decreased among this group, and the cost of the therapy was approximately 25 percent less than treatment with antibiotics. The researchers reported, "Ozone treatment improved glycemic control, prevented oxidative stress, normalized levels of organic peroxides, and activated superoxide dismutase [which catalyzes the dismutation of superoxide into oxygen and hydrogen peroxide and therefore is important in antioxidant defense]."[16]

The glucose concentrations of the group treated with antibiotics did not change, while hypoglycemia decreased and glucose concentrations moved within the normal range in the group treated with ozone. The researchers wrote, "This 'antidiabetic' effect produced by ozone treatment seems to be associated with the antioxidant properties of ozone, increasing insulin sensitivity even when taking into account the resistance to hypoglycemic drugs that these patients demonstrated before the beginning of the ozone treatment."[17]

These remarkable clinical results show that medical ozone treatment can be an effective, safe, and cost-efficient way to help manage diabetes, either alone or as a complimentary therapy in treating diabetics and their related complications. When combined with diet and exercise, it would be useful to explore if ozone can also be an effective form of preventive therapy in light of the growing number of individuals who suffer from this debilitating and often devastating disease.

Can Ozone Cure AIDS?

There is evidence that ozone (as well as hydrogen peroxide, since ozone becomes transformed into hydrogen peroxide in the body) can destroy lipid-enveloped viruses, both outside and within the body, including those related to hepatitis, Epstein-Barr virus, cancer, herpes, cytomegalovirus, and HIV.

The results of a study coordinated by the Canadian Armed Forces and published in the *Canadian Medical Association Journal* showed that ozone kills HIV, the hepatitis and herpes viruses, and other harmful agents in the blood used for transfusion. The author of the article added, "The systemic use of ozone in the treatment of AIDS could not only reduce the virus load, but also possibly revitalize the immune system." Although a related study on AIDS patients proved inconclusive, Commander Michael E. Shannon, a doctor and one of the coordinators of the original study, wrote, in a personal letter, "Of interest, however, the three patients (out of ten volunteers) who responded to minor autohemotherapy in the first trial, are still alive after four years post treatment, with CD4 counts in excess of two hundred. These patients should have theoretically succumbed to AIDS within a year post-treatment."[18]

In several clinics in Germany, AIDS patients have been treated successfully with different types of ozone therapies, including rectal insufflation, ozone bagging, and autohemotherapy.

In Europe, oxygen therapies have been an important part of holistic treatment for HIV-related problems, including lower T-cell counts, opportunistic infections, and AIDS-related diarrhea. Dan's (a pseudonym) was one such case. He was diagnosed HIV-positive, and his T-cell count had dropped below 600. After only one month of ozone therapy as part of a protocol including vitamin supplements, antiviral compounds, and intestinal cleansing, his T-cell count rose to 900 and his swollen lymph nodes shrank for the first time in years.

Although there have been other cases of improvement of AIDS patients after regular ozone treatments (and several documented cases of people who were HIV-positive reverting to HIV-negative status), ozone and hydrogen peroxide should not be considered as a "magic bullet" against HIV and AIDS.

According to Shallenberger, "Ozone therapy works in AIDS by acting as an immune system modulator. In this capacity, it is very effective, safe, inexpensive and readily available. Proper therapy for AIDS will be directed at early intervention (i.e., CD4 count > 300), ozone plus other synergistic immune-augmented therapy, intestinal cleansing is paramount due to the immuno-suppressive aspect of parasites."[19]

Dr. Silvia Menéndez, the cofounder and former director of research at Cuba's Ozone Research Center (part of the prestigious National Center for Scientific Research) in Havana, suggested that ozone works best when administered as soon as possible after HIV infection, before the virus has penetrated the lymphatic system and bone marrow. The personal, economic, and social ramifications of this possibility cannot be underestimated, especially in developing countries where HIV and AIDS continue to have a devastating effect on society.

Dental Cavity Reversal

Traditional dentistry has long employed the "drill-and-fill" approach to removing dental caries. This can be an uncomfortable and occasionally painful procedure for patients, and treated cavities often become decayed again. They then require additional drilling and filling, while in serious cases, the entire tooth is removed or root canals or crowns are required.

One of the most exciting developments in ozone therapy involves the work of Dr. Edward Lynch, professor of restorative dentistry and gerodontology at the School of Dentistry in Belfast, Northern Ireland. He developed an innovative procedure to reverse tooth decay by applying ozone directly to the affected tooth.

Using a novel ozone-delivery system (HealOzone,* developed by KaVo, a German company), a ten-second application is given to the decayed tooth at a concentration of approximately 2,100 parts per million. The ozone is delivered through a hand-held device containing a disposable silicone cup that fits tightly around the tooth so that ozone cannot escape. After treatment, a suction mechanism draws out the gas to an ozone neutralizer that converts it into oxygen. This simple technique has been found to not only disinfect the cavity and remove dead tissue without drilling, but to actually promote remineralization of the tooth itself.

Many clinical studies have evaluated this method of treatment, and I will cite a few of them here. In one study, Lynch and his research team found out that after just ten seconds of ozone treatment, 99 percent of the tooth's microorganisms were eliminated and over 70 percent of the cavities were either reversed or improved. Not a single lesion deteriorated. By contrast, 80 percent of the cavities among a control group deteriorated.[20]

Research done by Lynch and Dr. Aylin Baysan of the School of

---

*HealOzone is a trademarked product.

Dentistry at the University of Birmingham in England studied twenty-six patients with seventy primary root carious lesions (PRCLs). After ten or twenty seconds of treatment, the total number of microorganisms in the PRCLs was dramatically reduced. Out of the sixty-five PRCLs reviewed over five and one-half months, thirty-three lesions had become hard, twenty-seven reversed to severity index 1 from severity index 2, and five lesions remained the same.[21]

Another randomized clinical study by Baysan and Lynch found that after twelve months of treatment with the HealOzone method, 47 percent of the root caries lesions ranked from severity index 1 to 0 (hard) became hard in the ozone group, while none of the caries lesions became hard in the control group. In addition, 52 percent of lesions reversed from severity index 2 to 1 in the ozone group, while only 11.6 percent of the control group experienced a similar reduction.[22]

A randomized controlled trial by Dr. Julian Holmes at the UKSmiles Dental Practice in England assessed the effects of this system on noncavitated leathery PRCLs. A total of eighty-nine patients were chosen for this study, each with two of these lesions. The two lesions were randomly assigned for treatment with either ozone or air in a double-blind design: patients were evaluated after three, six, twelve, and eighteen months. Here are the results:

- **After three months:** Among members of the ozone group, sixty-one PRCLs (69 percent) had become hard and none deteriorated, while among the control group, 4 percent had become worse.
- **After six months:** In the ozone group, seven PRCLs (8 percent) remained leathery and the remaining eighty-two (92 percent) remained hard; among the control group, ten PRCLs (11 percent) became worse and one had become hard.
- **After twelve months:** Two subjects in the study had dropped out. Of the remaining eighty-seven participants, two PRCLs among the ozone group remained leathery while eighty-five (98 percent) had hardened; among the control group, twenty-one (24 percent) of the PRCLs had progressed from leathery to soft, sixty-five (75 percent) were still leathery, and one remained hard.

- **After eighteen months:** Among those treated with ozone, eighty-seven (100 percent) of the PRCLs were hard, while in the control group, thirty-two lesions (37 percent) of the PRCLs became soft, fifty-four (62 percent) remained leathery, and one became hard.

Holmes concluded, "Leathery non-cavitated primary root caries can be arrested non-operatively with ozone and remineralizing products. This treatment regime is an effective alternative to conventional 'drilling and filling.'"[23]

The future of this safe, effective, and noninvasive therapy is promising. Treating dental cavities with ozone requires no anesthesia, and uncomfortable drilling and filling can be avoided completely. In addition to treating dental cavities, this method could be used as an important part of preventive dentistry: treatments can be given to help avoid decay and strengthen teeth. This method is now available in several European countries (including the United Kingdom and Germany) as well as Canada. Hopefully, it will soon be widely available in the United States as well.

This new device will be welcomed by American dental patients. In his article in *Dentistry Today,* Dr. Russell Beggs, a dentist from California, wrote, "The ozone treatment has significant implications when dealing with new decay, recurrent decay, and an aging population. This is a new paradigm for dentistry."[24]

Musculoskeletal Problems

Ozone and hydrogen peroxide have been used to treat musculoskeletal disorders for over thirty years. One of the major methods used involves injecting small amounts of ozone or hydrogen peroxide into the joints, either alone or with other therapeutic substances. Medically, it is known as either *regenerative injection therapy* or *proliferative therapy.*

A broad-spectrum German study of the value of ozone therapy in treating orthopedic problems was undertaken by Dr. C. H. Siemsen, a specialist in orthopedics and sports medicine and a lecturer in biomedical technology at the Polytechnic College in Hamburg.

Fifty-nine male and female patients were chosen for the study. Patients were suffering from acute and chronic joint diseases including active inflammatory gonarthrosis, stiffness of the shoulder and shoulder area, and chronic diseases of the shoulder joint with calcification and painful restrictions of movement. Patients also suffered from lateral and medial epicondylitis (tennis elbow), chronic adductor insertion endopathia (known as footballer's hip in Europe), and malformations of the hip including acute and chronic bursitis trochanteria. Ozone treatment was carried out after all other forms of medical therapy were deemed unsuccessful.

Over a period of several weeks, fifty patients were given an average total of ten interarticular injections of ozone and oxygen in the affected areas preceded by a local anesthetic. Nine patients suffering from therapy-resistant systemic conditions were given a course of autohemotherapy as well. Patients were examined the day after each treatment.

The patients were assessed with scores produced by adding the numbers 1 to 6 to form quotients: a value of 1.9 (i.e., good) was a measure for the knee joint (activated gonarthrosis), and a value of 2.5 (i.e., good to satisfactory) was assigned to shoulder joint problems. After the course of treatment, all patients improved to a "good" quotient level. It was noted that none of the patients required corticosteroids. Siemsen concluded, "The application of ozone in orthopedics and in the treatment of acute, chronic or therapy-resistant painful diseases of the joints with involvement of the articular and periarticular regions is a good alternative treatment method for obtaining rapid pain relief, subsidence of inflammation and an increase in motility."[25]

Joint Pain and Prolozone Therapy

Derived from the word *ozone* and the Latin word *proli* (to regenerate or rebuild), Prolozone* therapy was developed by Shallenberger. It involves injecting a mixture of ozone gas, procaine, vitamin B_{12}, and selected homeopathic preparations into soft tissues, ligaments, or tendons, where they attach to the bone. This causes a localized inflammation and anabolic (muscle building) effect in these weak areas, which then increases the blood supply and stimulates the deposition of fibroblasts, the cells

---

*This is a trademarked product.

that the body uses to repair damaged connective tissue. Shallenberger reports, "Ozone stimulates the cells called fibroblasts and chondroblasts to lay down more collagen and cartilage, and in this way actually heals damaged joints and ligaments. Many patients, who were told 'you need a total knee or hip replacement,' are still out running around years later after a series of ozone injections. Injecting ozone into injured or degenerated backs, hips, knees, shoulders, or necks is very rewarding."[26]

Shallenberger uses this method to treat patients suffering from a wide variety of chronic pain syndromes, including neck pain, whiplash, degenerated or herniated discs, carpal tunnel syndrome, torn tendons, temporomandibular joint syndrome, sciatica, heel spurs, neuromas, tennis elbow, rotator cuff tears, knee injuries, and other sports injuries. He also finds Prolozone useful in reducing scar tissue due to accidents or surgery. Shallenberger writes, "When Prolozone therapy is administered correctly, there is an 85 percent chance for the chronic pain sufferer to become completely pain free."[27]

ARE THESE THERAPIES SAFE?

Although ozone and hydrogen peroxide are highly toxic in their purified state, they have been found to be both safe and effective when diluted to therapeutic levels for medical use. When administered in prescribed amounts by a qualified practitioner, the chances of experiencing adverse reactions to oxidative therapies are extremely small. For example, a German study on 384,775 patients evaluating the adverse side effects of over 5 million medically administered ozone treatments found that the rate of adverse side effects was only 0.0007 per application. This figure is far lower than for any other type of medical therapy.[28]

The main dangers were through the use of direct intravenous ozone injection, which involved injecting ozone gas directly into a vein. Flooding the body with ozone, hydrogen peroxide, or even oxygen can bring about chronic oxidative stress. This can not only render the treatments ineffective, but can actually depress immune system function. In some cases, repeated overdoses of ozone or hydrogen peroxide can lead to serious illness or even death. This method also exposes the patient to the risk of a deadly embolism, the sudden obstruction of blood by an air bubble. This is one reason why direct intravenous application of ozone is illegal in Germany and other European countries. Other ozone delivery methods, like autohemotherapy, rectal insufflation, and BOEX, do not create such a risk.

Well over 10 million people (primarily in Germany, Russia, and Cuba) have been given oxidative therapies over the past seventy years to treat over fifty different diseases. In some cases, oxygen therapies are administered alone, while in others, they are used in addition to traditional medical procedures (such as surgery or chemotherapy) or as adjuncts to alternative health practices like megavitamin therapy, acupuncture, or herbal medicine.

BARRIERS TO WIDER USE

Despite the fact that both ozone and hydrogen peroxide therapies have been proved in clinical trials (and in regular clinical practice) to be safe and effective in Germany, Austria, Cuba, Mexico, Italy, and Russia, very few people have heard about oxygen therapies in the United States and Canada. Although an estimated fifteen thousand European practitioners legally use oxygen therapies in their practices, the number of physicians using these therapies in North America is probably fewer than five hundred. This is partly due to the fact that information about medical ozone and hydrogen peroxide is not provided in medical schools, and students simply do not learn about them. In addition, the medical establishment (and especially provincial and state medical boards) often discourages or prevents licensed physicians from using them in their medical practice.

Some, like the late Dr. Robert Atkins, the author of the popular book *Dr. Atkins' Diet Revolution,* have been threatened with having their licenses revoked if they administer hydrogen peroxide or ozone. Clinics have been closed down, and practitioners have been threatened with jail.

Why is there so much prejudice against these therapies by the medical establishment? A major reason for this lack of interest in oxidative therapies is that ozone and hydrogen peroxide are *nonpatentable* substances that are very inexpensive to manufacture and use. In Germany, Russia, and Cuba, physicians have successfully treated many serious and chronic conditions (including cancer and heart disease) without expensive surgery. The net cost of the materials for a treatment of autohemotherapy or a medical infusion of hydrogen peroxide is under twenty dollars. Even though physicians must include professional fees and the use of their offices and equipment, oxidative therapies administered in a medical setting cost up to 50 percent less than traditional therapies, especially for patients suffering from chronic and degenerative diseases. Self-administered treatments by patients themselves, while not recommended, can cost far less.

For these reasons, ozone and hydrogen peroxide pose a threat to the continued dominance of the medical establishment: the pharmaceutical industry, medical centers, and physicians who are accustomed to providing expensive drugs, complex medical procedures, and long hospital stays.

LACK OF CLINICAL TRIALS

Because government health agencies are often influenced by the pharmaceutical industry and medical lobbies, objective investigation and development of effective protocols for bio-oxidative therapies have been difficult to undertake. However, the Canadian government has shown a greater willingness to investigate these therapies than American government agencies like the FDA or the National Institutes of Health (NIH), as shown by the HIV studies cited in the "Can Ozone Cure AIDS?" section on page 191. However, like the American press, the Canadian media largely ignored the important findings that ozone can completely remove HIV, hepatitis, and herpes viruses from the blood supply.

OXYGEN THERAPIES: THE FUTURE

Over the past few years, interest in therapeutic ozone and hydrogen peroxide has been embraced by the medical and scientific community. In the first half of 2012 alone, PubMed, the NIH's database of citations from the medical and scientific literature, listed over fifty research papers from peer-reviewed journals on the use of oxygen therapies in medicine. These articles covered a wide range of therapeutic applications, including peritonitis, cholesterol, asthma, joint inflammation, fibromyalgia, dental caries, osteonecrosis of the jaw, and renal ischemia and reperfusion injury.

At the same time, the legislatures of over a dozen states have passed "freedom of medicine" laws that allow the use of experimental therapies by licensed practitioners. (For updates, visit the website of the National Health Freedom Coalition at www.nationalhealthfreedom.org; accessed November 21, 2012.) Many physicians from Canada, the United States, and other countries are sharing their clinical data, with the goal of presenting their findings to government agencies like the NIH and FDA.

Medical ozone and hydrogen peroxide form the cutting edge of a new healing paradigm, involving safe, effective, natural, and less costly forms of medical therapy. As increasing numbers of lay people discover the value of these therapies, there will be greater consumer demand. Because oxidative therapies like hydrogen peroxide and ozone hold great promise in treating both minor health problems and some of the most devastating diseases confronting humanity today, including cardiovascular disease, cancer, and HIV-related problems, at low cost, they can go far to help solve our national health care crisis.

In an age of increasing medical specialization, complex and sometimes questionable medical procedures, and expensive, often ineffectual medications, people want to get back to basics. Interest is high in medical therapies for both major and minor health problems that are safe and effective and that can naturally enhance our innate healing powers. We are looking for therapies that will cause a minimum of side effects and that will not bring about financial ruin. As more health care consumers—and physicians—become acquainted with the value of these therapies, they will become a valuable part of mainstream medical practice.

PART 3

About Our Food Supply

All of humanity ate organic food until the early part of the twentieth century, yet we've been on a chemical binge diet for about eighty years—an eye blink in planetary history— and what do we have to show for it? We've lost one-third of America's original topsoil; buried toxic waste everywhere; and polluted and depleted water systems, worsened global warming, and exacerbated ailments ranging from cancer to diabetes to obesity.

GARY HIRSHBERG

The average American meal has traveled about 1,500 miles before it arrives on your plate. All told, the U.S. food system uses the equivalent of more than 450 billion gallons of oil every year.

COLD FOODS CAMPAIGN

Globally, thirty-three percent of the world's cereal harvests and ninety percent of the world's soy harvest are now being raised for animal feed. Feed crop farmers are heavily dependent on fossil fuels, used to power the on-farm machinery as well as used in the production of the petroleum-based chemicals to protect against pests, stave off weeds, and foster soil fertility on large-scale monoculture fields. . . . Globally, seventy percent of the world's available fresh-water is being diverted to irrigation-intensive agriculture.

ANNA LAPPÉ

In just one hour in the United States, more than 1 million land animals are killed for food. Before their slaughter, most of these farm animals—about 10 billion each year—endure lives of abuse with virtually no legal protection at all.

THE HUMANE SOCIETY OF THE UNITED STATES

The U.S. Department of Agriculture strictly prohibits mixing different types of pesticides for disposal due to the well-known process of the individual chemicals combining into new, highly toxic chemical compounds. There are no regulations regarding pesticide mixture on a consumer product level even though, in a similar manner, those same individual pesticide residues interact and mix together into new chemical compounds when conventional multiple ingredient products are made. . . . None of these chemicals are present in organic foods.

ORGANIC CONSUMERS ASSOCIATION

Unless someone like you cares a whole awful lot,
Nothing is going to get better. It's not.

DR. SEUSS

Whether we and our politicians know it or not, Nature is party to all our deals and decisions, and she has more votes, a longer memory, and a sterner sense of justice than we do.

WENDELL BERRY

7

CHOOSING TO LIVE

ENVIRONMENTAL TOXINS AS MAJOR HEALTH ISSUES

Joseph D. Weissman, M.D.

The Lord giveth and the Lord taketh away, but He is no longer the only one to do so.

ALDO LEOPOLD

My research reveals that many diseases have developed within the last two hundred years as probable by-products of the Industrial Revolution. The very technology we have created to make our lives easier and to rid ourselves of disease is now attacking us through toxic chemicals that have been introduced into our environment and food supply, both intentionally and accidentally, without our realizing their full cumulative effects. There is virtually no soil or water supply in the developed world that remains unpolluted by these toxins, and consequently they are also in almost all the food we eat, the water we drink, and the air we breathe.

How, then, can we choose to avoid these poisons and live active, vibrant, longer, and healthier lives? The solution is not to rid ourselves of our technology and industry; we are now dependent on the marvels we have created. In the long run, for the sake of our children and grandchildren, we must find ways to have our technology without the toxins, but that will surely take longer than our own lifetime to accomplish.

Most people have been aware for some time that obesity, the use of tobacco and alcohol, and a lack of proper exercise can be harmful to health. Much less familiar are the dangers related to animal food sources, drinking water, beverages, and processed foods, all of which contain toxic chemicals associated with our technological society. These toxins and their actions within our bodies are what we must avoid to remain healthy.

Consider these facts from one hundred years ago:

1. **Coronary artery disease** (also called coronary heart disease) was virtually unknown throughout the world. The first description of coronary occlusion (blockage associated with coronary artery disease) and heart attack appeared in the medical literature in 1910. Today, coronary artery disease is the leading cause of death.

2. **Cancer** caused approximately 3.4 percent of all deaths in Europe, and less in America. A century earlier, it was responsible for less than 1 percent. Now cancer is the second leading contributor to death, claiming one out of every four men and one out of every five women.

3. **Diabetes** was extremely rare; two out of every one hundred thousand Americans had the disease, compared with one in fifteen today (more than 26 million Americans are afflicted). Diabetes and its complications are the fifth most common cause of death.

4. **Alzheimer's disease** did not exist. The condition was first recognized in 1907 by the German physician Alois Alzheimer. Today, 5.3 million people in the United States are living with Alzheimer's disease, and a new case is discovered every seventy seconds. Alzheimer's disease is now the sixth leading cause of death.

Where have all these conditions come from? Certainly not from the aging process alone. Young people today acquire them, whereas older people in previous generations did not.

THE X FACTOR
IN DISEASE

Over the past two hundred years the world has undergone a unique period of rapid industrialization. The Industrial Revolution brought with it new man-made chemicals: chlorine and its compounds, coal-tar derivatives, pharmaceuticals, and petrochemicals, among others. Steam and electrical power, the internal combustion engine, and the mass-production of consumer and industrial goods made their debut.

All industry, past and present, creates by-products and wastes that require disposal. The only means of eliminating them are burning (with the consequent development of toxic smoke), disposal in nearby waterways, or burial. The emergence of industrialization, with its production of masses of waste, coincides with the discovery—and presumably the first appearance—of many new diseases.

Underground waste disposal ultimately intrudes on water aquifers, and burning wastes pollutes the air; thus toxic materials are deposited in farming areas and finally make their way into water and food supplies. All foods are affected: fruits, vegetables, grain, fish, poultry, meat, eggs, and dairy products. Some foods store more toxins than others, for some are bioconcentrators and biomagnifiers. Generally, *all* animals are bioconcentrators—from fish, mollusks, and birds to cattle, sheep, and humans. The absorption and retention of poisons in animals is far greater than in plants. The greatest concentrations of toxins occur in animal fat and cholesterol, for many chemical toxins are fat soluble; muscle tissue, eggs, and milk are not exempt, however (figure 7.1).

The various toxic substances in the environment constitute the X factor. This term derives from the Greek *xenobiotics,* a word research scientists use to describe substances foreign and harmful to living creatures, including man. Though some xenobiotics occur naturally in the environment (for example, ultraviolet irradiation from the sun, certain chemicals found in plants or created by volcanic activity), by far the greater number owe their existence to human intervention; these include man-made poisons, pollutants, reactive chemicals, free

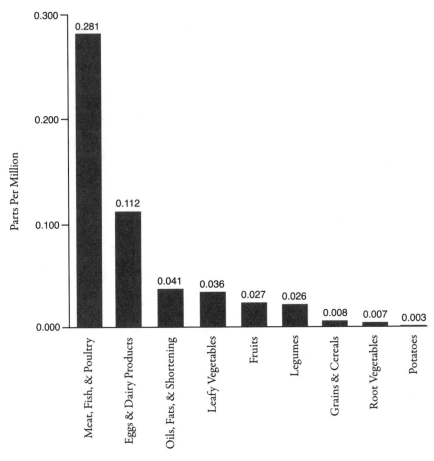

Fig. 7.1. Pesticide residues in parts per million

radicals,* radioactive substances, heavy metals, and most pharmaceuticals and chemical food additives. It is the intrusion of the X factor that has been the major cause of both the decline of infections and the appearance of the new man-made diseases.

Most medical theories that attempt to explain the causes of various diseases do not adequately account for the absence of these diseases historically and in existing primitive societies. Our ancestors, like present-day primitive people, were virtually free of "degenerative" diseases. Even

---

*Free radicals are very unstable, highly reactive molecules with odd numbers of electrons. They are created from stable compounds (and xenobiotics) by heat, radiation, chemical reactions, sonic vibration, and other means. Free radicals can be destructive to DNA, RNAa, and tissue membranes; they are carcinogenic and are probably responsible for other diseases.

meat-consuming peoples such as the Eskimo, Pygmy, Masai, Samburu, and Navajo have had no multiple sclerosis or lupus, little coronary artery disease, and very little cancer. Heredity does not explain it, since their relatives who migrated to industrial areas of the world began to develop "diseases of civilization."

In addition to exercise, one crucial factor appears to explain the lack of degenerative diseases in these groups: they have, or did have, relatively pure sources of food and water. They drank water that was not altered by chlorine or other disinfectants. Their food sources—cattle, camels, birds, and fish—had access to pure water and food untainted by industrial smoke and pesticide residues. In other words, they were not exposed to the X factor.

From this brief survey, a pattern begins to emerge. The major noninfectious diseases of our era do not appear to be a natural, unavoidable part of life or of the aging process. And they seem to be relatively new or modern diseases. Those that did not originate after the Industrial Revolution at least seem to have been rare before that period. Almost all began very slowly at the beginning of the nineteenth century, with many starting a dramatic rise thereafter as the traditional infectious diseases declined.

It must be noted that we now seem to be witnessing a reversal in the pattern of decline of infectious disease. We know that bacteria are capable of developing strains resistant to our most potent antibiotics. Insects, carriers of disease, also develop hardier offspring through mutation—their answer to our ever more exotic poisons. Today, as if out of nowhere, new viruses are emerging to defy the historic trend and to cause a variety of very serious illnesses: AIDS, Epstein-Barr virus, hepatitis, viral leukemia, cytomegalovirus, and others. As far as we know, their viral ancestors did not cause disease in earlier days. I believe that the recent resurgence of infectious disease is due to the chemical and other toxic wastes that have been saturating our environment since the Industrial Revolution.

It is more than possible that these pollutants have created all the right conditions for pathogens to adapt and reproduce in increasingly virulent forms while the human immune system falters under their combined assault. Even tuberculosis is on the rise again, reversing its centuries-long decline.

The clear historical association between the accumulation of toxins in the environment and the emergence or recession of various diseases is not a pattern to be ignored in searching for the causes of—and the solution to—these diseases. Once we link the ills of mankind to xenobiotics, the implications are enormous. The evidence suggests that we as a species are responsible for many of our diseases and that we must adjust our attitudes accordingly and adopt new methods of dealing with them.

CAUSES OF MANMADE DISEASES

For at least the past two hundred years we have been eating, drinking, and breathing low-grade poisons from our environment in increasing amounts. They accumulate and interact within our bodies, causing chemical changes that may be responsible for many of our present-day diseases.

The industrial nations of the world are being overwhelmed by xenobiotics and free-radical producers: ultraviolet irradiation, nuclear irradiation, X-rays, microwave energy, acid rain, cosmic irradiation, radon emissions, singlet oxygen, and many others. Many of these we can do very little about. But there is also an ever-increasing number of man-made substances with toxic potential. Heading the list are tobacco smoke and tars, dyes, industrial chemical wastes, the halogens (chlorine, bromine, fluorine, iodine), and halogenated hydrocarbons, followed by ozone and nitrous oxides in smoke, gasoline, solvents, automobile and jet engine exhausts, petrochemicals, and pesticides, including organophosphates, methylisocyanate, aldicarb, dieldrin, and dichlorodiphenyltrichloroethane (DDT). Then there are the synthetic food additives: colorings, flavorings, sweeteners, and preservatives.

SOME COMMON XENOBIOTICS

There are far too many common sources of contaminants to list them all. Every day we come into contact with engine exhaust, tobacco smoke, dyes, lead, cosmetics, petrochemical toners in copying machines, and hundreds of other toxins. What follows is a discussion of some of the more widespread industrial and chemical xenobiotics that appear to cause the greatest health hazards.

Chlorine

Chlorine has seemed an unlikely villain because of its value in disinfection. The addition of chlorine to drinking water beginning around 1900 was an important health breakthrough. Swiftly many of the dreaded water-borne diseases that had been major killers in previous centuries were virtually eliminated. However, some researchers suspect that chlorine was one of the factors responsible for the appearance of coronary artery disease around 1910.

Research done at the turn of the last century indicated that chlorine was very effective against bacteria without causing any ill effects in humans. For this reason, people have always had confidence in the supposed purity of tap water. But this early research was concerned primarily with disinfection and chlorine's ability to fight coliform bacteria and disease-causing germs, not with the possible effects of prolonged use of chlorinated water.

There are now indications that many public water supplies are of questionable purity. Chlorine is not inert; it interacts with other chemicals and even simple organic matter such as algae, bacteria, and humic acid. These chemical reactions sometimes produce chloroform and other known carcinogens. In addition, industrial waste, sewage, and agricultural runoff mix into our water supplies. The result is that there are literally thousands of toxic chemicals in the water, some of which also react with chlorine to create even more toxic compounds.

Pesticides

DDT, lindane, dieldrin, dibromochloropropane (DBCP), and numerous other pesticides have been used for years in industrialized societies. Pesticides were introduced to eliminate insects, rodents, mold, and other threats to agriculture and crops. DDT was also used in jungle areas to kill mosquitoes, which transmit malaria and other diseases.

DDT has now been shown to accumulate in the flesh of fish and birds, causing abnormally fragile eggshells and reproductive difficulties. The effects on humans are not quite so obvious. Unless one is exposed to a large amount of DDT all at once—enough to cause acute poisoning—

TABLE 7.2. TOXIC CHEMICALS IN DRINKING WATER

KNOWN AND SUSPECTED CARCINOGENS IN DRINKING WATER	
vinyl chloride	aldrin
carbon tetrachloride	heptachlor epoxide
trichloroethylene	diphenylhydrazine
bis (2-chloroethyl) ether	benzene
dieldrin	benzo[a]pyrene
heptachlor	1,4-dioxane
chlordane	methyl iodide
DDT	DDE
beta-BHC	1,2-dichlorethane
alpha-BHC	1,1,2-trichlorethane
chlorinated biphenyls	simazine
chloroform	tetrachloroethylene
bromodichloromethane	acrylonitrile
chlordibromomethane	1-bromobutane
bromoform	fluoroform
bromodifluoromethane	trifluoroethylene
TOXIC COMPOUNDS FORMED IN DRINKING WATER BY REACTION WITH CHLORINE	
chloroform	trichloroacetic acid
bromodichloromethane	trichloroacetaldehyde
chlorodibromomethane	chlorophenols
bromoform	chlorobenzenes
dichloromethanes	α-chloroketones
bis (2-chloroethyl) ether	chlorinated aromatic acid
trichloroethylene	chlorinated purines
tetrachloroethylene	chlorinated pyrimidines
1,1,1-trichloroethane	nonhalogenated compounds

the DDT is stored in body tissue and does its damage years later, in most cases not even suspected as the culprit.

The pesticide carbaryl (Sevin) can produce birth defects, cancer, and mutations. When workers involved in its production were tested, an extraordinary number had lower sperm counts and damaged sperm, and were sterile to all intents. The U.S. Environmental Protection Agency (EPA), however, has not banned Sevin, which is sprayed indiscriminately on crops throughout America. A highly toxic ingredient of Sevin, methylisocyanate, was involved in a serious industrial accident on December 4, 1984, in Bhopal, India; several thousand people died, and many more were left with permanent blindness and chronic respiratory illnesses.

Since the early 1950s, pesticide use in the United States has increased tenfold, yet we still lose about a third of our crops to pests—the same proportion we lost before the pervasive use of chemicals. The actual percentage of vegetables lost to insects has doubled, mainly because the chemicals are indiscriminate in their killing. Birds, natural enemies of insects, also die, as do useful insects that eat other insects. The lower forms of life, including insects, have a unique ability to mutate and evolve within a few generations, producing offspring that are totally resistant to our poisons. Such was the case with DDT; the hardy *Anopheles* mosquito survived the DDT onslaught, and malaria, once thought to have been eliminated, is on the rise again.

Faced with insect resilience, the chemical companies keep providing new and even deadlier compounds to farmers and consumers, thus creating a toxic spiral in which the insects are the ultimate winners. Pesticides can cause cancer, birth defects, mutations, and sterility. We have only seriously tested 10 percent of them, but whether we test them or not, these poisons can hardly be expected to improve human health, and their cumulative and combined effects cannot be predicted.

Today many of the most dangerous pesticides, including DDT, aldrin, β-hexachlorocyclohexane, chlordane, and lindane are banned in the United States, though their manufacture and export is not banned. Ironically, even DDT, which has been banned since the early 1970s, is still used in the third world countries on coffee beans and tropical fruits that are then imported by the United States. Mexican fruits and vegetables, which make up 90 percent of the U.S. produce supply from December to May, contains six times the level of pesticide residue considered acceptable by the U.S. Department of Agriculture, which is helpless to control their import.

The pesticide DBCP, used in the United States until it was banned in 1983, is now known to have contaminated more than two thousand wells in California's San Joaquin Valley, one of the largest agricultural areas in the country. Discovery of its presence in these wells shattered the belief that DBCP would evaporate or degrade and not migrate through the soil to the groundwater. A positive link has been established between DBCP contamination of drinking water and increased deaths from leukemia, stomach cancer, and thyroid cancer. In analyzing water from three thousand California wells, the California Assembly Office of Research has also found fifty-six other pesticides.

A rodenticide known as ethylene dibromide (EDB) was used for fifty years as a fumigant in grain storage. A proven carcinogen, it was banned for use in the United States in 1984 by the EPA. Yet trace amounts are still permitted, and this toxin shows up in our breakfast cereals, cake mixes, and bread.

Mercury

Mercury has entered the food chain in various parts of the world, notably the St. Clair River area of Michigan near the Canadian border and Minimata Bay in Japan. In these areas, industries discarded mercury wastes into the water, the mercury was absorbed by fish, and people who ate the fish developed severe neurological and other disorders. Mercury is also found frequently in ocean waters and in the tissue of ocean fish like swordfish, shark, and tuna; the older and larger the fish, the higher the concentration of mercury. The mercury scare of the early 1970s involving tuna and swordfish has been forgotten, but the mercury remains. In the nineteenth century, felt hat manufacturers discarded mercury into rivers, polluting some water supplies; they themselves often suffered from mercury poisoning, which causes blind staggers—hence the expression "mad as a hatter," a phrase made famous by Lewis Carroll's 1865 children's book, *Alice in Wonderland.*

Fire Retardants and Insulating Materials

Fire retardants known as polybromated biphenyls (PBBs) were accidentally shipped to farmers in Michigan in 1973 in place of animal feed. Masses of livestock were poisoned, and the farmers had to destroy over twenty-five thousand dairy cows and huge numbers of poultry and eggs. The only way to get rid of the carcasses was to bury the animals in mass graves. However, PBBs are very stable, so they are still in the soil and will reenter the food chain at some point. Farmers and their families who ate some of the tainted meat experienced a variety of complaints, including chloracne, joint pane, neurological difficulties, and an increased incidence of abortions and birth defects.

Far more common than the PBBs are the PCBs (polychlorinated biphenyls). This group of chemicals, widely used as fire retardants and insulating materials, has become one of the most feared of the toxic wastes. PCBs were first synthesized in 1881 and first used industrially fifty years later when their useful properties were recognized. Since 1929, 1.4 billion pounds of PCBs have been produced in the United States alone. The manufacture of these compounds was banned in 1977, but reliable estimates suggest that there may be 750 million pounds still in use. Although production of PCBs has ceased, the EPA has allowed their continued use in closed (theoretically leakproof) systems. Despite this restriction, significant amounts of PCBs have recently been found contaminating fuel oil shipped via pipeline in direct defiance of the EPA regulations.

The first major PCB accident occurred in Japan in 1968 when PCBs leaking from a heat exchanger contaminated rice oil. Over 1,200 people who consumed the oil became ill. They experienced such symptoms as swollen and painful joints, severe skin rashes, unusual discharges from the eyes, and gum discoloration. Since the early 1970s, there has been a PCB-related ban on sport and commercial fishing in the Hudson River in New York State. Because PCBs are so stable, tons of them will remain in the sediment of the Hudson and other American waterways for an untold period of time. PCBs have long since worked their way into the food chain, and the EPA has estimated that over 90 percent of all Americans have detectable traces of PCBs in their bodies.

Household Toxins

Various household products may cause a range of problems, some more serious than others. Penta (pentachlorophenol),* used in homes and on playground equipment, decks, and picnic tables to preserve wood and prevent termite infestation, was linked to birth defects more than fifty years ago. Penta contains a form of dioxin that may cause cancer, and the EPA attempted in 1984 to prevent the over-the-counter sale of the chemical. However, the decision has been appealed and continues to be tied up in toxic tort litigations in California. Meanwhile, Penta is still on the market. The only warning on its label states that it is toxic to fish.

Another dangerous chemical found in home-use products is captan, a close relative of the drug thalidomide, which caused a wave of birth defects some years ago. The safety tests that allow captan to be placed on the market were proved to be fraudulent and those who perpetrated the fraud went to jail, but the deadly chemical is still available. It is used as a spray for grapes and garden tomatoes and as an ingredient in cosmetics, shampoo, and some foods. In 1980 the EPA began a study of captan and has since classified it as "a probable human carcinogen." Even if the EPA decides to ban captan, the appeals process will permit it to remain on the market for many years.

Another serious xenobiotic often found in the home is benomyl (butylcarbamoyl-benzimidazole carbamate), which is used to kill fungus or mold on lawns and on peach crops prior to harvesting. Benomyl is linked to birth and genetic defects as well as infertility. Lindane, mentioned in the "Pesticides" section on page 209, is used in many home products, including medicines, floor wax, and pet dip.

Nitrates

Nitrate contamination of groundwater is one of the fastest-growing toxin problems today. Such contamination is primarily due to runoff from agri-

---

*Trade names for pentachlorophenol include Dowicide, PCP, Penchlorol, Penta, Penta Plus, Pentachloral, Pentacon, Penwar, Priltox, Santobrite, Santophen, Sinituho, and Weedone.

cultural fertilizer, either chemical or natural, abetted by septic tank percolation and land disposal of organic wastes. The nitrate problem is another toxic time bomb.

In the past, nitrate contamination was primarily a rural problem. While it is still true that the most heavily affected areas are agricultural, nitrate contamination has spread everywhere because of the growth of agribusiness. It has become the number one reason for shutting down public water wells in the United States.

The problem arises because nitrogen compounds used as fertilizer (ammonia, chemical preparations, animal waste products) are converted to nitrites and then to nitrates by aerobic bacteria in the soil. The nitrates and nitrites percolate down though the soul into the groundwater, often accompanied by bacteria. This affects the farm's well water and also the aquifers that supply cities and near farming areas.

The mixture of nitrates, nitrites, and bacteria in water is particularly dangerous to infants under the age of six months, because their poorly developed gastrointestinal tracts allow the further conversion of nitrates into nitrites, which are able to combine vigorously with infant hemoglobin. The result is methemoglobinemia (one form of the phenomenon popularly known as blue baby syndrome), a condition that prevents the infant from using oxygen readily and gives a bluish cast to the skin (cyanosis).

Unfortunately, boiling does not get rid of nitrates in water; in fact, it concentrates them. And it is just as important for nursing mothers to avoid nitrates as for babies, for nitrates can be passed on to the infant through the mother's milk. The U.S. Centers for Disease Control has a website that contains information on nitrates, how they can get into drinking water, how to tell if they are in your drinking water, and methods you can use to get rid of them.[1]

The main problem with high nitrate levels is that they can be converted into nitrosamines in the gastrointestinal tract. Nitrosamines are xenobiotics that have been implicated in the development of birth defects, stomach cancers, and esophageal cancers.

THE X FACTOR IN THE FOOD CHAIN

The chemicals we are putting into the environment can show up in virtually anything we eat or drink—water, meat, fish, poultry, eggs, coffee, dairy products, alcoholic beverages, fruits, vegetables, and grains. Some of our food sources, however, are more likely than others to carry large doses of toxins; animals—from mollusks to humans—are bioconcentrators and biomagnifiers of the X factor.

Animals and humans absorb nutrients through the gastrointestinal tract, which is also the entry point for most of the modern-day xenobiotics. However, considerable amounts of such chemicals as solvents, chlorine, and chloramines can be absorbed through the skin, especially during industrial contact or prolonged bathing, swimming, or use of chlorinated spas. We also absorb various poisons by breathing.

Our gastrointestinal tract is designed to absorb or digest just about anything; for this reason it cannot serve as a defense against xenobiotics (nor can the gastrointestinal systems of the animals we eat). From the gastrointestinal tract food is absorbed into the bloodstream and goes directly to the liver, where a complex series of enzymes continue to process the fats, carbohydrates, and amino acids before they are distributed to the rest of the body for further metabolism. The liver, with its cytochrome P-450 complex of detoxifying enzymes, is also the first organ to encounter any xenobiotics ingested along with the food.

The liver's numerous enzyme systems can often neutralize poisons in small amounts and arrange for them to pass out with bile juices or pass to the kidneys and out with the urine. But sometimes the liver is perplexed when it comes into contact with poisons it cannot defuse, and these end up in the fatty tissue or cholesterol while the liver tries to come up with a strategy for handling them. The insecticide DDT is one such poison. Occasionally the liver is also unable to entirely detoxify certain xenobiotics drugs, which can cause Parkinson's disease, cirrhosis, systemic lupus, and other man-made disasters.

Sometimes the detoxification process backfires. The liver has just so many enzymes to deal with an increasing number of xenobiotics.

Although insects are equipped to mutate rapidly and adapt to new poisons in a few generations, the same is not true for humans. Allow a few hundred thousand years, and our livers might evolve to cope with the poisons of progress over the past two hundred years. But as it is, through the process called biotransformation, our uneducated liver enzymes may foul up the detoxification process and convert a relatively innocuous chemical into a toxic substance, usually a free radical. For example, the liver might take a stable chlorinated hydrocarbon compound and unknowingly convert it into a free radical that will attack DNA or other vital cell structures. This has been shown to occur with carbon tetrachloride and dibenzanthracene.

At present, scientists suspect that the highly reactive singlet oxygen and peroxide free radicals transformed by oxygen metabolism contribute to the aging process and the development of several of the degenerative diseases, but it is important to broaden our thinking and investigate all the xenobiotics that enter the human body. While it is true that oxygen metabolism, a normal body process, generates free radicals as intermediate by-products, the countless toxins we ingest are much more likely suspects as causes of disease.

Most Americans consume in excess of five pounds of food additives each year. Thus, it is also important to question official reassurances that food additives "pose no threat" to us—that tiny amounts of captan will not be deleterious over a lifetime, nor a little bit of the Federal Food, Drug, and Cosmetic Act's (FD&C) #3 food dye each day, nor below-tolerance levels of dieldrin, nor any of the other poisons that fill our stores and our homes.

MONITORING THE X FACTOR

The governments of the industrialized nations attempt in various ways to control the pollutants and poisons in food, water, and air, but most of these controls are ineffective. However, it would be unfair to accuse government officials of negligence, for most do make a valiant effort within the constraints imposed on them by commercial interests, bureaucracy, and inadequate laws. In the United States, there are two important agencies concerned with the regulation of chemical pollutants: the EPA and the Food and Drug Administration (FDA).

The EPA was formed as an independent part of the executive branch in 1970 by President Richard Nixon. Its duties include air pollution control, solid waste management, drinking water quality control, water pollution oversight, and the establishment of environmental radiation protection standards and tolerance levels for pesticides.

Part of the EPA's mandate is setting standards of water quality. However, the mere existence of standards does not necessarily result in significant improvements. Pollutants in the waterways have not been eliminated, just regulated. Industries and municipalities have not stopped discharging waste; they can continue to do it as long as they have a permit. The permit is supposed to insure that the waste is treated before disposal, but this is not easily monitored, and even treated waste is suspect. There are also polluters who manage to escape the EPA's notice. In addition, the amounts of pollution discharged legally are often much higher than an already polluted body of water can tolerate. This is especially true in industrialized urban areas. The EPA is virtually powerless to deal with previously contaminated rivers, streams, and aquifers.

Some headway has been made against air pollution over the past two decades, including a decrease in levels of ambient lead, ozone, carbon monoxide, and sulfur dioxide. However, even with these modest improvements, acid rain from industrial emissions continues to be a major problem in the United States, Canada, and Europe.

Americans are hooked on disposables. For years, we have discarded boxes, containers, old furniture, paint cans, aerosol cans, and countless other items no longer of use—billions of tons of waste. In most cases, this waste has been buried in the ground in "safe" sanitary landfills—which have proved unsafe after all, as they frequently leach into underground water aquifers. The problem of solid waste disposal is certain to grow worse with time; toxic waste landfills have already produced several catastrophes, notably Love Canal in New York and the Stringfellow Acid Pits near San Bernardino, California. We need new technology to dispose of wastes, not new burial sites that will contaminate fragile soil and water aquifers.

The U.S. Congress has established a Superfund to be used by the EPA for the cleanup of contaminated areas. However, the EPA bureaucracy generally delegates investigation and cleanup to state officials and local EPA officers. The amount of money spent and the effectiveness of cleanup operations, then, depend on the vigor and ambition of these local groups. At this point, 1,305 sites across the nation have been identified as dangerous enough to qualify for Superfund money. However, in 1985 and 1987 the Government Accounting Office issued two reports estimating the potential number of toxic waste sites in the United States to be in the range of 130,000 to 425,000. In 1985 the Office of Technical Assistance took a more pessimistic view, estimating the number of active and inactive toxic sites that pose threats to health and the environment to be around 600,000.

The passage of the Pure Food and Drug Act in 1906 permitted the federal government to regulate food and drugs for the first time. It was an important step in rectifying the unsanitary conditions commonplace in the burgeoning food processing industry and in cracking down on worthless nostrums, patent medicines, and dangerous drugs such as opium, cocaine, heroin, and morphine. The act came about primarily through the efforts of Dr. Harvey W. Wiley, chief of the Bureau of Chemistry of the Department of Agriculture. His department administered the law until 1927, when the Food, Drug, and Insecticide Administration was formed. It was ultimately renamed the Food and Drug Administration and was transferred from the Department of Agriculture to what is today the Department of Health and Human Services.

For its time, the Pure Food and Drug Act was a strong law, but with the rapid emergence of technology in the twentieth century, it quickly became outdated. Amendments to the law became necessary to increase the authority of the FDA. After diethylene glycol, a poisonous solvent in sulfanilamides, caused the deaths of 107 people, mostly children, the Federal Food, Drug, and Cosmetic Act was passed in 1938 to regulate drugs prior to marketing. This act also broadened the FDA's mandate:

cosmetics and medical devices were now to be regulated, false claims for drugs could be suppressed without proof of intent to defraud, drug manufacturers were required to provide scientific proof that new products were safe before putting them on the market, and the addition of poisonous substances to food was prohibited or, where unavoidable or required in production, restricted to prescribed tolerance levels.

The thalidomide tragedy of the early 1960s brought about additional changes in drug regulation. Thalidomide was a mild additive declared safe after stringent, long-term testing on thirty-five thousand animals. It was sold without prescription in Europe and was made available with FDA approval to about 1,200 American physicians for clinical trials. Thalidomide remains one of the most vivid examples of the inadequacy of testing as a method of detecting drug toxicity.

Most people in the United States assume that they are protected by the FDA and the EPA. However, that belief should be examined. The EPA and the FDA see no harm in the fact that the standards they set for bottled water companies are no better than tap water standards; neither agency considers chlorine and the trace elements absorbed by water from pipes and surrounding soil to be a major problem.

A reading of the FDA laws on food additives also gives one pause. According to the FDA definition, "Food additives are substances which by their intended use may become components of food, or which otherwise affect the characteristics of the food."[2] Specifically exempt by law from the definition are the following: "(1) substances generally recognized as safe by qualified experts" [the GRAS (Generally Regarded as Safe) list includes such 'safe' chemicals as the sulfating agents, which have since been implicated in numerous allergic reactions and several deaths; (2) substances used in accordance with a previous approval; (3) pesticide chemicals in or on raw agricultural products; (4) a color additive; and (5) a new animal drug].[3]

The FDA does not usually undertake the testing of new drug preparations but only evaluates the results in deciding whether to approve the drug. Researchers from universities or pharmaceutical companies generally do the testing, first on animals and eventually on humans. Although the FDA is concerned about drug safety, experience has shown that even drugs believed to be safe can have disastrous consequences. There are also numerous instances of unscrupulous researchers and companies falsifying data.

With so much potential for outright fraud or disaster through error, it is no wonder that the EPA and the FDA have not given much consideration to subtle low-grade poisons that may have long-range effects. Rather than require the elimination of many of these poisons from food and water, both the EPA and the FDA have set up tolerance levels. In many instances the determining of "safe" levels of poisons is not based on reliable scientific evidence but on guesswork or estimates from incomplete animal studies.

When it is finally recognized that current tolerance levels for pesticides and other poisons may be too high to prevent long-term damage, perhaps we can expect a change in attitude. The FDA considers that it "has a double responsibility to protect the public from harm and to encourage technological advances that hold promise of benefit to society." We must bear in mind, however, that technological innovations have been responsible for both good and bad, and will probably continue to be so. We must reassess the damage that inevitably results from the disposal of chemicals into our fragile environment, and we must find new ways to contain, reuse, or eliminate them. Above all, we must insure that technological advances are truly advances, demonstrably safe now and in future generations, and that their "promise of benefit to society" is a promise they can keep.

TAKING RESPONSIBILITY FOR ONE'S OWN HEALTH

While we wait for society as a whole to behave responsibly and repair the ecological damage we have done, it is important for individuals to take responsibility for themselves and to avoid drinking, eating, or breathing the chemical poisons that threaten them. Because it is impossible to avoid all xenobiotics, other steps, such as taking vitamin and mineral supplements and giving the body proper exercise, are also necessary to fight or counteract the dangers.

Of course, the average person cannot be expected to recognize all the enemies from the generalized picture presented so far. There are far too many threatening villains, with names even more complicated than those of the prehistoric beasts faced by our primitive ancestors. Just as it was not necessary for our ancestors to recognize the frightening beast as a *Tyrannosaurus rex,* we do not have to know the term *butylcarbamoyl-benzimidazole carbamate* to be aware that a household fungicide may be harmful to us.

The objective of the following recommendations is to get all the essential nutrients without also ingesting toxic poisons.

FIBER AND HEALTH

One recommendation that will be familiar to most readers is to concentrate on fiber consumption—but not for the usual reasons.

The current popularity of fiber, bran, or roughage in the diet is partially based on studies investigating why primitive people do not suffer from the killing degenerative diseases of technological societies. Most primitive people do eat a considerable amount of vegetables or fruits that are high in fiber, and this has been the focus of most of the researchers, beginning with Drs. Denis Burkitt and Hugh Trowell, who first suggested the link between the high-fiber diet and the absence of disease in the 1950s. But this research has paid little attention to those primitive peoples who have a high-fat, low-fiber diet yet remain just as healthy. The standard arguments for high fiber made sense but seem to leave something out.

Plant foods are formed within a fibrous cell wall composed of cellulose, hemicellulose, and lignins. None of these substances are broken down by the digestive juices, so they are not absorbed through the gastrointestinal tract and cannot be considered essential nutrients in the human diet. The undigested plant fiber, along with a small amount of undigested protein and fat, passes through the human intestinal tract as part of fecal material. Typically, primitive Africans eat about twenty-five grams of fiber a day. In the average American diet, the amount of fiber consumed is very low—three to five grams per day.

To explain why a high-fiber diet is beneficial, researchers compared rural African schoolchildren with English schoolchildren, whose diets offered a strong contrast by being especially low in fiber. They found that the transit time, or the time it takes for stools to pass through the intestinal tract after a meal, was considerably shorter in African than in English schoolchildren (for the Africans, thirty-five to forty-five hours, for the English, fifty to seventy). The researchers also found that the stools among the Africans tended to be far heavier and bulkier and were passed without effort or strain, in contrast to the "civilized" stools, which were smaller, more concentrated, and more difficult to pass. The conclusion was that the rapid passage of stools was a protective factor against intestinal diseases.

By contributing to the rapid passage of stools, fiber helps rid the intestinal tract of bacteria—especially anaerobic bacteria, which are dangerous because they can increase deoxycholic acid, a potential cause of cancer. High fiber in the diet seems to aid in preventing constipation, hemorrhoids, diverticulosis, hiatal hernia, appendicitis, colon cancers, and a host of other intestinal ills.

High fiber, then, has value as a sort of rapid-transit system (though some forms of fiber, such as gums and pectins, prolong the stool's transit time rather than speeding it). It also appears to have one other beneficial effect. Fiber acts like a glue, attracting and accumulating bile digestive juices that are the starting point for the production of cholesterol. This suggests that fiber may be important for lowering high blood levels of cholesterol.

But the flaw in the high-fiber theory is that many primitive tribes manage to avoid the degenerative diseases without consuming high-fiber diets. The theory cannot adequately explain why peoples such as the Eskimo and the Masai, who eat large amounts of meat and virtually no fiber or roughage, do not suffer the ailments associated with meat and cholesterol. The Chinese before 1940, and our own ancestors before the

1900s, also consumed diets high in fat and cholesterol without suffering coronary heart disease. This evidence should be an embarrassment to the high-fiber, low-fat theorists, though they somehow manage to ignore it.

There is one common denominator among all these peoples, whether they are meat eaters or pure high-fiber vegetarians: the absence of chemical additives or pollutants in their food and water supplies.

Water in primitive lands—as in developed countries before the late nineteenth century—is not disinfected. There are no industries and factories pouring waste pollutants into the immediate environment, so plants, marine life, and land animals are not tainted by dangerous chemicals. Finally, primitive peoples have not incorporated food additives, excessive salt, bleached sugar, and bleached flour into their diet.

It has been well documented that underdeveloped societies undergo a change in health patterns once they adopt the diet and lifestyle of developed societies. When the early Spaniards came to the American Southwest, they brought sheepherding to the Navajo Indians. But the change to a high-fat diet of lamb and mutton did not introduce the degenerative diseases to the Navajo. They continued their sheepherding for centuries after the Spaniards left, with no ill effects. In the twentieth century they acquired automobiles and other amenities of civilization. They were able to leave their Arizona and New Mexico reservations to buy food, alcohol, and tobacco products, and at that point their health patterns began to change. They now suffer from the same degenerative ailments as other Americans.

Clearly there are too many inconsistencies in the evidence to support high fiber as the single most important factor in prevention of the man-made diseases. When we add bran or fiber to our diet while continuing to eat all the meats and cheese we did before, we do experience some improvement in bowel function, but not much happens to lower our blood cholesterol levels. We cannot even hope to approximate the good health of the fat-consuming Eskimos or that of our ancestors only a few generations back.

The answer lies in the chemical pollutants in our environment. But how is it possible that they can contaminate our food sources so easily?

BIOCONCENTRATORS
AND DISEASE

As pointed out in "The X Factor in Disease" section on page 205, all animals, including humans, are bioconcentrators and biomagnifiers. Pesticides and other poisonous chemicals do enter the food chain from the soil to fruits and vegetables, but in most cases the toxins absorbed by plants remain at the same level of concentration as in the original soil. However, animals concentrate and store the poisons they eat. Many of these toxins are fat soluble and make their home in the fatty tissue and cholesterol areas of the host animal. Biomagnification causes the amount of these poisons to increase dramatically over time, since the animal continues to ingest and store more poisons. Older and larger cattle, fish, and poultry have greater amounts of toxins than younger ones.

While the greatest concentration of toxins is in the cholesterol and fatty tissues, other tissues are also affected. Xenobiotics appear in liver and muscle tissues as well as in milk and eggs. Eating lean beef or restricting the animal food intake to fish, egg whites, nonfat milk, or skinned white meat of poultry solves little and is a compromise of dubious value.

If our meat, fish, and poultry were as free of toxins as the animal products consumed by primitive peoples in the undeveloped world, we might be able to continue to be omnivorous. However, the contamination of our soil and water now seems to be nearly total, and the problem is increasingly a global one; there is little unpolluted grazing land left to us. This problem is, of course, complicated by the development of agribusiness, in which cattle and poultry are raised en masse and fattened by the use of hormones, waste tallow supplements, antibiotics, and chemically sprayed grain and feed.

But if humans are bioconcentrators, don't we still accumulate toxic substances from fruits and vegetables? Yes, we do. But by emphasizing plant foods in our diet, eating as low in the evolutionary chain as possible, and eliminating animal foods, we are minimizing the dangers as much as possible. The toxin levels in animals are many times—in some studies, as much as sixteen times—those in plants.

And those in plants are high enough. For example, a study by the

Natural Resources Defense Council found that 44 percent of fruit and vegetable produce contained residues of nineteen different pesticides; 42 percent of the samples contained more than one pesticide, some as many as four. The consumption of foods containing two or more pesticides is especially risky, for synergistic action can take place, with the toxic effects of one pesticide being enhanced by exposure to other toxins.

Pesticide monitoring is carried out daily in the United States by the FDA and the Department of Agriculture. But this monitoring is simply that—monitoring. It does not prevent pesticides from being used. There are currently more than three hundred pesticides registered for use on food crops. When we consider that they are used on plant food for animals and are then concentrated and magnified within the cows, pigs, or chickens, interacting with the hormones and antibiotics they are given, we can begin to comprehend the magnitude of our own toxin consumption. Combine the lower levels of toxins from our plant foods with the concentrated and magnified toxins from animal foods, and we are literally poisoning ourselves each time we eat.

It is true that most food contains only infinitesimal amounts of synthetic colors, preservatives, fertilizers, pesticides, hormones, and antibiotics, but most of these substances do not leave our bodies. They remain stored within us to combine with toxins from our next meal and our next, until there are enough to affect our health adversely.

In my own medical practice I have seen low-toxin programs help patients with such conditions as coronary artery disease, cancer, rheumatoid arthritis, gout, systematic lupus, Crohn's disease, ulcerative colitis, spastic colitis, diabetes, duodenal ulcers, chronic hives, eczema, and hypertension. My results clearly point to the urgent need for medical science to give priority to further research into the effect of xenobiotics in the genesis of these diseases.

In my book, *Choose to Live,* I outlined an ten-week program for the elimination of toxins and the recovery of health. Others have suggested variations to prevent or treat a variety of conditions. For example, the late Nathan Pritikin pioneered a similar program based on different reasoning. In the mid-1950s Pritikin developed progressive heart disease.

Receiving little help from his physicians, he began his own research and concluded, among other things, that dietary fat and cholesterol were significant contributors to coronary heart disease. He promptly dropped them from his diet and made a full recovery. The program he originated has since helped many others.

In *Recalled by Life*, Dr. Anthony J. Sattilaro recounts his personal defeat of advanced cancer with the aid of a macrobiotic diet (a Far Eastern version of a low-toxin diet) after the failure of surgery, radiation, and chemotherapy. The National Cancer Institute and the American Heart Association also offer dietary guidelines, but these are less restrictive than the low-toxin diet, and in my opinion less effective.

For the most part, the dietary recommendations of the major medical organizations are rather tame. The medical profession has been notoriously slow in accepting the role of nutrition and xenobiotics in disease and health. Statistics show that coronary heart disease, cancer, and other conditions occur with equal frequency among physicians, their families, and the general public. It is apparent that doctors, too, need to change their lifestyles and viewpoints on nutrition.

THE TEN-POINT LOW-TOXIN PROGRAM

1. Avoid tobacco and restrict or eliminate the use of alcohol.
2. Drink pure water, preferably distilled water.
3. Take antioxidant vitamins and mineral supplements.
4. Develop and follow a regimen of exercise.
5. Keep your weight down, since body fat is a storage area for toxins.
6. Avoid processed foods.
7. Avoid animal food sources.
8. Base your diet on plant sources for food.
9. When possible, avoid drugs of all types (illicit, prescription, and nonprescription), radioactive isotopes, and x-rays.
10. Be aware of the toxic dangers in your environment and minimize those you can control.

THE DANGERS OF GENETICALLY MODIFIED ORGANISMS (GMOS)

Up till now all technologies were controllable. Electricity, even nuclear power can be turned off. GM is the first irreversible technology in human history. When a GMO is released it is out of our control; we have no means to call it back. . . . Since GMOs are self-replicating, releasing them might have dire consequences for human and animal health and for the environment and can change evolution.

PROFESSOR SUSAN BARDOCZ

The products of genetic engineering today are still at the level of a dinosaur technology. We use genes, which are foreign to a species, not knowing where they are inserted or what else will change in the whole chain from gene to protein.

CESAER OGESSLAR

Living organisms interact with the environment, they behave quite differently under different weather and soil conditions, they cross-pollinate, and they have a large range of natural genetic variability. . . . Genetically modified plants are alive, and cannot be regulated with a system developed for inert chemicals.

BILL FREESE

Next time you hear a scientist asserting that gene splicing is safe, remind yourself that there is no scientific evidence for that statement. We are profoundly ignorant about what we are doing to the code that generates all life. And unfortunately some scientists, including those entrusted with public safety, are willing to lie.

DONELLA H. MEADOWS

Context is critical. Yet genetic manipulation of food ignores millions of years of evolutionary context, and that could have serious implications in the future. We aren't dealing with an insignificant change to our diets here, we're dealing with a revolutionary technology being used in our food supply—affecting us, future generations, and the ecosystems on which we depend.

DAVID SUZUKI

There is something profoundly amiss in our stampede down the biotech path for every trivial application. The level of the change now possible, the speed at which we can make these dramatic alterations and the potential consequences for animals, the environment and ourselves—for the world as we know it—ought to give us great pause. It is naïve to think that this research, unbridled, will have only a trivial impact.

AUTUMN FIESTER

The situation is like the tobacco industry. They knew about it but they suppressed that information. They created misleading evidence that showed that the problem wasn't so serious. And all the time they knew how bad it was. Tobacco is bad enough. But genetic modification, if it is going to be problematic, if it is going to cause us real health problems, then tobacco will be nothing in comparison with this. The size of genetic modification and problems it may cause us are tremendous.

ARPAD PUSZTAI

A captive elk escaped and took up residence in our crops of organic corn and soy. It had total access to the neighboring fields of GM crops, but never went into them.

SUSAN AND MARK FITZGERALD, MINNESOTA

8

STATE-OF-THE-SCIENCE ON THE HEALTH RISK OF GM FOODS

WHAT YOU NEED TO KNOW ABOUT THE LACK OF ADEQUATE FEDERAL OVERSIGHT

Jeffrey M. Smith

It's impressive, the way so many communities affected by biotechnology are resisting a technology supported by so many huge economic institutions. In fact, the massive and well-organized resistance to this technology by such large numbers of people worldwide has never been equaled in human history.

DAVID SUZUKI

Nature never deceives us; it is always we who deceive ourselves.

JEAN JACQUES ROUSSEAU

We all know stories of tobacco, asbestos, and DDT. Originally declared safe, they caused widespread death and disease. Although their impact was vast, most of the population was spared. The same cannot be said for sweeping changes in the food supply. Everyone eats; everyone is affected. The increase in several diseases in North America may be due to the profound changes in our diet. The most radical change occurred a little over a decade ago when genetically modified (GM) crops were introduced. Their influence on health has been largely ignored, but recent studies show serious problems. Genetically modified organisms (GMOs) have been linked to thousands of toxic or allergic-type reactions, thousands of sick, sterile, and dead livestock animals, and damage to virtually every organ and system studied in lab animals.[1] Nearly every independent animal feeding safety study shows adverse or unexplained effects.

GM foods were made possible by a technology developed in the 1970s whereby genes from one species are forced into the DNA of other species. Genes produce proteins, which in turn can generate characteristics or traits. The promised traits associated with GMOs have been sky high—vegetables growing in the desert, vitamin-fortified grains, and highly productive crops feeding the starving millions. None of these are available. In fact, the only two traits that are found in nearly all commercialized GM plants are herbicide tolerance and pesticide production.

Herbicide-tolerant soy, corn, cotton, and canola plants are engineered with bacterial genes that allow them to survive otherwise deadly doses of herbicides. This gives farmers more flexibility in weeding and gives the GM seed company lots more profit. When farmers buy GM seeds, they sign a contract to buy only that seed producer's brand of herbicide. Herbicide-tolerant crops comprise about 80 percent of all GM plants. The other 20 percent are corn and cotton varieties that produce a pesticide in every cell. This is accomplished due to a gene from a soil bacterium called *Bacillus thuringiensis,* or Bt, which produces a natural insect-killing poison called Bt-toxin. In addition to crops with these two traits, there are also disease-resistant GM Hawaiian papaya, zucchini, and crook-neck squash, which make up well under 1 percent of GMO acreage.

THE FOOD AND
DRUG ADMINISTRATION'S
"NONREGULATION" OF GM FOODS

Rhetoric from the United States government since the early 1990s proclaims that GM foods are no different from their natural counterparts that have existed for centuries. The Food and Drug Administration (FDA) has labeled them "generally recognized as safe" (GRAS). This status allows a product to be commercialized without any additional testing. According to U.S. law, to be considered GRAS the substance must be the subject of a substantial amount of peer-reviewed published studies (or the equivalent) and there must be overwhelming consensus among the scientific community that the product is safe. GM foods had neither. Nonetheless, in a precedent-setting move in 1992 that some experts contend was illegal, the FDA declared that GM crops are GRAS as long as their producers say they are. Thus, the FDA does not require *any* safety evaluations or labeling of GMOs. A company can even introduce a GM food to the market without telling the agency.

Such a lenient approach was largely the result of the influence of large agricultural corporations. According to Henry Miller, who had a leading role in biotechnology issues at the FDA from 1979 to 1994, "In this area, the U.S. government agencies have done exactly what big agribusiness has asked them to do and told them to do."[2] The ag biotech company with the greatest influence was clearly Monsanto. According to the *New York Times,* "What Monsanto wished for from Washington, Monsanto and, by extension, the biotechnology industry got. . . . When the company abruptly decided that it needed to throw off the regulations and speed its foods to market, the White House quickly ushered through an unusually generous policy of self-policing."[3]

This policy was heralded by Vice President Dan Quayle on May 26, 1992. He chaired the Council on Competitiveness, which had identified GM crops as an industry that could boost U.S. exports. To take advantage, Quayle announced "reforms" to "speed up and simplify the process of bringing" GM products to market without "being hampered by unnecessary regulation."[4] Three days later, the FDA policy on nonregulation was unveiled.

The person who oversaw its development was the FDA's deputy commissioner for policy, Michael Taylor, whose position had been created especially for him in 1991. Prior to that, Taylor was an outside attorney for both Monsanto and the Food Biotechnology Council. After working at the FDA, he became Monsanto's vice president. The Obama administration has put Taylor back into the FDA as the U.S. food safety czar.

THE FDA COVERS UP HEALTH RISKS

Taylor's GMO policy needed to create the impression that unintended effects from GM crops were not an issue. Otherwise their GRAS status would be undermined, and they would need the extensive testing and labels that are normally required for food additives. But internal memos made public from a lawsuit showed that the overwhelming consensus among the agency's scientists was that GM crops can have unpredictable, hard-to-detect side effects. Various departments and experts spelled these out in detail, listing allergies, toxins, nutritional effects, and new diseases as potential dangers. They urged superiors to require long-term safety studies.[5] In spite of the warnings, according to public interest attorney Steven M. Druker, who studied the FDA's internal files, "References to the unintended negative effects of bioengineering were progressively deleted from drafts of the policy statement (over the protests of agency scientists)."[6]

FDA microbiologist Louis J. Pribyl, Ph.D., wrote about the policy, "What has happened to the scientific elements of this document? Without a sound scientific base to rest on, this becomes a broad, general, 'What do I have to do to avoid trouble-type document. . . . It will look like and probably be just a political document. . . . It reads very pro-industry, especially in the area of unintended effects."[7]

The scientists' concerns were not only ignored, their very existence was also denied. The official FDA policy stated, "The agency is not aware of any information showing that foods derived by these new methods differ from other foods in any meaningful or uniform way."[8] In sharp contrast, an *internal* FDA report stated, "The processes of genetic engineering and traditional breeding are different and according to the technical experts in the agency, they lead to different risks."[9] The FDA's deceptive notion of no difference was coined "substantial equivalence" and formed the basis of the U.S. government position on GMOs.

Many scientists and organizations have criticized the U.S. position. The National Academy of Sciences and even the pro-GM Royal Society of London[10] describe the U.S. system as inadequate and flawed. The editor of the prestigious journal *The Lancet* said, "It is astounding that the US Food and Drug Administration has not changed their stance on genetically modified food adopted in 1992. . . . The policy is that genetically modified crops will receive the same consideration for potential health risks as any other new crop plant. This stance is taken despite good reasons to believe that specific risks may exist. . . . Governments should never have allowed these products into the food chain without insisting on rigorous testing for effects on health."[11] The Royal Society of Canada described substantial equivalence as "scientifically unjustifiable and inconsistent with precautionary regulation of the technology."[12]

GMOS ARE INHERENTLY UNSAFE

There are several reasons why GM plants present unique dangers. The first is that the *process* of genetic engineering itself creates unpredicted alterations, irrespective of which gene is transferred. The gene insertion process, for example, is accomplished by either shooting genes from a "gene gun" into a plate of cells or using bacteria to infect the cell with foreign DNA. Both create mutations in and around the insertion site and elsewhere.[13] The "transformed" cell is then cloned into a plant through a process called tissue culture, which results in additional hundreds or thousands of mutations throughout the plant's genome. In the end, the GM plant's DNA can be a staggering 2–4 percent different from its natural parent.[14] Native genes can be mutated, deleted, or permanently turned on or off. In addition, the insertion process causes holistic and not-well-understood changes among large numbers of native genes. One study revealed that up to 5 percent of the natural genes altered their levels of protein expression as a result of a single insertion.

The Royal Society of Canada acknowledged that "the default prediction" for GM crops would include "a range of collateral changes in expression of other genes, changes in the pattern of proteins produced and/or changes in metabolic activities."[15] Although the FDA scientists evaluating GMOs in 1992 were unaware of the extent to which GM DNA is damaged or changed, they too described the potential consequences. They reported, "The possibility of unexpected, accidental changes in genetically engineered plants" might produce "unexpected high concentrations of plant toxicants."[16] GM crops, they said, might have "increased levels of known naturally occurring toxins" and the "appearance of new, not previously identified" toxins.[17] The same mechanism can also produce allergens, carcinogens, or substances that inhibit assimilation of nutrients.

Most of these problems would pass unnoticed through the safety assessments on GM foods, which are largely designed on the false premise that genes are like Legos that cleanly snap into place. But even if we disregard unexpected changes in the DNA for the moment, a properly functioning inserted gene still carries significant risk. Its newly created GM protein, such as the Bt-toxin, may be dangerous for human health. Moreover, even if that protein is safe in its natural organism, once it is transferred into a new species it may be processed differently. A harmless protein may be transformed into a dangerous or deadly version. This happened with at least one GM food crop under development, GM peas, which were destroyed before being commercialized.

FDA scientists were also quite concerned about the possibility of inserted genes spontaneously transferring into the DNA of bacteria inside our digestive tract. They were particularly alarmed at the possibility of antibiotic-resistant marker (ARM) genes transferring. ARM genes are employed during gene insertion to help scientists identify which cells successfully integrated the foreign gene.

These ARM genes, however, remain in the cell and are cloned into the DNA of all the GM plants produced from that cell. One FDA report wrote in all capital letters that ARM genes would be "A SERIOUS HEALTH HAZARD," due to the possibility that they might transfer to bacteria and create super diseases, untreatable with antibiotics. *Although the biotech industry confidently asserted that gene transfer from GM foods was not possible, the only human feeding study on GM foods later proved that it does take place. The genetic material in soybeans that make them herbicide tolerant transferred into the DNA of human gut bacteria and continued to function.*[18] *That means that long after we stop eating a GM crop, its foreign GM proteins may be produced inside our intestines.* It is also possible that the foreign genes might end up inside our own DNA, within the cells of our own organs and tissues.

Another worry expressed by FDA scientists was that GM plants might gather "toxic substances from the environment" such as "pesticides or heavy metals"[19] or that toxic substances in GM animal feed might bioaccumulate into milk and meat products. While no studies have looked at the bioaccumulation issue, herbicide-tolerant crops certainly have higher levels of herbicide residues. In fact, many countries had to increase their legally allowable levels—by up to fifty times—in order to accommodate the introduction of GM crops.

The overuse of the herbicides due to GM crops has resulted in the development of herbicide-resistant weeds. Statistics from the U.S. Department of Agriculture show that herbicide use is rapidly accelerating. Its use was up by 383 million pounds in the first thirteen years of GM crops.[20] But the rate of application is accelerating due in large part to the emergence of herbicide-tolerant weeds. According to a study by Charles Benbrook, research professor at the Center for Sustaining Agriculture and Natural Resources at Washington State University. "Crop years 2007 and 2008 accounted for 46% of the increase in herbicide use over thirteen years across the three HT [herbicide tolerant] crops. Herbicide use on HT crops rose a remarkable 31.4% from 2007 to 2008." And as Roundup becomes less effective, farmers are now using more toxic herbicides, such as 2-4D, the use of which increased by 237 percent from 2004 to 2006.[21]

All of the above risks associated with GM foods are magnified for high-risk groups, such as pregnant women, children, the sick, and the elderly. The following sections highlight some of the problems that have been identified.

GM DIET SHOWS TOXIC REACTIONS IN THE DIGESTIVE TRACT

The very first crop submitted to the FDA's voluntary consultation process, the FlavrSavr tomato, showed evidence of toxins. Out of twenty female rats fed the GM tomato, seven developed stomach lesions.[22] The director of the FDA's Office of Special Research Skills wrote that the tomatoes did not demonstrate a "reasonable certainty of no harm," which is their normal standard of safety.[23] The Additives Evaluation Branch agreed that "unresolved questions still remain."[24] The political appointees, however, did not require that the tomato be withdrawn.*

According to Arpad Pusztai, Ph.D., one of the world's leading experts in GM food safety assessments, the type of stomach lesions linked to the tomatoes "could lead to life-endangering hemorrhage, particularly in the elderly who use aspirin to prevent [blood clots]."[25] Pusztai believes that the digestive tract, which is the first and largest point of contact with foods, can reveal various reactions to toxins and should be the first target of GM food risk assessment. He was alarmed, however, to discover that studies on the FlavrSavr never looked past the stomach to the intestines. Other studies that did look found problems.

Mice fed potatoes engineered to produce the Bt-toxin developed abnormal and damaged cells, as well as proliferative cell growth in the lower part of their small intestines (ileum).[26] Rats fed potatoes engineered to produce a different type of insecticide—Galanthus nivalis agglutinin (GNA)—lectin from the snowdrop plant) also showed proliferative cell growth in both the stomach and intestinal walls (figure 8.1).[27] Although

---

*Calgene had submitted data on two lines of GM tomatoes, both using the same inserted gene. They voluntarily elected to market only the variety that was not associated with the lesions. This was not required by the FDA, which did not block approvals on the lesion-associated variety. The FlavrSavr tomato has since been taken off the market. After the FlavrSavr, no other biotech company has submitted such detailed data to the FDA.

Stomach Lining   Intestinal Wall

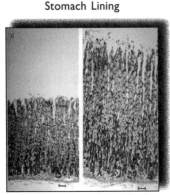

Fig. 8.1. Rats fed GM potatoes showed proliferative cell growth in the stomach and intestines.

Non-GM   GM   Non-GM   GM

the guts of rats fed GM peas were not examined for cell growth, the intestines were mysteriously heavier, possibly as a result of such growth.[28] Cell proliferation can be a precursor to cancer and is of special concern.

GM DIETS CAUSE LIVER DAMAGE

The state of the liver—a main detoxifier for the body—is another indicator of toxins.

- Rats fed the Galanthus nivalis agglutinin lectin potatoes, described on page 237, had smaller and partially atrophied livers.[29]
- Rats fed Monsanto's MON 863 corn, engineered to produce Bt-toxin, had liver lesions and other indications of toxicity.[30]
- Rabbits fed GM soy showed altered enzyme production in their livers as well as higher metabolic activity.[31]
- The livers of rats fed Roundup Ready canola were 12–16 percent heavier, possibly due to liver disease or inflammation.[32]
- Microscopic analysis of the livers of mice fed Roundup Ready soybeans revealed altered gene expression and structural and functional changes.[33] Many of these changes reversed after the mice diet was switched to non-GM soy, indicating that GM soy was the culprit. The findings, according to molecular geneticist Michael Antoniou, Ph.D., "are not random and must reflect some 'insult' on the liver

by the GM soy." Antoniou, who does human gene therapy research in King's College London, said that although the long-term consequences of the GM soy diet are not known, it "could lead to liver damage and consequently general toxemia."[34]

- Rats fed Roundup Ready soybeans also showed structural changes in their livers.[35]

GM-FED ANIMALS HAD HIGHER DEATH RATES AND ORGAN DAMAGE

In the FlavrSavr tomato study, *a note in the appendix* indicated that seven of forty rats died within two weeks and were replaced.[36] In another study, chickens fed herbicide-tolerant Liberty Link corn died at twice the rate of those fed natural corn.[37] But in these two industry-funded studies, the deaths were dismissed without adequate explanation or follow-up.

In addition, the cells in the pancreas of mice fed Roundup Ready soy had profound changes and produced significantly less digestive enzymes;[38] in rats fed a GM potato, the pancreas was enlarged.[39] In various analyses of kidneys, GM-fed animals showed lesions, toxicity, altered enzyme production, or inflammation.[40,41] Enzyme production in the hearts of rabbits was altered by GM soy.[42] And GM potatoes caused slower growth in the brain of rats.[43] A team of independent scientists reanalyzed the raw data in three Monsanto ninety-day rat feeding studies and saw signs of toxicity in the liver and kidneys, as well as effects in the heart, adrenal glands, spleen, and blood.[44]

REPRODUCTIVE FAILURES AND INFANT MORTALITY

The testicles of both mice and rats fed Roundup Ready soybeans showed dramatic changes. In rats, the organs were dark purple instead of pink (figure 8.2).[45] In mice, young sperm cells were altered.[46] Embryos of GM soy-fed mice also showed temporary changes in their DNA function, compared with those whose parents were fed non-GM soy.[47]

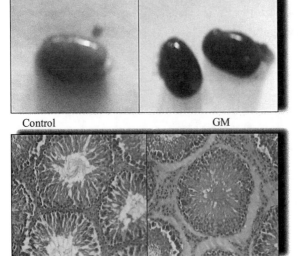

Control   GM

Fig. 8.2. The testicles of rats fed Roundup Ready soybeans were dark purple (top right) instead of pink (top left), and the structure of the cells was significantly altered (compare bottom left with bottom right).

An Austrian government study showed that mice fed GM corn (Bt and Roundup Ready) had fewer babies and smaller babies.[48] More dramatic results were discovered by a leading scientist at the Russian National Academy of Sciences. Female rats were fed GM soy, starting two weeks before they were mated, with the following results:

- Over a series of three experiments, 51.6 percent of the offspring from the GM-fed group died within the first three weeks, compared with 10 percent from the non-GM soy group and 8.1 percent for non-soy control group.
- "High pup mortality was characteristic of every litter from mothers fed the GM soy flour."[49]
- The average size and weight of the GM-fed offspring was quite a bit smaller (figure 8.3).[50]
- In a preliminary study, the GM-fed offspring were unable to conceive.[51]

After the three feeding trials, the supplier of rat food used at the Russian laboratory began using GM soy in its formulation. Since all the rats housed at the facility were now eating GM soy, no non-GM-fed

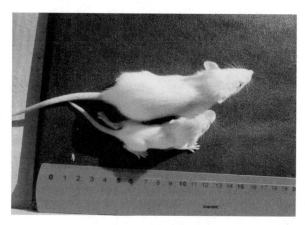

Fig. 8.3. The twenty-day-old smaller rat, born of a mother fed GM soy, is quite a bit smaller than the nineteen-day-old rat from the control group.

control subjects were available for subsequent GM feeding trials; follow-up studies were canceled. *After two months on the GM soy diet, however, the infant mortality rate of rats throughout the facility had skyrocketed to 55.3 percent (99 of 179).*[52]

FARMERS REPORT LIVESTOCK STERILITY AND DEATHS

About two dozen farmers reported that their pigs had reproductive problems when fed certain varieties of Bt corn. Pigs were sterile, had false pregnancies, or gave birth to bags of water. Cows and bulls also became sterile. Bt corn was also implicated by farmers in the deaths of cows, horses, water buffaloes, and chickens.[53]

When Indian shepherds let their sheep graze continuously on Bt cotton plants, within five to seven days, one out of four sheep died. There were an estimated ten thousand sheep deaths in the region in 2006, with more reported in 2007. Postmortems on the sheep showed severe irritation and black patches in both intestines and the liver (as well as enlarged bile ducts). Investigators said preliminary evidence "strongly suggests that the sheep mortality was due to a toxin . . . most probably Bt-toxin."[54] In a small feeding study, 100 percent of sheep fed Bt cotton died within thirty days. Those fed natural plants had no symptoms.

Buffalo that have grazed on natural cotton plants for years without incident react to the Bt variety. In one village in Andhra Pradesh, India, for example, thirteen buffalo grazed on Bt cotton plants for a single day. All died within three days.[55] Investigators in the state of Haryana, India, report that most buffalo that ate GM cottonseed had reproductive complications such as premature deliveries, abortions, infertility, and prolapsed uteruses. Many young calves and adult buffaloes died.

GM CROPS TRIGGER IMMUNE REACTIONS AND MAY CAUSE ALLERGIES

Allergic reactions occur when the immune system interprets something as foreign, different, and offensive, and reacts accordingly. All GM foods, by definition, have something foreign and different. And several studies show that they provoke reactions. Rats fed Monsanto's GM corn, for example, had a significant increase in blood cells related to the immune system.[56] Also, GM potatoes caused the immune system of rats to respond more slowly.[57] And GM peas provoked an inflammatory response in mice, suggesting that they might cause deadly allergic reactions in people.[58]

It might be difficult to identify whether GM foods are triggering allergic responses in the population, since very few countries conduct regular studies or keep careful records. One country that does have an annual evaluation is the United Kingdom. *Soon after GM soy was introduced into the British diet, researchers at the York Laboratory reported that allergies to soy had skyrocketed by 50 percent in a single year.*[59] Although no follow-up studies were conducted to see if GM soy was the cause, there is evidence showing several ways in which it might have contributed to the rising incidence of allergies:

- The only significant variety of GM soy is Monsanto's Roundup Ready variety, planted in 89 percent of U.S. soy acres. A foreign gene from bacteria (with parts of virus and petunia DNA) is inserted, which allows the plant to withstand Roundup herbicide. The protein produced by the bacterial gene has never been part of the human food supply. Because people aren't usually allergic to a food until they have eaten it several times, it would be difficult to know in advance if the protein is an allergen. Without a surefire method to identify allergenic GM crops, the World Health Organization (WHO) and others recommend examining the properties of the protein to see if it shares characteristics with known allergens. One method is to compare the amino acid sequence of the novel protein with a database of allergens. If there is a match, according to the WHO, the GM crop should either not be commercialized or additional testing should be done. Sections of the protein produced in GM soy *are* identical to shrimp and dust mite allergens,[60] but the soybean was introduced before WHO criteria were established, and the recommended additional tests were not conducted. If the protein does trigger reactions, the danger is compounded by the finding that the Roundup Ready gene transfers into the DNA of human gut bacteria and may continuously produce the protein from within our intestines.[61]

- In addition to the herbicide-tolerant protein, GM soybeans contain a unique, unexpected protein, which likely came about from the changes incurred during the genetic engineering process. Scientists found that this new protein was able to bind with IgE antibodies, suggesting that it may provoke dangerous allergic reactions. The same study revealed that one human subject showed a skin-prick immune response only to GM soy, but not to natural soy.[62] These results must be considered preliminary, as the non-GM soy was a wild type and not necessarily comparable with the GM variety. Another study showed that the levels of one known soy allergen, called trypsin inhibitor, were as much as seven times higher in cooked GM soy compared with a non-GM control soy.[63] This was Monsanto's own study, and it did use comparable control soy.

- GM soy also produces an unpredicted side effect in the pancreas of mice: the amount of digestive enzymes produced is dramatically reduced.[64] If a shortage of enzymes causes food proteins to breakdown more slowly, then they have more time to trigger allergic reactions. Thus, digestive problems from GM soy might promote allergies to a wide range of proteins, not just soy.

- The higher amount of Roundup herbicide residues on GM soy might create reactions in consumers. In fact, many of the symptoms identified in the UK soy allergy study are among those related to glyphosate exposure. (The allergy study identified irritable bowel syndrome, digestion problems, chronic fatigue, headaches, lethargy, and skin complaints, including acne and eczema, all related to soy consumption. Symptoms of glyphosate exposure include nausea, headaches, lethargy, skin rashes, and burning or itchy skin. It is also possible that glyphosate's breakdown product aminomethylphosphonic acid [AMPA], which accumulates in GM soybeans after each spraying, might contribute to allergies.)

It is interesting to note that in the five years immediately after GM soy was introduced, U.S. peanut allergies doubled. It is known that a protein in natural soybeans cross-reacts with peanut allergies (i.e., soy may trigger reactions in some people who are allergic to peanuts).[65] Given the startling increase in peanut allergies, scientists should investigate whether this cross-reactivity has been amplified in GM soy.

BT-TOXIN, PRODUCED IN GM CORN AND COTTON, MAY CAUSE ALLERGIES

For years, organic farmers and others have sprayed crops with solutions containing natural Bt bacteria as a method of insect control. The toxin creates holes in the insects' stomach and kills them. Genetic engineers take the gene that produces the toxin in bacteria and insert it into the DNA of crops so that the plant does the work, not the farmer. The fact that we consume that toxic pesticide in every bite of Bt corn is hardly appetizing.

Biotech companies claim that Bt-toxin has a history of safe use, is quickly destroyed in our stomach, and wouldn't react with humans or mammals in any event. Studies verify, however, that natural Bt-toxin is *not* fully destroyed during digestion and *does* react with mammals. Mice fed Bt-toxin, for example, showed an immune response as potent as a response to cholera toxin,[66] became immune sensitive to formerly harmless compounds,[67] and had damaged and altered cells in their small intestines.[68] A 2008 Italian government study found that Bt corn provoked immune responses in mice.[69] Moreover, when natural Bt was sprayed over areas around Vancouver and Washington State to fight gypsy moths, about five hundred people reported reactions—mostly allergy or flu-like symptoms.[70,71] Farm workers and others also report serious reactions,[72–76] and authorities have long acknowledged that "people with compromised immune systems or preexisting allergies may be particularly susceptible to the effects of Bt."[77]

The Bt-toxin produced in GM crops is "vastly different from the bacterial [Bt-toxins] used in organic and traditional farming and forestry."[78] The plant-produced version is designed to be more toxic than natural varieties,[79] and is about three thousand to five thousand times more concentrated than the spray form. And just like the GM soy protein, the Bt protein in GM corn varieties has a section of its amino acid sequence that is identical to a known allergen (egg yolk). The Bt protein also fails other allergen criteria recommended by the WHO (i.e., the protein is too resistant to break down during digestion and heat.)

If Bt-toxin causes allergies, then gene transfer carries serious ramifications. *If Bt genes relocate to human gut bacteria, our intestinal flora may be converted into living pesticide factories, possibly producing Bt-toxin inside of us year after year.* The UK Joint Food Safety and Standards Group also described gene transfer from a different route. They warned that genes from inhaled pollen might transfer into the DNA of bacteria in the respiratory system.[80] Although no study has looked into that possibility, pollen from a Bt cornfield appears to have been responsible for allergic-type reactions.

In 2003, during the time when an adjacent Bt cornfield was pollinating, virtually an entire village of about one hundred people in the Philippines was stricken by mysterious skin, respiratory, and intestinal reactions.[81] The symptoms started with those living closest to the field and spread to those farther away. Blood samples from thirty-nine individuals showed antibodies in response to Bt-toxin, supporting—but not proving—a link. When the same corn was planted in four other villages the following year, however, the symptoms returned in all four areas—only during the time of pollination.[82]

Bt-toxin might also trigger reactions by skin contact. In 2005, a medical team reported that hundreds of agricultural workers in India were developing allergic symptoms when exposed to Bt cotton, but not when exposed to natural varieties.[83] They say reactions come from picking the cotton, cleaning it in factories, loading it onto trucks, or even leaning against it. Their symptoms were virtually identical to those described by the five hundred people in Vancouver, Washington, and Washington State who were sprayed with Bt.

GOVERNMENT EVALUATIONS MISS MOST HEALTH PROBLEMS

Although the number of safety studies on GM foods is quite small, they have validated the concerns expressed by FDA scientists and others. Unfortunately, government safety-assessment agencies worldwide are not competent to even *identify* most of the potential health problems described above, let alone protect their citizens from the effects.[84]

A 2000 review of approved GM crops in Canada by Professor E. Ann Clark, Ph.D., for example, reveals that 70 percent (28 of 40) "of the currently available GM crops . . . have not been subjected to any actual lab or animal toxicity testing, either as refined oils for direct human consumption or indirectly as feedstuffs for livestock. The same finding pertains to all three GM tomato decisions, the only GM flax, and to five GM corn crops." In the remaining 30 percent (12 of 40) of the crops, which were tested, animals were *not* fed the whole GM feed. They were given just the isolated GM protein that the plant was engineered to produce.

But even this protein was not extracted from the actual GM plant. Rather, it was manufactured in genetically engineered bacteria. This method of testing would never identify problems associated with collateral damage to GM plant DNA, unpredicted changes in the GM protein, transfer of genes to bacteria or human cells, excessive herbicide residues, or accumulation of toxins in the food chain, among others. Clark asks, "Where are the trials showing lack of harm to fed livestock, or that meat and milk from livestock fed on GM feedstuffs are safe?"[85]

Epidemiologist and GM safety expert Judy Carman, Ph.D., M.P.H., shows that assessments by Food Safety Australia New Zealand also overlooked serious potential problems, including cancer, birth defects, and long-term effects of nutritional deficiencies.[86]

Carman also wrote:

> A review of twelve reports covering twenty-eight GM crops—four soy, three corn, ten potatoes, eight canola, one sugar beet and two cotton—revealed no feeding trials on people. In addition, one of the GM corn varieties had gone untested on animals. Some seventeen foods involved testing with only a single oral gavage (a type of forced-feeding), with observation for seven to fourteen days, and only of the substance that had been genetically engineered to appear [the GM protein], not the whole food. Such testing assumes that the only new substance that will appear in the food is the one genetically engineered to appear, that the GM plant-produced substance will act in the same manner as the tested substance that was obtained from another source [GM bacteria], and that the substance will create disease within a few days. All are untested hypotheses and make a mockery of GM proponents' claims that the risk assessment of GM foods is based on sound science. Furthermore, where the whole food was given to animals to eat, sample sizes were often very low— for example, five to six cows per group for Roundup Ready soy—and they were fed for only four weeks.[87]

Carman points out that GM "experiments used some very unusual animal models for human health, such as chickens, cows, and trout. Some of the measurements taken from these animals are also unusual measures of human health, such as abdominal fat pad weight, total de-boned breast meat yield, and milk production." In her examination of the full range of submittals to authorities in Australia and New Zealand, she says that there was no proper evaluation of "biochemistry, immunology, tissue pathology, and gut, liver, and kidney function."[88] Writing on behalf of the Public Health Association of Australia, Carman says, "The effects of feeding people high concentrations of the new protein over tens of years cannot be determined by feeding 20 mice a single oral gavage of a given high concentration of the protein and taking very basic data for 13–14 days."[89]

THE FDA'S FAKE
SAFETY ASSESSMENTS

Submissions to the FDA may be worse than in other countries, since the agency doesn't actually require *any* data. Its policy says that biotech companies can determine if their own foods are safe. Anything submitted is voluntary and, according to former Environmental Protection Agency scientist Doug Gurian-Sherman, Ph.D., "often lack[s] sufficient detail, such as necessary statistical analyses needed for an adequate safety evaluation." Using Freedom of Information Act requests, Gurian-Sherman gathered and analyzed more than one-fourth of the data summaries (14 of 53) of GM crops reviewed by the FDA. He says, "The FDA consultation process does not allow the agency to require submission of data, misses obvious errors in company-submitted data summaries, provides insufficient testing guidance, and does not require sufficiently detailed data to enable the FDA to assure that GE [genetically engineered] crops are safe to eat."[90] Similarly, a Friends of the Earth (FOE) review of company and FDA documents concluded:

> If industry chooses to submit faulty, unpublishable studies, it does so without consequence. If it should respond to an agency request with deficient data, it does so without reprimand or follow-up. . . . If a company finds it disadvantageous to characterize its product, then its properties remain uncertain or unknown. If a corporation

chooses to ignore scientifically sound testing standards . . . then faulty tests are conducted instead, and the results are considered legitimate. In the area of genetically engineered food regulation, the "competent" agencies rarely, if ever, (know how to) conduct independent research to verify or supplement industry findings.[91]

At the end of a consultation, the FDA doesn't actually approve the crops. Rather, they issue a letter that includes a statement such as the following: "Based on the safety and nutritional assessment you have conducted, it is our understanding that Monsanto has concluded that corn products derived from this new variety are not materially different in composition, safety, and other relevant parameters from corn currently on the market, and that the genetically modified corn does not raise issues that would require premarket review or approval by FDA. . . . As you are aware, it is Monsanto's responsibility to ensure that foods marketed by the firm are safe, wholesome and in compliance with all applicable legal and regulatory requirements."[92]

COMPANY RESEARCH IS SECRET, INADEQUATE, AND FLAWED

The unpublished industry studies submitted to regulators are typically kept secret based on the claim that they contain "confidential business information." The Royal Society of Canada is one of many organizations that condemn this practice. They wrote:

In the judgment of the Expert Panel, the more regulatory agencies limit free access to the data upon which their decisions are based, the more compromised becomes the claim that the regulatory process is "science based." This is due to a simple but well-understood requirement of the scientific method itself—that it be an open, completely transparent enterprise in which any and all aspects of scientific research are open to full review by scientific peers. Peer review and independent corroboration of research findings are axioms of the scientific method, and part of the very meaning of the objectivity and neutrality of science.[93]

Whenever private submissions *are* made public through lawsuits or Freedom of Information Act requests, it becomes clear why companies benefit from secrecy. The quality of their research is often miserable, incompetent, and unacceptable for peer review. In 2000, for example, after the potentially allergenic StarLink corn was found to have contaminated the food supply, the corn's producer, Aventis CropScience, presented wholly inadequate safety data to the EPA's scientific advisory panel. One frustrated panel member, Dr. Dean Metcalfe—the government's top allergist—said during a hearing, "Most of us review for a lot of journals. And if this were presented for publication in the journals that I review for, it would be sent back to the authors with all of these questions. It would be rejected."[94]

UNSCIENTIFIC ASSUMPTIONS ARE THE BASIS OF APPROVALS

Clark, who analyzed submissions to Canadian regulators, concluded, "Most or all of the conclusions of food safety for individual GM crops are based on inferences and assumptions, rather than on actual testing." For example, rather than actually testing to see if the amino acid sequence produced by their inserted gene is correct, "the standard practice," according to research analyst Bill Freese, "is to sequence just 5 to 25 amino acids," even if the protein has more than six hundred in total.[95] If the short sample matches what is expected, they assume that the rest are also fine. If they are wrong, however, a rearranged protein could be quite dangerous.

Monsanto's submission to Australian regulators on their high-lysine GM corn provides an excellent example of overly optimistic assumptions used in place of science. The gene inserted into the corn produces a protein that is naturally found in soil. Monsanto claimed that since people consume small residues of soil on fruits and vegetables, the protein has a history of safe consumption. Based on the amount of GM corn protein an average U.S. citizen would consume (if all his or her corn were Monsanto's variety), he or she would eat up to 4 trillion times the amount normally consumed through soil. In other words, "for equivalent exposure" of the protein from soil "people would have to eat . . . nearly as much as 10,000kg [22,000 pounds, every] second 24 hours a day seven days a week."[96]

STUDIES ARE RIGGED
TO AVOID FINDING PROBLEMS

In addition to relying on untested assumptions, industry-funded research is often designed specifically to force a conclusion of safety. In the high-lysine corn described above, for example, the levels of certain nutritional components (i.e., protein content, total dietary fiber, acid detergent fiber, and neutral detergent fiber) were far outside the normal range for corn. Instead of comparing their corn with normal control varieties, which would reveal this disparity, Monsanto compared it with obscure corn varieties that were also substantially outside the normal range *on precisely these values*. Thus, their study found no statistical differences *by design*.

When Monsanto learned that independent researchers were to publish a study in 1999 showing that GM soy contains 12–14 percent less cancer-fighting phytoestrogens, the company responded with its own study, concluding that soy's phytoestrogen levels vary too much to even carry out a statistical analysis. The Monsanto researchers failed to disclose, however, that they had instructed the laboratory to use an obsolete method of detection—one that had been prone to highly variable results.[97] When Aventis CropScience prepared samples to see if the potential allergen in StarLink corn remained intact after cooking, instead of using the standard thirty-minute treatment, they heated the corn for two hours.[98]

To show that pasteurization destroys bovine growth hormone in milk from cows treated with recombinant bovine growth hormone (rGBH) scientists pasteurized the milk 120 times longer than normal. Unable to destroy more than 19 percent, they then spiked the milk with a huge amount of the hormone and repeated the long pasteurization, destroying 90 percent.[99] (The FDA reported that pasteurization destroys 90 percent of the hormone.)[100]

To demonstrate that injections of rbGH did not interfere with cows' fertility, Monsanto apparently added cows to the study that were pregnant prior to injection.[101]

And in order to prove that the protein from their GM crops breaks down quickly during simulated digestion, biotech companies used thousands of times the amount of digestive enzymes and a much stronger acid compared with that recommended by the WHO.[102]

Other methods used to hide problems are varied and plentiful. For example, researchers:

- Use highly variable animal starting weights to hinder detection of food-related changes
- Keep feeding studies short to miss long-term impacts
- Test effects of Roundup Ready soybeans that have not been sprayed with Roundup
- Avoid feeding animals the actual GM crop, but give them instead a single dose of the GM protein that was produced inside GM bacteria
- Use too few subjects to derive statistically significant results
- Use poor statistical methods or simply leave out essential methods, data, or statistics
- Use irrelevant control groups and employ insensitive evaluation techniques.

ROUNDUP READY SOYBEANS: CASE STUDY OF FLAWED RESEARCH

Monsanto's 1996 *Journal of Nutrition* articles on Roundup Ready soybeans provide plenty of examples of scientific transgressions.[103,104] Although the study has been used often by the industry as validation for safety claims, experts working in the field were not impressed. For example, Pusztai was commissioned at the time by the UK government to lead a twenty-member consortium in three institutions to develop rigorous testing protocols on GM foods—protocols that were never implemented. Pusztai, who had published several studies in that same nutrition journal, said the Monsanto paper was not "up to the normal journal standards." He said, "It was obvious that the study had been designed to avoid finding any problems. Everybody in our consortium knew this." Let's look at some of these flaws.

For instance, researchers tested GM soy on mature animals, not young ones. Young animals use protein to build their muscles, tissues, and organs. Problems with GM food could therefore show up in organ and body weight. But adult animals use the protein for tissue renewal and energy. "With a nutritional study on mature animals," says Pusztai, "you would never see any difference in organ weights even if the food turned out to be anti-nutritional. The animals would have to be emaciated or poisoned to show anything."

Also, if there were an organ-development problem, the study wouldn't have picked it up since the researchers didn't even weigh the organs.

In one of the trials, researchers substituted only one-tenth of the natural protein with GM soy protein. In two others, they diluted their GM soy six- and twelvefold.[105]

Scientists Ian Pryme, Ph.D., of Norway and Rolf Lembcke, Ph.D., of Denmark, who published a paper in *Nutrition and Health* that analyzed all published peer-reviewed feeding studies on GM foods (ten, as of 2003), wrote that the "level of the GM soy was too low, and would probably ensure that any possible undesirable GM effects did not occur." They also pointed out that the percentage of protein in the feed used in the Roundup Ready study was "artificially too high." This "would almost certainly mask, or at least effectively reduce, any possible effect of the [GM soy]." They said it was "highly likely that all GM effects would have been diluted out."[106]

Proper compositional studies filter out effects of weather or geography by comparing plants grown at the same time in the same location. Monsanto, however, pooled data from several locations, which makes it difficult for differences to be statistically significant. Nonetheless, the data revealed significant differences in the ash, fat, and carbohydrate content. Roundup Ready soy meal also contained 27 percent more trypsin inhibitor, a potential allergen. Also, cows fed GM soy produced milk with a higher fat content, demonstrating another disparity between the two types of soy.

One field trial, however, did grow GM and non-GM plants next to each other, but data from that trial were not included in the paper. Years after the study appeared, medical writer Barbara Keeler recovered the data that had been omitted. They showed that Monsanto's GM soy had significantly lower levels of protein, a fatty acid, and phenylalanine, an essential amino acid. Also, toasted GM soy meal contained nearly twice the amount of a lectin—a substance that may interfere with the body's ability to assimilate other nutrients. And the amount of trypsin inhibitor in cooked GM soy was as much as seven times higher than in cooked non-GM control soy.

The study also omitted many details normally required for a published paper. According to Pryme and Lembcke, "No data were given for most of the parameters."

And when researchers tested the effects of Roundup Ready protein on animals, they didn't extract the protein from the soybeans. Instead, they derived it from GM bacteria, claiming the two forms of protein were equivalent. There are numerous ways, however, in which the protein in the soy may be different. In fact, nine years after this Monsanto's soybean study was published, another study showed that the gene inserted into the soybeans produced unintended aberrant RNA strands, meaning that the protein may be quite different than what was intended.[107]

In Pryme and Lembcke's analysis, it came as no surprise that this Monsanto study, along with the other four peer-reviewed animal feeding studies that were "performed more or less in collaboration with private companies," reported no negative effects of the GM diet. "On the other hand," they wrote, "adverse effects were reported (but not explained) in [the five] independent studies." They added, "It is remarkable that these effects have all been observed after feeding for only 10–14 days."[108]

TOXIC GM FOODS COULD HAVE
BEEN APPROVED

Two GM foods whose commercialization was stopped because of negative test results give a chilling example of what may be getting through. Rats fed GM potatoes had potentially precancerous cell growth in the stomach and intestines (see figure 8.1 on page 238), less developed brains, livers, and testicles, partial atrophy of the liver, and damaged immune systems.[109] GM peas provoked an inflammatory response in mice, suggesting that the peas might trigger a deadly anaphylactic shock in allergic humans.[110] Both of these dangerous crops, however, could easily have been approved. The problems were only discovered because the researchers used advanced tests that were never applied to GM crops already on the market. Both would have passed the normal tests that companies typically use to get their products approved.

Ironically, when Monsanto was asked to comment on the pea study, their spokesperson said it demonstrated that the regulatory system works. He failed to disclose that none of his company's GM crops had been put through such rigorous tests.

RAMPANT, UNRELENTING
INDUSTRY BIAS

Industry-funded research that favors the funders is not new. Bias has been identified across several industries. In pharmaceuticals, for example, positive results are four times more likely if the drug's manufacturer funds the study.[111] When companies pay for the economic analyses of their own cancer drugs, the results are eight times more likely to be favorable.[112] Compared with drug research, the potential for industry manipulation in GM crop studies is considerably higher. Unlike pharmaceutical testing, GM research has no standardized procedures dictated by regulators. GM studies are not usually published in peer-reviewed journals and are typically kept secret by companies and governments. There is little money available for rigorous independent research, so company evidence usually goes unchallenged and unverified. Most importantly, whereas drugs *can* show serious side effects and still be approved, GM food cannot. There is no tolerance for adverse reactions; feeding trials *must* show no problems.

Thus, when industry studies show problems (in spite of their efforts to avoid them), serious adverse reactions and even deaths among GM-fed animals are ignored or dismissed as "not biologically significant" or due to "natural variations." In the critical arena of food safety research, the biotech industry is without accountability, standards, or peer review. They've got bad science down to a science.

PROMOTING AND REGULATING DON'T MIX

While such self-serving behavior may be expected from corporations, why do government bodies let such blatant scientific contortions pass without comment? One reason is that several regulatory agencies are also charged with promoting the interests of biotechnology. This is the official position of the FDA and other U.S. government bodies, for example. Suzanne Wuerthele, Ph.D., an EPA toxicologist, says, "This technology is being promoted, in the face of concerns by respectable scientists and in the face of data to the contrary, by the very agencies which are supposed to be protecting human health and the environment. The bottom line in my view is that we are confronted with the most powerful technology the world has ever known, and it is being rapidly deployed with almost no thought whatsoever to its consequences."[113]

Canadian regulators are similarly conflicted. The Royal Society of Canada reported:

> In meetings with senior managers from the various Canadian regulatory departments . . . their responses uniformly stressed the importance of maintaining a favorable climate for the biotechnology industry to develop new products and submit them for approval on the Canadian market. . . . The conflict of interest involved in both promoting and regulating an industry or technology . . . is also a

factor in the issue of maintaining the transparency, and therefore the scientific integrity, of the regulatory process. In effect, the public interest in a regulatory system that is 'science based'. . . is significantly compromised when that openness is negotiated away by regulators in exchange for cordial and supportive relationships with the industries being regulated.[114]

Many scientists on the European Food Safety Authority (EFSA) GMO Panel are personally aligned with biotech interests. According to the FOE:

One member has direct financial links with the biotech industry and others have indirect links, such as close involvement with major conferences organized by the biotech industry. Two members have even appeared in promotional videos produced by the biotech industry. . . . Several members of the Panel, including the chair Professor Kuiper, have been involved with the EU-funded ENTRANSFOOD project. The aim of this project was to agree [to] safety assessment, risk management, and risk communication procedures that would 'facilitate market introduction of GMOs in Europe, and therefore bring the European industry in a competitive position.' Professor Kuiper, who coordinated the ENTRANSFOOD project, sat on a working group that also included staff from Monsanto, Bayer CropScience, and Syngenta.[115]

In a statement reminiscent of reactions to the deceptive policy statement of the FDA, the FOE report concludes that the EFSA is "being used to create a false impression of scientific agreement when the real situation is one of intense and continuing debate and uncertainty."

The European Commission repeats the same ruse. According to leaked documents obtained by FOE, while they privately appreciate "the uncertainties and gaps in knowledge that exist in relation to the safety of GM crops, . . . the Commission normally keeps this uncertainty concealed from the public whilst presenting its decisions about the safety of GM crops and foods as being certain and scientifically based." For example, the commission privately condemned the submission information for one crop as "mixed, scarce, delivered consecutively all over years, and not convincing." They said there is "no sufficient experimental evidence to assess the safety."[116]

With an agenda to promote GM foods, regulators regularly violate their own laws. In Europe, the law requires that when the EFSA and member states have different opinions, they "are obliged to co-operate with a view to either resolving the divergence or preparing a joint document clarifying the contentious scientific issues and identifying the relevant uncertainties in the data."[117] According to FOE, in the case of *all* GM crop reviews, none of these legal obligations were followed.[118] The declaration of GRAS status by the FDA also deviated from the Food, Drug, and Cosmetic Act and years of legal precedent. Some violations are more blatant. In India, one official tampered with the report on Bt cotton to increase the yield figures to favor Monsanto.[119] In Mexico, a senior government official allegedly threatened a University of California professor, implying, "We know where your children go to school," trying to get him not to publish incriminating evidence that would delay GM approvals.[120] In Indonesia, Monsanto gave bribes and questionable payments to at least 140 officials, attempting to get their GM cotton approved.[121]

MANIPULATION OF PUBLIC OPINION

When governments fail in their duty to keep corporations in check, the "protector" role should shift to the media, which act as a watchdog to expose public dangers and governmental shortcomings. But mainstream media around the world have largely overlooked the serious problems associated with GM crops and their regulation. The reasons for this oversight are varied and include contributions from an aggressive public relations and disinformation campaign by the biotech industry, legal threats by biotech companies, and in some cases, the fear of losing advertising accounts. This last reason is particularly prevalent within the farm press, which receives much of its income from the biotech industry.

Threatening letters from Monsanto's attorneys have resulted in the cancellation of a five-part news series on their genetically engineered bovine growth hormone scheduled for a Fox TV station in Florida, as well as the cancellation of a book critical of Monsanto's GMO products. A printer also shredded fourteen thousand copies of the *Ecologist* magazine issue titled "The Monsanto Files," due to fear of a Monsanto lawsuit. (See the chapter "Muscling the Media" in *Seeds of Deception*[122] for more examples.)

The methods that biotech advocates use to manipulate public opinion research have become an art form. Consumer surveys by the International Food Information Council, for example, whose supporters include the major biotech seed companies, offer conclusions such as, "A growing majority of Americans support the benefits of food biotechnology as well as the US Food and Drug Administration's (FDA) labeling policy." But Communications Professor James Beniger, a past president of the American Association for Public Opinion Research, described the surveys as "so biased with leading questions favoring positive responses that any results are meaningless."[123] A 2003 survey, for example, included gems such as: "All things being equal, how likely would you be to buy a variety of produce, like tomatoes or potatoes, if it had been modified by biotechnology to taste better or fresher?" and "Biotechnology has also been used to enhance plants that yield foods like cooking oils. If cooking oil with reduced saturated fat made from these new plants was available, what effect would the use of biotechnology have on your decision to buy this cooking oil?"[124]

A similar tactic was used at a December 11, 2007, focus group in Columbus, Ohio, "designed" to show that consumers wanted to make it illegal for dairies to label their milk as free from Monsanto's genetically engineered hormone recombinant bovine somatotropin (rBST). The facilitator said, "All milk contains hormones. There is no such thing as hormone-free milk. The composition of both types of milk is the same in all aspects. Now what do you think of a label that says 'no added hormones'? Don't you think it is deceiving and inappropriate to put 'rBST-free' on labels?" Not only was the facilitator "leading the witness," he presented false information. Milk from cows treated with rBST has substantially higher levels of insulin-like growth factor-1,*[125] which has been linked to higher risk of cancer[126] and higher incidence of fraternal twins.[127] It also has higher levels of bovine growth hormone, pus, and in some cases, antibiotics.

Another example of manipulated consumer opinion was found in a 2003 article in the *British Food Journal,* authored by four advocates of GM foods.[128] According to the peer-reviewed paper, when shoppers in a Canadian farm store were confronted with an informed and unbiased choice between GM corn and non-GM corn, most purchased the GM variety. This finding flew in the face of worldwide consumer resistance to GM foods, which had shut markets in Europe, Japan, and elsewhere. It also challenged studies that showed that the more information on GMOs consumers have, the *less* they trust them.[129] The study, which was funded by the biotech-industry front group, the Council for Biotechnology Information, and the industry's trade association, the Crop Protection Institute of Canada (now Croplife Canada), was given the journal's prestigious Award for Excellence for the Most Outstanding Paper of 2004 and has been cited often by biotech advocates.

Stuart Laidlaw, a reporter from Canada's *Toronto Star,* visited the farm store several times during the study and described the scenario in his book *Secret Ingredients.* Far from offering unbiased choices, key elements appeared rigged to favor GM corn purchases. The consumer education fact sheets were entirely pro-GMO, and Doug Powell, the lead researcher, enthusiastically demonstrated to Laidlaw how he could convince shoppers to buy the GM varieties. He confronted a farmer who had already purchased non-GM corn. After pitching his case for GMOs, Powell proudly had the farmer tell Laidlaw that he had changed his opinion and would buy GM corn in his next shopping trip.

Powell's interference with shoppers' "unbiased" choices was nothing compared with the effect of the signs placed over the corn bins. The sign

---

*According to an article in *The Lancet,* estimates of increased IGF-1 levels vary considerably; in some instances IGF-1 levels were up to ten times higher. The methods used may also underestimate IGF-1 levels considerably.

above the non-GM corn read, "Would you eat wormy sweet corn?" It further listed the chemicals that were sprayed during the season. By contrast, the sign above the GM corn stated, "Here's what went into producing quality sweet corn." It is no wonder that 60 percent of shoppers avoided the "wormy corn." In fact, it may be a testament to people's distrust of GMOs that 40 percent still went for the "wormy" option.

Powell and his colleagues did not mention the controversial signage in their study. They claimed that the corn bins in the farm store were "fully labelled"—either "genetically engineered Bt sweet corn" or "regular sweet corn." When Laidlaw's book came out, however, Powell's "wormy" sign was featured in a photograph,[130] exposing what was later described by Cambridge University's Richard Jennings, Ph.D., as "flagrant fraud." Jennings, who is a leading researcher on scientific ethics, says, "It was a sin of omission by failing to divulge information which quite clearly should have been disclosed."[131]

In his defense, Powell claimed that his signs merely used the language of consumers and were "not intended to manipulate consumer purchasing patterns." He also claimed that the "wormy" corn sign was only there for the first week of the trial and was then replaced by other educational messages. But eyewitnesses and photographs demonstrate the presence of the sign long after Powell's suggested date of replacement.[132]

Several scientists and outraged citizens say the paper should be withdrawn, but the journal refused. In fact, the journal's editor has not even agreed to reconsider its Award for Excellence. A blatant propaganda exercise still stands validated as exemplary science.

CRITICS AND INDEPENDENT
SCIENTISTS ARE ATTACKED

One of the most troubling aspects of the biotech debate is the attack strategy used on GMO critics and independent scientists. Not only are adverse findings by independent scientists often suppressed, ignored, or denied, researchers who discovered problems from GM foods also have been fired, stripped of responsibilities, deprived of tenure, and even threatened. Consider Pusztai, the world's leading scientist in his field, who inadvertently discovered in 1998 that unpredictable changes in GM crops caused massive damage in rats. He went public with his concerns, was a hero at his prestigious institute for two days, and then, after the director received two phone calls allegedly from the UK prime minister's office, was fired after thirty-five years and silenced with threats of a lawsuit. False statements were circulated to trash his reputation, which are still recited by GMO advocates today.

After University of California Professor Ignacio Chapela, Ph.D., published evidence that GM corn had contaminated Mexico's indigenous varieties, two fictitious characters created by Monsanto's PR firm, the Bivings Group, initiated a brutal Internet smear campaign, lying about Chapela and his research.

Irina Ermakova, Ph.D., a leading scientist at the Russian National Academy of Sciences, fed female rats GM soy and was stunned to discover that more than half their offspring died within three weeks—compared with only 10 percent from mothers fed non-GM soy. Without funding to extend her analysis, she labeled her work "preliminary," published it in a Russian journal, and implored the scientific community to repeat the study. Two years later, no one has repeated it, but advocates have used false or irrelevant arguments to divert attention from the shocking results and have tried to vilify Ermakova.

A member of New Zealand's parliament testified at the 2001 Royal Commission of Inquiry on Genetic Modification, "I have been contacted by telephone and e-mail by a number of scientists who have serious concerns . . . but who are convinced that if they express these fears publicly . . . or even if they asked the awkward and difficult questions, they will be eased out of their institution." Indeed in 2007, after Professor Christian Velot, Ph.D., raised the difficult questions on GMOs at public conferences, his 2008 research funds were confiscated, his student assistants were reassigned, and his position at the University of Paris-Sud faced early termination.

WE'RE THE GUINEA PIGS

Since GM foods are not properly tested before they enter the market, consumers are the guinea pigs. But this doesn't even qualify as an experiment. There are no controls and no monitoring. Given the mounting evidence of harm, it is likely that GM foods are contributing to the deterioration of health in the United States, Canada, and other countries where they are consumed. But without postmarketing surveillance, the chances of tracing health problems to GM foods are low. The incidence of a disease would have to increase dramatically before it was noticed, meaning that millions may have to get sick before a change is investigated. Tracking the impact of GM foods is even more difficult in North America, where the foods are not labeled.

Regulators at Health Canada announced in 2002 that they would monitor Canadians for health problems from eating GM foods. A spokesperson said, "I think it's just prudent and what the public expects, that we will keep a careful eye on the health of Canadians." But according to CBC TV news, Health Canada "abandoned that research less than a year later saying it was 'too difficult to put an effective surveillance system in place.'" The news anchor added, "So at this point, there is little research into the health effects of genetically modified food. So will we ever know for sure if it's safe?"[133]

Not with the biotech companies in charge. Consider the following statement in a report submitted to county officials in California by pro-GM members of a task force: "[It is] generally agreed that long-term monitoring of the human health risks of GM food through epidemiological studies is not necessary because there is no scientific evidence suggesting any long-term harm from these foods."[134] Note the circular logic: because no long-term epidemiological studies are in place, we have no evidence showing long-term harm. And since we don't have any evidence of long-term harm, we don't need studies to look for it.

What are these people thinking? Insight into the pro-GM mind-set was provided by Dan Glickman, the U.S. Secretary of Agriculture under President Clinton.

What I saw generically on the pro-biotech side was the attitude that the technology was good, and that it was almost immoral to say that it wasn't good, because it was going to solve the problems of the human race and feed the hungry and clothe the naked. . . . And there was a lot of money that had been invested in this, and if you're against it, you're Luddites, you're stupid. That, frankly, was the side our government was on. Without thinking, we had basically taken this issue as a trade issue and they, whoever "they" were, wanted to keep our product out of their market. And they were foolish, or stupid, and didn't have an effective regulatory system. There was rhetoric like that even here in this department. You felt like you were almost an alien, disloyal, by trying to present an open-minded view on some of the issues being raised. So I pretty much spouted the rhetoric that everybody else around here spouted; it was written into my speeches.[135]

Fortunately, not everyone feels that questioning GM foods is disloyal. On the contrary, millions of people around the world are unwilling to participate in this uncontrolled experiment. They refuse to eat GM foods. Manufacturers in Europe and Japan have committed to avoid using GM ingredients. And the U.S. natural foods industry, not waiting for the government to test or label GMOs, is now engaged in removing all remaining GM ingredients from their sector using a third-party verification system.* The Campaign for Healthier Eating in America circulates non-GMO shopping guides in stores nationwide so that consumers have clear, healthy non-GMO choices. With no governmental regulation of biotech corporations, it is left to us as consumers to protect ourselves.

---

*For a guide to avoiding GMOs, please see www.NonGMOShoppingGuide.com (accessed November 26, 2012).

9

ORGANIC FOODS

HOW TO EAT HEALTHY AND PROTECT THE ENVIRONMENT

Melvin D. Epp, Ph.D.

A significant part of the pleasure of eating is in one's accurate consciousness of the lives and the world from which the food comes.

WENDELL BERRY

The act of putting into your mouth what the earth has grown is perhaps your most direct interaction with the earth.

FRANCES MOORE LAPPÉ

INTRODUCTION

The sales of organic foods and beverages have progressively increased in the United States. Organics cannot be dismissed as a fleeting fad anymore. In 1990, organic food sales exceeded $1 billion, and they increased to exceed $20 billion by 2007. Organic food sales in 2008 were $22.9 billion, while organic nonfood sales grew by an astounding 39.4 percent to reach $1.6 billion. Organic foods sales now account for approximately 3.5

percent of all food product sales in the United States. Sales increases are expected to continue for many years.[1]

In addition to fresh products such as vegetables, fruits, grains, and meats, there are also value-added foods manufactured with organic ingredients. Organic ready-to-eat meals were forecasted to grow at an annual compound rate of almost 25 percent.[2]

Organic production can also be implemented for flower production and lawn care. Organic fibers (cotton, wool, and linen) are used to manufacture organic fabrics and organic clothing. Organic cosmetic and skin care lines are available, as well as organic household cleaning products. Organic pet food can be procured. However, this chapter will focus on human food considerations.

HISTORY

The concept of organic food was defined uniformly nationwide with the implementation of the U.S. Department of Agriculture's Program (USDA; NOP) on October 21, 2002. The NOP was mandated under the Organic Foods Production Act of 1990. No longer are there varying community or statewide definitions of organics; the parameters became uniformly defined.

Products certified as manufactured or produced compliant to the NOP can be identified with a product seal (figure 9.1).

The seal, either in color or in black-and-white, readily conveys spe-

Fig. 9.1. The seal verifying a product's inclusion in the National Organic Program

cific product information: (1) Synthetically compounded fertilizers and pesticides were not used in production except in rare approved instances. (2) The land used in organic production had no applications of synthetically formulated fertilizers or pesticides for three years prior to organic production. (3) Raw manure was not applied directly to growing plants but rather applied to the soil, followed by a soil-fallow period of ninety or 120 days, depending on whether the product grows in contact with the soil or the manure was composted with defined temperature parameters for specific periods of time prior to application. (4) Sewage sludge was not used as a fertilizer. (5) Irradiation was not used to sterilize or preserve the product. (6) There were no genetically modified organism (GMO) plant varieties or products used. (7) No antibiotics or growth hormones were used in livestock or poultry production, and both livestock and poultry had access to outdoor space. And finally, (8) processed foods with the seal have 95–100 percent organic ingredients.[3]

The NOP is implemented through the participation of fifty-six domestic accredited certifying agencies; this includes thirty-six state organic certifying programs. There are forty-four foreign accredited NOP certifying agencies.[4]

The Organic Materials Review Institute (OMRI), founded in 1997 as a nonprofit organization, provides organic certifiers, growers, manufacturers, and suppliers an independent review of products intended for use in certified organic production, handling, and processing. They review products against the NOP standards, and acceptable products are OMRI Listed* and appear on the OMRI Products List.[5]

Another demarcation of organic produce is the grocery store label on many pieces of produce. These small stick-on labels include numerical codes called price-look-up codes (PLUs), which are used by the checkout clerks and also often list the produce cultivar name and the country of origin. PLUs provide additional informational for shoppers: if the PLU has four digits, the produce was grown conventionally, but if the PLU has five digits and the first is a 9 followed by four other numbers, the produce

---

*"OMRI Listed" is a registered trademark.

was grown organically. If the starting number is an 8 followed by four other numbers, the produce is genetically modified, a GMO.[6]

Why the interest in organic foods? With awareness growing that organic food is better for us and for the environment, about 70 percent of Americans buy organic food occasionally, and nearly one-quarter buy it every week.[7] Young mothers often ask themselves how can they provide the best food for their young infants and children. This question portends far more than just an emotional reaction.

Children take in more toxic chemicals relative to body weight than adults and have developing organ systems that are more vulnerable and less able to detoxify such chemicals.[8] The Environmental Protection Agency's (EPA) "Guidelines for Carcinogen Risk Assessment" suggest that children receive fifty percent of their lifetime cancer risks in the first two years of life.[9]

Measurements of urine samples of children eating primarily organic diets showed significantly lower (almost none) organophosphorous (OP) pesticide exposure compared with children consuming primarily conventional diets. In a follow-up experiment the same research team then conducted a second experiment with twenty-three school-aged children. The second study included three phases of testing for OP insecticidal metabolites in urine. During the first phase, the children consumed a diet containing conventionally grown foods. The second phase involved a predominantly organic diet, and the testing was performed only five days into the second phase; phase three returned to a conventional diet. All twenty-three children had OP insecticidal metabolites in their urine in phase one testing, while levels were below the limit of detection during phase two for all children following the consumption of mostly organic food for just five days. With the resumption of a conventional diet in phase three, the levels of OP insecticidal metabolites in their urine returned to those found in phase one. There were two key conclusions: (1) on a daily basis, the majority of the exposures to OP insecticides among children are coming through the diet, and (2) consuming food grown using organic methods can virtually eliminate exposures to a dangerous class of insecticides known to disrupt neurological development in infants and children.[10]

How do organic foods stack-up? For the 2009 growing season, First Lady Michelle Obama initiated an organic vegetable garden, digging up a 1,100-square-foot area of the South Lawn at the White House, where the garden would be visible to passersby on E Street. Her stated objective was to provide food for her own family, but to also use the garden to educate children about healthful, locally grown fruits and vegetables during this period when obesity and diabetes have become a national plight.[11,12] This garden was also featured on Food Network's White House episode of *Iron Chef America,* with chefs Mario Batali, Cristeta Comerford, Bobby Flay, and Emeril Lagassi embracing the first lady's challenge to harvest produce from the White House garden and showcase the good taste of fresh organic produce, honey from the White House beehive, and locally produced meats.[13]

Organic versus Natural

All mankind ate organic and natural food until the early years of the twentieth century, and for only about the past eighty years have we in the United States been on a chemical binge diet—equivalent to a blink of an eye in global history. Yet what do we have to show for this "advancement" in our diet: one-third of America's topsoil lost, buried toxic waste everywhere, polluted and depleted water systems, worsened global warming, and exacerbated health concerns ranging from cancer to diabetes to obesity.[14]

All organic foods are natural, but not all natural foods are organic. Organic foods are raised and produced as defined by the NOP. Items labeled "natural" are generally undefined, and the term specifies nothing of consistent or meaningful value. That being said, some small producers at farmers markets whose size does not warrant the expense of organic certification will vend their goods as "all-natural," having applied organic techniques in their operations.[15] But the organic food business is the rare industry that actively seeks increased government regulations to remedy the consumer confusion about the meaning of "organic."

Less Pesticide Residue on Organic Produce

In response to the public concerns over the apple pesticide Alar (damino-zide), the USDA's Pesticide Data Program (PDP) was funded by Congress in 1991. The USDA lacked good data on actual residues in food; conse-quently, the EPA lacked the essential information for carrying out mean-ingful pesticide dietary risk assessments. Since its inception the PDP tests annually about twelve thousand to fifteen thousand samples of foods pre-pared to reflect residues in "as eaten" food.

Two external reviews have been issued using the PDP data.[16] These measurements show that during the period from 1993 to 2006 more than 60 percent of the samples from nonorganic, conventionally produced fruits and vegetables had pesticide residues, while the samples of organically produced fruits and vegetables had less than 20 percent positive results for pesticide residues. Expressed in another way, during this fourteen-year period of testing, nonorganic fruit was about 3.2 times more likely than organic fruit to contain a pesticide residue; likewise, nonorganic vegeta-bles were 3.5 times more likely to test positive for pesticide residue. The pesticide-sampling program in Great Britain reflected a similar pattern.

Some find it disturbing that there are any pesticide residues on certi-fied organic produce at all. But a low level of pesticides is expected since a few pesticides are approved for use on organic food: spinosad, sulfur, cop-per fungicides, oils, several botanicals, *Bacillus thuringiensis* (Bt), soaps, certain microbial pesticides, and pheromones. The PDP only routinely tests for spinosad since the other active ingredients are regarded as safe and are exempt from the requirement that a tolerance level be established to cover residues. Conventional pesticide residue vulnerability on organic produce emanates from conventional pesticides drifting from adjacent conventional production fields, the use of contaminated irrigation water, soil-bound residues of persistent pesticides used years ago prior to organic production, and cross-contamination with postharvest fungicides applied in storage facilities or later along the food supply chain.

Many PDP samplings detected multiple residues. Conventionally grown peaches, a soft-skinned fruit, tended to average more residues per sample than any other fruit. In 2006, 98.8 percent of the peaches sampled had residues, with 5.6 percent reflecting only one residue; almost one-half of the samples (46.6 percent) contained five or more residues. This is why the peach appears on lists of relatively high-pesticide-risk foods. Apples in 2004 tested for three or more residues in 73 percent of 743 samples, while the organic apple samples had 80 percent with no detectable residues. Conventional lettuce in 2004 showed 35 percent with four or more residues, and two lettuce samples had nine residues. Two conventional pepper samples contained twelve different residues, and three samples had eleven. About 22 percent of the samples had six or more residues; only 3.4 percent had none. Of the organic sweet bell pepper samples tested, 91 percent had no pesticide residues. In 2006 PDP testing, conventional fruits and vegetables were about eight times more likely than organic samples to have multiple residues. Fortunately, multiple residues are rare in many other crops and foods.

With regrettable frequency, most Americans, including infants and children, are exposed to pesticides via their diet and drinking water. It is estimated that average Americans consume three or four residues daily just through fresh fruits and vegetables, another two or three residues via milk, and another two to three from other foods, juices, and beverages, for a total of seven to ten from food. Drinking water is another major source of pesticide exposure, particularly in the Midwest and other farming regions. Water is thought to add another three exposures per day, bringing the average American exposure to ten to thirteen pesticide residues on a daily basis from food and drinking water. Fortunately, the levels are very low in most cases, and the residues pose modest if any risks.[17] This is no doubt true for healthy adults, but scientific evidence supports the contention that some residues are high enough to pose clear risks at vulnerable periods of fetal development, during the first years of life, or when a person is coping with an illness.

For organic production, synthetic chemical substances and most synthetic pesticides are prohibited; most natural substances, including botanical pesticides, copper fungicides, and sulfur, are allowed with some relatively toxic natural substances prohibited or severely restricted. Organic farmers must follow both the product label and any additional restrictions imposed by their organic certifiers. Organic farmers must also submit to their certifiers preseason plans of any pesticides they expect to use to handle projected pest problems. Midseason on-site inspections are an integral component in the organic production protocol. But it must be remembered that all pesticides are toxic to at least some organism, and applications must be timed to deal with the target organism and not beneficial insects. Some formulations of a relatively new biochemical insecticide called spinosad have been approved for organic crop uses. While far less risky to most organisms than the high-risk organophosphate and carbamate insecticides of conventional farming, spinosad is among the most toxic pesticides ever used to bees. All farmers must use discretion when applying spinosad to assure that foraging bees are not in the vicinity. Organic production is not pesticide free; the important caveat is that, on average, pesticides used in organic production are applied at a rate lower than rates used with conventional pesticides, are less toxic per pound of ingredient, and have very short residual periods—normally measured in hours.

Consistently over the last decade about 80 percent of organic samples tested by the USDA's PDP have contained no detectable residues; the dietary risks for these foods are reduced essentially 100 percent or to zero. Calculating a Dietary Risk Index score and including the 20 percent of organic samples with detectable residues, taking into account the amount of residue and its toxicity, it is calculated that a switch from conventional to organic produce in one's diet reduces the dietary risks by nearly 97 percent overall.[18]

Organic Produce Is More Nutritionally Dense

It has been an arduous process to establish convincingly that organic produce delivers a higher level of nutrients. Extra effort was needed to conduct valid experiments where comparisons of organic and conventional produce were made using the same soil types within the same climactic conditions, using identical growth management protocols with similar irrigation patterns, and using identical harvesting and sampling procedures. Only in more recent years have longer-term organic production areas been available that could be contrasted with adjacent conventional production areas separated spatially at an NOP-defined distance to maintain the integrity of the organic areas. Similar levels of available nitrogen needed to be available to minimize the differences in plant physiological responses to low and high levels of nitrogen within the confines of organic production that uses organic sources of nitrogen in contrast to chemical nitrogen sources used in conventional production. The plant genetic component needed to be minimized by using the same cultivar in both production methods. By eliminating many of the factors that can influence extraneous mineral uptake and physiological responses, the response to the two production methodologies could be compared in pairwise evaluations.

The Organic Center has recently issued a State of Science Review: Nutritional Superiority of Organic Foods. Reviewing the published scientific literature and evaluating it for valid paired results, their thorough analysis showed that the antioxidants evaluated for organic produce tended to have higher levels more frequently; this included total phenolics, total antioxidant capacity, quercetin, and kaempferol. The vitamins tested in paired analyses showed that ascorbic acid (vitamin C) and α-tocoperol (vitamin E) were both higher more frequently in organic produce; β-carotene did not show a preference for cultural technique. The mineral phosphorus was higher more frequently in organic production, while potassium was higher more frequently in conventional production. Nitrates were also higher much more frequently in conventional production, but such levels are considered undesirable for human food consumption and reflect the readily available nitrogen from the chemical fertilizer; likewise protein levels were higher more frequently in conventional production. These analyses also found that the magnitude of the advantage in nutrient density within the organic samples was far greater than the magnitude of differences in those conventional samples that contained higher levels of nutrients. The conclusions from this rigorous study were that, indeed, organic plant-based foods are, on average, more nutritious in terms of their nutrient density for compounds validated by this study's methodology and that an average serving of organic plant-based food contains about 25 percent more of the nutrients encompassed in this study than a comparable-sized serving of the same food produced by conventional farming methods.[19]

Environmental Implications of Organic Foods

In 2005, Jessica Prentice coined the word *locavore,* which was voted the 2007 "Word of the Year" by Oxford University Press. *Locavore* was coined to describe and promote the practice of eating a diet consisting of food harvested from within an area bounded by a one-hundred-mile radius. Prentice was the director of education at the Ferry Plaza Farmers Market in San Francisco at the time and wanted to encourage food lovers to enjoy what they eat while still appreciating the impact they have on the environment. Locavorism projects positive considerations: (1) the traditional pleasures of eating real, fresh foods grown and prepared in the context of community, (2) reducing the distance that food is transported using fossil fuels, which now on average is 1,500 miles from farm to table, (3) providing an alternative to factory farms that exploit workers and the Earth, abuse animals, and contribute to a society in which factory-processed foods have become staples, creating a population that is simultaneously overfed and undernourished, and (4) creating strong local food systems that support environmental sustainability, food security, social equity, and the economic vitality of thriving communities.[20]

If you join the many Americans who turned to food gardening after the 2009 economic recessionary year and grow your own food, you would control the soil composition and the pesticide load and insure that the produce was handled with clean hands. There is no place more local than your own backyard. Your produce is as fresh and nutritionally dense as it can be, if used shortly after harvesting.

With the NOP defining the requirements for organic production, multinational corporations have changed their production methods to conform to the definition, but still end up shipping the produce many, many miles to reach your fork. By shopping for local produce, either by reviewing the PLUs at the grocery store or frequenting local farmers markets, the carbon footprint of organic produce procurement can be reduced. There has been an increase recently in the interest and locations of farmers' markets, as well as a revival of small farms.[21]

Food safety also impinges on concepts of locavorism. The consequences of a contamination problem in our highly concentrated national food system are far greater; when there was *E. coli* in spinach, *E. coli* in hamburger, *Salmonella* in peppers, or *Salmonella* in peanut butter, to how many states were the contaminated food products distributed prior to product recalls? Smaller, more localized production and processing systems are less attractive to potential (bio)terrorists as well.[22]

Since most of us living in America are living in a temperate climate, another technique to insure wholesome organic produce year round will require systems of food preservation. Most county extension services have bulletins that can be downloaded that describe methodologies for canning, freezing, and other preservation.[23]

In spite of the fact that fresh whole fruits and vegetables usually deliver the most nutrients per serving, during the winter months when only imported, conventional, fresh produce is available, consumers should consider choosing canned or frozen domestically grown fruits and vegetables. Processed apples, grapes, peaches, pears, green beans, peas, and tomatoes have a substantially reduced pesticide load compared with fresh, imported, conventional, nonorganic produce.[24]

Another major contribution of organic gardening and production deals with recycling organic wastes into soil-amending compost. Composted organic wastes are materials that do not need to overburden local refuge-disposal systems. Recent results of a Sedgwick County (Kansas, including Wichita) residential waste characterization study reported a breakdown analysis of refuse, which included 21.8 percent paper, 11.8 percent food waste, and 31 percent yard waste. Much of this waste could have been composted. There are guidelines for insuring the papers are free of heavy metal ions, the food waste does not include meat or fat scraps, and the yard wastes are free of applied pesticides and herbicides. Dog and cat wastes are not recommended for use in vegetable garden compost due to possible parasite carryover.[25]

SOME OTHER MAJOR
FOOD GROUPS

There are also organic guidelines for the production of poultry, eggs, pork, and beef products. Included is the humane treatment of animals in settings where the animals have room to exercise with access to outdoor space and where health is maintained on diets that do not rely on anti-biotics for survival. Organic feedstocks must be used.[26] In the past ten years, a number of books have been written that evaluate segments of the American food production systems and focus increasingly on the care of the animals that provide our meat. Some of these publications are high-lighted in the Additional Resources section. There have also been two documentaries released recently that focus on the food system that clarify the problems and make suggestions for improvements.[27]

Most oils, meats, and poultry products contain few detectable pes-ticides (other than residues of long-banned insecticides like DDT) and contribute modestly to the overall pesticide dietary exposures and risk. Very few pesticide residues were found in milk by the PDP between 1996 and 1998; about 15 percent of the samples tested positive for residues, and 95 percent of the residues were DDE, a breakdown product of the persistent DDT in many soils—a substance banned from agricultural use in the early 1970s. Farmers can do little to avoid DDE residues in milk, but fortunately, the levels will incrementally decline and become less of a concern.[28]

The industrialization of meat production has introduced confined animal feeding operations that have provided inexpensive meat in vast quantities. This efficiency in efforts to feed a vast nation with low-cost food is not without environmental costs and concerns about the health-fulness of the products generated.

Cattle and corn are transported many miles to established confined animal feeding operations for the final "finishing." During this period when the cattle are readied for slaughter, the predominant diet of corn gives the meat the marbling texture that tenderizes and flavors the meat with fat deposits between the muscle fibers. But bovines are designed by nature to forage grasses and can only survive a concentrated corn or grain diet with the supplementation of low levels of antibiotics. This creates a major public health concern, because bacteria (primarily *E. coli*) exposed to continuous, low-level antibiotics can become resistant and may contaminate meat products through contact with fecal matter during the slaughtering process. The American Medical Association, American Public Health Association, and the National Institutes of Health all describe antibiotic resistance as a growing public health concern. A decrease in resistance has been reported in European countries that have banned the use of antibiotics in animal production. Seventy percent of all antimicrobials used in the United States are fed to livestock. This involves 25 million pounds of antibiotics annually, more than eight times the amount used to treat disease in humans.[29]

Additionally, with FDA and USDA approval, factory farms in the United States use hormones to promote growth in beef cattle and to promote milk production in dairy cattle. It is estimated that two-thirds of all U.S. cattle raised for slaughter are injected with growth hormones. The Europeans banned growth hormones for beef in 1988. The European Commission appointed a committee to study the impact on humans of meat consumed from hormone-enhanced cattle and in 1999 reported that residues in meat from injected animals could affect the hormonal balance of humans, causing reproductive issues and breast, prostate, or colon cancer. The European Union has prohibited the importation of all beef treated with hormones, which means it does not accept any U.S. beef. Approximately 22 percent of all dairy cows in the United States and 54 percent of large herds use recombinant bovine growth hormone (rBGH) to get an 8–17 percent increase in milk production. Its use has increased bacterial udder infections in cows by 25 percent, necessitating the use of antibiotics to treat the infections. The milk of cows injected with rBGH has higher levels of another hormone called insulin-like growth factor-1, which in humans is linked to colon and breast cancer.[30]

Regulations prohibit the use of hormones in pigs and poultry, but antibiotics are used routinely. The tight confinement of pigs and chickens encourages the use of prophylactic low levels of antibiotics to promote growth, to insure health, and to minimize the spread of infectious diseases within the populations of crowded chickens and pigs. This perpetual use of antibiotics can impact not only the consumers of eggs and meats, but the animal caretakers also are more likely to acquire multi-drug-resistant *E. coli.*

Organic production of animal products does not permit the use of growth hormones or the prophylactic use of antibiotics. Milk from dairy cows on organic farms, particularly pasture-based operations, contains significantly higher levels of conjugated linoleic acids (CLAs). These levels in organic milk are often 30 percent higher or more than in conventional milk, but this CLA advantage is modulated by the time of year, quality of pasture, levels of production, and herd health and management. The human health benefits of CLAs include reducing the propensity to store fat (especially abdominal fat), inhibiting tumor development, promoting cellular sensitivity to insulin, increasing immune response against viral antigens, and modulating inflammatory processes. The reliance of organic beef farmers on pasture and forage grasses increases the CLA level in meat as well. A European study has shown that nursing mothers who consume mostly organic milk and meat products have about 50 percent higher levels of rumenic acid in their breast milk. Rumenic acid is the CLA responsible for most of the health benefits of CLAs in milk and meat. Meat is an excellent dietary source of iron and vitamin B_{12}; additionally, meat, eggs, and milk from pastured animals also contain higher levels of omega-3 essential fatty acids that are indispensable for human neurological health.[31]

FEEDING OURSELVES AND OUR CHILDREN WHOLESOMELY

Now that we are aware of the state of the foods available, there are opportunities to maximize the quality of the foods we consume. Through careful selection and astute buying, the quality of foods can be improved. There are also opportunities for some families to become involved in the production of wholesome vegetables by growing vegetables in pots on a patio, by converting some lawn space into a seasonal garden, or by participating in a community garden project. Another option is to locate farmers within driving distance who practice organic farming that can provide these food items for you.

Let's begin with a trip to the local grocery store. It is wonderful to see many large grocery stores now offering organic produce. But the choice to purchase organic versus conventional vegetables and fruits involves a consideration of costs and benefits for many families. The Environmental Working Group has used the USDA's PDP data from 2000 to 2007 and ranked produce using six measures of contamination. The ranking is based on the likelihood of being consistently contaminated with the greatest number of pesticides at the highest levels. Using the rankings, a shopper's guide to pesticides is suggested. This list is updated annually.

Among the twelve most contaminated (the Dirty Dozen) were seven fruits (peaches, apples, nectarines, strawberries, cherries, imported grapes, and pears) and five vegetables (sweet bell peppers, celery, kale, lettuce, and carrots). This study suggests that by substituting produce from the list of least contaminated fruits and vegetables the buyers can reduce their consumption of pesticides by 80 percent. Among the sixteen least contaminated produce items were seven fruits (avocados, pineapples, mangos, kiwi, papayas, watermelon, and grapefruit) and nine vegetables (onions, sweet corn, asparagus, frozen sweet peas, cabbage, eggplant, broccoli, tomatoes, and sweet potatoes).[32]

This study also suggests that purchasing the Dirty Dozen organically would eliminate most pesticide residues. Purchasing the sixteen least contaminated produce items organically would reduce the pesticide load only minimally. For the produce listed between the most and least contaminated, the choice of organic or conventional would be a cost versus benefit consideration. The situation of choice would be the availability of organic selections of all produce year round.

Increasingly, families are looking to alternative sources for seasonal produce and meats. There is no produce as fresh and nutritionally dense as that which is harvested from an organic kitchen garden and consumed within minutes of harvest. The number of families that are involved in vegetable gardening continues to increase. Surveys report that 44 percent of households in 2009 expected to grow some produce; this compares with 39 percent in 2008 and 32 percent in 2007. This trend has been encouraged by rising gas prices, increased food costs, the overall sluggish economy, and the local food movement. During World War II, home-based "victory gardens," which were championed by First Lady Eleanor Roosevelt, produced 40 percent of the produce consumed by Americans.[33]

But fresh produce grown locally can also be procured at local farmers markets. You can locate one in your area at www.localharvest.org (accessed November 26, 2012) or www.eatwellguide.com (accessed November 26, 2012). Also listed are family farms and other sources of sustainably grown produce and grass-fed meats. Opportunities also exist to preserve by canning, freezing, drying, or other methods of preservation of local produce when it is in season to extend the availability of prime, nutritionally dense produce for year-round consumption. Local foods will be fresher than fresh produce transported thousands of miles, even if it is grown organically in its country of origin.

There is an ever-increasing awareness of the ethics of food. Gardens, particularly organic gardens, can remind us that our relationship to our planet can be sustainable. As long as the sun shines and people plant seeds we can find ways to provide for our nutritional needs without adversely impacting the world.

NOTES

FOREWORD

1. Albert Szent-Györgyi, *Introduction to a Submolecular Biology* (New York: Academic Press, 1960).

2. Werner Heisenberg, *Physics and Philosophy: The Revolution in Modern Science* (1958; repr., Amherst, N.Y.: Prometheus Books, 1999). Contains text of lectures delivered at the University of St. Andrews, Scotland, winter 1955–1956.

3. Evan Esar and Nicolas Bentley, *The Treasury of Humorous Quotations* (London: Phoenix House, 1951).

INTRODUCTION. EMERGING PARADIGMS IN HEALTH AND HEALING

1. Pim van Lommel, *Consciousness beyond Life: The Science of Near-Death Experience* (New York: HarperOne, 2011).

CHAPTER 1. MOVING BEYOND THE "ENERGY CRISIS" IN MEDICINE

1. The Official Web Site of the Nobel Prize, "The Nobel Prize in Physiology or Medicine 1937: Albert Szent-Györgyi," www.nobelprize.org/nobel_prizes/medicine/laureates/1937/szent-gyorgyi.html (accessed July 1, 2010).

2. Willy Kühne, *Untersuchungen über das Protoplasma und die Contractilitat* (Leipzig: W. Engelmann, 1864).

3. Albert Szent-Györgyi, *Chemistry of Muscular Contraction* (New York: Academic Press, 1951).

4. Albert Szent-Györgyi, "Lost in the Twentieth Century," *Annual Reviews of Biochemistry* 32 (1963): 1–13.

5. Albert Szent-Györgyi, "Bioenergetics," *Science* 124, no. 3227 (1956): 873–75.

6. W. Einthoven, G. Fahr, and A. de Waart, "Über die Richtung und die manifeste Grösse der Potentialschwankungen im menschlichen Herzen und über den Einfluss der Herzlage auf die Form des Elektrokardiogramms," *Archiv für die gesammte Physiologie des Menschen und der Thiere* 150 (1913): 275–315.

7. James L. Oschman, *Energy Medicine in Therapeutics and Human Performance* (Edinburgh: Butterworth-Heinemann, 2003).

8. Ramzi S. Cotran, "Inflammation: Historical Perspectives," in *Inflammation: Basic Principles and Clinical Correlates,* 3rd ed., ed. John I. Gallin and Ralph Snyderman, 5 (Philadelphia, Pa.: Lippincott Williams & Wilkins, 1999).

9. Albert Szent-Györgyi, *Electronic Biology and Cancer: A New Theory of Cancer* (New York and Basel: Marcel Dekker, 1976).

10. J. T. Edsall, "In Reminiscences on Szent-Györgyi," *Biological Bulletin* 174 (1988): 230.

11. Albert Szent-Györgyi, "Looking Back," *Perspectives in Biology and Medicine* 15, no. 1 (1971): 1–4.

12. Albert Szent-Györgyi, "Dionysians and Apollonians" *Science* 176 (1972): 966.

13. Ibid.

14. A. A. Berezin, "Hampering the Progress of Science by Peer Review and by the 'Selective' Funding System," *Science Tribune,* December 1996.

15. Central Intelligence Agency, "Country Comparison: Life Expectancy at Birth," *The World Factbook,* www.cia.gov/library/publications/the-world-factbook/2102rank.html (accessed June 13, 2010).

16. Albert Szent-Györgyi, *Introduction to a Submolecular Biology* (New York: Academic Press, 1960).

17. Albert Szent-Györgyi, *Bioelectronics* (New York: Academic Press, 1968).

18. Franco Bistolfi, *Biostructures and Radiation Order Disorder* (Torino, Italy: Edizioni Minerva Medica, 1991).

19. Włodzimierz Sedlak, *Bioelektronika* (Warsaw, Poland: Instytut Wydawniczy Pax, 1979). In Polish, with English summaries at the ends of the chapters.

20. Konstantin Korotkov, ed. *Measuring Energy Fields: State-of-the-Science* (Fair Lawn, N.J.: Backbone Publishing Company, 2004).

21. P. R. C. Gascoyne, R. Pethig, and A. Szent-Györgyi, "Water Structure-Dependent Charge Transport in Proteins," *Proceedings of the National Academy of Sciences* 78 (1981): 261–65.

22. F. Rosenberg and E. Postow, "Semiconduction in Proteins and Lipids—Its Possible Biological Import," *Annals of the New York Academy of Sciences* 158 (1969): 161–90.

23. N. S. Hush, "An Overview of the First Half-Century of Molecular Electronics," *Annals of the New York Academy of Sciences* 1006 (2003): 1–20.

24. A. C. Ober and J. L. Oschman, "Method of treating inflammation and autoimmune diseases," US Patent 7,724,491, issued May 25, 2010.

25. Alfred Pischinger, *The Extracellular Matrix and Ground Regulation: Basis for a Holistic Biological Medicine* (Berkeley: North Atlantic Books, 2007).

26. Hartmut Heine, Lehrbuch der biologischen Medizin. Grundregulation kund *Extrazellulare Matrix* (Stuttgart, Germany: Hippokrates Verlag, 2007).

27. Andrew Taylor Still, *The Philosophy of Osteopathy.* (Kirksville, Mo.: 1899), 86.

28. Rudolf Virchow, *Die Cellularpathologie in ihrer Begründung auf physiologische und pathologische Gewebelehre* (1858; English translation, 1860).

29. Alfred Pischinger and Hartmut Heine, *The Extracellular Matrix and Ground Regulation* (Berkeley: North Atlantic Books, 2007).

30. J. L. Oschman, "Structure and Properties of Ground Substances," *American Zoologist* 24, no. 1 (1983): 199–215.

31. M. S. Bretscher, "A Major Protein which Spans the Human Erythrocyte Membrane," *Journal of Molecular Biology* 59 (1971): 351–57; M. S. Bretscher, "Major Human Erythrocyte Glycoprotein Spans the Cell Membrane," *Nature New Biology* 231 (1971): 229–32.

32. R. Berezney and D. S. Coffey, "Isolation and Characterization of a Framework Structure from Rat Liver Nuclei," *Journal of Cell Biology* 73 (1977): 616–37.

33. J. L. Oschman, and Nora H. Oschman, "Matter, Energy, and the Living Matrix," *Rolf Lines* (the news magazine for the Rolf Institute, Boulder, Colorado), October 1993, 55–64.

34. Kiiko Matsumoto and Stephen Birch, *Hara Diagnosis: Reflections on the Sea* (Brookline, Mass.: Paradigm Publications, 1988).

35. Oschman, *Energy Medicine*.

36. D. M. Eisenberg, R. C. Kessler, C. Foster, et al., "Unconventional Medicine in the United States—Prevalence, Costs, and Patterns of Use," *New England Journal of Medicine* 328 (1993): 246–52.

37. D. M. Eisenberg, R. B. Davis, S. L. Ettner, et al., "Trends in Alternative Medicine Use in the United States, 1990–1997: Results of a Follow-up National Survey," *Journal of the American Medical Association* 280, no. 18 (1998): 1569–75.

38. G. Chevalier and K. Mori, "The Effect of Earthing on Human Physiology. Part II. Electrodermal Measurements," *Subtle Energies and Energy Medicine* 18, no. 3 (2010): 11–34.

39. Clinton Ober, Stephen T. Sinatra, and Martin Zucker, *Earthing: The Most Important Health Discovery Ever?* (Laguna Beach, Calif.: Basic Health Publications, 2010).

40. M. Ghaly and D. Teplitz, "Biological Effects of Grounding the Human Body during Sleep, as Measured by Cortisol Levels and Subjective Reporting of Sleep, Pain, and Stress," *Journal of Alternative Complementary Medicine* 10 (2004): 767–76.

41. Szent-Györgyi, "Lost in the 20th Century," 1–15.

42. Hans Selye, *The Stress of Life* (New York: McGraw Hill, 1978).

43. John I. Gallin and Ralph Snyderman, "Overview," in *Inflammation: Basic Principles and Clinical Correlates,* 3rd ed., ed. John I. Gallin and Ralph Snyderman, 1 (Philadelphia, Pa.: Lippincott Williams & Wilkins, 1999).

44. H. Selye, "On the Mechanism through which Hydrocortisone Affects the Resistance of Tissues to Injury: An Experimental Study with the Granuloma Pouch Technique," *Journal of the American Medical Association* 152, no. 13 (1953): 1207–13.

45. R. H. Davis, H. S. Pitkow, and K. A. Shovlin, "Anti-inflammatory Effect of Tryptophan in Selye Pouch," *Journal of the American Podiatry Association* 71, no. 12 (1981): 690–91.

46. Selye, *The Stress of Life.*

47. George E. Meinig, *Root Canal Cover-Up,* 2nd ed. (Ojai, Calif.: Bion Publishing, 1994).

48. Ida P. Rolf, *Rolfing: Reestablishing the Natural Alignment and Structural Integration of the Human Body for Vitality and Well-Being* (Rochester, Vt.: Healing Arts Press, 1989), 129.

49. C. R. McMakin, "Microcurrent Therapy: A Novel Treatment Method for Chronic Low Back Myofascial Pain," *Journal of Bodywork and Movement Therapies* 8, no. 2 (2004): 143–53.

50. C. A. L. Bassett, "Bioelectromagnetics in the Service of Medicine," in *Electromagnetic Fields: Biological Interactions and Mechanisms,* Advances in Chemistry Series 250, ed. Martin Blank (Washington, D.C.: American Chemical Society, 1995): 261–75.

51. James L. Oschman and Judy Kosovich, "Energy Medicine and Matrix Regeneration," in *Anti-Aging Therapeutics,* vol. 10, ed. Robert M. Klatz and Robert Goldman (Chicago: American Academy of Anti-Aging Medicine, 2007), 247–53.

52. Oschman and Oschman, "Matter, Energy, and the Living Matrix," 55–64.

53. T. Tanaka, "Gels," *Scientific American* 244 (1981): 124–38.

CHAPTER 2.
LIFE'S MUSICAL BLUEPRINT

1. H. P. Blavatsky, *The Secret Doctrine,* vols. I and II (Pasadena, Calif.: Theosophical University Press, 1970).

2. Alain Daniélou, *Music and the Power of Sound: The Influence of Tuning and Interval on Consciousness* (Rochester, Vt.: Inner Traditions, 1995).

3. Ibid.

4. Theo Paijmans, *Free Energy Pioneer: John Worrell Keely* (Kempton, Ill.: Adventures Unlimited Press, 2004).

5. Dale Pond, *The Physics of Love* (Santa Fe, N. Mex.: The Message Company, 1996); Dale Pond, *Universal Laws Never before Revealed: Keely's Secrets* (Santa Fe, N. Mex.: The Message Company, 2004).

6. Leonard G. Horowitz, *DNA: Pirates of the Sacred Spiral* (Amsterdam: Tetrahedron Publishing, 2004).

7. Leonard G. Horowitz, *Walk on Water* (Amsterdam: Tetrahedron Publishing, 2006).

8. Soma Energetics, "What Are the Ancient Solfeggio Tones?" www.somaenergetics.com/Solfeggio_Frequencies.php (accessed October 31, 2012).

9. Leonard G. Horowitz and Joseph S. Puleo, *Healing Codes for the Biological Apocalypse* (Amsterdam: Tetrahedron Publishing, 2001).

10. Ibid., 73, 156.

11. Harold Aspden, *Modern Aether Science* (Southampton, England: Sabberton Publications, 1972).

12. Ervin Laszlo, *Science and the Akashic Field: An Integral Theory of Everything* (Rochester, Vt.: Inner Traditions, 2007).

13. Thomas E. Bearden, *Energy from the Vacuum* (Santa Barbara, Calif.: Cheniere Press, 2002); Thomas E. Bearden, *Gravitobiology: A New Biophysics* (Santa Barbara, Calif.: Cheniere Press, 1991); Thomas E. Bearden, *Oblivion: America at the Brink* (Santa Barbara, Calif.: Cheniere Press, 2005).

14. Lynne McTaggart, *The Field: The Quest for the Secret Force of the Universe* (New York: HarperPaperbacks, 2008).

15. James L. Oschman, *Energy Medicine: The Scientific Basis* (Edinburgh: Churchill Livingstone, 2000).

16. Peggy Phoenix Dubro and David P. Lapierre, *Elegant Empowerment: Evolution of Consciousness* (Sedona, Ariz.: Platinum Publishing House, 2002).

17. See also William A. Tiller, Walter E. Dibble Jr., and Michael J. Kohane, *Conscious Acts of Creation: The Emergence of a New Physics* (Walnut Creek, Calif.: Pavior Publishing, 2001).

18. Worth reading in this regard are: Michael Hayes, *High Priests, Quantum Genes* (London: Black Spring Press Ltd., 2004); Barbara Hand Clow and Gerry Clow, *Alchemy of Nine Dimensions: Decoding the Vertical Axis, Crop Circles, and the Mayan Calendar* (Newburyport, Mass.: Hampton Roads Publishing Company, 2004); and John Consemulder, *Blauwdruk: de Multidimensionale Werkelijkheid van Creatie en Manifestatie* (Deventer, The Netherlands: Ankh-Hermes BV, 2008).

19. Bearden, *Energy from the Vacuum*; Bearden, *Gravitobiology*; and Bearden, *Oblivion*.

20. Oschman, *Energy Medicine*.

21. Bearden, *Energy from the Vacuum*.

22. Two papers by Edmund Taylor Whittaker are "On the Partial Differential Equations of Mathematical Physics," *Mathematische Annalen* 57 (1903): 333–55; and "On an Expression of the Electromagnetic Field Due to Electrons by Means of Two Scalar Potential Functions," *Proceedings of the London Mathematical Society* 1, series 2 (1904): 367–72.

23. Bearden, *Oblivion*.

24. Consemulder, *Blauwdruk*.

25. Bearden, *Gravitobiology*, 53.

26. Ibid., 2.

27. Ibid., 13.

28. Ibid.

29. Francisco J. Yndurain, *Quantum Chromodynamics: An Introduction to the Theory of Quarks and Gluons* (London: Springer-Verlag, 1983).

30. Jacobs, R., "21st Century Medicine," *Kindred Spirits* 3, no. 10 (1997): 37–40.

31. Consemulder, *Blauwdruk*.

32. Valerie V. Hunt, *Infinite Mind: Science of the Human Vibrations of Consciousness* (Malibu, Calif.: Malibu Publishing, 2000).

33. Bearden, *Gravitobiology*, 40.

34. Ibid., 48, 49.

35. Ibid., 46.

36. Bearden, *Gravitobiology*.

37. Ibid., 47, 48.

38. Lifescientists web page (in German), www.lifescientists.de (in German; accessed October 31, 2012).

39. Stephen Linsteadt and Maria Elena Boekemeyer, *The Heart of Health: The Principles of Physical Health and Vitality* (La Quinta, Calif.: Natural Healing House Press, 2003).

40. Bruce H. Lipton, *The Biology of Belief: Unleashing the Power of Consciousness, Matter, and Miracles* (Carlsbad, Calif.: Hay House, 2008).

41. I. Miller and R. A. Miller, "From Helix to Hologram: An Ode on the Human Genome," *Nexus* 10, no. 5 (2003).

42. Horowitz, *DNA*, 428.

43. Horowitz, *DNA*.

44. The Fractal Field web site, www.fractalfield.com (accessed October 31, 2012).

45. Jeremy Narby, *The Cosmic Serpent: DNA and the Origins of Knowledge* (New York: Tarcher, 1999).

46. P. P. Gariaev, K. V. Grigor'ev, A. A. Vasil'ev, et al., "Investigation of the Fluctuation Dynamics of DNA Solutions by Laser Correlation Spectroscopy," *Bulletin of the Lebedev Physics Institute*, no. 11–12 (1992): 23–30; Pjotr P. Gariaev, *Wave Genome* (Public Profit, 1994); and Consemulder, *Blauwdruk*.

47. Herbert Fröhlich, *Biological Coherence and Response to External Stimuli* (New York: Springer, 1988).

48. Consemulder, *Blauwdruk*.

49. Ibid.

50. Miller and Miller, "From Helix to Hologram."

51. G. Rein and R. McCraty, "Structural Changes in Water and DNA Associated with New Physiologically Measured States," *Journal of Scientific Exploration* 8, no. 3 (1994): 438.

52. Consemulder, *Blauwdruk*.

53. Sol Luckman, *Conscious Healing: Book One of the Regenetics Method* (n.p.: Crow Rising Transformational Media, 2009).

54. Horowitz, *DNA*.

55. J. J. Hurtak, *The Book of Knowledge: The Keys of Enoch* (n.p.: The Academy for Future Science, 1987).

56. Gregg Braden, *The God Code* (Carlsbad, Calif.: Hay House, 2005).

57. Horowitz, *DNA*, 483.

58. Bearden, *Gravitobiology*, 57.

59. Ibid.

60. Consemulder, *Blauwdruk*.

61. Miller and Miller, "From Helix to Hologram."

62. Consemulder, *Blauwdruk*.

63. R. A. Miller, B. Webb, and D. Dickson, "A Holographic Concept of Reality," *Psychoenergetic Systems* 1 (1975): 55–62.

64. Michael Talbot, *The Holographic Universe* (New York: Harper Perennial, 1992).

65. Michael Hyson in Horowitz, *Pirates of the Sacred Spiral*.

66. Jonathan Goldman, *Shifting Frequencies* (Flagstaff, Ariz.: Light Technology Publishing, 1998).

67. Jonathan Goldman, *Healing Sounds: The Power of Harmonics* (Rochester, Vt.: Healing Arts Press, 2002).

68. Dhyani Ywahoo, *Voices of Our Ancestors* (Boston: Shambhala, 1987).

69. Oschman, *Energy Medicine*.

70. Robert O. Becker and Gary Selden, *The Body Electric: Electromagnetism and the Foundation of Life* (New York: Quill, 1985).

71. Consemulder, *Blauwdruk*.

72. Hans Jenny, *Cymatics: A Study of Wave Phenomena and Vibrations* (Newmarket, N.H.: Macromedia Publishing, 2001).

73. Goldman, *Shifting Frequencies*.

74. Laszlo, *Science and the Akashic Field*.

75. Daniélou, *Music and the Power of Sound*, 3.

76. John Beaulieu, *Music and Sound in the Healing Arts* (Barrytown, N.Y.: Station Hill Press, 1995).

77. Consemulder, *Blauwdruk*.

CHAPTER 3.
CONSCIOUSNESS AND HEALING

1. Larry Dossey, *Healing Words: The Power of Prayer and the Practice of Medicine* (San Francisco: HarperSanFrancisco, 1993).

2. Martha Walden, review of *Healing Words,* by Larry Dossey, *Raising Power,* Spring 1995.

3. Benjamin Jowett, "In Conversation with Logan Pearsall Smith," in *Unforgotten Years,* Logan Pearsall Smith, 169 (Boston: Little, Brown and Company, 1939).

4. Albert Einstein (attributed), Wikiquote, http://en.wikiquote.org/wiki/Albert_Einstein (accessed May 21, 2008).

5. F. Galton, "Statistical Inquiries into the Efficacy of Prayer," *Fortnightly Review* 12 (1872): 125–35.

6. John C. Polkinghorne, *Science and Providence: God's Interactions with the World* (Boston: New Science Library/Shambhala, 1989), 75.

7. Willard Sterne Randall, *George Washington: A Life* (New York: Holt, 1998).

8. Dossey, *Healing Words*, 172.

9. Ibid., 170–79.

10. R. Byrd, "Positive Therapeutic Effects of Intercessory Prayer in a Coronary Care Unit Population," *Southern Medical Journal* 81, no. 7 (1988): 826–29.

11. Dossey, *Healing Words*, 179–86.

12. Larry Dossey, "Distance Healing: Evidence," in *The Parapsychology Revolution: A Concise Anthology of Paranormal and Psychical Research*, ed. Robert M. Schoch and Logan Yonavjak (New York: Tarcher/Penguin, 2008), 216–32.

13. Ibid., 226–229.

14. Wayne B. Jonas and Cindy C. Crawford, *Healing, Intention, and Energy Medicine* (New York: Churchill Livingstone, 2003), xv–xix.

15. Dossey, "Distance Healing," 216–31.

16. Daniel J. Benor, *Healing Research,* vol. 1 (Southfield, Mich.: Vision, 2002).

17. L. Dossey and D. B. Hufford, "Are Prayer Experiments Legitimate? Twenty Criticisms," *Explore* 1, no. 2 (2005): 109–17.

18. Jonas and Crawford, *Healing, Intention, and Energy Medicine*, xv–xix.

19. "The Pertinence of the Princeton Engineering Anomalies Research (PEAR) Laboratory to the Pursuit of Global Health," ed. Robert G. Jahn and Brenda J. Dunne, special issue, *Explore: The Journal of Science and Healing* 3, no. 3 (2007): 191–345.

20. Edward O. Wilson, *Consilience: The Unity of Knowledge* (New York: Knopf, 1998).

21. H. Benson, J. A. Dusek, J. B. Sherwood, et al., "Study of the Therapeutic Effects of Intercessory Prayer (STEP) in Cardiac Bypass Patients: A Multicenter Randomized Trial of Uncertainty and Certainty of Receiving Intercessory Prayer," *American Heart Journal* 151 (2006): 934–42.

22. M. W. Krucoff, S. W. Crater, and K. L. Lee. "From Efficacy to Safety Concerns: A STEP Forward or a Step Back for Clinical Research and

Intercessory Prayer? The Study of Therapeutic Effects of Intercessory Prayer (STEP)," *American Heart Journal* 151, no. 4 (2006): 762–64.

23. Larry Dossey, *Be Careful What You Pray For* (San Francisco: HarperSan-Francisco, 1997), 165–92.

24. M. Jain, quoted in: "Largest Study of Third-Party Prayer Suggests Such Prayer Not Effective in Reducing Complications following Heart Surgery," news release from Harvard Medical School Office of Public Affairs, March 31, 2006, web.med.harvard.edu/sites/RELEASES/html/3_31STEP.html (accessed June 5, 2008).

25. Dossey, *Healing Words*, 189–95.

26. H. Ariel, L. Dvorkin, Y. Steinman, et al., "Intercessory Prayer: A Delicate Celestial Orchestration between Spiritual and Physical Worlds," letter to the editor, *Journal of Alternative and Complementary Medicine* 14, no. 4 (May 2008): 351–52.

27. C. Bethea, quoted in: W. J. Cromie, "Prayers Don't Help Surgery Patients," *Harvard University Gazette,* April 6, 2006, www.hno.harvard.edu/gazette/2006/04.06/05-prayer.html (accessed June 5, 2008).

28. J. A. Dusek, quoted in: W. J. Cromie, "Prayers Don't Help Surgery Patients," *Harvard University Gazette,* April 6, 2006, www.hno.harvard.edu/gazette/2006/04.06/05-prayer.html (accessed June 5, 2008).

29. John Palmer, "Confronting the Experimenter Effect," in *Psi Research Methodology: A Re-examination; Proceedings of an International Conference Held in Chapel Hill, North Carolina,* October 29–30, 1988, ed. L. Coly and J. D. S. McMahon (New York: Parapsychology Foundation; 1993): 44–64.

30. R. Wiseman and M. Schlitz, "Experimenter Effects and the Remote Detection of Staring," *Journal of Parapsychology* 61 (1997): 197–208.

31. I. Stevenson, "Thoughts on the Decline of Major Paranormal Phenomena," presidential address to the Society for Psychical Research, 1989, *Proceedings of the Society for Psychical Research* 57 (1990): 149–62.

32. R. A. White, "The Influence of Persons Other than the Experimenter on the Subject's Scores in Psi Experiments," *Journal of the Society for Psychical Research* 70 (1976): 133–66.

33. K. J. Batcheldor, "Report on a Case of Table Levitation and Associated Phenomena," *Journal of the Society for Psychical Research* 43 (1966): 339–56.

34. Iris M. Owen and Margaret Sparrow, *Conjuring Up Philip: An Adventure into Psychokinesis* (New York: Harper and Row, 1976).

35. G. R. Schmeidler, "Predicting Good and Bad Scores in a Clairvoyance

Experiment: A Preliminary Report," *Journal of the Society for Psychical Research* 37 (1943): 103–10.

36. Ibid., 210–21.

37. G. R. Schmeidler, "Evidence for Two Kinds of Telepathy," *International Journal of Parapsychology* 3 (1961): 5–48.

38. G. R. Schmeidler, "Are There Two Kinds of Telepathy?" *Journal of the Society for Psychical Research* 55 (1961): 87–97.

39. Stevenson, "Thoughts on the Decline of Major Paranormal Phenomena," 149–62.

40. Dossey, *Be Careful What You Pray For*, 165–92.

41. N. Adams, "Remarkable Mesmeric Phenomena," *The Zoist* 7 (1849–1850): 79–80.

42. P. Janet, "Note sur Quelques Phénomènes de Somnambulisme," *Revue Philosophique de la France et de l'Etranger* 21 (1886): 190–98.

43. P. Janet, "Deuxième Note sur le Sommeil Provoqué a Distance et la Suggestion Mentale Pendant l'Etat Somnambulique," *Revue Philosophique de la France et de l'Etranger* 22 (1886): 212–23.

44. C. Richet, "Un Fait de Somnambulisme à Distance," *Revue Philosophique de la France et de l'Etranger* 21 (1886): 199–200.

45. Leonid Leonidovich Vasiliev, *Experiments in Distant Influence* (New York: E. P. Dutton and Co., 1976).

46. L. Dossey, "Hypnosis: A Window into the Soul of Healing," *Alternative Therapies in Health and Medicine* 6, no. 2 (2000): 12–17, 102–11.

47. Dossey, *Be Careful What You Pray For*, 53–133.

48. Gallup poll reported in *Life* magazine, March 1994.

49. Russell Targ and Harold E. Puthoff, *Mind-Reach: Scientists Look at Psychic Ability* (New York: Delta, 1977), 169.

50. "Scanning the Issue," editorial, *Proceedings of the IEEE* LXIV, no. 3 (March 1976): 291.

51. Marilyn M. Schlitz and Dean Radin, "Prayer and Intention in Distant Healing," *Measuring the Immeasurable,* ed. Tami Simon (Boulder: Sounds True, 2008): 387–404.

52. J. Achterberg, K. Cooke, T. Richards, et al., "Evidence for Correlations between Distant Intentionality and Brain Function in Recipients: A Functional Magnetic Resonance Imaging Analysis," *Journal of Alternative and Complementary Medicine* 11, no. 6 (2005): 965–71.

53. L. Dossey and D. B. Hufford. "Are Prayer Experiments Legitimate? Twenty Criticisms, *Explore* 1, no. 2 (2005): 109–17; L. Dossey, "Spirituality,

Prayer, and Medicine: What Is the Fuss Really About?" *Virtual Mentor* (the American Medical Association journal of ethics) 7, no 5 (May 2005), www.virtualmentor.ama-assn.org/2005/05/oped2-0505.html (accessed November 1, 2012).

54. L. Dossey, "Spirituality, Prayer, and Medicine: What Is the Fuss Really About?" *Virtual Mentor* (the American Medical Association journal of ethics) 7, no. 5 (May 2005), www.virtualmentor.ama-assn.org/2005/05/oped2-0505.html (accessed November 1, 2012).

55. J. Achterberg, K. Cooke, T. Richards, et al., "Evidence for Correlations between Distant Intentionality and Brain Function in Recipients: A Functional Magnetic Resonance Imaging Analysis," *Journal of Alternative and Complementary Medicine* 11, no. 6 (2005): 965–71.

56. Edward F. Kelly, Emily Williams Kelly, Adam Crabtree, et al., *Irreducible Mind: Toward a Psychology for the 21st Century* (Lanham, Md.: Rowman and Littlefield, 2007), xxvii–xxix.

57. Russell Targ and Jane Katra. *Miracles of Mind: Exploring Non-local Consciousness and Spiritual Healing* (Novato, Calif.: New World Library, 1998), 81–82.

58. Caryle Hirshberg and Mark Ian Barasch. *Remarkable Recovery: What Extraordinary Healings Tell Us About Getting Well and Staying Well* (New York: Riverhead, 1995).

59. F. Sicher, E. Targ, D. Moore, and H. S. Smith. "A Randomized Double-Blind Study of the Effect of Distant Healing in a Population with Advanced AIDS—Report of a Small-Scale Study," *Western Journal of Medicine* 169, no. 6 (1998): 356–63.

60. J. Achterberg, K. Cooke, T. Richards, et al., "Evidence for Correlations between Distant Intentionality and Brain Function in Recipients: A Functional Magnetic Resonance Imaging Analysis," *Journal of Alternative and Complementary Medicine* 11, no. 6 (2005): 965–71.

61. Ibid.

62. Sicher, Targ, Moore, and Smith. "A Randomized Double-Blind Study of the Effect of Distant Healing in a Population with Advanced AIDS—Report of a Small-Scale Study," 356–63.

63. Ibid.

64. David Ian Miller, "Parapsychology Researcher Dean Radin on ESP, Spirituality, and How the Consciousness of Individuals Is Connected," *San Francisco Chronicle,* February 25, 2008, www.sfgate.com/cgi-bin/article.cgi?f=/g/a/2008/02/25/findrelig.DTL (accessed May 23, 2008).

65. M. W. Krucoff, S. W. Crater, D. Gallup, et al. "Music, Imagery, Touch, and Prayer as Adjuncts to Interventional Cardiac Care: The Monitoring and Actualization of Noetic Trainings (MANTRA II) Randomized Study," *Lancet* 366 (2005): 211–17.

66. Sicher, Targ, Moore, and Smith, "A Randomized Double-Blind Study of the Effect of Distant Healing in a Population with Advanced AIDS—Report of a Small-Scale Study," 356–63.

67. W. J. Matthews, J. M. Conti, and S. G. Sireci, "The Effects of Intercessory Prayer, Positive Visualization, and Expectancy on the Well-Being of Kidney Dialysis Patients," *Alternative Therapies in Health and Medicine* 7, no. 5 (2001): 42–52.

68. Sicher, Targ, Moore, and Smith, "A Randomized Double-Blind Study of the Effect of Distant Healing in a Population with Advanced AIDS—Report of a Small-Scale Study," 356–63.

69. E. F. Keller, *A Feeling for the Organism: The Life and Work of Barbara McClintock* (San Francisco: W. H. Freeman, 1983).

70. Benor, *Healing Research,* vol. 1.

71. Jonas and Crawford, *Healing, Intention, and Energy Medicine,* xv–xix.

72. Ibid.

73. Gloria A. Gronowicz, Ankur Jhaveri, L. W. Clarke, et al. "Therapeutic Touch Stimulates the Proliferation of Human Cells in Culture," *The Journal of Alternative and Complementary Medicine* 14, no. 3 (April 1, 2008): 233–39.

74. Thomas S. Kuhn, *The Structure of Scientific Revolutions,* 3rd ed. (Chicago: University of Chicago Press, 1996).

75. Stevenson, "Thoughts on the Decline of Major Paranormal Phenomena," 149–62.

76. L. Kaiser, "Spirituality and Healthcare: A Candid Talk about Possibilities. Interview by Bonnie J. Horrigan, *Explore: The Journal of Science and Healing* 1, no. 1 (2005): 48–56.

77. D. Radin, "Time-Reversed Human Experience: Experimental Evidence and Implications," Boundary Institute, July 31, 2000, www.boundaryinstitute .org/articles/timereversed.pdf (accessed June 8, 2008).

78. William James, *The Correspondence of William James,* vol. 11, gen. ed. John J. McDermott; ed. Ignas K. Skrupskelis, Elizabeth Berkeley, and Frederick H. Burkhardt (Charlottesville, Va.: University of Virginia Press, 1992–2004), 143–44.

79. L. Nemeth and Charlie McGuire, "Love Is the Essence of Healing," *Beginnings,* Spring 2008, 56.

80. J. Katra, obituary of Elisabeth F. Targ, Findarticles.com, http://findar
ticles.com/p/articles/mi_m2320/is_4_66/ai_97754940/pg_1 (accessed
May 31, 2008); L. Dossey, "Healing Research: What We Know and Don't
Know," *Explore: The Journal of Science and Healing* 4, no. 5 (2008):
341–52.

CHAPTER 4.
RIFE THERAPY

1. James L. Oschman, *Energy Medicine: The Scientific Basis* (Edinburgh and
New York: Churchill Livingstone, 2000), 121, 123.

2. Royal Raymond Rife, a written reply to 137-question deposition from
John Crane's lawyer, for Crane's trial, March 7, 1961, Website of Royal
Rife, www.rife.org/crane/johncranetrial.html (accessed November 9,
2007).

3. Royal Rife Technologies Homepage, www.rt66.com/~rifetech (accessed
October 21, 2007).

4. James Bare, e-mail correspondence, October 21, 2007.

CHAPTER 5.
HARMONIZING THE ENERGIES
OF BODY, MIND, AND ENVIRONMENT
WITH PULSOR MICROCYRSTALS

1. George T. F. Yao, *Pulsor: Miracle of Microcrystals* (Murrieta, Calif.: Gyro
International, 1986), xv.

2. Ibid.

3. World Health Organization, Electromagnetic Fields and Public Health Fact
Sheet No. 322, June 2007, www.who.int/mediacentre/factsheets/fs322/en/
index.html (accessed January 1, 2013).

4. World Health Organization International Agency for Research on Cancer,
"Electromagnetic Fields and Public Health: Extremely Low Frequency
Fields and Cancer, 2001, October," https://apps.who.int/inf-fs/en/fact263
.html (accessed January 1, 2013).

5. Franz Adlkofer, project coordinator, "The REFLEX Project: Risk Evaluation of Potential Environmental Hazards from Low Energy Electromagnetic Field (EMF) Exposure Using Sensitive in Vitro Methods,"
www.ec.europa.eu/research/quality-of-life/ka4/pdf/report_reflex_en.pdf
(accessed November 1, 2012).

6. Andrew Goldsworthy, "The Dangers of Electromagnetic Smog," www

.hese-project.org/hese-uk/en/papers/electrosmog_dangers.pdf (accessed November 1, 2012).

7. Irving L. Janis, *Psychological Stress* (New York: John Wiley & Sons, 1958).

8. Yao, *Pulsor: Miracle of Microcrystals*, 8.

9. Ibid.

10. Joseph B. Michaelson, "Preliminary Screening of the Effects of Fluorescent Radiation on Blood Chemistries of Rats in the Presence and Absence of Pulsor Anti-radiation Devices," monograph, March 1980, www.health improvement.nl/pulsoronderzoeken.php?val=lab (accessed January 11, 2013).

11. Christa Uricher, "Elektrosmog" [Electromagnetic Pollution], *Umwelt-magazin Kreise,* no. 9 (2005).

CHAPTER 6.
OZONE AND HYDROGEN PEROXIDE
IN HEALING

1. J. W. Finney, H. C. Urschel, G. A. Balla, et al., "Protection of the Ischemic Heart with DMSO Alone or DMSO with Hydrogen Peroxide," *Annals of the New York Academy of Sciences* 151 (1967): 231–41.

2. H. C. Urschel Jr., "Cardiovascular Effects of Hydrogen Peroxide." *Circulation* 31, suppl. 2 (1965): 203–10.

3. Ibid., 187–88.

4. Velio Bocci, *Ozone: A New Medical Drug* (Dordrecht, Netherlands: Springer, 2005), 28.

5. Ibid., 22–24, 27.

6. Frank Shallenberger, "Intravenous Ozone Therapy in HIV Related Disease," *Proceedings: Fourth International Bio-Oxidative Medical Conference* (April 1993).

7. C. H. Farr, *Protocol for the Intravenous Administration of Hydrogen Peroxide* (Oklahoma City, Okla.: International Bio-Oxidative Medicine Foundation, 1993), 32.

8. Nathaniel Altman, *Oxygen Healing Therapies* (Rochester, Vt.: Healing Arts Press, 1998), x–xi.

9. Velio Bocci, *Oxygen-Ozone Therapy: A Critical Evaluation* (Dordrecht, Netherlands: Kluwer Academic Publishers, 2002), 213–14.

10. Renate Viebahn-Hänsler, *The Use of Ozone in Medicine,* 4th English ed. (Iffezheim, Germany: Odrei Publishers, 2002), 44.

11. Gerard Sunnen, "Ozone in Medicine: Overview and Future Direction," *Journal of Advancement in Medicine* 1, No. 3 (Fall 1988).

12. Nathaniel Altman, *The Oxygen Prescription* (Rochester, Vt.: Healing Arts Press, 2007), 19–20.

13. Bocci, *Oxygen-Ozone Therapy*, 122.

14. R. Giunta, A. Coppola, C. Luongo, et al., "Ozonized Autohemotransfusion Improves Hemorheological Parameters and Oxygen Delivery to Tissues in Patients with Peripheral Occlusive Arterial Disease," *Annals of Hematology* 80 (December 2001): 745–48.

15. B. Clavo, J. L. Pérez, L. López, et al., "Effect of Ozone Therapy on Muscle Oxygenation," *The Journal of Alternative and Complementary Medicine* 9, no. 2 (April 2003): 251–56.

16. G. Martínez-Sánchez, S. M. Al-Dalain, S. Menéndez, et al., "Therapeutic Efficacy of Ozone in Patients with Diabetic Foot," *European Journal of Pharmacology* 523, nos. 1–3 (October 31, 2005): 151.

17. Ibid., 156.

18. Michael E. Shannon, letter, January 21, 1994.

19. Dr. Frank Shallenberger, letter, December 9, 1993.

20. Julian Holmes, "New Technologies for Dental Care," *Dentistry*, May 16, 2002, 14.

21. Aylin Baysan and Edward Lynch, "Effect of Ozone on the Oral Microbiota and Clinical Severity of Primary Root Caries," *American Journal of Dentistry* 17 (February 2004): 56.

22. Aylin Baysan and Edward Lynch, "The Use of Ozone in Dentistry and Medicine," *Primary Dental Care* 12 (April 2005): 51.

23. Julian Holmes, "Clinical Reversal of Root Caries Using Ozone, Double-Blind, Randomized, Controlled 18-Month Trial," *Gerodontology* 20 (December 2003): 106–14.

24. Russell Beggs, "Reliable Caries Reversal: Another Paradigm Shift?" *Dentistry Today* 23 (February 2004): 16.

25. C. H. Siemsen, "The Use of Ozone in Orthopedics," in *Proceedings: Ozone in Medicine, 12th World Congress of the International Ozone Association,* 125–30 (Zurich: International Ozone Association, 1995).

26. Frank Shallenberger, *The Principles and Applications of Ozone/UVB Therapy* (Carson City, Nev.: Frank Shallenberger, 1999).

27. Frank Shallenberger, *Prolozone Therapy* (Carson City, Nev.: Frank Shallenberger, 2003).

28. Marie Thérès Jacobs, "Adverse Effects and Typical Complications in Ozone-Oxygen Therapy," *Ozonachrichten*, no. 1 (1982): 193–201.

CHAPTER 7.
CHOOSING TO LIVE

1. U.S. Centers for Disease Control, "Nitrate and Drinking Water from Private Wells," www.cdc.gov/healthywater/drinking/private/wells/disease/nitrate.html (accessed November 23, 2012).
2. U.S. Food and Drug Administration, "Federal Food, Drug, and Cosmetic Act (FD&C Act)," www.fda.gov/regulatoryinformation/legislation/federal-fooddrugandcosmeticactfdcact/default.htm (accessed January 1, 2013).
3. Ibid.

CHAPTER 8.
STATE-OF-THE-SCIENCE ON THE
HEALTH RISK OF GM FOODS

1. Jeffrey M. Smith, *Genetic Roulette: The Documented Health Risks of Genetically Engineered Foods* (Fairfield, Iowa: Yes! Books, 2007).
2. Kurt Eichenwald, et al., "Biotechnology Food: From the Lab to a Debacle," *New York Times*, January 25, 2001.
3. Ibid.
4. Dan Quayle, speech, Indian Treaty Room of the Old Executive Office Building, Washington, D.C., May 26, 1992.
5. For copies of FDA memos, see the Alliance for Bio-Integrity website, www.biointegrity.org (accessed November 2, 2012).
6. Steven M. Druker, "How the U.S. Food and Drug Administration Approved Genetically Engineered Foods Despite the Deaths One Had Caused and the Warnings of Its Own Scientists about Their Unique Risks," Alliance for Bio-Integrity, www.biointegrity.org/ext-summary.html (accessed November 2, 2012).
7. Louis J. Pribyl, "Comments on Biotechnology Draft Document, 2/27/92," Alliance for Bio-Integrity, www.biointegrity.org/FDAdocs/04/view1.html (accessed November 2, 2012).
8. "Statement of Policy: Foods Derived from New Plant Varieties," *Federal Register* 57, no. 104 (May 29, 1992): 22991; www.fda.gov/Food/GuidanceComplianceRegulatoryInformation/GuidanceDocuments/Biotechnology/ucm096095.htm (accessed January 11, 2013).
9. Linda Kahl to James Maryanski, memorandum, January 8, 1992, regarding *Federal Register* document titled "Statement of Policy: Foods from Genetically Modified Plants," Alliance for Bio-Integrity, www.biointegrity.org

(accessed November 27, 2012); www.responsibletechnology.org/fraud/fda-quotes (accessed January 11, 2013).

10. See, for example, "Good Enough to Eat?" *New Scientist,* February 9, 2002, 7.

11. "Health Risks of Genetically Modified Foods," editorial, *Lancet* 29 (May 1999).

12. "Elements of Precaution: Recommendations for the Regulation of Food Biotechnology in Canada; An Expert Panel Report on the Future of Food Biotechnology, Prepared by the Royal Society of Canada at the Request of Health Canada, Canadian Food Inspection Agency, and Environment Canada," Royal Society of Canada, January 2001. http://rsc-src.ca/en/expert-panels/rsc-reports/elements-precaution-recommendations-for-regulation-food-biotechnology-in (accessed December 20, 2102).

13. J. R. Latham, A. K. Wilson, and R. A. Steinbrecher, "The Mutational Consequences of Plant Transformation," *The Journal of Biomedicine and Biotechnology* 2 (2006): article ID 25376, 1–7; see also A. K. Wilson, J. R. Latham, and R. A. Steinbrecher, "Transformation-Induced Mutations in Transgenic Plants: Analysis and Biosafety Implications," *Biotechnology and Genetic Engineering Reviews* 23 (December 2006): 209–37.

14. P. H. Bao, S. Granata, S. Castiglione, et al., "Evidence for Genomic Changes in Transgenic Rice (*Oryza sativa L.*) Recovered from Protoplasts," *Transgenic Research* 5 (1996): 97–103; M. Labra, C. Savini, M. Bracale, et al., "Genomic Changes in Transgenic Rice (*Oryza sativa L.*) Plants Produced by Infecting Calli with *Agrobacterium tumefaciens,*" *Plant Cell Reports* 20 (2001): 325–30.

15. "Elements of Precaution: Recommendations for the Regulation of Food Biotechnology in Canada; An Expert Panel Report on the Future of Food Biotechnology, Prepared by the Royal Society of Canada at the Request of Health Canada, Canadian Food Inspection Agency, and Environment Canada," Royal Society of Canada, January 2001.

16. Edwin J. Mathews, Ph.D., to the Toxicology Section of the Biotechnology Working Group, memorandum, October 28, 1991, "Subject: Analysis of the Major Plant Toxicants."

17. Division of Food Chemistry and Technology and Division of Contaminants Chemistry, "Points to Consider for Safety Evaluation of Genetically Modified Foods: Supplemental Information," November 1, 1991, www.biointegrity.org (accessed November 27, 2012); www.responsibilitetechnology.org/fraud/fda-quotes (accessed January 11, 2013).

18. T. Netherwood, S. M. Martín-Orúe, A. G. O'Donnell, et al., "Assessing the

Survival of Transgenic Plant DNA in the Human Gastrointestinal Tract," *Nature Biotechnology* 22, no. 2 (2004): 204–9.

19. Division of Food Chemistry and Technology and Division of Contaminants Chemistry, "Points to Consider for Safety Evaluation of Genetically Modified Foods: Supplemental Information," November 1, 1991, www.bio integrity.org/FDAdocs/10/index.html (accessed December 20, 2012); www .responsibletechnology.org/fraud/fda-quotes (accessed January 11, 2013).

20. Charles Benbrook, "Impacts of Genetically Engineered Crops on Pesticide Use: The First Thirteen Years," Organic Center, www.organic-center.org/ science.latest.php?action=view&report_id=159 (accessed November 2, 2012).

21. Center for Food Safety, AC21 Ag Biotech Committee Meeting, August 1, 2007.

22. Fred A. Hines to Linda Kahl, U.S. Food and Drug Administration, Department of Veterinary Medicine, memorandum, June 16, 1993. As quoted in: "FLAVR SAVR Tomato . . . : Pathology Branch's Evaluation of Rats with Stomach Lesions from Three Four-Week Oral (Gavage) Toxicity Studies . . . and an Expert Panel's Report," Alliance for Bio-Integrity, www .biointegrity.org/FDAdocs/17/view1.html (accessed November 2, 2012).

23. Robert J. Scheuplein to the U.S. Food and Drug Administration biotechnology coordinator and others, memorandum, October 27, 1993, "Response to Calgene Amended Petition," Alliance for Bio-Integrity, www.bioin-tegrity.org (accessed November 27, 2012); www.responsibletechnology.org/ fraud/fda-quotes (accessed January 11, 2013).

24. Carl B. Johnson to Linda Kahl and others, memorandum, December 7, 1993, "Flavr Savr Tomato: Significance of Pending DHEE Question," Alliance for Bio-Integrity, www.biointegrity.org (accessed November 27, 2012); www.responsibletechnology.org/fraud/fda-quotes (accessed January 11, 2013).

25. Arpad Pusztai, "Genetically Modified Foods: Are They a Risk to Human/ Animal Health?" Action Bioscience, www.actionbioscience.org/biotech/ pusztai.html (accessed November 2, 2012).

26. Nagui H. Fares and Adel K. El-Sayed, "Fine Structural Changes in the Ileum of Mice Fed on Delta-Endotoxin-Treated Potatoes and Transgenic Potatoes," *Natural Toxins* 6, no. 6 (1998): 219–33.

27. Stanley W. Ewen and Arpad Pusztai, "Effect of Diets Containing Genetically Modified Potatoes Expressing *Galanthus nivalis* Lectin on Rat Small Intestine," *Lancet* 354, no. 9187 (October 16, 1999): 1353–54.

www.thelancet.com/journals/lancet/article/PIIS0140-6736(98)05860-7/ abstract (accessed December 20, 2012).

28. Arpad Pusztai, "Facts Behind the GM Pea Controversy," Epigenetics, Transgenic Plants, and Risk Assessment Conference, December 1, 2005 (Frankfurt am Main, Germany: Literaturhaus, 2005).

29. Arpad Pusztai, "Can Science Give Us the Tools for Recognizing Possible Health Risks of GM Food," *Nutrition and Health* 16 (2002): 73–84.

30. John M. Burns, "13-Week Dietary Subchronic Comparison Study with MON 863 Corn in Rats Preceded by a 1-Week Baseline Food Consumption Determination with PMI Certified Rodent Diet #5002," www.greenpeace .de/fileadmin/gpd/userupload/themen/gentechnik/MonsantoRatten- fuetterungsstudie.pdf (accessed December 20, 2012).

31. R. Tudisco, P. Lombardi, F. Bovera, et al., "Genetically Modified Soya Bean in Rabbit Feeding: Detection of DNA Fragments and Evaluation of Meta- bolic Effects by Enzymatic Analysis," *Animal Science* 82 (2006): 193–99.

32. Comments to Australia New Zealand Food Authority (ANZFA) about applications A346, A362, and A363 from the Food Legislation and Regulation Advisory Group (FLRAG) of the Public Health Association of Australia (PHAA) on behalf of the PHAA, "Food Produced from Glyphosate-Tolerant Canola Line GT73," Institute of Health and Environ- mental Research, Inc.

33. M. Malatesta, C. Caporaloni, S. Gavaudan, et al., "Ultrastructural Morpho- metrical and Immunocytochemical Analyses of Hepatocyte Nuclei from Mice Fed on Genetically Modified Soybean," *Cell Structure and Function* 27 (2002): 173–80.

34. Jeffrey M. Smith, *Genetic Roulette: The Documented Health Risks of Geneti- cally Engineered Foods* (Fairfield, Iowa: Yes! Books, 2007).

35. Irina Ermakova, "Experimental Evidence of GMO Hazards" (presentation at "Scientists for a GM Free Europe," European Union Parliament, Brussels, June 12, 2007).

36. Arpad Pusztai, "Can Science Give Us the Tools for Recognizing Possible Health Risks for GM Food?" *Nutrition and Health* 16 (2002): 73–84.

37. S. Leeson, "The Effect of Glufosinate Resistant Corn on Growth of Male Broiler Chickens," Department of Animal and Poultry Sciences, University of Guelph, report no. A56379, July 12, 1996.

38. M. Malatesta, C. Caporaloni, L. Rossi, et al., "Ultrastructural Analysis of Pancreatic Acinar Cells from Mice Fed on Genetically modified Soybean," *Journal of Anatomy* 201, no. 5 (November 2002): 409–15; see also

M. Malatesta, M. Biggiogera, E. Manuali, et al., "Fine Structural Analyses of Pancreatic Acinar Cell Nuclei from Mice Fed on GM Soybean," *European Journal of Histochemistry* 47 (2003): 385–88.

39. Arpad Pusztai, "Can Science Give Us the Tools for Recognizing Possible Health Risks of GM Food?" *Nutrition and Health,* 16 (2002): 73–84.

40. R. Tudisco, P. Lombardi, F. Bovera, et al., "Genetically Modified Soya Bean in Rabbit Feeding: Detection of DNA Fragments and Evaluation of Metabolic Effects by Enzymatic Analysis," *Animal Science* 82 (2006): 193–99.

41. John M. Burns, "13-Week Dietary Subchronic Comparison Study with MON 863 Corn in Rats Preceded by a 1-Week Baseline Food Consumption Determination with PMI Certified Rodent Diet #5002," www.greenpeace .de/fileadmin/gpd/userupload/themen/gentechnik/MonsantoRatten fuetterungsstudie.pdf (accessed December 20, 2012).

42. R. Tudisco, P. Lombardi, F. Bovera, et al., "Genetically Modified Soya Bean in Rabbit Feeding: Detection of DNA Fragments and Evaluation of Metabolic Effects by Enzymatic Analysis," *Animal Science* 82 (2006): 193–99.

43. Arpad Pusztai, "Can Science Give Us the Tools for Recognizing Possible Health Risks of GM Food?" *Nutrition and Health* 16 (2002): 73–84.

44. J. S. de Vendômois F. Roullier, D. Cellier, and G. E. Séralini, "A Comparison of the Effects of Three GM Corn Varieties on Mammalian Health," *International Journal of Biological Sciences* 5 (2009): 706–26, www.biolsci.org/ v05p0706.htm (accessed November 2, 2012).

45. I. V. Ermakova, "Experimental Evidence of GMO Hazards" (presentation at "Scientists for a GM Free Europe," European Union Parliament, Brussels, June 12, 2007).

46. L. Vecchio, B. Cisterna, M. Malatesta, et al, "Ultrastructural Analysis of Testes from Mice Fed on Genetically Modified Soybean," *European Journal of Histochemistry* 48, no. 4 (October–December 2004): 449–54.

47. Oliveri, et al., "Temporary Depression of Transcription in Mouse Pre-implantion Embryos from Mice Fed on Genetically Modified Soybean" (paper presented at forty-eighth Symposium of the Society for Histochemistry, Lake Maggiore, Italy, September 7–10, 2006).

48. Alberta Velimirov and Claudia Binter, "Biological Effects of Transgenic Maize NK603xMON810 Fed in Long Term Reproduction Studies in Mice," Forschungsberichte der Sektion IV. Report-Federal Ministry of Health, Family and Youth, 2008. wwwbiosicherheit.de/pdf/aktuell/zentek_studie 2008.pdf (accessed January 11, 2013).

49. I. V. Ermakova, "Genetically Modified Organisms and Biological Risks," in

Proceedings of International Disaster Reduction Conference (IDRC), Davos, Switzerland, August 27–September 1, 2006, 168–72. http://eco-irinaermakova.narod.ru/eng/art/art16.html (accessed January 11, 2013).

50. Ermakova, "Genetically Modified Soy Leads to the Decrease of Weight and High Mortality of Rat Pups of the First Generation. Preliminary Studies," 4–9.

51. Ermakova, "Experimental Evidence of GMO Hazards."

52. I. V. Ermakova "GMO: Life Itself Intervened into the Experiments," letter, *Ecosinform* N2 (2006): 3–4.

53. Smith, *Genetic Roulette.*

54. "Mortality in Sheep Flocks after Grazing on Bt Cotton Fields—Warangal District, Andhra Pradesh," report of the preliminary assessment, April 2006, GM Watch, http://gmwatch.org/latest-listing/1-news-items/6416-mortality-in-sheep-flocks-after-grazing-on-bt-cotton-fields-warangal-district-andhra-pradesh-2942006.

55. Personal communication and visit by Jeffrey Smith with village members, near Warangal, Andhra Pradesh, January 2009.

56. John M. Burns, "13-Week Dietary Subchronic Comparison Study with MON 863 Corn in Rats Preceded by a 1-Week Baseline Food Consumption Determination with PMI Certified Rodent Diet #5002," December 17, 2002, www.monsanto.com/monsanto/content/sci_tech/prod_safety/full-ratstudy.pdf (accessed January 11, 2013); see also Stéphane Foucart, "Controversy Surrounds a GMO," *Le Monde,* December 14, 2004; and Jeffrey M. Smith, "Genetically Modified Corn Study Reveals Health Damage and Cover-up," www.greenpeace.de/fileadmin/gpd/userupload/themen/gentechnik/MonsantoRattenfuetterungsstudie.pdf (accessed December 20, 2012).

57. Arpad Pusztai, "Can Science Give Us the Tools for Recognizing Possible Health Risks of GM Food?" *Nutrition and Health* 16 (2002): 73–84.

58. V. E. Prescott, P. M. Campbell, A. Moore, et al., "Transgenic Expression of Bean Alpha-Amylase Inhibitor in Peas Results in Altered Structure and Immunogenicity," *Journal of Agricultural and Food Chemistry* 53, no. 23 (2005): 9023–30.

59. Mark Townsend, "Why Soya Is a Hidden Destroyer" (report on yearly food-sensitivity assessment of York Laboratory), *Daily Express,* March 12, 1999.

60. G. A. Kleter and A. A. C. M. Peijnenburg, "Screening of Transgenic Proteins Expressed in Transgenic Food Crops for the Presence of Short Amino Acid Sequences Identical to Potential, IgE-Binding Linear Epitopes of Allergens," *BMC Structural Biology* 2 (2002): 8–19.

61. T. Netherwood, S. M. Martín-Orúe, A. G. O'Donnell, et al., "Assessing the Survival of Transgenic Plant DNA in the Human Gastrointestinal Tract," *Nature Biotechnology* 22, no. 2 (2004): 204–9.

62. Hye-Yung Yum, Soo-Young Lee, Kyung-Eun Lee, et al., "Genetically Modified and Wild Soybeans: An Immunologic Comparison," *Allergy and Asthma Proceedings* 26, no. 3 (May–June 2005): 210–16.

63. S. R. Padgette, N. B. Taylor, D. L. Nida, et al., "The Composition of Glyphosate-Tolerant Soybean Seeds Is Equivalent to That of Conventional Soybeans," *Journal of Nutrition* 126, no. 3 (April 1996): 702–16, including data in the journal archives from the same study; see also A. Pusztai and S. Bardocz, "GMO in Animal Nutrition: Potential Benefits and Risks," in *Biology of Nutrition in Growing Animals,* ed. R. Mosenthin, J. Zentek, and T. Zebrowska; tech. ed. P. Gregory (Edinburgh and New York: Elsevier, 2006).

64. M. Malatesta, C. Caporaloni, L. Rossi, et al, "Ultrastructural Analysis of Pancreatic Acinar Cells from Mice Fed on Genetically Modified Soybean," *Journal of Anatomy* 201, no. 5 (November 2002): 409; see also M. Malatesta, M. Biggiogera, E. Manuali, et al., "Fine Structural Analyses of Pancreatic Acinar Cell Nuclei from Mice Fed on GM Soybean," *European Journal of Histochemistry* 47 (2003): 385–88.

65. See for example, S. H. Sicherer, A. Muñoz-Furlong, H. A. Sampson, et al., "Prevalence of Peanut and Tree Nut Allergy in the United States Determined by Means of a Random Digit Dial Telephone Survey: A 5-Year Follow-up Study," *Journal of Allergy and Clinical Immunology* 112, no. 6 (December 2003): 1203–7; and Ricki Helm, A. Wesley Burks, and Eliot Herman, "Hypoallergenic Foods—Soybeans and Peanuts," *Information Systems for Biotechnology News Report,* October 1, 2002.

66. R. I. Vázquez-Padrón, L. Moreno-Fierros, L. Neri-Bazán, et al., "Intragastric and Intraperitoneal Administration of Cry1Ac Protoxin from *Bacillus thuringiensis* Induces Systemic and Mucosal Antibody Responses in Mice," *Life Sciences* 64, no. 21 (1999): 1897–1912; R. I. Vázquez-Padrón, L. Moreno-Fierros, L. Neri-Bazán, et al., "Characterization of the Mucosal and Systemic Immune Response Induced by Cry1Ac Protein from *Bacillus thuringiensis* HD 73 in Mice," *Brazilian Journal of Medical and Biological Research* 33 (2000): 147–55.

67. R. I. Vázquez, L. Moreno-Fierros, L. Neri-Bazán, et al., "*Bacillus thuringiensis* Cry1Ac Protoxin Is a Potent Systemic and Mucosal Adjuvant," *Scandinavian Journal of Immunology* 49 (1999): 578–84. See also R. I.

Vazquez-Padron, et al. (2000b) Characterization of the mucosal and systemic immune response induced by CrylAc protein from Bacillus thuringiensis HD 73 in mice. *Brazilian Journal of Medical and Biological Research* 33, 147–155.

68. Nagui H. Fares and Adel K. El-Sayed, "Fine Structural Changes in the Ileum of Mice Fed on Endotoxin Treated Potatoes and Transgenic Potatoes," *Natural Toxins* 6, no. 6 (1998): 219–33.

69. A. Finamore, M. Roselli, S. Britti, et al., "Intestinal and Peripheral Immune Response to MON810 Maize Ingestion in Weaning and Old Mice," *Journal of Agriculture and Food Chemistry* 56, no. 23 (2008): 11533–39.

70. Washington State Department of Health, *Report of Health Surveillance Activities: Asian Gypsy Moth Control Program* (Olympia, Wash., 1993).

71. M. Green, M. Heumann, R. Sokolow, et al., "Public Health Implications of the Microbial Pesticide *Bacillus thuringiensis:* An Epidemiological Study, Oregon, 1985–86," *American Journal of Public Health* 80, no. 7 (1990): 848–52.

72. M. A. Noble, P. D. Riben, and G. J. Cook, *Microbiological and Epidemiological Surveillance Program to Monitor the Health Effects of Foray 48B BTK Spray* (Vancouver, B.C.: Ministry of Forests, Province of British Columbia, September 30, 1992).

73. A. Edamura, M.D., "Affidavit of the Federal Court of Canada, Trial Division. Dale Edwards and Citizens against Aerial Spraying vs. Her Majesty the Queen, Represented by the Minister of Agriculture" (May 6, 1993); as reported in Carrie Swadener, "*Bacillus thuringiensis* (B.t.)," *Journal of Pesticide Reform* 14, no. 3 (Fall 1994).

74. J. R. Samples and H. Buettner, "Ocular Infection Caused by a Biological Insecticide," *Journal of Infectious Diseases* 148, no. 3 (1983): 614; as reported in Carrie Swadener, "*Bacillus thuringiensis* (B.t.)," *Journal of Pesticide Reform* 14, no. 3 (Fall 1994).

75. M. Green, M. Heumann, R. Sokolow, et al., "Public Health Implications of the Microbial Pesticide *Bacillus thuringiensis:* An Epidemiological Study, Oregon, 1985–86," *American Journal of Public Health* 80, no. 7 (1990): 848–52.

76. A. Edamura, M.D., "Affidavit of the Federal Court of Canada, Trial Division. Dale Edwards and Citizens against Aerial Spraying vs. Her Majesty the Queen, Represented by the Minister of Agriculture," (May 6, 1993); as reported in Carrie Swadener, "*Bacillus thuringiensis* (B.t.)," *Journal of Pesticide Reform* 14, no. 3 (Fall 1994).

77. Carrie Swadener, "*Bacillus thuringiensis* (B.t.)," *Journal of Pesticide Reform* 14, no. 3 (Fall 1994).

78. Terje Traavik and Jack Heinemann, *Genetic Engineering and Omitted Health Research: Still No Answers to Ageing Questions* (2006). Cited in their quote was: G. Stotzky, "Release, Persistence, and Biological Activity in Soil of Insecticidal Proteins from *Bacillus thuringiensis*," in *Genetically Engineered Organisms: Assessing Environmental and Human Health Effects*, ed. Deborah K. Letourneau and Beth E. Burrows (Boca Raton, Fla.: CRC Press LLC, 2002), 187–222.

79. See, for example, A. Dutton, H. Klein, J. Romeis, and F. Bigler, "Uptake of Bt-Toxin by Herbivores Feeding on Transgenic Maize and Consequences for the Predator *Chrysoperla carnea*," *Ecological Entomology* 27 (2002): 441–47; and J. Romeis, A. Dutton, and F. Bigler, "*Bacillus thuringiensis* Toxin (Cry1Ab) Has No Direct Effect on Larvae of the Green Lacewing *Chrysoperla carnea* (Stephens) (Neuroptera: Chrysopidae)," *Journal of Insect Physiology* 50, no. 2–3 (2004): 175–83.

80. N. Tomlinson of the UK MAFF's [Ministry of Agriculture, Fisheries and Food] Joint Food Safety and Standards Group 4, December 1998 letter to the U.S. Food and Drug Administration, commenting on its draft document, "Guidance for Industry: Use of Antibiotic Resistance Marker Genes in Transgenic Plants."

81. Jeffrey M. Smith, "Bt-Maize (corn) During Pollination May Trigger Disease in People Living Near the Cornfield," press release, February 2004, Seeds of Deception, www.responsibletechnology.org/gmo-dangers/health-risks/articles-about-risks-by-jeffrey-smith/Genetically-Engineered-Foods-May-Cause-Rising-Food-Allergies-Genetically-Engineered-Corn-June-2007; and Allen V. Estabillo, "Farmer's Group Urges Ban on Planting Bt Corn; Says It Could Be Cause of Illnesses," Mindanews, October 19, 2004, www.gmwatch.org/latest-listing/43-2004/5635-farmers-group-urges-ban-on-planting-bt-corn-20102004.

82. Mae-Wan Ho, "GM Ban Long Overdue, Dozens Ill and Five Deaths in the Philippines," Institute of Science in Society press release, June 2, 2006, www.i-sis.org.uk/GMBanLongOverdue.php (accessed January 11, 2013).

83. Ashish Gupta, et al., "Impact of Bt Cotton on Farmers' Health (in Barwani and Dhar District of Madhya Pradesh)," *Investigation Report,* October–December 2005.

84. Smith, *Genetic Roulette*.

85. E. Ann Clark, "Food Safety of GM Crops in Canada: Toxicity and

Allergenicity," GE Alert, 2000, www.plant.uoguelph.ca/research/ homepages/eclark/safety.htm (accessed January 11, 2013).

86. Food Legislation and Regulation Advisory Group of the Public Health Association of Australia on behalf of the Public Health Association of Australia, "Comments to ANZFA about Applications A372, A375, A378, and A379."

87. Judy Carman, "Is GM Food Safe to Eat?" in *Recoding Nature: Critical Perspectives on Genetic Engineering,* ed. Richard Hindmarsh and Geoffrey Lawrence, 82–93 (Sydney: UNSW Press, 2004).

88. Ibid.

89. Food Legislation and Regulation Advisory Group, "Comments to ANZFA about Applications A346, A362, and A363," Institute of Health and Environmental Research, Inc., www.iher.org.au (accessed November 3, 2012).

90. Doug Gurian-Sherman, "Holes in the Biotech Safety Net, FDA Policy Does Not Assure the Safety of Genetically Engineered Foods," Center for Science in the Public Interest, www.cspinet.org/new/pdf/fda_report__final.pdf (accessed November 3, 2012).

91. Bill Freese, "The StarLink Affair, Submission by Friends of the Earth to the FIFRA [Federal Insecticide, Fungicide, and Rodentcide Act] Scientific Advisory Panel Considering Assessment of Additional Scientific Information Concerning StarLink Corn," July 17–19, 2001.

92. Alan M. Rulis, Office of Premarket Approval, Center for Food Safety and Applied Nutrition, U.S. Food and Drug Administration, letter to Dr. Kent Croon, regulatory affairs manager, Monsanto Company, September 25, 1996. See Letter for BNF No. 34 at www.fda.gov/Food/Biotechnology/ Submissions/ucm161107.htm (accessed January 11, 2013).

93. "Elements of Precaution: Recommendations for the Regulation of Food Biotechnology in Canada; An Expert Panel Report on the Future of Food Biotechnology, Prepared by the Royal Society of Canada at the Request of Health Canada, Canadian Food Inspection Agency, and Environment Canada," Royal Society of Canada, January 2001, www.canadians.org/ food/documents/rsc_feb05.pdf (accessed January 11, 2013).

94. FIFRA Scientific Advisory Panel, open meeting, July 17, 2001, www.epa. gov/scipoly/sap/meetings/2001/july/julyfinal.pdf (accessed January 11, 2013).

95. Bill Freese, "Crop Testing," letter to the editor, *New Scientist,* no. 2530, December 17, 2005.

96. M. Cretenet, J. Goven, J. A. Heinemann, et al., "Submission on the DAR for Application A549 Food Derived from High-Lysine Corn LY038:

To Permit the Use in Food of High-Lysine Corn," Centre for Integrated Research in Biosafety, www.inbi.canterbury.ac.nz (search for article title; accessed November 3, 2012).

97. Marc Lappé and Britt Bailey, "ASA Response: June 25, 1999," Center for Ethics and Toxics, www.environmentalcommons.org/cetos/articles/asaresponse.html (accessed November 3, 2012).

98. Bill Freese, "The StarLink Affair, Submission by Friends of the Earth to the FIFRA Scientific Advisory Panel Considering Assessment of Additional Scientific Information Concerning StarLink Corn," July 17–19, 2001.

99. Paul P. Groenewegen, Brian W. McBride, John H. Burton, and Theodore H. Elsasser. "Bioactivity of Milk from bST-Treated Cows." *Journal of Nutrition* 120 (1990): 514–19.

100. Judith C. Juskevich and C. Greg Guyer. "Bovine Growth Hormone: Human Food Safety Evaluation." *Science* 249 (August 24, 1990): 875–84.

101. Pete Hardin, "rbGH: Appropriate Studies Haven't Been Done," *The Milkweed*, July 2000.

102. See, for example, Doug Gurian-Sherman, "Holes in the Biotech Safety Net, FDA Policy Does Not Assure the Safety of Genetically Engineered Foods," Center for Science in the Public Interest, www.cspinet.org/new/pdf/fda_report__final.pdf (accessed November 3, 2012).

103. S. R. Padgette, N. B. Taylor, D. L. Nida, et al., "The Composition of Glyphosate-Tolerant Soybean Seeds Is Equivalent to That of Conventional Soybeans," *Journal of Nutrition* 126 (1996): 702–16.

104. B. G. Hammond, J. L. Vicini, G. F. Hartnell, et al., "The Feeding Value of Soybeans Fed to Rats, Chickens, Catfish, and Dairy Cattle Is Not Altered by Genetic Incorporation of Glyphosate Tolerance," *Journal of Nutrition* 126 (1996): 717–27.

105. A. Pusztai and S. Bardocz, "GMO in Animal Nutrition: Potential Benefits and Risks," in *Biology of Nutrition in Growing Animals,* ed. R. Mosenthin, J. Zentek, and T. Zebrowska; tech. ed. P. Gregory (Edinburgh and New York: Elsevier, 2006).

106. Ian F. Pryme and Rolf Lembcke, "In Vivo Studies on Possible Health Consequences of Genetically Modified Food and Feed—with Particular Regard to Ingredients Consisting of Genetically Modified Plant Materials," *Nutrition and Health* 17 (2003): 1–8.

107. Andreas Rang, Bettina Linke, and Bärbel Jansen, "Detection of RNA Variants Transcribed from the Transgene in Roundup Ready Soybean," *European Food Research and Technology* 220 (2005): 438–43.

108. Pryme and Lembcke, "In Vivo Studies on Possible Health Consequences of Genetically Modified Food and Feed," 1–8.

109. Arpad Pusztai, "Can Science Give Us the Tools for Recognizing Possible Health Risks of GM Food?" *Nutrition and Health* 16 (2002): 73–84; Stanley W. B. Ewen and Arpad Pusztai, "Effect of Diets Containing Genetically Modified Potatoes Expressing *Galanthus nivalis* Lectin on Rat Small Intestine," *Lancet* 354, no. 9187 (October 16, 1999): 1353–54; Arpad Pusztai, "Genetically Modified Foods: Are They a Risk to Human/Animal Health?" Action Bioscience, www.actionbioscience.org/biotech/pusztai .html (accessed November 3, 2012); and A. Pusztai and S. Bardocz, "GMO in Animal Nutrition: Potential Benefits and Risks," in *Biology of Nutrition in Growing Animals,* ed. R. Mosenthin, J. Zentek, and T. Zebrowska; tech. ed. P. Gregory (Edinburgh and New York: Elsevier, 2006).

110. Prescott, Campbell, Moore, et al., "Transgenic Expression of Bean Alpha-Amylase Inhibitor in Peas Results in Altered Structure and Immunogenicity," 9023–30.

111. J. Lexchin, L. A. Bero, B. Djulbegovic, and O. Clark, "Pharmaceutical Industry Sponsorship and Research Outcome and Quality: Systematic Review," *BMJ* 326 (2003): 1167–76.

112. M. Friedberg, B. Saffran, T. J. Stinson, et al., "Evaluation of Conflict of Interest in Economic Analyses of New Drugs Used in Oncology," *Journal of the American Medical Association* 282, no. 15 (1999): 1453–57.

113. Suzanne Wuerthele quoted here: http://archive.sare.org/sanet-mg/archives/ html-home/23-html/0195.html (accessed January 11, 2013).

114. "Elements of Precaution: Recommendations for the Regulation of Food Biotechnology in Canada; An Expert Panel Report on the Future of Food Biotechnology, Prepared by the Royal Society of Canada at the Request of Health Canada, Canadian Food Inspection Agency, and Environment Canada," Royal Society of Canada, January 2001, www.canadians.org/ food/documents/rsc_feb05.pdf (accessed January 11, 2013).

115. Friends of the Earth Europe, "Throwing Caution to the Wind: A Review of the European Food Safety Authority and Its Work on Genetically Modified Foods and Crops," November 2004. www.gmfreeireland.org/resources/ documents/FOE/EFSAreport.pdf (accessed December 20, 2012).

116. European Communities submission to World Trade Organization dispute panel, January 28, 2005, reported in "Hidden Uncertainties— Risks of GMOs," April 23, 2006, www.non-gm-farmers.com/news_print .asp?ID=2731 (accessed January 11, 2013).

117. European Union Regulation 178/2002 (Article 30.4), http://europa
.eu/legislation_summaries/consumers/consumer_information/f80501_
en.htm#amendingact (accessed January 11, 2013).

118. Friends of the Earth Europe, "Throwing Caution to the Wind: A Review of
the European Food Safety Authority and Its Work on Genetically Modified
Foods and Crops."

119. "Greenpeace Exposes Government-Monsanto Nexus to Cheat Indian
Farmers: Calls on GEAC to Revoke BT Cotton Permission," press release,
March 3, 2005, Greenpeace International, www.greenpeace.org/india/en/
news/greenpeace-exposes-government/ (accessed December 20, 2012).

120. Jeffrey M. Smith, *Seeds of Deception: Exposing Industry and Government
Lies about the Safety of the Genetically Engineered Foods You're Eating* (Fairfield, Iowa: Yes! Books, 2003), 224.

121. Third World Network Malaysia, "Monsanto Bribery Charges in Indonesia
by DoJ and USSEC," Mindfully, www.mindfully.org/GE/2005/Monsanto-
Indonesia-Bribery27jan05.htm (accessed November 3, 2012).

122. Smith, *Seeds of Deception*.

123. Karen Charman, "The Professor Who Can Read Your Mind," *PR Watch
Newsletter* 6, no. 4 (fourth quarter 1999).

124. www.gmwatch.org/latest-listing/41-2002/3068-support-for-food-biotech
nology-holds-in-the-us (accessed January 11, 2013).

125. T. B. Mepham, P. N. Schofield, W. Zumkeller, and A. M. Cotterill, "Safety of
Milk from Cows Treated with Bovine Somatotropin," *Lancet* 344, no. 8934
(1994):1445-46; see also Samuel S. Epstein, "Unlabeled Milk from Cows
Treated with Biosynthetic Growth Hormones: A Case of Regulatory Abdi-
cation," *International Journal of Health Services* 26 (1996): 173–85; and Samuel
S. Epstein, *What's In Your Milk?* (Victoria, B.C., Canada: Trafford Publishing,
2006), 197–204.

126. For a review of literature linking elevated levels of IGF-1 with increased
risks of breast, colon, and prostate cancers, see Samuel S. Epstein, *What's
In Your Milk?* (Victoria, B.C., Canada: Trafford Publishing, 2006),
197–204.

127. Gary Steinman, "Mechanisms of Twinning: VII. Effect of Diet and
Heredity on the Human Twinning Rate," *Journal of Reproductive Medicine* 51, no. 5 (May 2006): 405–10; S. E. Echternkamp, A. J. Roberts,
D. D. Lunstra, et al., "Ovarian Follicular Development in Cattle Selected
for Twin Ovulations and Births," *Journal of Animal Science* 82 no. 2
(2004): 459–71; and S. E. Echternkamp, L. J. Spicer, K. E. Gregory, et al.,

"Concentrations of Insulin-Like Growth Factor-I in Blood and Ovarian Follicular Fluid of Cattle Selected for Twins," *Biology of Reproduction* 43, no. 1 (1990): 8–14.

128. D. A. Powell, K. Blaine, S. Morris, and J. Wilson, "Agronomic and Consumer Considerations for Bt and Conventional Sweet-Corn," *British Food Journal* 105, no. 10 (November 2003): 700–713.

129. "GM Nation? The Findings of the Public Debate," GM Nation, www.gmnation.org.uk/ut_09/ut_9_6.htm#summary (accessed November 3, 2012).

130. To see the *Toronto Star* photo in Stuart Laidlaw's book, go to www.gmwatch.org/p1temp.asp?pid=72&page=1 (accessed August 2007).

131. "Corn Fakes," *Private Eye,* no. 1194, September 28–October 11, 2007, GM Watch, http://independentsciencenews.org/news/corn-fakes (accessed January 11, 2013).

132. Tim Lambert, "Would You Eat Wormy Sweet Corn?" Science Blogs, www.scienceblogs.com/deltoid/2007/09/would_you_eat_wormy_sweet_corn.php (accessed November 3, 2012).

133. "Genetically Modified Foods, Who Knows How Safe They Are?" CBC News and Current Affairs, September 25, 2006.

134. Mike Zelina, Teresa Campbell, Andrew Christie, et al., "The Health Effects of Genetically Engineered Crops on San Luis Obispo County: A Citizen Response to the SLO Health Commission GMO Task Force Report." www.slocounty.ca.gov/Assets/PH/HealthCommission/GMOTaskForce/Citizen+Response+on+the+Health+Effects+of+GE+Crops.pdf (accessed December 20, 2012).

135. Bill Lambrecht, *Dinner at the New Gene Café* (New York: St. Martin's Press, 2001), 139.

CHAPTER 9. ORGANIC FOODS

1. "OTA FY09 Annual Report," Organic Trade Association, www.ota.com/fy2009.html#growth (accessed January 3, 2010).

2. "U.S. Organic Market Projected to Exceed $30 Billion by 2007," *Organic Processing,* April/June 2004, 10.

3. United States Department of Agriculture, Agricultural Marketing Service, www.ams.usda.gov/nop (go to Organic Standards and click on Organic Regulations); accessed January 2, 2010).

4. United States Department of Agriculture, Agricultural Marketing Service, www.ams.usda.gov/nop (go to Organic Certification & Accreditation and click on List of Certifying Agents); accessed January 2, 2010).

5. Organic Materials Review Institute home page, www.omri.org (accessed January 2, 2010.

6. *Vegetarian Times*, March 2005, 112.

7. Jessica DeCostole, "The Truth about Organic Foods," *Redbook,* www .redbookmag.com/print-this/truth-about-organic-foods (accessed January 3, 2010).

8. U.S. Environmental Protection Agency, Office of the Administrator, *Environmental Health Threats to Children,* EPA 175-F-96-001, September 1996; National Research Council, National Academy of Science, *Pesticides in the Diets of Infants and Children* (Washington, D.C.: National Academy Press, 1993): 184–85.

9. U.S. Environmental Protection Agency, *Draft Final Guidelines for Carcinogen Risk Assessment,* EPA/630/P-30/001A, 2003.

10. C. L. Curl, R. A. Fenske, and K. Elgethun, "Organophosphorous Pesticide Exposure of Urban and Suburban Pre-school Children with Organic and Conventional Diets," *Environmental Health Perspectives* 111, no. 3 (2003): 377–82; C. Lu, K. Toepel, R. Irish, et al., "Organic Diets Significantly Lower Children's Dietary Exposure to Organophosphorous Pesticides," *Environmental Health Perspectives* 114, no. 2 (2006): 260–63, www.organ icconsumers.org/organic/ehpstudy.pdf (accessed January 15, 2010); Organic Consumer Association, "Exposure to Pesticides: A Fact Sheet," in *Food, Inc.,* ed. Karl Weber, 103 (New York: PublicAffairs, 2009), www.organiccenter .org/science.hot/php?action=view&report_id=26 (accessed January 6, 2010).

11. Marian Burros, "Obamas to Plant Vegetable Garden at White House," *New York Times,* March 20, 2009, www.nytimes.com/2009/03/20/ dining/20garden.html (accessed January 3, 2010).

12. "The White House Garden," Food Network, www.foodnetwork.com/ food/cda/article_print/0,1983,FOOD_32086_6023528_ARTICLE-STORY,00.html (accessed January 4, 2010).

13. Food Network, www.foodnetwork.com/search/delegate.do?fnSearchString=iron +chef+america+at+the+White+House&fnSearchType=site (accessed January 8, 2010).

14. G. Hirshberg, "Organics—Healthy Food, and So Much More," in *Food, Inc.,* ed. Karl Weber, 47 (New York: PublicAffairs, 2009).

15. Certified Naturally Grown Programs, www.naturallygrown.org/programs (accessed January 19, 2010).

16. B. P. Baker, C. M. Benbrook, E. Groth III, and K. L. Benbrook, "Pesticide Residue in Conventional, Integrated Pest Management (IPM)-Grown, and

Organic Foods: Insights from Three U.S. Data Sets," *Food Additives and Contaminants* 19, no. 5 (2002): 427–46; C. Benbrook, "Simplifying the Pesticide Risk Equation: The Organic Option," Organic Center, *State of Science Review*, March 2008, www.organiccenter.org/reportfiles/Pesticide_SSR_2008.pdf (accessed January 6, 2010).

17. Mayo Clinic staff, "Organic Foods: Are They Safer? More Nutritious?" Mayo Clinic, www.mayoclinic.com/health/organic-food/NU00255 (accessed January 3, 2010).

18. Benbrook, "Simplifying the Pesticide Risk Equation."

19. C. Benbrook, X. Zhao, J. Yáñez, et al., "New Evidence Confirms the Nutritional Superiority of Plant-Based Organic Foods," Organic Center, *State of Science Review*, March 2008, www.organiccenter.org/science.nutri.php?action=view&report_id=126 (accessed January 22, 2010).

20. "The *Oxford Dictionary* Word of the Year Is 'Locavore,'" Cooltown Studios, www.cooltownstudios.com/2007/11/15 (accessed February 24, 2009); "The Birth of Locavore," Oxford University Press, OUPblog, http://blog.oup.com/2007/11/prentice (accessed February 24, 2009).

21. *Businessweek*, www.businessweek.com/print/bwdaily/dnflash/content/may2008 (accessed February 24, 2009).

22. Zheng Yang, "Are You a Locavore? If So, You Are Either a 'Local Hero' or 'Indulgent and Hedonistic,'" Cornell University, *Chronicle Online*, www.news.cornell.edu/stories/March08/local.foods.talk.zy.html (accessed February 24, 2009).

23. www.riley.ksu.edu/DesttopDefault.aspx?tabid=252 (accessed January 25, 2010).

24. Benbrook, Zhao, Yáñez, et al., "New Evidence Confirms the Nutritional Superiority of Plant-Based Organic Foods," see Table 10.

25. "The Master Gardener, News and Information for Sedgwick County Extension Master Gardeners," January 2010, insert on p. 1, www.hfrr.ksu.edu/DesktopModules/ViewDocument.aspx?DocumentID=1757 (accessed January 25, 2010).

26. U.S. Department of Agriculture, Agricultural Marketing Service home page, www.ams.usda.gov (accessed December 31, 2009). See National Organic Program, NOP regulations, and addition regulations per specific certifiers.

27. *Food, Inc.,* DVD, directed by Robert Kenner, produced by River Road Entertainment, Participant Media, and Magnolia Pictures, www.foodincmovie.com (accessed November 5, 2012), with a companion book, Karl Weber,

ed., *Food, Inc.* (New York: PublicAffairs, 2009); *Fresh: New Thinking about What We're Eating,* DVD, directed by Ana Sophia Joanes, produced by Ripple Effect Productions, www.freshthemovie.com (accessed November 5, 2012). A review of these two films is available: C. Benbrook, "A Tale of Two Films: The Full Commentary," Organic Center, July 7, 2009, www.organic-center.org/reportfiles/TTF_Commentary_Full.pdf (accessed January 6, 2010).

28. Benbrook, Zhao, Yáñez, et al., "New Evidence Confirms the Nutritional Superiority of Plant-Based Organic Foods."

29. Food and Water Watch, "Food Safety Consequences of Factory Farms," in *Food, Inc.,* ed. Karl Weber, 19 (New York: PublicAffairs, 2009); Sustainable Table, "Questions for a Farmer," in *Food, Inc.,* ed. Karl Weber (New York: PublicAffairs, 2009), 197.

30. Ibid., 19.

31. A. Angel, guest ed., "The Role of Conjugated Linoleic Acid in Human Health: Proceedings of a Workshop. Winnipeg, Canada, March 13–15, 2003," *American Journal of Clinical Nutrition* 79, no. 6 suppl. (2004): 1131S–1120S; L. Rist, A. Mueller, C. Barthel, et al., "Influence of Organic Diet on the Amount of Conjugated Linoleic Acids in Breast Milk of Lactating Women in the Netherlands," *British Journal of Nutrition* 97, no. 4 (2007): 735–43; C. Benbrook and A. Greene, "The Link between Organic and Health: New Research Makes the Case for Organic Even Stronger," *Organic Processing* 5, no. 2 (2008): 40–49; Michael Pollan, *The Omnivore's Dilemma: A Natural History of Four Meals* (Penguin Group, NY., 2006).

32. www.foodnews.org (accessed January 22, 2010).

33. "More People Planning Vegetable Gardens," March 21, 2008, http://mynortherngarden.wordpress.com/2008/03/21 (accessed January 29, 2010); Garden Writers Association home page, www.gardenwriters.org (accessed January 29, 2010); Michael Pollen, "Why Bother?" in *Food, Inc.,* ed. Karl Weber, 169 (New York: PublicAffairs, 2009).

ADDITIONAL RESOURCES

FOREWORD

Please visit http://stores.homestead.com/HEALTHYMEDICINEACADEMY for DVDs of Dr. Maret's lecture on "Electromagnetic Fields and Cancer" (accessed December 20, 2012).

INTRODUCTION. EMERGING PARADIGMS IN HEALTH AND HEALING

Bailey, Alice A. *Esoteric Healing.* Lucis Publishing Co., reprint 2007.

CHAPTER 1.
MOVING BEYOND THE "ENERGY CRISIS" IN MEDICINE

Books and Periodicals

Becker, Robert O., and Gary Selden. *The Body Electric: Electromagnetism and the Foundation of Life.* Harper Paperbacks, 1998.

Burr, Harold Saxton. *The Fields of Life: Our Links with the Universe.* Ballantine Books, 1972.

Gerber, Richard. *Vibrational Medicine: The #1 Handbook of Subtle-Energy Therapies.* 3rd ed. Bear & Company, 2001.

Greene, Debra. *Endless Energy: The Essential Guide to Energy Health.* MetaComm Media, 2009.

Ho, Mae-Wan. *The Rainbow and the Worm: The Physics of Organisms.* 3rd ed. World Scientific Publishing Company, 2008.

Miwa, Satomi, Kenneth B. Beckman, and Florian L. Muller. *Oxidative Stress in Aging: From Model Systems to Human Diseases.* Humana Press, 2008.

Ober, Clinton, Stephen T. Sinatra, and Martin Zucker. *Earthing.* Basic Health Publications Inc., 2010.

Oschman, James L., *Energy Medicine: The Scientific Basis.* Churchill Livingstone, 2000.

———. *Energy Medicine in Therapeutics and Human Performance.* Harcourt Health Sciences/Butterworth Heinemann, 2003.

Pethig, Ronald. *Dielectric and Electronic Properties of Biological Materials.* John Wiley & Sons, 1979.

Popp, Fritz-Albert, and Lev Vladimirovich Beloussov, eds. *Integrative Biophysics: Biophotonics.* Kluwer Academic, 2003.

Rosch, Paul J., and Marko S. Markov. *Bioelectromagnetic Medicine.* Marcel Dekker, 2004.

Tavera, Matteo. *Sacred Mission.* Translated from the French by George Verdon. www.earthinginstitute.net/tavera/mt_sacred_mission.pdf (accessed January 21, 2013).

Thomas, Linnie. *The Encyclopedia of Energy Medicine.* Fairview Press, 2010.

Websites

Energy Research home page: www.energyresearch.us (accessed November 5, 2012). Website of the author, with lecture schedule, resources, and bio.

CHAPTER 2.
LIFE'S MUSICAL BLUEPRINT

Ashton, Anthony. *Harmonograph: A Visual Guide to the Mathematics of Music.* Wooden Books Ltd., 2003.

Bailey, Alice A. *A Treatise on White Magic.* Lucis Publishing Company, 1998.

Bearden, T. E., *Gravitobiology: A New Biophysics.* Chenier Press, 1991.

———. *Energy from the Vacuum.* Chenier Press, 2002.

———. *Oblivion: America at the Brink.* Chenier Press, 2005.

Becker, Robert O., and Gary Selden. *The Body Electric: Electromagnetism and the Foundation of Life.* Quill, 1985.

Bell, Fred. *Rays of Truth—Crystals of Light.* Pyradyne Publishing, 1999.

Beloussov, L. V., V. L. Voeikov, and R. Van Wijk, eds. *Biophotonics and Coherent Systems.* Moscow University Press, 2000.

Bentov, Itzhak. *Stalking the Wild Pendulum.* E. F. Dutton, 1977.

Berendt, Joachim Ernst. *The World Is Sound: Nada Brahma; Music and the Landscape of Consciousness.* Destiny Books, 1991.

Bernstein, Nikolai Aleksandrovich. *The Mathematical Apparatus of Biological Cybernetics.* CCM Information Corp., 1964.

Bischof, Marco. *Biophotons: The Light in Our Cells.* Zweitausendeins, 1995.

———. "Introduction to Integrative Biophysics." In *Integrative Biophysics—Biophotonics,* edited by Fritz-Albert Popp and Lev Vladimirovich Beloussov. Kluwer Academic Publishers, 2003.

Blavatsky, H. P. *The Secret Doctrine.* Theosophical University Press, 1970.

———. *Isis Unveiled: A Master-Key to the Mysteries of Ancient and Modern Science and Theology.* Theosophical University Press, 1998.

———. *Occultism of the Secret Doctrine.* Kessinger Publishing, LLC, 2004.

Bohm, David. *Wholeness and the Implicate Order.* Routledge, 2002.

Braden, Gregg. *The Isaiah Effect: Decoding the Lost Science of Prayer and Prophecy.* Three Rivers Press, 2000.

———. *The God Code: The Secret of Our Past, the Promise of Our Future.* Hay House, 2004.

———. *The Divine Matrix: Bridging Time, Space, Miracles, and Belief.* Hay House, 2007.

Braud, William. *Distant Mental Influence: Its Contributions to Science, Healing, and Human Interactions.* Hampton Roads, 2003.

Campbell, Don G., *The Mozart Effect.* Quill, 2001.

———. *The Roar of Silence.* 1st ed. Quest Books, 1989.

Cardeña, Etzel, Steven J. Lynn, and Stanley Krippner, eds. *Varieties of Anomalous Experience: Examining the Scientific Evidence.* American Psychological Association, 2000.

Cayce, Edgar, John Keely, Rudolf Steiner, and Dale Pond. *The Physics of Love: The Ultimate Universal Laws.* Message Company, 1996.

Chang, Jiin-Ju, Joachim Fisch, and Fritz-Albert Popp. *Biophotons.* Springer, 2002.

Coats, Callum. *Living Energies: An Exposition of Concepts Related to the Theories of Viktor Schauberger.* 1st ed. Gateway Books, 1995.

Cook, Nick. *The Hunt for Zero Point: Inside the Classified World of Antigravity Technology.* Broadway Books, 2003.

Cousto, Hans. *The Cosmic Octave: Origin of Harmony.* LifeRhythm Publication, 2000.

Daniélou, Alain. *Music and the Power of Sound.* Inner Traditions International, 1995.

Davies, Paul. *How to Build a Time Machine.* Viking, 2001.

Deane, Ashayana. *Voyagers,* vol. 1, *The Sleeping Abductees.* Granite Publishing, 1999.

———. *Voyagers,* vol. 2, *The Secrets of Amenti.* Wild Flower Press, 2002.

Emoto, Masaru. *The Secret Life of Water.* Atria Books, 2005.

Free, Wynn, with David Wilcock. *The Reincarnation of Edgar Cayce?: Interdimensional Communication and Global Transformation.* Frog Ltd., 2004.

Fröhlich, Herbert. *Biological Coherence and Response to External Stimuli.* Springer, 1988.

Gariaev, Pjotr P., *Wave Genome.* Public Profit, 1994.

Gariaev, P. P., K. V. Grigorev, A. A. Vasilev, et al. "Investigation of the Fluctuation Dynamics of DNA Solutions by Laser Correlation Spectroscopy." *Bulletin of the Lebedev Physics Institute,* no. 11–12 (1992): 23–30.

Gariaev, P. P., and V. P. Poponin. "Vacuum DNA Phantom Effect In Vitro and Its Possible Rational Explanation. *Nanobiology* (1995).

Garnett, Merrill. *First Pulse: A Personal Journey in Cancer Research.* First Pulse Projects, 1998.

Gerber, Richard. *Vibrational Medicine: New Choices for Healing Ourselves.* Updated ed. Bear & Company, 1996.

Godwin, Joscelyn. *The Mystery of the Seven Vowels.* Phanes Press, 1991.

———. *Harmonies of Heaven and Earth: The Spiritual Dimensions of Music from Antiquity to the Avant-Garde.* Inner Traditions International, 1995.

Goldman, Jonathan. *Shifting Frequencies.* Light Technology Publishing, 1998.

———. *Healing Sounds: The Power of Harmonics.* Healing Arts Press, 2002.

Govinda, Lama Anagarika. *Foundations of Tibetan Mysticism.* Samuel Weiser, 1974.

———. *Creative Meditation and Multi-Dimensional Consciousness.* Quest Books, 1976.

Grof, Stanislav. *When the Impossible Happens: Adventures in Non-ordinary Reality.* Sounds True, 2006.

Grove, William Robert. *The Correlation of Physical Forces.* Dynamics Publishing, 1874.

Harper, John Jay. *Tranceformers: Shamans of the 21st Century.* Reality Press, 2006.

Ho, Mae-Wan. *The Rainbow and the Worm: The Physics of Organisms.* 2nd ed. World Scientific Publishing Co., 2006.

Ho, Mae-Wan, Fritz-Albert Popp, and Ulrich Warnke. *Bioelectrodynamics and Biocommunication.* World Scientific Publishing Company, 1994.

Holtje, Dennis. *From Light to Sound: The Spiritual Progression.* Masterpath Inc., 1995.

Horowitz, Leonard G. *Emerging Viruses: AIDS and Ebola; Nature, Accident, or Intentional?* Limited ed. Tetrahedron Publishing Group, 1996.

———. *DNA: Pirates of the Sacred Spiral.* Tetrahedron Publishing Group, 2004.

———. *Walk on Water: Technology of the Creator.* Tetrahedron Publishing Group, 2006; Horowitz, Leonard G., and Joseph Puleo. *Healing Codes for the Biological Apocalypse.* Tetrahedron Publishing Group, 2001.

Hunt, Valerie V. *Infinite Mind: Science of the Human Vibrations of Consciousness.* 2nd ed. Malibu Publishing, 2000.

Hurtak, J. J., *The Book of Knowledge: The Keys of Enoch.* The Academy of Future Science, 1987.

———. *Consciousness, Energy, and Future Science.* The Academy of Future Science, 2004.

Jenny, Hans. *Cymatics: A Study of Wave Phenomena and Vibration.* MacroMedia Publishing, 2001.

Kaku, Michio. *Hyperspace: A Scientific Odyssey through Parallel Universes, Time Warps, and the 10th Dimension.* Anchor Books, 1995.

———. *Parallel Worlds: A Journey through Creation, Higher Dimensions, and the Future of the Cosmos.* Anchor Books, 2006.

Keyes, Laurel Elizabeth. *Toning the Creative Power of the Voice.* Devorss Publishing, 1997.

Khan, Hazrat Inayat. *The Music of Life.* Omega Publications, 1983.

———. *The Mysticism of Sound and Music.* Shambhala Publications, Inc., 1991.

Khan, Vilayat Inayat. *Toward the One.* Harper & Row Publishers, 1959.

King, Moray B. *Quest for Zero Point Energy: Engineering Principles for Free Energy.* Adventures Unlimited Press, 2001.

Lauterwasser, Alexander. *Water Sound Images: The Creative Music of the Universe.* Macromedia, 2007.

Leeds, Joshua. *The Power of Sound: How to Be Healthy and Productive Using Music and Sound.* Healing Arts Press, 2001.

Linsteadt, Stephen, and Maria Elena Boekemeyer. *The Heart of Health: The Principles of Physical Health and Vitality.* Natural Healing House Press, 2003.

Lipton, Bruce H. *The Biology of Belief: Unleashing the Power of Consciousness, Matter, and Miracles.* Hay House, 2005.

Lipton, Bruce H., and Mitchell Jay Rabin. *Fractal Evolution: The Biology of Consciousness,* DVD. Released by A Better World, 2004.

Liu, K., J. D. Cruzan, and R. J. Saykally. "Water Clusters." *Science* 271 (February 16, 1996): 929–31.

McTaggart, Lynne. *The Intention Experiment: Using Your Thoughts to Change Your Life and the World.* Free Press, 2007.

———. *The Field: The Quest for the Secret Forces of the Universe.* Harper Paperback, 2008.

Miller, I., and R. A. Miller. "From Helix to Hologram: An Ode on the Human Genome." *Nexus,* August–September 2003.

Müller, Hartmut. *Raum und Zeit, Special 1: Free Energy—Global Scaling.* Ehlers Verlag GmbH, 2002.

———. *Theory of Global Scaling.* Institute for Space-Energy Research, Leonard Euler, Ltd., and Global Scaling Applications, Inc., 2002.

Myers, David P., and David S. Percy. *Two-Thirds: A History of our Galaxy.* Aulis Publishers, 1999.

Narby, Jeremy. *The Cosmic Serpent: DNA and the Origins of Knowledge.* J. P. Tarcher, 1998.

Ornstein, Robert. *The Evolution of Consciousness: The Origins of the Way We Think.* Touchstone, 1991.

Ornstein, Robert, and David Sobel. *The Healing Brain: Breakthrough Discoveries about How the Brain Keeps Us Healthy.* Touchstone, 1988.

Oschman, James L. *Energy Medicine: The Scientific Basis.* Churchill Livingstone, 2000.

Ouspensky, Peter D. *A New Model of the Universe.* Vintage, 1971.

Paijmans, Theo. *Free Energy Pioneer: John Worrell Keely.* Adventures Unlimited Press, 2004.

Penrose, Roger. *The Road to Reality: A Complete Guide to the Laws of the Universe.* Alfred A. Knopf Publishing, 2004.

Pond, Dale, John Keely, Nikola Tesla, et al. *Universal Laws Never Before Revealed: Keeley's Secrets.* Message Company, 2004.

Presman, Aleksandr Samuilovich. *Electromagnetic Fields and Life.* Plenum Press, 1970.

Radin, Dean. *The Conscious Universe: The Scientific Truth of Psychic Phenomena.* HarperEdge, 1997.

———. *Entangled Minds: Extrasensory Experiences in a Quantum Reality.* Paraview Pocket Books, 2006.

Rein G., "Storage of Non-Hertzian Frequency Information in Water." In *Proceedings of the International Tesla Society,* edited by S. Elswick. Tesla Society Publishing, 1992.

———. "A Bioassay for Negative Gaussian Fields Associated with Geometric Patterns." In *Proceedings of the Academy of New Energy,* May 1997.

———. "Biological Effects of Scalar Acoustic Energy: Modulation of DNA." In *Proceedings of the U.S. Psychotronics Association,* July 1998.

———. "Bioinformation within the Biofield: Beyond Bioelectromagnetics." *Journal of Alternative and Complementary Medicine* 10, no. 1 (February 2004): 59–68.

Rein, G., T. A. Gagnon. "The Biological Significance of Water Structured with Non-Hertzian Time Reversed Waves." *Journal of the U.S. Psychotronics Association* 4 (1990): 26–31.

Rein, G., R. McCraty. "Local and Non-local Effects of Coherent Heart Frequencies on Conformational Changes of DNA." In *Proceedings of the Joint USPA/IAPR Conference,* 1993.

———. "Structural Changes in Water and DNA Associated with New Physiologically Measured States." *Journal of Scientific Exploration* 8, no. 3 (1994): 438.

Saraydarian, Torkom. *The Creative Sound: Sacred Music, Dance, and Song.* T. S. G. Publishing Foundation, Inc., 1999.

Schlitz, Marilyn, Tina Amorok, and Marc Micozzi. *Consciousness and Healing: Integral Approaches to a Mind-Body Medicine.* Elsevier Inc., 2005.

Sheldrake, Rupert. *The Presence of the Past: Morphic Resonance and the Habits of Nature.* Fontana, 1988.

———. *The Sense of Being Stared At.* Hutchinson, 2003.

Sheppard, Asher R., and Merril Eisenbud. *The Biological Effects of Electric and Magnetic Fields of Extreme Low Frequency.* New York University Press, 1997.

Smith, Cyril W., and Simon Best. *Electromagnetic Man: Health and Hazard in the Electrical Environment.* St. Martin's Press, 1989.

Sparks, Jim. *The Keepers: An Alien Message for the Human Race.* Wild Flower Press, 2006.

Swartz, Tim R. *The Lost Journals of Nikola Tesla: HAARP—Chemtrails and the Secret of Alternative 4.* Inner Light-Global Communication, 2000.

Talbot, Michael. *The Holographic Universe.* HarperPerennial, 1992.

Tart, C. T., Harold E. Puthoff, and Russell Targ, eds. *Mind at Large.* Hampton Roads, 2002.

Tiller, William A. *Science and Human Transformation: Subtle Energies, Intentionality, and Consciousness.* Pavior Publishing, 1997.

Tiller, William A., W. E. Dibbel, and J. G. Fandel. *Some Science Adventures with Real Magic.* Pavior Publishing, 2005.

Tomatiz, Alfred A. *The Conscious Ear: My Life of Transformation through Listening.* Station Hill Press, 1992.

Tracy, Kathleen. *Barbara McClintock: Pioneering Geneticist (Unlocking the Secrets of Science).* Mitchell Lane Publishers, 2001.

Valone, Thomas. *Bioelectromagnetic Healing: A Rationale for Its Use.* Rev. ed. Integrity Research Institute, 2006.

Van Dyke, Deborah. *Travelling the Sacred Sound Current: Keys for Conscious Evolution.* Sound Current Music, 2001.

Van Erkelens, Herbert. *De Dertien Tonen van de Schepping.* Symbolon, 2006.

White, John, and Stanley Krippner. *Future Science: Life Energies and the Physics of Paranormal Phenomena.* 1st ed. Anchor Books, 1977.

Yogananda, Paramahansa. *Autobiography of a Yogi.* 60th ann. ed. Self-Realization Fellowship Publishers, 2006.

CHAPTER 3.
CONSCIOUSNESS AND HEALING

Benor, Daniel J. *Healing Research,* vol. 1. Vision, 2002.

Broderick, Damien. *Outside the Gates of Science: Why It's Time for the Paranormal to Come In from the Cold.* Thunder's Mouth Press/Avalon Publishing Group, 2007, 175.

Broughton, Richard S. *Parapsychology: The Controversial Science.* Ballantine, 1991.

Cardeña, Etzel, Steven J. Lynn, and Stanley Krippner, eds. *Varieties of Anomalous Experience: Examining the Scientific Evidence.* American Psychological Association, 2000.

Dossey, Larry. *Space, Time, and Medicine.* New Science Library, 1982.

———. *Beyond Illness.* New Science Library, 1984.

———. *Recovering the Soul.* Bantam, 1989.

———. *Meaning and Medicine.* Bantam, 1991.

———. *Healing Words: The Power of Prayer in the Practice of Medicine.* HarperSanFrancisco, 1993.

———. *Prayer Is Good Medicine.* HarperSanFrancisco, 1996.

———. *Be Careful What You Pray For.* HarperSanFrancisco, 1997.

———. *Reinventing Medicine.* HarperSanFrancisco, 1999.

———. *Healing Beyond the Body.* Shambhala, 2001.

———. *The Extraordinary Healing Power of Ordinary Things.* Harmony/ Random House, 2006.

———. *The Power of Premonitions: How Knowing the Future Can Shape Our Lives.* Dutton/Penguin, 2009. Available also in an eight-CD set, in MP3 format, and in Kindle.

Explore: The Journal of Science and Healing. www.explorejournal.com (accessed November 6, 2012). *Explore* Journal regularly publishes articles that deal with the nature of consciousness and its role in healing, in addition to covering the field of complementary and integrative medicine.

Gronowicz, Gloria A., Ankur Jhaveri, Libbe W. Clarke, et al. "Therapeutic Touch Stimulates the Proliferation of Human Cells in Culture." *Journal of Alternative and Complementary Medicine* 14, no. 3 (April 1, 2008): 233–39.

Jahn, Robert. G., and Brenda J. Dunne. *Margins of Reality: The Role of Consciousness in the Physical World.* ICRL Press, 2009.

Jonas, Wayne B., and Cindy C. Crawford. *Healing, Intention, and Energy Medicine.* Churchill Livingstone, 2002.

Kelly, Edward. F., Emily Williams Kelly, Adam Crabtree, et al. *Irreducible Mind: Toward a Psychology for the 21st Century.* Rowman and Littlefield, 2007.

Mayer, Elizabeth Lloyd. *Extraordinary Knowing: Science, Skepticism, and the Inexplicable Powers of the Human Mind.* Bantam/Random House, 2007.

Radin, Dean. *The Conscious Universe: The Scientific Truth of Psychic Phenomena.* HarperEdge, 1997.

———. *Entangled Minds: Extrasensory Experiences in a Quantum Reality.* Paraview Pocket Books, 2006.

Schoch, Robert M., and Logan Yonavjak. *The Parapsychology Revolution: A Concise Anthology of Paranormal and Psychical Research.* Tarcher/Penguin, 2008.

Schwartz, Stephen A. *Opening to the Infinite: The Art and Science of Nonlocal Awareness.* Nemoseen, 2007.

Targ, Russell. *Do You See What I See?* Hampton Roads Publishing, 2008.

Targ, Russell, and Jane Katra. *Miracles of Mind: Exploring Non-local Consciousness and Spiritual Healing.* New World Library, 1998, 273.

CHAPTER 4. RIFE THERAPY

Books and Periodicals

Sylver, Nenah, *The Rife Handbook of Frequency Therapy and Holistic Health*. Desert Gate Productions, 2011.
Online order: www.rifehandbook.com
Mail order: Barner Books, 3 Church Street, New Paltz, New York 12561
Phone order: 845-255-2635

This hardcover, illustrated, 768-page book has been hailed by licensed health professionals, device manufacturers, and laypersons as "the bible of holistic medicine for the 21st century," "the best written and most informative book I've ever seen on resonant frequency therapy," and "destined to become the definitive reference on attaining self-directed, holistic health."

Frequency Devices

GB-4000 Frequency Generator
AAA Production Inc.
P.O. Box 277
Moroni, Utah 84646
Phone: 888-486-4420 (toll free, North America) or 435-436-5235
Website: www.gbgenerators.com

The GB-4000 reaches up to 20 MHz, has a 2.4 MHz carrier frequency, and can output up to eight frequencies simultaneously to 40,000 Hz. It does regular sweeps, converge sweeps, and gating (with a variable pulse rate from 5 Hz to 2,200 Hz and a variable pulse duty cycle of 10–90 percent). It runs sine and square waves, and its square wave duty cycle ranges from 10 percent to 90 percent. The GB-4000 has two thousand programmable channels, each with up to forty-eight frequencies, and comes with a one-year parts and labor warranty. The MOPA (Master Oscillator Power Amplifier) is a radiant plasma tube attachment.

BioWave devices
Medi Gen Technology Ltd.
Leiten 3
D-83556 Griesstätt, Germany
Contact: Peter Franke
Phone: + 49-8039-90 75 01
Website: www.medi-gen.com (in German)

The BioWave devices, certified in Europe for medical use, have a frequency range of 1 Hz to 1 MHz. The low-cost BioWave 21 Liquid Crystal Display (LCD) for home use can run preprogrammed chip cards for a variety of conditions, as well as master chip cards that have been programmed on the BioWave 77. The BioWave 77, the professional unit for therapists, can be programmed with up to thirty frequencies—either manually or from database chip cards containing frequencies advanced by Royal Raymond Rife, Hulda Clark, Ph.D., and Alan Baklayan, N.D. Master chip cards can also store individual programs that can then be used on the BioWave 21 LCD.

Pulsed Technologies
Pulsed Technologies Research LLC
3003 Brookshire Drive
Plano, Texas 75075

Pulsed Technologies Romania
Bioenergetics and Pulsed Technologies SRL
Aleea Mizil 46G, sector 3
Bucharest, 032347, Romania
Phone, U.S. and international: 214-453-0095 or 800-801-4798 (general: sales, support, technical); 888-669-3198 (research and development only)
Phone, outside the U.S.: +40-314-057-986; +40-722-643-640 (mobile cell)
E-mail: info@pulsedtech.com
Website: www.PulsedTech.com

The PFG Series 2 (Precision Function Generator) devices are portable (6" × 1" × 3½") frequency units emitting complex, precision waveforms via company-supplied software and a user-supplied personal computer. The PFG2 units operate with electrodes, plasma tubes, or other available accessories. The P3 (Precision Pulsed Plasma) tube units are controlled by the PFG series generators. The P3+ and P3 Pro (special order) machines include built-in PFG2 frequency generators. Optional custom systems and accessories are available, such as an immersible electrode and an imprintable colloidal silver attachment or specialized custom configurations for specialized research applications. Software for all the equipment allows for extensive user configuration and can easily import frequencies from other sources.

F-Scan devices
Health Balances
10814 206th Street E
Graham, Washington 98338
Contact: Richard Loyd, Ph.D.
Phone: 206-244-1383
Website: www.royalrife.com

There are two sizes of F-Scan: the F-Scan 2 (which is quite portable) and the Compact (small enough to fit into a pocket). The F-Scan 2 can be controlled by a computer using the included software, or it can be used as a stand-alone device. In the DIRP mode, it can scan the body for the frequencies of pathogens, and then apply the frequencies in any range from 1 Hz to 15 MHz. There are two Compact models, one that can do DIRP and one that can't. The one with DIRP capabilities scans frequencies from 80,000 Hz to 560,000 Hz. Both Compacts can produce and apply frequencies of up to 5 million Hz. The F-Scan and both Compact units produce sine, square, and pulsed DC waves (similar to those of a zapper). All models can transmit frequencies via electrodes, or they can be the frequency source for radiant plasma devices.

PERL (Photon Emission Resonant Light) plasma light unit
Resonant Light Technology, Inc.
4875 North Island Highway
Courtenay, British Columbia V9N 5Y9 Canada
Contact: Edna Anne (Eddie) Tunney
Phone: 250-338-4949; toll free in North America: 1-877-338-4949
Fax: 250-338-1399
Website: www.resonantlight.com
E-mail: info@resonantlight.com

The PERL plasma light unit is equipped with a leaded silica, argon-filled glass tube lit with a 27.125 MHz radiofrequency carrier wave. The PERL's multi-signaling feature can use up to three ProGen II frequency generators simultaneously, which allows the user to reduce the time required to run a particular protocol or frequency set. Effective emissions range up to thirty feet. Frequency selection is from 1 Hz to 999,999 Hz, with square, sine, or triangular waveforms (accurate to 0.001 Hz). It comes with preprogrammed protocols and computer software for creating and downloading frequencies. Optional accessories include contact electrodes and LEDs.

BCX Ultra device

Whitman Technology

Contact: Roger Whitman

Phone: 530-623-1935

The BCX Ultra device transmits frequencies via two handheld noble gas–filled tubes, with a 45 KHz radiofrequency carrier wave, hand-held electrodes and foot plates (with several different carrier waves), a coiled freestanding plasma tube, LEDs, and footbath. Functions include customizable gate, duty cycle, and different waveforms. In addition to the 1,236 preprogrammed channels, up to 255 frequencies can be manually programmed (frequency range up to 100,000 Hz). All functions can be seen in a digital readout. There is a warranty and 30- to 60-day buy-back guarantee.

Microscopes

Ergonom microscopes

Grayfield Optical Inc.

Kohlenstrasse 23

50825 Cologne, Germany

Phone: UK, +44 20 8133 4321; Europe, +49 221 20046970

Website: www.grayfieldoptical.com

Ergonom microscopes have a higher resolution ability and greater depth of field than Rife's best microscope (while being much easier to use). All Grayfield instruments feature variable depth of field—independent of magnification—as well as extended working distance and full contrast in true color, without any need for staining or oil immersion. These features allow for the observation of living organisms in real time.

Websites

Website of Royal Rife: www.rife.org

Webmaster: Stanley Truman Jr.

The most complete collection of Rife historical records: scientific papers; letters to and from Rife; newspaper, magazine, and journal articles; Rife's lab notes; photos of Rife and his wife, his colleagues, and his lab equipment; and slides of specimens seen through the Universal Microscope.

Rife Resources Ltd. Website: www.royalrife.com

Webmaster: Richard Loyd, Ph.D.

This site features an eclectic and very sophisticated collection of material pertaining to health and electromedicine (including Rife's technology). Some of the material is innovative and hard to find. A number of articles were written by Loyd on such important topics as mold and Lyme toxins.

CHAPTER 5. HARMONIZING THE ENERGIES OF BODY, MIND, AND ENVIRONMENT WITH PULSOR MICROCRYSTALS

Davidson, John. *Subtle Energy.* The C. W. Daniel Company Limited, 1987.

Levitt, B. Blake. *Electromagnetic Fields: A Consumer's Guide to the Issues and How to Protect Ourselves.* Backinprint.com, 2007.

McTaggart, Lynn. *The Field: The Quest for the Secret Force of the Universe.* Harper Paperbacks, 2008.

Oschman, James L. *Energy Medicine: The Scientific Basis.* Churchill Livingstone, 2000.

Yao, George T. F. *Pulsor: Miracle of Microcrystals.* Gyro International, 1986.

CHAPTER 6. OZONE AND HYDROGEN PEROXIDE IN HEALING

Books and Periodicals

Bocci, Velio, *Oxygen-Ozone Therapy: A Critical Evaluation.* Kluwer Academic Publishers, 2002. An exhaustive (and breakthrough) treatise on all aspects of ozone therapy written primarily for clinical researchers, physicians, and ozone therapists by the world's leading authority on oxidative medicine. Includes protocols and clinical guidance.

———. *Ozone: A New Medical Drug.* Springer, 2005. A somewhat simplified version of Bocci's previous book, this book will be better understood by lay readers with a solid scientific background. Includes protocols and clinical guidance.

Viebahn-Hänsler, Renate. *The Use of Ozone in Medicine.* 5th English ed. Iffezheim, Germany: Odrei Publishers, 2007. This book is a classic text by one of the world's most respected practitioners, and it includes protocols and clinical guidance. New editions are published every few years. Her *Ozon-Handbuch* is currently available only in German.

Websites

Oxygen Healing Therapies
www.oxygenhealingtherapies.com

This website contains information about different aspects of oxygen therapies, including Dr. Frank Shallenberger's course schedule and a list of practitioners who have attended his seminars. Note: This site is not affiliated with Nathaniel Altman or the book *Oxygen Healing Therapies*.

International Ozone Association—Pan-American Group

www.io3a.org

Founded in 1973, the International Ozone Association is a nonprofit educational and scientific organization dedicated to the collection and dissemination of information on, and to promote research in, any and all aspects of ozone and related oxygen species technologies. The IOA sponsors seminars and international conferences on medical ozone.

CHAPTER 7. CHOOSING TO LIVE

Bortz, Walter M., and Randall Stickrod. *The Roadmap to 100: The Breakthrough Science of Living a Long and Healthy Life*. Palgrave Macmillan, 2010.

Hass, Elson, and Daniella Chace. *The New Detox Diet: The Complete Guide for Lifelong Vitality with Recipes, Menus, and Detox Plans*. Celestial Arts, 2004.

Ignarro, Louis. *No More Heart Disease*. St. Martin's Griffin, 2005.

Weissman, Joseph D. *Choose to Live*. Penguin Books, 1988.

CHAPTER 8. STATE-OF-THE-SCIENCE ON THE HEALTH RISK OF GM FOODS

Books and Periodicals

Smith, Jeffrey M. *Seeds of Deception: Exposing Industry and Government Lies about the Safety of the Genetically Engineered Foods You're Eating*. Yes! Books, 2003.

———. *The GMO Trilogy and Seeds of Deception Set*, DVD. Yes! Books, 2006.

———. *Genetic Roulette: The Documented Health Risks of Genetically Engineered Foods*. Chelsea Green Publishing, 2007.

DVDs

Food, Inc. A Robert Kenner Film, Magnolia Home Entertainment, 2009.

The Future of Food. Virgil Films and Entertainment, 2007.

The World According to Monsanto. Yes! Books, 2008.

CHAPTER 9. ORGANIC FOODS

Books and Periodicals

Berry, Wendell. *The Unsettling of America: Culture and Agriculture.* Sierra Club Books, 2004.

Burke, Cindy. *To Buy or Not to Buy Organic.* Marlowe and Company, 2007.

Coleman, Eliot. *The New Organic Grower: A Master's Manual of Tools and Techniques for the Home and Market Gardener.* Chelsea Green Publishing, 1995.

Goodall, Jane. *Harvest for Hope: A Guide to Mindful Eating.* Wellness Central/ Hachette, 2006.

Gussow, Joan Dye. *This Organic Life.* Chelsea Green Publishing, 2002.

Heron, Katrina, ed. *Slow Food Nation's Come to the Table: The Slow Food Way of Living.* Modern Times, 2008.

Kingsolver, Barbara, with Steven L. Hopp and Camille Kingsolver. *Animal, Vegetable, Miracle: A Year of Food Life.* HarperCollins, 2007.

Nestle, Marion. *Food Politics: How the Food Industry Influences Nutrition.* University of California Press, 2003.

Patel, Raj. *Stuffed and Starved: The Hidden Battle for the World Food System.* Melville House, 2008.

Pollan, Michael. *The Botany of Desire: A Plant's-Eye View of the World.* Random House, 2001.

———. *The Omnivore's Dilemma: A Natural History of Four Meals.* Penguin, 2006.

———. *In Defense of Food: An Eater's Manifesto.* Penguin, 2008.

———. *Food Rules: An Eater's Manual.* Penguin, 2009.

Salatin, Joel. *Everything I Want to Do Is Illegal: War Stories from the Local Food Front.* Polyface, Inc., 2007.

Schlosser, Eric. *Fast Food Nation: The Dark Side of the All-American Meal.* Houghton Mifflin, 2001.

Shabecoff, Philip, and Alice Shabecoff. *Poisoned for Profit.* Chelsea Green Publishing, 2010.

Winne, Mark. *Closing the Food Gap: Resetting the Table in the Land of Plenty.* Beacon Press, 2008.

Websites

Organic Growers Association
www.organicconsumers.org
This group campaigns for health, justice, sustainability, peace, and democracy.

CONTRIBUTORS

Nathaniel Altman traveled to Germany and Cuba and interviewed scientists from Russia, France, Italy, and the United States to document scientific evidence and clinical findings on the role of oxygen therapies as detoxifying agents and immunoregulators. In addition to *The Oxygen Prescription* (Healing Arts Press, 2007), Altman has written more than a dozen books on health and healing, including *What You Can Do About Asthma; Healing Springs; The Twelve Stages of Healing;* and *The Honey Prescription*. He lives in Brooklyn, New York. www.nathanielaltman.com.

John Consemulder, M.Sc., is a neuropsychologist and consciousness researcher, research journalist, and radio host (www.healingsound-movement.com/radio.html). His radio broadcasts focus mainly on the fields of intention, heart coherence, nonlocal and infinite consciousness, information medicine, healing, and bioenergetics. He is also an international music producer of energetic and contemporary healing music and has produced more than fifteen healing music albums. He is also a live artist, certified sound healer, and an author of spiritual and scientific articles and books. Consemulder also organizes a variety of workshops, concerts, spiritual events, and conferences, as well as the Avatar Festival in the Netherlands. With his wife, singer and choreographer Renske Skills, he has initiated a global consciousness and world peace initiative for children of the world: www.worldpeacechild.com, and he also has his own HealingSoundMovement TV show. He maintains a website for his healing work: www.healingsoundmovement.com.

Larry Dossey, M.D., is a former internist, former chief of staff of Medical City Dallas Hospital, and former cochair of the Panel on Mind/ Body Interventions, National Center for Complementary and Alternative Medicine, National Institutes of Health. He is executive editor of the peer-previewed journal *Explore: The Journal of Science and Healing.* He is the author of eleven books on the role of consciousness and spirituality in health, most recently *The Power of Premonitions: How Knowing the Future Can Shape Our Lives.* He lives in New Mexico and lectures around the world.

Melvin D. Epp, Ph.D., is a Wheaton College graduate and holds a master's degree in botany from the University of Connecticut and a Ph.D. in genetics from Cornell University. As a Damon Runyon Fellow, he learned the techniques of plant tissue culture. He has been a research scientist working on botanical and production problems for corporate America, including working on tropical plantations in the Philippines and in temperate agriculture and horticulture in the United States. Epp has served as the president of the Wichita Organic Garden Club since 2002 and continues to give lectures on gardening activity, with an emphasis on organic techniques. He is widely published; his current book, *The Petals of a Kansas Sunflower: A Mennonite Diaspora,* is an anthology of his late mother's Kansas prairie poetry written between 1929 and 1991.

Finley Eversole, Ph.D., is a philosopher, educator, activist, and advocate for the role of the arts in the evolution of consciousness. In the 1960s he was active in the civil rights and women's movements and participated in organizing the first Earth Day in New York City in 1970. As executive director of the Society for the Arts, Religion, and Contemporary Culture, he worked with such cultural leaders as Joseph Campbell, W. H. Auden, Allan Watts, Marianne Moore, and Alfred H. Barr Jr. A former university professor and a small business owner for ten years, Eversole edited and contributed to *Christian Faith and the Contemporary Arts,* is the author of *Art and Spiritual Transformation*, and edited *Infinite Energy Technologies: Tesla, Cold Fusion, Antigravity and the Future of Sustainability.* Eversole is listed in Marquis' *Who's Who in the World 2011–3013* and in their thirty-year *Pearl Anniversary Edition.*

Karl Maret, M.D., is president of the Dove Health Alliance, a nonprofit foundation focused on the creation and promotion of global research and education networks in energy medicine. He practices complementary medical modalities—including nutrition, functional medicine, and energy medicine at the Dove Center for Integral Medicine in Aptos, California. He trained in both electrical and biomedical engineering before undertaking medical studies in Canada and completed a four-year postdoctoral research fellowship at the University of California, San Diego, where he developed all the instrumentation for the successful American Medical Research Expedition to Mt. Everest in 1981. Maret is a partner in Heart-Mind Communications and a former director of the International Society for the Study of Subtle Energy and Energy Medicine. He has recently has begun educating physician groups specifically on the biological impacts of communication technologies, such as cell phones, wireless technologies, and smart meters.

R. Carole Morginsky, Ph.D., is a practitioner and teacher specializing in the use of Pulsor technology. Introduced to Pulsors in 1991, she found that wearing and using these devices increased her ability to function effectively in a highly stressful work environment and in her personal life. She became so impressed with the benefits of Pulsors that they eventually became an essential component of her life's work—helping people to function at their optimum levels. She was trained and designated by George T. F. Yao (Pulsor inventor) as an official Pulsor representative and international diplomat and has devoted the last twenty years to the practice of Pulsor vortex energy balancing and Pulsor environmental treatment. She has also conducted seminars to teach others about the development and use of Pulsors. www.Lifebalancings.com.

James L. Oschman, Ph.D., is a pioneer in the exploration of the scientific basis for complementary and alternative medicine (CAM). He has both the academic credentials and the background in CAM to carry out his explorations. He has published approximately one hundred articles, both in leading scientific journals and in journals of complementary medicine. Oschman has also written two books on energy medicine, both published by Elsevier, in 2000 and 2003. He lectures and gives workshops internationally on the theoretical and practical significance of energy medicine and the living matrix. In 2009 he was president of the International Society for the Study of Subtle Energies and Energy Medicine, and he received a Career Honor from the Second International Fascia Research Congress, held in Amsterdam.

Jeffrey M. Smith is the leading spokesperson on the health dangers of genetically modified organisms (GMOs). His first book, *Seeds of Deception,* became the world's bestselling and number-one-rated book on GMOs. His second, *Genetic Roulette: The Documented Health Risks of Genetically Engineered Foods,* is an authoritative work that presents irrefutable evidence that GMOs are harmful. Smith has counseled world leaders from every continent, lectured in more than thirty countries, and been quoted by hundreds of media outlets, including the *New York Times, Washington Post, BBC World Service, Los Angeles Times,* and *Time* magazine. He is executive director of the Institute for Responsible Technology, whose Campaign for Healthier Eating in America is designed to achieve the tipping point of consumer rejection of GMOs—forcing them out of the market. www.ResponsibleTechnology.org; www.NonGMOShoppingGuide .com.

Nenah Sylver, Ph.D., is an internationally published writer, educator, and consultant. She received her Ph.D. in psychology and holistic health from the Union Institute. When faced with health challenges, she learned about—and eventually became an expert in—Rife Therapy. Dr. Sylver's writing on psychology, natural health, and electromedicine has appeared in textbooks, journals, and anthologies in English, German, Korean,

Polish, and Spanish, including *The New Internationalist, Beiträge zum Werk von Wilhelm Reich (Contributions to the Work of Wilhelm Reich), Natural Living Today, Natural Food & Farming, Nexus, Townsend Letter,* and *Women, Culture, and Society: Readings in Women's Studies* (Simon & Schuster). Her books include *The Holistic Handbook of Sauna Therapy* (2004) and the 768-page *Rife Handbook of Frequency Therapy and Holistic Health* (2011). Dr. Sylver is interviewed regularly on radio, gives educational seminars on holistic health and electromedicine, and is a featured speaker on Rife Therapy worldwide. www.rifehandbook.com.

Dr. Joseph D. Weissman was an early pioneer in longevity research, specializing in preventive medicine, immunology, and the treatment of allergies. His 1988 book, *Choose to Live,* published by Penguin Books, was highly influential. Weissman received his medical degree from the State University of New York, Downstate Medical Center, Brooklyn. He was a clinical assistant professor of medicine at UCLA School of Medicine and in private practice in Torrance, California. He was a captain in the U.S. Army Medical Corps from 1957 to 1960, and is a member of the American Board of Internal Medicine, the American Board of Pediatrics, and a fellow of the American Academy of Allergy and Immunology. He is an avid long-distance runner and has run in more than fifty-five marathons, including three ultramarathons of forty-five to fifty miles.

INDEX